Central America

LATIN AMERICAN HISTORIES

JAMES R. SCOBIE, EDITOR

Central America

A NATION DIVIDED

SECOND EDITION

RALPH LEE WOODWARD, JR.

New York · Oxford
OXFORD UNIVERSITY PRESS
1985

Oxford University Press
Oxford London New York Toronto
Delhi Bombay Calcutta Madras Karachi
Kuala Lumpur Singapore Hong Kong Tokyo
Nairobi Dar es Salaam Cape Town
Melbourne Auckland
and associated companies in
Beirut Berlin Ibadan Mexico City Nicosia

Copyright © 1976, 1985 by Oxford University Press, Inc.
Published by Oxford University Press, Inc., 200 Madison Avenue
New York, New York 10016

Library of Congress Cataloging in Publication Data

Woodward, Ralph Lee.
Central America, a nation divided.

(Latin American histories)
Bibliography: p.
Includes index.
1. Central America—History. I. Title. II. Series.
F1436.W66 1985   972.8   84-27213
ISBN 0-19-503592-5
ISBN 0-19-503593-3 (pbk.)

Printing (last digit): 9 8 7 6 5 4 3
Printed in the United States of America

Foreword to the Second Edition

Nearly a decade has passed since the first edition of this book. In the intervening period tumultous events, ranging from a devastating earthquake in Guatemala to major social revolutions in Nicaragua and El Salvador, have attracted world attention to the isthmus. Yet despite the recent crises, little has happened to require revision of the basic themes of this work. On the contrary, the present political conflicts are but the latest manifestations of a challenge to the oligarchies established by the Liberal revolutions of about a century ago. Efforts at regional cooperation have continued to be frustrated by the elites of the individual states, despite irresistible arguments in favor of reunion, and the progress toward union made earlier has been reversed in the last ten years. The worldwide economic recession, exacerbated by higher prices for petroleum, has accelerated the inevitable social revolutions and challenges to the old orders. That challenge, begun in the 1920s and continued after World War II, has broken forth with new fury in the 1980s. At the same time, the role of the United States on the isthmus, never small, but less heavy handed in the 1970s, has once more become the target of widespread criticism, both within the United States and abroad.

The revisions in the latter chapters of this work seek to incorporate the events of the past decade without sacrificing the principal goal of this volume, which is to acquaint the reader with Central American history from pre-Columbian times to the present. The revisions, therefore, have sought as much to relate the trends of the last decade to their historical antecedents and to attempt to explain events in their regional and global context as to provide a detailed chronology. Those wishing greater detail than these chapters or the updated "Political Chronology" (pp. 284 - 307) provide, should consult the "Selective Guide to the Literature" on pp. 308 - 61. The recent crises have produced extensive, if frequently myopic, publication. A completely revised bibliographical essay incorporates this new literature on contemporary Central America as well as less voluminous, but probably more durable, recent publication on earlier Central American history.

In addition to those named in the Foreword to the first edition, I wish to thank especially the following students and colleagues for their insights and assistance in preparing this edition: Pablo Mateu, Michael Fry, Virginia Garrard, Jorge Eduardo Arellano, Regina Wagner, William Swezey, Will Andrews, Jorge Mario Salazar Mora, and Rodolfo Pastor Fasquelle. I am also most grateful for the assistance and support, tangible and intangible, of my wife and daughter, Sue McGrady and Laura Woodward.

New Orleans, La.   R.L.W, Jr.
September 1984

Foreword

1976 EDITION

The concept of a united isthmus of Central America dates at least from the beginning of Iberian rule there. In fact, the idea of a Central American nation might even be attributed to some pre-Columbian inhabitants and conquerors. Yet the reality of such a nation has repeatedly eluded the peoples of the isthmus. This work rests on the premise that national union potentially exists for the five Central American republics of Guatemala, El Salvador, Honduras, Nicaragua, and Costa Rica. The social and economic history of the isthmus suggests that its peoples share considerably in their problems and circumstances, even though their political experience has been diverse. But it is also clear that their social and economic unity has been limited by their political disunity.

The problems inherent in describing as a "nation" an area that has developed as several sovereign states are numerous. Factual data become minutiae if they are detailed for each of the separate political divisions, yet generalizations always suffer from exceptions in one or another of the states. The goal here has been to provide representative examples of general trends rather than a comprehensive or detailed chronicle, while also explaining the major political, social, and economic events of the region's history. The Political Chronology provides additional detail. Sources for Central America are not as available as they are for much of the rest of Latin America. Destruction of libraries and archives has imposed severe limitations on historians of El Salvador, Nicaragua, and Belize, and the availability and classification of historical materials is uneven in the other states. If Guatemala appears to receive more than its share of the space in this volume, it is in part a reflection of that circumstance, but also a reflection of the fact that Guatemala is the largest and traditionally the most important of the Central American states. Panama has for the most part been excluded from this study, although at some points its history blends with that of Central America. It has been treated peripherally on those occasions. The same is true for Chiapas and the Yucatán peninsula, which today are part of Mexico, but once were integral parts of Central America.

This work is based on nearly two decades of research on Central America and its institutions. Many people have contributed to its completion. I am especially grateful to Ms. Marjorie LeDoux and her staff at the Latin American Library of Tulane University. Also helpful were the directors and staffs of all of the Central American national archives and libraries, the Archivo General de Indias in Seville, and the Latin American Collection of the University of Texas Library. Among many others to whom I am grateful are William J. Griffith, Richard E. Greenleaf, Robert Wauchope, Carlos Meléndez, Doris Zemurray Stone, Victoria Bricker, John P. Bell, Nancy Farriss, James R. Scobie, Caroline Taylor, and Guillermo Cochez. I also wish to thank several students: Kenneth Finney, Gene Yaeger, David McCreery, Henry Ackerman, Joanne Weaver, Wilbur Meneray, Alvaro Taboada, Stephen Webre, James Bingham, and Barry Holt. Their comments and suggestions have been important to the writing of this book, but responsibility for the final version rests entirely with the author.

New Orleans, La.   R.L.W., Jr.
September 1975

Contents

Maps

Chart

Tables

Central America

Chapter 1 • The Isthmus

Ever since the sixteenth century, Central America has been described by residents and travelers alike as a region of abundant fertility, a potential paradise with a delicious climate, a land where man might easily satisfy his needs and still produce ample surpluses for export. Yet, over the last three hundred years and more, no such Eden has been fashioned. Even now, in the late twentieth century, the isthmus is one of the most underdeveloped areas of the world, a land of poverty, not prosperity. Measured by any economic and social criterion, the Central American republics rank among the poorest of all the Latin American states.

Explanations of Central America's failure to modernize successfully and to achieve the promise of its geography are numerous. They range from geographic or climatic determinism, where the tropics become the principal villain; through racist condemnations of Hispanic heritage, Spanish character, or Indian lethargy; to attacks on European or North American imperialism. But the causes of Central America's backwardness are more complex than these single-cause analyses usually suggest.

It is true, of course, that the great fertility of the soil and a year-round temperate climate bless much of the isthmus. But steaming rain forests, jagged mountains, and scorched arid zones have been greater geographic determinants in the development of the country than have the regions to which the designation of "paradise" might upon first impression be applied. Centuries of uncontrolled exploitation laid waste much of the Central American forests, while generations of farmers using slash-and-burn methods caused the erosion and depletion of millions of acres of arable land.

The dominant geographical feature of Central America is the imposing range of volcanic mountains which runs from Mexico through Panama. Rugged, wild, and shifting, these mountains present major obstacles to communication and cultivation, while at the same time they provide the elevation which assures much of the isthmus its eternal springtime climate. In the past, these mountains were bastions for the Indians, allowing them to resist their enemies; later the Indians' conquerors used them as forts against their European rivals. The volcanic cones which punctuate the spine of the isthmus reach their greatest heights in Guatemala, where Tajumulco is nearly 14,000 feet above sea level and many other volcanoes rise to more than 10,000 feet, and in Costa Rica, where several peaks exceed 12,000 feet. In several of the other states there are volcanoes over 7000 feet high. In Honduras, Nicaragua, and Panama, however, there are breaks in the chain, and for centuries Central Americans, lured by the potential profits of world commerce, dreamed of striking through them to create an interoceanic passage.

Picturesque lakes dot the isthmus, particularly in Guatemala and El Salvador. Guatemala's Lake Atitlán, which lies more than 5000 feet above sea level, is one of the most beautiful on Earth. More remote, but rivaling Atitlán in their misty tranquillity, are the tiny highland lakes north of Huehuetenango. Lake Amatitlán, a popular resort near the Guatemalan capital, combines breathtaking views with warm mineral-water springs. In the tropical lowlands are Lake Izabal, which is connected to the Gulf of Honduras and the Caribbean via the exotic Río Dulce, and Lake Petén-Itzá, in the midst of which lies the island village of Flores. (Near Petén-Itzá are the ancient Mayan ruins of Uaxactún and Tikal.) El Salvador's Lakes Cojutepeque and Ilopango are also spectacular. West central Honduras has Lake Yojoa, while in Nicaragua the large Lake Nicaragua and smaller Lake Managua, both lovely, have been used for navigation. The natural beauty of the isthmus, however, has mesmerized many observers into overlooking the staggering poverty of its people and the cruel racial injustice they endure.

Central America has no major navigable rivers, although several streams, principally the Motagua and Polochic in Guatemala, the Ulúa in Honduras, the San Juan in Nicaragua, and the Chagres in Panama, have at times provided channels from the Caribbean into the interior. In most cases, however, they are not navigable as far up as the highlands, where the population centers are. The steep, Pacific watershed offers virtually no possibilities for navigation; there only the Lempa in El Salvador permits minor service.

The bulk of the population lived between 3000 and 8000 feet, and the tropical lowlands along both coasts remained sparsely settled and undeveloped, isolating the highlands from the rest of the world. Despite two long coastlines, neither shore offers good natural harbors, and the search for safe, deep-water anchorages met with frustration and defeat for much of Central America's history. On the Pacific coast, only Puntarenas and Panama City offered reasonable protection for shipping, and both had other shortcomings. Elsewhere, ports were simply wharves stretching out over the beach into deeper water. Although the Caribbean coast offered better natural harbors, the tropical heat, the marshy lowlands, and the concomitant diseases retarded port development there. Even those ports which did develop were little more than unsanitary outposts of the societies of the highlands, far from the problems and dangers of the lowlands. There are some important population centers at or near sea level now, among them Panama City, San Pedro Sula, Belize, Managua, León, and Granada. Yet most of the major cities of Central America developed at the higher elevations of the Pacific mountain chain. San Salvador is 2238 feet above sea level, Tegucigalpa just over 3000, and San José nearly 4000. The

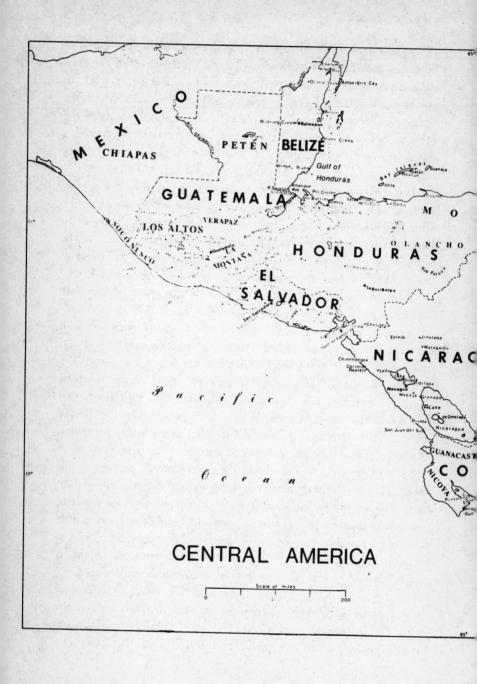

CENTRAL AMERICA

Scale of miles

0   200

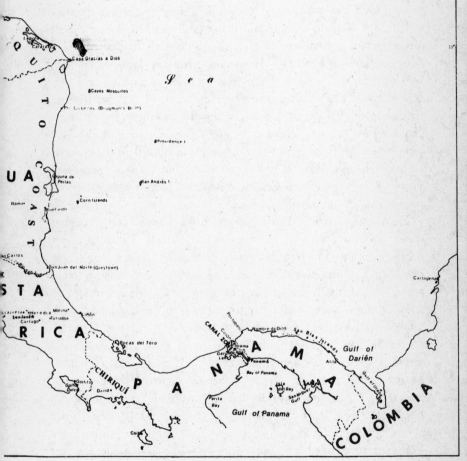

JAMAICA

Caribbean

Sea

Laguna
Caratasca
Cape Gracias a Dios

Cayos Mosquitos

Pto. Cabezas (Bragman's Bluff)

Providence I.

Laguna de
Perlas

San Andrés I.

Ramas

Bluefields

Corn Islands

San Carlos

San Juan del Norte (Greytown)

Cartagena

ST A

Alajuela
Heredia Matina
San José
Cartago
Turrialba
Limón

Portobelo
Hombre de Dios

San Blas Islands

Gulf of
Darién

R I C A

CANAL ZONE
Colón

Bocas del Toro

Panama
Gatun Lake
Panamá

Acla

Gulf of Uraba

CHIRIQUÍ

Golfito
Golfo
Dulce

David

Bay of Panama

Isla
del Rey
San Miguel
Gulf

COLOMBIA

Parita
Bay

Gulf of Panama

P A N A M A

Coibi

highest cities are in Guatemala, where the capital is nearly 5000 feet above sea level and Quezaltenango is at 7710 feet.

Yet the highlands, too, had their problems and dangers. Despite the temperate climate and more salubrious conditions, diseases still took their toll—besides smallpox and plague, there were cholera, dysentery, typhoid, and other waterborne diseases. Nor were the mosquitoborne diseases, such as yellow fever and malaria, completely unknown in the highlands, particularly at the lower elevations. The tropics, highland and lowland, so lush in vegetation, also supported a wide range of plant diseases and insect pestilence, hindering the development of agriculture. The coming of rainfall in a single rainy season—often in torrential downpours—which is followed by long droughts, created additional problems for both production and communication. Streams which are either dry or no more than trickling brooks much of the year after heavy rains become deep, raging rivers, changing their course capriciously. The difficulty of road and bridge-building under these conditions not only contributed to the isolation of the highlands from the rest of the world, but even separated each province from the others. Central American products could not compete in markets they could not reach.

From time to time, natural disasters have changed both the geography of Central America and the living conditions of its inhabitants, bringing misery and tragedy to whole cities and states. Each year, from May to November, the rains bring storms and flooding to many areas. On the coasts, violent hurricanes whip rain, wind, and sea, destroying crops, roads, bridges, and buildings. In the highlands, earthquakes and volcanoes are even more formidable enemies. The volcanoes lie along a major fault line. Many of them are old, but still active, and new ones appear periodically. They present a dramatic landscape, but they also give awesome testimony of the destructive forces of nature. Lava flows disrupt agriculture and communications. During the 1960's the eruption of the long-dormant Volcán Pacaya in Guatemala destroyed land where peaceful villages once thrived, and Volcán Irazú polluted the Costa Rican air with volcanic dust for most of that decade. Volcanic eruptions and earthquakes destroyed the original León, Nicaragua, forcing its abandonment in 1610. In 1902, Quezaltenango, Guatemala, and countless near-by villages were badly damaged. Elsewhere, quakes, along with the floods and fires that often accompany them, have wreaked havoc on nearly every Central American city at one time or another. Construction of the capital of Guatemala had only begun when a great torrent of mud, rocks, and water crashed down the side of Volcán Agua, sweeping away the town and most of its inhabitants, including its new Governor, Doña Beatriz de la Cueva, widow of conquistador Pedro de Alvarado, in 1541. The new colonial capital, now named Antigua, rebuilt several miles away, suffered serious tremors in 1575, 1577, 1585-86, 1607, 1621, 1640, 1651, 1687, 1717, and 1751. Then, in 1773, earthquakes struck there, causing such devastation that the capital was finally removed to its present site in the Hermita Valley. Earthquakes throughout the nineteenth century demonstrated that this site was no safer. Few structures in the present capital antedate the earthquakes of December and January of 1917-18. Cartago, Costa Rica, suffered a fate similar to Antigua; there was widespread ruin there in 1841. Granada, Comayagua, Panama, San Salvador, Ciudad Real (San Cristóbal de las Casas, Chiapas), and other cities endured comparable devastation at various times. Little in Managua, Nicaragua, survived the great earthquake and fire of March 1931, yet that city experienced even greater destruction in the earthquake of December 1972.

Inevitably, the frequency of natural disaster has conditioned the Central Americans' views of life and development. Stoicism may be said to be part of their national mentality, tempering their attitudes toward the future. Death and tragedy always seem close in Central America. The primitive states of communication, transportation, and production, and the insecurity of human life, have been major determinants in the region's history, contributing to the separation of Central Americans from the rest of the world, just as they have contributed to the disunity of the isthmus.

The narrowness of the Central American isthmus has also conditioned its international role, making it the focal point of a link between the two oceans. At the same time, its rugged terrain creates a serious land barrier between the two American continents. The route across Panama first became important to the Europeans early in the sixteenth century. When Peruvian gold and silver began to funnel through its narrow paths, its importance as one of the world's great transfer points became evident to Spain and her rivals. The strategic significance of the isthmus has affected international politics ever since.

Human elements were at least as important as geographic ones in forming Central America. Although the isthmus was united under Spanish rule for three hundred years, its cohesion was more apparent than real. For much of the Hispanic period the region from Chiapas through Costa Rica formed a single Spanish kingdom, but each province had its own loyalties, interests, and jealousies, all of which were aggravated by the geographical obstacles. Before the Spanish Conquest the Indian tribes of the isthmus competed and often warred against one another, and the conquistadores simply continued and exploited this tradition of disunion.

The isthmus is an archaeological bridge between the two continents; it contains the ruins of a variety of nomadic and sedentary cultures. Central America was the home of the Maya, the most civilized of all pre-Columbian Americans, but their influence extended only slightly beyond Chiapas, Yucatán, Guatemala, El Salvador, and Honduras. Nor were the Maya themselves notable for their unity or cohesion. Unlike the Aztec and Inca, who evolved highly developed central states ruling large territories, the Maya had individual cities, or city-states, which retained autonomy, or almost complete autonomy. What unity existed was cultural rather than political.

Civilization, stimulated by influences from both north and south, emerged as early as the second millennium B.C. Evidence of human life dates from several thousand years earlier. The earliest pottery, found in the Parita bay region of Panama, dates from about 2130 B.C. It reflects South American cultural influence, which began to promote change as far north as Chiapas and Guatemala. Mexican influence in Chiapas dates from at least 1500 B.C., perhaps earlier. Thereafter it extended as far south as Nicaragua and the Nicoya peninsula of Costa Rica. Central America thus became the meeting ground for Meso-american, South American, and Caribbean cultures. During the first millennium B.C., organized, sedentary tribes flourished in many places. Although the details are lost in obscurity, we do know that an active commerce and communication developed among the Indians of Cen-tral America and Mexico. Relations were not always peaceful, and conquests modified or obliterated some tribal characteristics. These tribes did not live in isolation, but within a larger economic and cul-tural world, one which encompassed the entire isthmus and beyond. They exerted substantial cultural influence one on another. Moreover, inconclusive archaeological clues in the Old World and the New point to the possibilities of contacts with Europe and Asia.

Whatever cultural influences were at work within Central Amer-ica, by the beginning of the Christian era there were thriving com-munities from one end of the isthmus to the other and there was considerable communication among them. They traded their goods—necessities as well as artistic and religious objects—far beyond the places of manufacture. The relics which have survived reveal complex social patterns and beliefs, diverse cultures, and trends toward civilized society. Although manioc and other tubers dominated much of the economic life of the Caribbean coastal region and substantial portions of Costa Rica, maize eventually became the commodity widely traded throughout the region as the staple food of most Indians. Beans were the usual accompaniment, but a variety of fruits, vegetables, small animals, fish, and chocolate rounded out the diet. Cacao beans had especially high value; in some regions they served as currency even long after the Spanish Conquest. The natives prepared maize in a variety of ways—they used it to make alcoholic beverages, among other things—but the round, flat, corn tortilla was and remains today the principal breadstuff of much of Central America.

After 500 B.C., an advanced civilization began to emerge in the highlands of Guatemala and El Salvador, where the Indian popula-tion remains large today. At Kaminaljuyú, in the outskirts of the present capital city of Guatemala, hundreds of mounds covering stone and adobe structures once contained thousands of pre-Columbian relics. Archaeologists had begun to excavate there, but before they could get far the builders of the expanding metropolis destroyed and bulldozed much of the site. Even so, it is evident that a large population lived there for a long period. Before the Christian era they had developed the beginnings of an extensive civilization, one greatly influenced by Olmec culture from the Veracruz-Tabasco coast of Mexico. Other centers emerged elsewhere, from Chiapas southeastward to Nicaragua, most notably around Santa Lucía Cotzumalhuapa in Guatemala and Quelepa in eastern El Salvador.

Early in the first millennium A.D. classical Maya civilization arose in the lowlands of the Petén. While this may have resulted from a substantial migration from the highlands to Uaxactún, Tikal, Quiriguá, Copán, and other, newer centers on the Caribbean lowlands, it is not at all likely that entire populations moved, for the highlands remained heavily populated. Moreover, pre-classical indigenous cultures also developed in the lowlands during the first millennium B.C., contemporaneously with such highland centers as Kaminaljuyú. Perhaps the Petén offered a new frontier for aggressive or footloose Indians who wished to escape what may have been an overcrowded situation in the highlands. In any case, trade and communication flourished between the highland and lowland regions of Central America. Olmec influence certainly provided the cultural stimuli to produce Maya civilization in both areas.

Later, Mexican immigrants of Nahuatl origin contributed additional cultural and social traits to Maya civilization. In first millennium A.D. the Nahuatl impact was greatest in the highlands, where it brought about substantial differences from lowland Mayan development. The Pipil of El Salvador migrated from central Mexico during this period, bringing with them new deities and artistic concepts from Teotihuacán in the Valley of Mexico and El Tajín in Veracruz. They had an enormous influence on Guatemala and El Salvador. Contacts between the people of the mountains and those of the lowlands continued as merchants carried cultural, economic, and social traits from one place to another. For example, Tazumal, in western El Salvador, was influenced by Copán, the Maya scientific center in the western Honduran lowlands. Throughout Central America during the first millennium A.D. major migrations occurred, and they spread cultural innovations in complex and interwoven patterns. After 500 A.D. new Mexican migrations began to exert cultural influences on the inhabitants of Nicaragua and Costa Rica, influences which can be seen in the changing styles of sculpture and pottery.

In the lowlands, which the Europeans later regarded as virtually uninhabitable because of the heat, humidity, insects, and disease, flourished the most civilized society in pre-Columbian America. It reached its zenith between 600 and 900 A.D. Although it was once called the "Old Maya Empire," it was not in fact politically organized into a single unit. That there was communication and commerce among the city-states is evident from the similarities of their culture —in architecture, carvings, painting, pottery, and writing—but there was variety in emphasis and talent.

By the third century A.D. Maya scientists had made sophisticated astronomical and mathematical discoveries comparable to those of the ancient Egyptian civilization. An elaborate system of hieroglyphs on stelae, stone monuments, which can be found at regular intervals throughout Maya territory, recorded data on their development. These stelae have explained much of the chronology of Maya history and tradition, although they provide scant specific biographical data. The artistic and scientific achievements of the Maya have few pre-Columbian equals, and they surpassed European achievement of the same era in many areas. Pottery, sculpture, weaving, and painting all reflected a highly developed aesthetic sensitivity. Through their advanced mathematical and astronomical knowledge the Maya developed an accurate calendar and complex systems of management. They also possessed an advanced system of writing, most of which is still undeciphered. Since it was written on parchment or bark paper—and was considered to be heretical by the Spanish priests—little of it survived the conquest. Technologically, however, the Maya were less advanced than their European counterparts. Their architectural achievements, remarkable as they were, were not the equal of those of ancient Graeco-Roman or medieval European builders. Moreover, the Maya failed to develop energy-saving machines, nor did they make practical use of the wheel, even though their children played with wheeled toys. Lacking readily domesticated animals, their society depended entirely on the labor of humans working directly with their hands, under the supervision of a small intellectual elite.

The classic period (c. 300 to c. 900) of the southern Maya lowlands was relatively short, and, for reasons not altogether clear, it decayed after the eighth century A.D. During late classic times, other centers of a new Maya civilization emerged in the Usumacinta Valley and in the Chiapas lowlands (notably at Palenque, Piedras Negras, Bonampak, Yaxchilán, and Altar de Sacrificios) and in the Yucatán peninsula (at Dzibilchaltún, Uxmal, Kabah, Sayil, and elsewhere). The people of these centers built striking architectural monuments, great stone structures which still stand, though surrounded by the jungle. In post-classic times Mexican Toltecs invaded Yucatán and made Chichén Itzá their capital. Scientific and artistic achievements continued, yet they were less remarkable than the earlier advances at Copán, Tikal, or Uaxactún. The terminal, or decadent, pre-Columbian period produced small centers, such as Mayapán. Technological innovations were sorely lacking, and the economy remained underdeveloped, depending principally on basic agriculture and primitive commerce. Internal civil war and intervention from central Mexican tribes sapped Maya strength and vitality. By the time of the Spanish Conquest, the Maya and their civilization were in thorough decline, yet they resisted subjugation longer than either the Aztec of Mexico or the Inca of Peru.

Meanwhile, something of a renaissance occurred in the older Maya areas. Migration back into the Petén from Yucatán resulted in the establishment of Tayasal, near Tikal. Tayasal produced no great archeological monuments; it was clearly a place of refuge at a time of decline. Yet it maintained Maya autonomy in the region until 1697. Elsewhere, the Lacandón, descendants of the people who had built the magnificent temples at Palenque and Bonampak, found security in remote jungle and mountain villages, and they defied pacification throughout the Hispanic period. They raided the Spanish-controlled areas from time to time. The Spaniards countered with expeditions from both Guatemala and Yucatán, but they were unsuccessful.

In the highlands, too, beginning in the twelfth or thirteenth centuries, several important tribes had grown in power. Mexican influence had reached major proportions, extending as far south as Panama. The Pipil influence stretched from Guatemala to Costa Rica. By the close of the fourteenth century three tribes dominated highland Guatemala. The Quiché, whose capital was at Utatlán, controlled the western highlands around modern-day Quezaltenango and Santa Cruz. To the east, centered at Iximché, near present-day Tecpán, were the Cakchiquel. And between the two, around Lake Atitlán, were the Zutugil. Intense rivalry, apparently fostered by Aztec traders and diplomats, simmered among these tribes. The Quiché were undoubtedly the strongest of the three, but in 1501 the Cakchiquel defeated the Zutugil at Zakcab. Although they failed to gain control of all Zutugil territory, they became a greater threat to the Quiché. Then, in 1512, the Cakchiquel made an alliance with Mexican forces. The war with the Quiché which resulted dragged on for seven years, weakening both sides. Early in the struggle, as the Cakchiquel seemed to be gaining the advantage, a severe locust plague struck the Cakchiquel region. The plague not only created famine and misery, it also checked the Cakchiquels' advance against the Quiché. Then, on top of this, a great fire destroyed the Cakchiquel capital, Iximché.

Rumors of the arrival of the Spaniards on the Caribbean coast led to a suspension of hostilities in 1519, and soon thereafter an epidemic of smallpox, which had been brought to the New World by the Spaniards, took a frightening toll on both sides, but particularly among the already weakened Cakchiquel. Perhaps taking advantage of the Cakchiquels' weakened condition, the Quiché resumed the war in 1521. The Cakchiquel, finding their Aztec allies now conquered, sent an emissary to the Spaniards to seek aid. Pedro de Alvarado and a conquering army brought that "aid" in 1524.

The Spaniards soon enslaved or made serfs of the highland Indians. By the time of their subjugation, the Indians had become efficient workers, and their labor was the most prized commodity among the conquerors. Spanish greed and brutality produced a major rebellion of their Cakchiquel allies, but the Spaniards finally forced them into servility and imprisoned, killed, or exiled their leaders.

Throughout the colonial period, some Indians fled in the face of the Spanish advance, while others continued to flee Spanish oppression. A steady trickle of Indians seeking freedom in northern Guatemala contributed to the growth of a maroon frontier region alongside the Lacandón. Never large in number, and living primitively, they played no major role in the country, other than to retard the Europeanization of that northern region by resisting conquest and pacification.

The existence of a tradition as well as a substantial amount of literary and historical art among these highland Indians has permitted more thorough study of their history and culture than of the other pre-Columbian peoples. Most of the Maya works were destroyed by the conquerors and their priests; if they had not been, we would undoubtedly know still more about that people. But several important works did survive, even though Spanish recorders, who may not have understood fully the Indian or his culture, perhaps distorted them somewhat. These works include the *Popol Vuh* and the *Title of the Lords of Totonicapán*, which relate the mythology and history of the Quiché, and the *Annals of the Cakchiquels*.

The pre-Columbian ruins of Central America, from Honduras to Yucatán, attest to the magnificence of Maya civilization and industry. Yet it is not their brilliant artistic, architectural, or scientific achievement which survives as part of Central American life today, but rather their characteristics and traditions of daily life.

The principal activity of most of the population of pre-Columbian Central America was then, as it is today, agriculture—the growing of maize, tubers, beans, fruits, vegetables, and cotton. The ruined Mayan cities reflect for the most part ceremonial, religious, or governmental activities which had relatively little to do with the daily life of the peasants who worked the soil and lived on the outskirts of these centers. The Indians' daily routine remains the same in Central American villages even now. Most lived in straw or palm-covered houses with walls made of adobe, wooden poles, or even cornstalks, depending on the climate and region. Only the important people in the great cities lived in houses of stone.

In the Indian villages of upper Central America which have survived, the pattern of life is probably not very different from that of the pre-Conquest days. A few "rich" families do own much land and animals. Although they are wealthy by village standards and occupy important positions in the village social and religious life, nevertheless, they continue to work with their hands—their counterparts in the white society do not. A large number, a sort of middle class, own some land, a few animals, and are assured generally of a modest but regular income, perhaps equivalent to $350 per year (1974). The poor, who are in the great majority, have tiny plots of land to work and generally enough to eat, but they live a day-to-day existence. They depend on charity and assistance from the community. The diet of nearly all the people remains much as it was before the Conquest. The Spaniards brought wheat, rice, and assorted fruits and vegetables, as well as livestock and poultry, and some of these commodities found their way into the Indian diet, but not nearly so regularly as Indian maize, beans, and native fruits appeared on the conquerors' tables. Chocolate, for example, was a drink quickly picked up by the Spanish soldiers, even though their priests condemned it and associated it with heresy.

The Indian men tended the maize and other crops. The women ran their households and manufactured utensils, clothing, and housewares. A high degree of specialization evolved, as each village developed a particular skill. Some engaged in cotton spinning and weaving, or pottery-making; others manufactured jewelry, or basketry, or musical instruments, or toys, or tools, or furniture. Merchants carried these objects far and wide to the village marketplaces, a practice which still continues in Guatemala. They raised and traded indigo, cochineal, and a wide assortment of dyewoods to give their clothing and bodies bright colors. Financing of this activity was at a primitive level. Barter

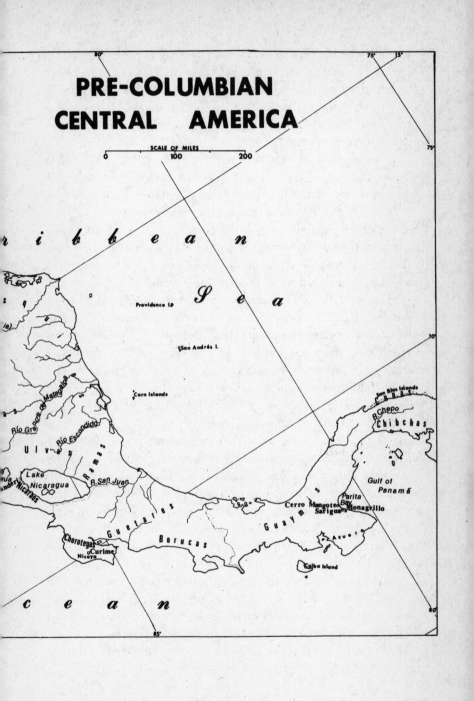

PRE-COLUMBIAN
CENTRAL   AMERICA

SCALE OF MILES

0   100   200

C a r i b b e a n

S e a

Providence I.9

ʠSan Andrés I.

ᵒCorn Islands

San Blas Islands

R.Chepo

C h i b c h a s

Río Grande de Matagalpa

Río Escondido

U l v a s

R a m a s

Lake
Nicaragua

R.San Juan

Nicaraos

G u e t a r e s

Chorotegas
ᵒCurime
Nicoya

B o r u c a s

G u a y m í s

Cerro Mangote
Sarigua
Parita Bay
Monagrillo

Azuero

ᵒCeiba Island

Gulf of
Panamá

O c e a n

was common, but semiprecious stones and cacao beans provided a kind of currency. There is no evidence that the Indians employed any advanced currency before the Spanish introduced metal coins in the sixteenth century; metalwork was not among the Maya accomplishments, although they did acquire some metal goods from other Indians to the north and south.

The cornfields, or *milpas,* were and are the key to life in the Indian villages, and around their ownership or use revolved the social and economic status of the individual Indian. Private ownership *per se* was not a highly developed concept in Indian society, although it seems to have been evolving by the time of the Conquest. Communally owned land was important, and such land ownership persisted into modern times. But the Spanish emphasis on privately owned land challenged and altered Indian landholding patterns.

For most of the Maya, education consisted of learning the vocations and practices of their parents. Only the children of the priests and the ruling classes received formal education. They learned reading, writing, and natural and social sciences, including the arts of war and government. In fact, their educational system was not unlike that of Europe of the same period, where only the privileged received education, and that closely supervised by religious authorities.

The Maya observed strict moral codes which, although they varied somewhat, regulated the sexual behavior of the people. Generally, each man had but one wife, although there were exceptions, notably among the Lacandón, where polygamy was common. Also, the chiefs and nobles often kept concubines. There were prostitutes, and they were recognized, but their social status was low. Fathers arranged marriages, but the children usually participated in the selection process. Marriages could be terminated relatively easily, and the child of a dissolved union accompanied the parent of his or her own sex. Harsh penalties proscribed fornication and other sexual offenses. An outraged husband had the right to smash the head of an adulterer with a large rock. Rape was also punishable by death. Other rules prohibited or restricted sexual relations with and among slaves.

Agricultural societies are seldom noted for their development of recreation or the arts, yet the Maya were. They played various kinds of ball games, although the formal ball fields of Maya ruins were primarily ritualistic or ceremonial centers, not amusement fields. They played several wind and percussion instruments (but not the marimba, so popular in modern Central America; it was probably adapted from African models). Their art reflected assorted athletic contests as well as a life-style closely connected with their religious beliefs. Painting must have been a popular art, for murals ornamented the great halls. The Maya also painted their pottery, both fine and crude, as well as the walls of private homes and even peasant huts. Religious and mythological motifs characterized much of this painting.

Religion permeated the life of the Maya. The priests were the most powerful members of Maya society. Government was theocratic, or almost completely so, as priests not only directed the religious and cultural development, but advised and dictated to the civil rulers as well. A philosophy of good opposed to evil, with appropriate gods representing elements and characteristics, was at the heart of the religion. The practice of human sacrifice was never really characteristic of the Maya, although it was common among the tribes of eastern Central America. The Aztec had introduced the practice in Maya territory, especially in Yucatán, by the time the Spanish arrived, and the horrified conquistadors wrote luridly about it. In some areas Christian teachings were combined with the native religions, so that crucifixion became an added means of human sacrifice.

While the priests developed a complex theology, the masses of the people clung to a simpler religion and concept of good versus evil. Omens, symbols, and superstition were important. Much of this symbolism, often mixed with Christian symbolism and mythology, survives in the mountains of Guatemala and Chiapas. Maya accounts of the origin of man and the universe, recorded after the Conquest, were similar to the Judeo-Christian mythology and were doubtless influenced by it. With the destruction of the Maya temples and formal religion, Spanish priests encouraged and then required the Indians to adopt Christianity. Conversion was often incomplete, for Spanish Catholicism and the Maya religion had much in common. Both recognized and emphasized an eternal conflict between good and evil. The multitude of saints was not incongruous with the multitude of nature gods and symbolic gods of the Indians. Conveniently for the Europeans, the cross had been the symbol of the vital Maya rain god in some areas. Both religions emphasized an authoritative status for priests and their close relation to political authority. Both peoples believed in life after death, yet both feared death, and both religions contained elaborate rituals for death and burial. Cremation was practiced among the Maya, although not universally. In essence, the teachings of the Spanish friars were not wholly alien or strange to the Maya, and, with the demise of their own religious leaders, the Indians accepted the Spanish clerics relatively easily—considerably more easily than they accepted the Spanish soldiers! Thus the Church came to play a vital role in the pacification of the Maya. Religious organizations became intertwined with village government and society. At the local level, fraternal, lay organizations, called *cofradías,* are still the most important social organizations in the Indian areas of Guatemala, and their counterparts are nearly as important throughout the rural, Indian regions of the rest of upper Central America. Even so, the folk religion of today often bears only slight resemblance to Catholicism as it is practiced in western Europe, the United States, or non-Indian parts of Latin America.

The Indians' religious traditions, with Christianity superimposed over them, together with the violence of the Conquest and the centuries of slavery or serfdom which followed, left clear impressions on the personality and mentality of the Central American Indian. To the outsider, including the Spaniard or creole in Central America, the Indian sometimes appears docile, obedient to authority, humble, and meek—as with lowered eyes and hat in hand he respectfully speaks to his landlord. Yet beneath these characteristics lie deeper qualities, and emotions of distrust and bitterness. He holds a view of the world which is oriented toward his own family and community, not toward the nation, which is alien to him. Patience, caution, stoicism, reserve —all characterize the modern Maya. Yet when he is in his own village he displays humor, gaiety, and a wide range of emotions. He may appear dull to outsiders, when in fact he is quick to learn. He is often volatile and insistent, perfectly capable of demanding his rights. Indian rebellions, from the sixteenth century through the twentieth, testify to the Indians' love of liberty. Each village is a complete unit, with only secondary ties to other places and to the national structure. The Indian residents of the village regard themselves as a "pueblo," a sovereign people, proudly clinging to their traditional beliefs and values. Though these characteristics have helped to preserve the Indian in Central America, they have also helped to maintain the cultural barriers which separate him from "modern" Central America. His isolation has never been absolute, however, and national policy and practice have inevitably impinged heavily on Indian lifestyles and conditions.

In lower Central America, some remnants of non-Maya tribes still survive today. Yet they do not make up so significant a part of the population or history and have not, therefore, exercised so great an influence on modern Central America as have the Maya peoples.

The Indians' relation to the *ladinos,* as mixed-bloods are called in Central America, and to the Europeans is often close and frequent, but there are significant differences between the ladinos and the Indians. The Indians, the conquered, have learned to cushion the burden they carry for their white and ladino masters, and their personalities and life-styles reflect centuries of oppression. The ladinos, on the other hand, have represented a growing middle sector—racially, culturally, economically, and socially—between the Indian serfs and the privileged, white, upper classes since the sixteenth century. Deprived of the deep traditional and racial roots of either the Indians or the Spaniards, and denied easy acceptance by either, the ladinos have been more mobile, more aggressive, than either. They represent and typify most of Central America as it has developed since independence. Even in communities where they are few in number, as in the western Guatemalan highlands, they are the more enterprising, the more aggressive, the more ambitious, and the more ruthless members of the community, seeking self-advancement by whatever means possible. They care little for abstract philosophical values, but are impressed by signs of material progress and by tangible means of joining in that progress. The ladinos are oriented toward the national life, toward the capital and sometimes beyond, while the Indians are oriented inwardly, toward their own immediate families and communities. Over the centuries these differences have become more cultural and economic than racial.

The peoples of Central America were already isolated and at war with one another when the Europeans arrived. The geographical position of each group—from the rest of the world and even from other groups within the isthmus—permitted them to develop agricultural communities separately, even though there had been much migration on the isthmus, probably because of natural disasters. Invasion and exploitation, principally from the north, did much to shape the culture and society the Spaniards found. The disunity among the indigenous nations which permitted such foreign incursions to occur so easily would continue to be a major characteristic of the isthmian peoples. Finally, the large segment of the sensitive and deeply religious pre-Columbian population which survived the Conquest guaranteed that Central America would develop a unique culture among Spanish-American nations, although its people would be slow to recognize and appreciate their Indian heritage.

Chapter 2 • The Kingdom of Guatemala

Less than a decade after his initial discovery of the New World, Christopher Columbus staked a Spanish claim to the isthmus. He was not the first to do so, however, for since 1495 others had sailed westward under license from the Castilian Crown. In March 1501, Rodrigo de Bastidas arrived at the mouth of the Magdalena River, in Colombia, and continued westward into the Gulf of Darién, near Colombia's modern boundary with Panama. Beset by mishaps, Bastidas had no hope of establishing a settlement, but he seized a few natives and their belongings and carried them back to Hispaniola. However, he lost most of his exotic cargo in a storm and arrived in Spain with relatively little of value other than the exaggerated tales which the conquistadores always brought back from the newly discovered lands.

Meanwhile, Columbus, on his fourth and final voyage in search of the East Indies, reached Guanaja, the easternmost of the Bay Islands in the Gulf of Honduras, at the end of July 1502. After a brief rest, the Admiral continued southeasterly along the Central American coast as far as Panama. He accumulated a small store of valuable objects and heard tales of much greater wealth and a vast ocean beyond the mountains to the southwest. Then hostile Indians attacked, forcing him to abandon Panama. More than a decade passed before effective colonization followed, but Columbus had contributed geographical data and many place names.

Juan Díaz de Solís and Vicente Yáñez de Pinzón followed up these early expeditions. They searched for wealth and a westward passage through the isthmus, but they found little to encourage further exploration. There were easier prey in the Caribbean and greater riches to be found in Mexico and the north coast of South America. Yet while other Spaniards conquered the Caribbean islands, enslaving or massacring the natives, a few navigators charted the coastline of the isthmus. The principal activity of those who sailed the Central American coast during the first decade of the sixteenth century, aside from their geographical work, was the capture of hundreds, perhaps thousands, of startled Indians, carried to the mines of Hispaniola as slaves to replace the native force which was rapidly dying out there. Spanish cruelty in the Caribbean evoked a strong reaction on the part of the clergy, and this led to a more humane royal policy by the time of Central America's colonization.

Settlement of the isthmus began as an extension of the colonization of Hispaniola. In 1509, Fernando V granted two concessions for settlement of the mainland. Alonso de Ojeda received Nueva Andalusia, from the Gulf of Darién eastward, and Diego de Nicuesa received Castilla del Oro, from Darién northward to Cape Gracias a Dios (at the modern Honduras-Nicaragua boundary). Both expeditions suffered staggering losses from disease, shipwrecks, and hostile natives. Ojeda, wounded, returned to Santo Domingo, leaving in command Francisco Pizarro, who would later become the Conqueror of Peru. When Ojeda died in the Franciscan monastery at Santo Domingo a year later, his partner, Martín Fernández de Enciso, brought reinforcements and relieved Pizarro. Enciso led the expedition to Darién—actually within the limits of Nicuesa's Castilla del Oro—where the Spaniards successfully defeated and captured a prosperous Indian village. There they established the town of Santa María la Antigua de Darién. Remnants of the battered Nicuesa expedition, which had established a meager post at Nombre de Dios, now joined them. Trouble arose immediately. The settlers at Darién denied Nicuesa's authority, and, in the end, they forced him to sail from the isthmus in a rotten and unsafe brigantine. He never reached civilization and his final fate is a mystery.

Enciso had been a good administrator in Santo Domingo, but as a frontier commander he had serious shortcomings. He increasingly depended for leadership upon a stowaway, Vasco Núñez de Balboa. Balboa had been a member of the 1501 Bastidas expedition to these coasts, and he had later taken up farming on Hispaniola, with ill success. He was now fleeing indebtedness. Balboa's experience and natural abilities allowed him gradually to assume authority. He finally arrested Enciso and sent him to Spain, accusing him of mismanagement and illegal usurpation of authority. Balboa then skillfully consolidated and extended the Darién colony. Through a combination of arms, terror, conciliation, and diplomacy, he overcame the Indians of the region and accumulated a considerable treasure of gold and pearls. He successfully turned his desperate troops into well-disciplined and hard-working colonists, and he also established a base for an agricultural economy, thus ending the threat of famine which had hung over the colony when it had had to depend on supply ships.

When reinforcements arrived from Santo Domingo, Balboa set out to find the "other sea," where, according to Indian accounts, several tribes lived in regal splendor. At the head of 190 Spaniards and several hundred allied Indians, he marched through dense jungle vegetation and enemy Indians. He reached the Pacific Ocean on September 29, 1513. Claiming for Spain all the lands which bordered upon his "South Sea," Balboa launched a new phase in the expansion of the Spanish Empire. He returned to Darién with great treasure after making extensive explorations. There he improved Indian relations and forged the first really productive European colony in America.

Meanwhile Enciso, in Spain, employed his legal talents not only to absolve himself of the charges made against him, but also to gain vengeance against Balboa. The Crown, displeased at the breach of authority implicit in Balboa's action but dubious of Enciso's command ability, ordered Pedro Arias de Avila (better known as Pedrarias Dávila) to relieve the erstwhile stowaway. Soon after, however, news arrived from Darién, telling of the great wealth Balboa had found and of his discovery of the South Sea. Fernando quickly issued new orders: Balboa became the *Adelantado* of the South Sea and Captain General of two provinces, Panama and Coiba, on the west coast, where he was to continue his explorations. Thus the pragmatic nature of royal administration of the Indies was vividly revealed, and not for the last time. The Crown evolved lofty theories of justice and policy, but theory gave way to expediency when it served the royal interest.

Although Balboa remained subordinate to Pedrarias, the new situation was untenable as far as the latter was concerned. Before the new royal order arrived, he had pushed Balboa into the background. Now Balboa received the two richest provinces in the colony and the opportunity to gain even more. An uneasy truce between the two conquerors lasted three years, as Balboa explored the Pacific coast and Pedrarias extended Spanish control of the isthmus northwestward. An undercurrent of mistrust persisted, however, and in 1517 Pedrarias accused Balboa of treason. A court of dubious justice quickly tried, convicted, and sentenced the Adelantado to death. All appeals were denied, and the discoverer of the South Sea and four of his associates were beheaded.

The loss of Balboa hurt the colony. Although far from gentle with the natives, he had gained their respect and reached important agreements with them. Pedrarias pursued a more ruthless policy. Despite royal orders to act humanely toward the Indians, Pedrarias was quick to enslave or murder them. But he extracted much gold from them, and the colony continued to prosper financially. Pedrarias established Panama City in 1519, and the new city, with its more healthful climate and location, became the seat of government and the entrepôt of the isthmus. Darién, hot and humid, with concomitant tropical diseases, was finally abandoned altogether in 1524.

Gil González Dávila, a soldier of wide experience, now received the King's commission to continue the explorations of Balboa. He arrived in Panama in 1519, but misfortune and differences with Pedrarias delayed the start of his expedition until 1522. He found the Pacific coast of Costa Rica a disappointment after hearing of the optimistic claims for that province made by Columbus, who had named the country on the basis of Indian reports. Continuing northwestward, he discovered the semicivilized Indians living along the shores of Lake Nicaragua. Although he made no settlements, González Dávila claimed to have secured Christian baptism of 32,000 souls before returning to Panama. Moreover, the expedition brought back a little gold, thus stimulating further interest in the region.

Pedrarias was especially so stimulated, and a bitter rivalry between him and González Dávila ensued. González finally fled with the treasure he had acquired, but he refused to abandon his claim on Nicaragua. Pedrarias, who encountered stiff Indian resistance in Chiriquí, delayed his overland march northward, but in 1524 he ordered a large force under the command of Francisco Hernández de Córdoba to move into Nicaragua. Sailing to the Gulf of Nicoya, Hernández established the town of Urutina (which survived only three years). Then he marched inland and founded Granada on Lake Nicaragua and León on Lake Managua.

Disputes among the conquerors now slowed the advance. González returned to Nicaragua from Santo Domingo and soundly defeated a detachment of Hernández's men. Hernández rebelled against Pedrarias and attempted to set up an independent kingdom in Nicaragua. Pedrarias then took to the field, and, after a year of civil war and intrigue, the rebel surrendered in 1526. Unforgiving, Pedrarias tried and executed Hernández. Pedrarias remained in León as Governor of Nicaragua. With the strongarm methods he had made notorious in Panama, he consolidated and extended his rule there until his death in 1531.

Meanwhile, other conquerors approached Central America to challenge Pedrarias's control. Spaniards first arrived on the Yucatán peninsula about 1511, when survivors of a shipwreck off Jamaica found their way there in a lifeboat. Most had been captured and sacrificed to Indian gods or eaten by cannibalistic Caribs, but two survived. One, Gonzalo Guerrero, won the respect of local chieftains and became in a sense the first military missionary to Latin America, as he taught them how to repel Spanish invaders. The other, Gerónimo de Aguilar, in 1519 welcomed rescue by Fernando Cortés, for whom he became a valuable interpreter. The first to attempt the conquest of the Maya was Francisco Fernández de Córdoba (not to be confused with Hernández de Córdoba, mentioned earlier), who led an expedition from Cuba in 1517. The Maya, perhaps coached by Guerrero, successfully defended their lands, and Fernández lost his life in the effort. Subsequent forays from Cuba resulted in skirmishes with the Maya and the collection of some gold and turquoise jewelry, but were otherwise indecisive except to maintain the interest of the Cuban Governor, Diego de Velásquez. Fernando Cortés, also sent by Velásquez, defeated the Aztec of Mexico in 1521, but in Yucatán he did little more than smash a few idols and rescue Aguilar. A series of expeditions begun in 1527 by Francisco de Montejo and his son finally subdued the Maya of Yucatán in 1546 after much bloodshed. However, final Spanish victory over the Maya did not come until 1697, when Tayasal, in the Guatemalan Petén, was captured.

With Aztec power broken, Cortés dispatched expeditions southward by sea and land. Cristóbal de Olid sailed to the Gulf of Honduras, established the town of Triunfo de la Cruz, and promptly declared himself independent of Cortés's authority, a practice becoming standard among the conquerors. At first, Cortés sent Francisco de las Casas with troops to relieve Olid. Then, deciding to trust no one but himself, he embarked upon a perilous march overland across the Petén to reprimand Olid in person. In the meantime, Olid found himself confronted with González Dávila, who was still pressing his claim against Pedrarias. Olid managed to capture González and Las Casas, but they escaped and turned the tables on him. After a bungled assassination attempt, they formally beheaded him with only ceremonial respect for the law. González now chose to negotiate for concessions from Cortés rather than contest his armed forces, and he permitted Las Casas to assume command. A Mexican tribunal sentenced both captains to death for the murder of Olid, but the sentences were never carried out. Indeed, upon his return from Honduras, Cortés promoted Las Casas and permitted González Dávila to return freely to Spain.

Cortés's arduous journey to Honduras had thus been unnecessary. The march had been costly in men and to his own health. Yet before returning to Mexico, in April 1526, Cortés consolidated his control against the continuing designs of Pedrarias. Las Casas had already ordered establishment of the port of Trujillo. Cortés now established, in September 1525, Puerto Natividad, later called Puerto Caballos. The Honduran government renamed it Puerto Cortés in 1869.

Cortés's ambitious but loyal second-in-command, Pedro de Alvarado, led the land expedition to Central America which resulted in the establishment of Guatemala as a Spanish kingdom. After a reconnaissance into southern Mexico, Alvarado left Mexico City with a large army in December 1523. Smallpox swept over the country before his advance, making resistance light or non-existent until he reached the Isthmus of Tehuantepec. There the natives forced the Spaniards to fight their way through the rugged highlands of Chiapas. In Guatemala the Cakchiquel and Quiché tribes were locked in civil war, with other tribes nominally allied to one or the other of these two powers. Alvarado took advantage of the enmities among the Indians, as had Cortés in Mexico, and he entered into an alliance with the Cakchiquel. Together they defeated the Quiché in April 1524. Alvarado himself is alleged to have killed the heroic Quiché chief, Tecúm-Umán, in hand-to-hand combat. Alvarado then established his capital at Iximché, the seat of Cakchiquel power, in July.

Iximché was built high on a plateau, advantageous for defense but otherwise inconvenient, and Alvarado searched for a more suitable site. In 1527 his brother, Jorge, relocated Guatemala City in the Almolonga Valley at the base of Volcán Agua, at a place today known as Ciudad Vieja. Pedro de Alvarado spent two more years conquering the remainder of Guatemala and El Salvador and suppressing Indian revolts. He founded several new settlements, but the Indians already had many towns and villages and these gradually became, to varying degrees, Hispanicized.

In Honduras, Alvarado confronted the forces of Pedrarias, and boundary disputes between the two captains led to dissension and disorder there for many years. In the mid-sixteenth century the Crown resolved the issue in a series of decrees which clarified the limits of the Kingdom of Guatemala. It included the land held by the modern-day republics of Costa Rica, Nicaragua, El Salvador, Honduras, and Guatemala, as well as British Honduras and the present Mexican state of Chiapas. Panama, with its important inter-oceanic transfer route, became a dependency of the Viceroyalty of Peru. As Peruvian gold and silver flowed across its narrow jungle paths in ever-increasing volume, it became one of the world's most strategic locations. Disputes over the boundary between Costa Rica and Panama, as well as over provincial boundaries within Central America, continued into the twentieth century.

After Alvarado made a triumphant visit to Spain, where in 1527 he received the title of Governor of Guatemala, he returned to the pacification of Central America. He was disappointed at the scarcity of precious minerals, and when word arrived of Pizarro's discoveries in Peru, he abandoned Guatemala for South America. Unsuccessful there, he returned once more to Spain, where he married into a prominent family. With his bride, Doña Beatriz de la Cueta, he returned to Guatemala in 1539, empowered to make new explorations. But news of golden cities in Cíbola (North America) lured him to the frontier of northern Mexico. There, he fought with his characteristic courage and recklessness, but his horse fell upon him and injured him fatally.

Uniquely, Alvarado's widow succeeded him as Governor of Guatemala. The rule of Doña Beatriz de la Cueva lasted but two days, however, as she died when a massive mudslide brought inundation and destruction to the capital city on the night of September 10, 1541. Construction of a new Guatemala City (present-day Antigua) began in the Panchoy Valley in 1543 under the direction of Doña Beatriz's brother, Francisco de la Cueva. From these frustrated beginnings emerged the magnificent capital known as Santiago de los Caballeros de Guatemala.

As the Conquest continued, a stream of settlers and adventurers flowed into the country from Spain, the Caribbean, and Mexico, establishing towns throughout the isthmus, exploiting the native labor, and turning to agriculture when mining failed. Indian resistance delayed the conquest of Costa Rica; not until 1561 did Juan de Cavallón finally lead a successful colonization party into that province. Although none of the settlements his small expedition founded in the Nicoya Bay region survived, he and his men began the first permanent Spanish occupation of Costa Rica. A year later Juan Vásquez de Coronado, with a larger and better-equipped force, took over as Governor of Nicaragua and Costa Rica and firmly established Spanish rule. He founded Cartago in 1564 as the Costa Rican capital.

The Indians were defeated, but not all were servile. Throughout the colonial era recurring Indian revolts consumed Spanish energies and resources. From Chiapas to Costa Rica the bloody and cruel suppression of the Indian populations stained the sixteenth century. The subjugation of these peoples passed through several phases: initial defeat, exploitation, suppression of insurgencies, and ideological subjection through conversion to Hispano-Christian culture.

The first great revolt came from Alvarado's allies, the Cakchiquel. It began in Sacatepéquez, in central Guatemala, as soon as Alvarado had moved on. Alvarado quickly returned from El Salvador to direct a bitter, four-year war of submission. By now the Conquest was economic as well as military. The Spaniards took the Indians' lands and properties, curtailed their freedoms, and reduced them to slavery or serfdom through the institution of the *encomienda*. Initially a tribute-collecting institution, the encomienda became the principal device by which this invading army settled on the land and developed a new society based on Indian labor. (We will consider the encomienda later.) Guatemala became the base of operations for subjugation of the natives in an ever-expanding region stretching into Chiapas, El Salvador, and Honduras, so that by 1540 the Indians were not only defeated, but also reduced to the status of Spanish social and economic vassals.

An important technique used by Alvarado and other conquerors to ensure the servility of newly conquered tribes was to seize and hold as hostages principal Indian chiefs, or *caciques*. Of these the most famous were the Quiché and Cakchiquel chiefs, Sequechul and Sinacam, whom Alvarado held for sixteen years. Fearing that they were directing continued uprisings even from captivity, Alvarado, in 1540, carried them into exile when he left Guatemala, ostensibly in search of the Spice Islands, but actually for Mexico. He took them into Jalisco, but after his death they escaped from there. They were never heard of again.

In subsequent years more Indian rebellions and raids plagued the colonists. Many expeditions were made against the fierce Lacandón of the Petén, even as late as the eighteenth century. But the sorties failed to stop their raids. Meanwhile, in Costa Rica, the settlers pushed back or exterminated the Indians of the Central Valley, leaving that small province almost exclusively inhabited by Iberians. On the Caribbean coasts other tribes, notably the Mosquito, maintained their independence from Spanish rule and prevented colonists in Nicaragua and Costa Rica from developing agriculture and commerce more fully on the Caribbean watershed. In the highlands, however, the Spanish succeeded in establishing their rule, though at the cost of thousands of Indian lives and heavy expenditures.

Yet the Conquest was not entirely military. There was one notable case in Central America of a peaceful approach by Christian friars to pacify and exploit the native population. The efforts of Bartolomé de las Casas, if not totally successful, suggest at least that there was another means of pacification that was less violent and more productive. Las Casas had entered the Dominican Order after witnessing the brutalities of the Spanish Conquest in the Caribbean. After his peaceful methods failed to subjugate the Indians at Cumaná (in modern Venezuela), he cloistered himself for several years in Hispaniola. He came to Central America via Mexico. In Nicaragua he organized a Dominican convent at Granada, where the cruel treatment of the Indians begun by Pedrarias had continued. Las Casas's preaching against such treatment was a thorn in the side of the civil officials there, but his efforts brought meager results, and toward the end of 1536 he abandoned Nicaragua and moved to Guatemala. There he became a vocal conscience for Alvarado and the Spanish administrators. Once more he conceived the idea of pacifying Indians unconquered by armed forces, and in 1537 he chose a region north of the capital known as the Land of War because of the Indians' successful resistance to Spanish arms.

Centering his activities at Tuzulutlán, he persuaded the caciques of the region to accept his friars, and his program appeared successful. The region became known as the Land of True Peace, or Verapaz. Las Casas then returned to Spain, where his success aided him. He persuaded the Crown to promulgate, in 1542, the New Laws of the Indies, an attempt to stop the ruthless encomienda system. Las Casas returned in 1544 as Bishop of Chiapas, under whose jurisdiction the Verapaz fell. He continued his efforts, but the colonial outcry against the New Laws made his work nearly impossible. The Dominican experiment in the Verapaz eventually failed, as Indians revolted and massacred the friars. The Dominicans still maintained monasteries and much land in the Verapaz, but the province gradually fell under the control of settlers seeking land and labor. Nevertheless, the influence of Bartolomé de las Casas remained strong in Guatemala, and his voice of humanity and compassion toward the Indians never died entirely.

Political jurisdiction over Central America evolved slowly. Conquistadores represented authorities in Mexico, Santo Domingo, and Panama, and it was several years before a unified administration ruled over a united colony. Rivalry among representatives of these seats of authority contributed heavily to the early disorder and turmoil in Central America, especially in Honduras and Nicaragua. Individual jealousies combined with geographic barriers to retard the unification of Central America in the sixteenth century. Several important and virtually autonomous administrative centers emerged on the isthmus. In addition to Alvarado's Santiago de Guatemala, there were Ciudad Real in Chiapas, Comayagua in Honduras, León and Granada in Nicaragua, and Panama City. Each new conquest justified a new government. This resulted in decentralization, despite royal efforts to maintain close control through its agents. The municipalities assumed authority, and the *ayuntamientos*, or town councils, were the most important governing bodies. In these early days they exercised jurisdiction over much wider areas than the towns themselves. By 1530 Guatemala, Nicaragua, Honduras, Chiapas, and Panama all functioned under separate royal orders.

Yet in the next decade increased knowledge about the isthmus, the death of Pedrarias Dávila in Nicaragua, and the growing prestige of Guatemala's Pedro de Alvarado all contributed to a royal inclination toward unifying the isthmus under a single jurisdiction. The establishment of the Viceroyalty of New Spain implied Mexican rule over the northern portions of the region, but the establishment of the Audiencia de Panamá in the same year (1535) continued the confusion over jurisdiction in Nicaragua. Not until 1543 did the Crown unify the entire region by creating the Audiencia de los Confines (Boundaries). The new court held jurisdiction from Tabasco and Yucatán to Panama. In selecting a centrally located seat, the Crown had originally thought in terms of Comayagua, but in 1544 it ordered the new Audiencia to be established at Gracias, which had been founded by Alvarado as a gold-mining center in western Honduras.

Immediately, the residents of both Santiago de Guatemala and Panama City sent representatives (*procuradores*) to Spain to argue against Gracias. That city flourished briefly, from both mining and its administrative importance, but its gold was soon exhausted and the city was otherwise isolated and poorly located. Honduras's early importance as a gold producer faded quickly. In 1548, therefore, the Crown ordered the Audiencia moved to Santiago. The following year the Audiencia took up offices in the episcopal palace of the new city. Soon thereafter, the Audiencia lost jurisdiction over Panama, Yucatán, and Tabasco. What remained, with only minor boundary modifications, became the colonial Kingdom of Guatemala. By that time there was nominal peace and order, although continued Indian revolts, new conquests, internal disputes, and attacks by foreign interlopers on the coasts would disrupt life on the isthmus periodically for more than two centuries thereafter.

In the 1560's the unity of Central America was once more administratively broken by the termination of the Audiencia de los Confines at Guatemala and the reestablishment of one at Panama with jurisdiction over Panama, Costa Rica, and Nicaragua. Honduras, Guatemala, and Chiapas were placed under the jurisdiction of the Audiencia of Mexico. The indignant protests of powerful cacao producers and civil and ecclesiastical leaders—including Bartolomé de las Casas, who

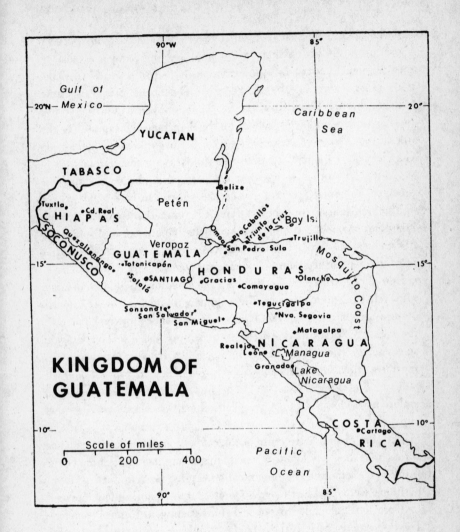

KINGDOM OF
GUATEMALA

believed that the Audiencia in Guatemala was a check against settlers' abuses of the Indian missions in Guatemala—brought rapid reversal of this decision. By 1570 the Audiencia had been restored to Guatemala, with jurisdiction over the Kingdom of Guatemala, stretching from Chiapas through Costa Rica. Its jurisdiction survived until the end of the Hispanic period. Meanwhile, Felipe II granted the capital city the title of the "very noble and loyal city of Santiago de los Caballeros de Goathemala." Panama City received a similar commendation in 1581.

Under the Audiencia, Guatemala emerged as the most important province. Provincial governments existed elsewhere and provided for local administration, but they suffered discrimination from the capital. Honduras' economic decline weakened its importance and influence. Nicaragua—and Costa Rica, which was a virtual dependency of that province—languished, and Chiapas was remote and ignored. Even within the province of Guatemala, the populous highland districts (Los Altos) centered around Quezaltenango and the Pacific districts around San Salvador felt the discriminatory practices of the officials in the capital. Not until the eighteenth century did El Salvador gain status as a separate province, and Los Altos failed altogether in its separatist endeavors. Inevitably, therefore, Guatemala was not only the political, but also the social and economic center of the kingdom, and ambitious colonists seeking to advance themselves gravitated to that city.

The administrative structure of the colony followed Spanish practice throughout the New World. Principal positions, including those of the Captain General and the provincial governors, as well as many lesser positions, were filled by trained appointees from Spain, although several had previous colonial experience before coming to Central America. Lesser positions, such as those of the *alcaldes mayores* and the *corregidores,* sometimes were staffed with creoles. Only in the ayuntamientos of the towns were the creole population adequately represented. In effect, a bureaucracy of Spanish officials was responsible for most aspects of government in the kingdom. Some of these officials remained in the colony and became founders of new creole families, but for the most part they formed a rotating bureaucratic corps which was separate from the local creole population. In the Indian areas of Guatemala, of course, caciques often remained in control of their tribes and villages, and, by effectively collaborating with the bureaucracy, they often thwarted creole ambitions.

While the Viceroyalty of New Spain nominally had jurisdiction over the Kingdom of Guatemala, in practice, since the bureaucracy was appointed directly from Spain and could communicate directly with the home government, bypassing viceregal authority, Guatemala operated as an autonomous Spanish dominion. Yet there were enough instances in which the viceregal authority attempted to intervene in Central America over the course of the colonial period that Central Americans developed some feelings of antagonism toward Mexico. The superior trade privileges and opportunities of Mexicans and the Central Americans' resentment of the viceregal status held by the inhabitants of Mexico compounded this animosity.

The most pervasive authority in the colony was the Audiencia, which was presided over by the President, who also was Captain General and Governor. The *oidores,* or justices, of the Audiencia served longer terms in the colony than other bureaucrats. Separately, they served as appellate judges for the various private and public courts that existed in the complex Spanish American judicial system. Collectively, they served in both legislative and judicial capacities, wielding enormous power over the colony. Throughout the sixteenth and seventeenth centuries, most of the presidents of the Kingdom were men trained in the law. A royal *cédula* of 1680 relieved the President of direct responsibility for presiding over the Audiencia, providing a regent to serve in his absence. This act reflected the colony's need for defense, and after 1680 it was more common for the Crown to appoint military officers to the position.

A vigorous and zealous Church participated with the State in administrative authority over society and economy, to their mutual advantage. Regular friars and secular priests accompanied the conquistadores and soon established convents and parishes from which to convert and instruct the indigenous population and minister to the settlers. Dedi-

cated missionaries, the products of a reform movement within the
Spanish Church which antedated the Protestant Reformation of northern Europe, worked tirelessly to temper the harsh aspects of the Conquest, while at the same time planting firmly the institution of Christianity in the new land. In the early years they established several
monasteries in Nicaragua and Guatemala, and soon thereafter they set
up dioceses. Honduras and Chiapas received bishops a little later, but
Central America had no archbishop until 1745. The Verapaz became
a diocese in 1559, with its see at Cobán, but the region failed to prosper, and it was reincorporated into the diocese of Guatemala in 1607.
Relations between Church and State, as we have already seen in the
case of the Dominican friar Las Casas, were not always cordial. The
Church served as the agent for the royal policy of humanitarian treatment of the natives, a role which often lead it into conflict with civil
officials and planters. Yet there were many cases in which Church and
State worked together harmoniously. For example, the first Bishop of
Guatemala, Francisco Marroquín, provided inspired leadership for the
Church as well as for the city of Guatemala during that town's difficult
early years.

As the religious orders established themselves in the kingdom, disputes over jurisdiction arose among them and between them and the
secular clergy. There was especial rivalry between the Dominicans and
Franciscans for control of the Indian population in Guatemala. By
1600 there were twenty-two Franciscan, fourteen Dominican, and six
Mercederian *conventos* in Guatemala alone. The Jesuits arrived in
1582, and, although they were never numerous in Central America,
they were important in education and in agricultural production, particularly of sugar.

The clergy did much more than provide for the spiritual needs of
the Indians and colonists. Both the monastic orders and the secular
establishment acquired considerable wealth, particularly in Guatemala
and Nicaragua, so that there was growing resentment of the clergy on
economic grounds. They ran large estates, served as bankers, and constructed roads and bridges; one friar even proposed construction of an
interoceanic canal through Central America early in the seventeenth

century. The Jesuits were more aggressive than the other orders, and their efforts to start schools and increase their properties in the isthmus earned them the antagonism of the other clergy.

One religious order, the result of the exemplary work and devotion of a Franciscan friar, Pedro de San José de Betancur (1626-67), originated in Guatemala during the years 1651-67. Sometimes referred to as the "St. Francis of the Americas," Betancur had come to Guatemala from the Canary Islands. He dedicated himself to the care of the poor and sick. In his will, he commanded his followers to form a cofradía to maintain his hospital in Guatemala, but his principal disciple, Rodrigo de la Cruz (formerly Rodrigo Arias Maldonado, Marquis of Talamanca and Interim Governor of Costa Rica), instead formed (in 1668) the Bethlehemite Order, which gained papal confirmation in 1672. Viewed unenthusiastically by the Spanish government, the new order remained small until the eighteenth century. By the close of the colonial era it was maintaining seventeen hospitals throughout Spanish America and one in the Canaries, as well as several colleges. The Bethlehemites, the only male religious order to originate in Spanish America, did not survive the anticlericalism of the nineteenth century, although a small female branch, organized in 1670, continues to exist.

In the seventeenth century, as civil authority weakened owing to a degenerating Spanish monarchy, the clergy assumed greater authority in civil and economic affairs. The century saw the construction of many new churches, basilicas, monasteries, and charitable institutions. These buildings made Santiago into one of America's loveliest cities. By the close of the 1600's it ranked behind only Mexico City and Lima in size and importance. Reflecting its dominant position within the kingdom, the Diocese of Guatemala (including El Salvador) by the end of the colonial era contained nearly 60 per cent of the churches in the kingdom (424 of 759). Honduras had 145, Chiapas 102, and Nicaragua and Costa Rica 88.

Notwithstanding the zeal of devout clergymen in converting the Indians, the principal motive for colonization in Central America was economic. The lure of easy wealth, preferably gold or silver, attracted

Spaniards to the isthmus, and the availability of Indian labor to build agricultural estates kept them there after mining proved less lucrative than they had hoped. The isthmus was not devoid of precious metals, however. Panama and Honduras had rich deposits, which accounted for early interest in those provinces. Guatemala and Nicaragua provided smaller quantities. The turbulent and bloody early political history of Honduras stemmed from the gold rush. As the opportunities for rapid enrichment diminished, so also did the ardor for political power.

Royal policy encouraged mining. Initially, the Crown maintained formal ownership of all mining activities, simply leasing concessions to individuals. The first "mining," of course, was simply robbing Indian treasure, and the conquerors were very thorough robbers. Placer mining followed, and this was lucrative in Panama and Honduras, but it soon exhausted the supply and gave way to underground mining, for which Indians were pressed into service. Occasional discoveries of new veins of silver caused flurries of excitement throughout the colonial years, but rarely did they offer more than small rewards. Central America did not become a large producer of precious metals. In the end, it was agricultural production rather than minerals which provided most Central Americans with their livelihood. Yet the Crown never abandoned the possibilities of greater mineral extraction. It periodically lowered the amount of royalty on precious metals in order to encourage mining, and after 1584 it permitted private ownership of mining properties.

Because of the feudal traditions of Spain, and the eventual predominance of agriculture in the isthmus, social and economic security and advancement in the colony depended upon landholding. From the beginning settlers fought and intrigued to secure land titles. The conquistadores made the initial grants to their loyal followers, but as new settlers arrived the municipalities made new grants, later to be confirmed by royal decree. Land tenure offers insight into much of the social and economic history of colonial Central America, for it reflects the rising and falling fortunes of the principal families.

Yet even more important than the land was control of the labor to work the land. Indians were the means to wealth, and all who came sought to exploit them. The conquistadores divided the labor of the Indians among themselves in a vicious system of forced labor. The requirement of tribute drove the Indians to seek work from the Spaniards in order to make their payments. Indian slavery was common during the Conquest, but it became relatively rare after 1550 as the encomienda—virtual serfdom—provided an alternative. The Spanish competed ruthlessly for encomiendas of Indians from near-by pueblos to work their lands.

The New Laws of 1542 formally abolished the encomienda system, but lax enforcement and evasion allowed the system to continue in Central America. The colonists vigorously protested the New Laws. They attacked Las Casas, whom they knew well from his criticisms of Indian treatment in Nicaragua and Guatemala. Reminding Carlos I that they had invested their lives and possessions in the Conquest and that the Crown, without risking a peso, had received enormous benefits, Guatemalan colonists petitioned the King to revoke the orders and to treat those who had served him so well with greater consideration. In Nicaragua the colonists reacted to the New Laws with an armed uprising and murdered a bishop who supported the Laws. Violence also erupted in Honduras. The authorities finally restored some measure of order, but while the King refused to revoke the New Laws, in effect the institution of the *repartimiento* subverted their intention.

The repartimiento required labor from Indian men between ages sixteen and sixty, excepting only the caciques and those Indians who were ill. As it evolved in Guatemala, the repartimiento generally conscripted a quarter of the men of a village each week. In theory, this left each man three weeks to take care of his own fields. In actual practice, Indians often spent more than a third of their time in repartimiento service, for travel from their villages to the place of work, sometimes considerable distances away, represented further loss of time for them. They often suffered losses in transit, and the long trips required rest time when they arrived. The Audiencia assigned the repartimientos to private individuals, religious institutions, municipalities, and government offices. By law, the Indians were to be paid, usually one *real* (one-eighth of a peso) per day, but in practice little money actually changed hands, as the employers "charged" the Indians for the goods they consumed. Toleration of this illegal practice helps to explain how debt slavery evolved in the eighteenth and nineteenth centuries.

Although enforcement was slow and somewhat uneven, the old encomienda did end. A measure of freedom for the Indians evolved, permitting them to live in their own villages, where the encomendero was prohibited from living. In the end, the new system benefited the landowners as greatly as had the encomienda. They rarely paid actual cash for the Indians' services, and they no longer had the obligation to protect the Indians, which the encomienda system had required. The New Laws themselves provided the basis for the new system, formalized into law by royal decrees in 1574 and 1601, which granted part of the tribute from Indian communities to the settlers as a reward for the Conquest. Although it was abolished in Mexico in 1633, Central American creoles, through their attorneys at the Spanish court, succeeded in legally maintaining the repartimiento through the eighteenth century.

The New Laws thus permitted Indians to live apart and contributed to a growing concentration of Indians in larger towns, many of which had few Spanish or ladino residents. Indian villages survived longer here than in Mexico, where debt slavery replaced the repartimiento system sooner. Among important Indian towns in Central America were Quezaltenango, Totonicapán, Cobán, Momostenango, Santa Cruz del Quiché, Sololá, and Escuintla in Guatemala; Santa Ana and Ahuachapán in El Salvador; Managua and Masaya in Nicaragua; and Nicoya in Costa Rica.

The repartimiento represented what has become one of the most pervasive qualities of Central American society and mentality. The system provided Indian labor for landholders, miners, and government officials. In some areas the system evolved into a technically free system of wage labor, but in reality it became debt peonage, as Indians began to live on the *fincas*, or haciendas, of Central America. In Guatemala, where the Indians were more numerous and continued to maintain their cultural identity and separateness, the repartimiento system survived beyond Independence, and similar systems of forced labor persist in the twentieth century. It was the principal means by which the

Spanish kept the Indians in subjugation and exploited their labor, thus maintaining the Indian in an inferior position for the remainder of the colonial period and well up to the present time. The repartimiento was the colonists' answer to the New Laws, and they successfully thwarted all royal efforts to provide opportunities for Indians to become full-fledged citizens of the kingdom.

Most of the inhabitants from Chiapas to Costa Rica were engaged in simple subsistence agriculture or in producing foodstuffs for local markets, yet it was in the production of export commodities that the economic future of the isthmus rested. Cacao was popular in pre-Columbian times. The Indians of the isthmus regularly drank chocolate, and cacao beans had served as currency before the Conquest, a practice which continued under Spanish rule in Costa Rica, where scarcity of coin was a serious problem even into the nineteenth century. Cacao grew along the Pacific slopes from Soconusco to Nicaragua and on the Caribbean slopes of Costa Rica. The major center for the cacao trade, Sonsonate, in southwestern El Salvador, in the late sixteenth century grew to become second in size only to Santiago de Guatemala. Merchants shipped most of the cacao overland through Oaxaca to Veracruz, although they shipped some from the Pacific ports of Realejo and Acajutla. By the beginning of the seventeenth century, other cacao-producing regions, notably Venezuela, with locations more accessible to Europe had challenged Central American producers. Because of devastating epidemics, the supply of Indian labor in the cacao-producing regions had diminished, and the new competition could not be overcome. The crop then lost its preeminent position in the Central American economy. The one exception was Costa Rica, which enjoyed a resurgence in production and export of cacao in the seventeenth century.

Indigo, grown principally in El Salvador, Guatemala, and Nicaragua, then replaced cacao as the leading export and source of hard currency for the isthmus. Indigo cultivation was developed through the harvesting of the wild *xiquilite,* mostly on the lower Pacific slopes, beginning late in the sixteenth century. The planters employed Indians for the difficult and dangerous work of cultivating and processing the indigo into blocks of deep blue dye, and only a population resurgence in the seventeenth century permitted expansion of the industry. At that time African slaves supplemented the native labor force. By 1635 San Vicente, El Salvador, was the major center for the indigo trade, although there were other important centers in Guatemala and Nicaragua. Indigo was the major export of the kingdom throughout the remainder of the colonial period, reaching its peak during the second half of the eighteenth century.

The vast bulk of agricultural production, however, was for domestic consumption. Fincas produced livestock, corn, wheat, and other crops for the local residents. Certain Indian communities, especially in the heavily populated valleys around the capital, specialized in the production of foodstuffs. Corn was the major crop, but important wheat-producing areas grew up around Cartago and Guatemala City. Sugar plantations, worked by African slaves, became important near Amatitlán. Beans and other vegetables and fruits were cultivated widely. The Spanish population, as well as an important segment of the ladinos, depended upon the Indians to produce their food. Large market-places in every village and town developed brisk internal trade in provisions. Indian traders brought their goods into the urban markets. Such markets are still an integral aspect of Central American life.

Conversely, manufacturing played a minor though essential role in the kingdom's economy. Spain itself lagged far behind its European neighbors in industry. Moreover, imperial policy did not favor colonial competition with the mother country. Royal encouragement came only to products not sufficiently available in the mother country, which for the most part meant tropical agricultural produce. Nevertheless, the isolation of the kingdom from the principal trade routes and the high cost of transporting European goods to Central America inevitably meant that many items had to be manufactured locally. Most such goods were produced on the fincas or in villages. Home manufacture of clothing, leather goods, housewares, and other everyday necessities was standard. In the larger towns and cities, small artisan shops produced such things for the urban population. The municipal regulations reflect close control of quality standards and prices for shoemakers, tailors, and other artisans. Organized into guilds, these craftsmen attempted to limit competition while at the same time maintaining standards, but they rarely sold their goods beyond their immediate vicinity. Mercantilistic royal decrees prohibited colonial manufacture of such products as wine or silk, in which there was recurrent colonial interest. On the other hand, Indian crafts—textiles, pottery, crude furniture, etc.—were marketed widely in native markets by traveling Indian merchants. Although the wealthy, who insisted on European finery, shunned these native-made goods, they gained acceptance among the ladino population.

Because of the importance of precious metals, cacao, and the immigration of settlers and the transport of slaves, Central America enjoyed considerable commercial activity in the early years, but after 1550 the kingdom settled down to a backwater position in the Spanish commercial empire. Early promise of prosperity in the isthmus gave way to a slower routine, and poverty became widespread. The principal exports continued to flow from the kingdom, but most commercial activity was local. Stifling regulations, taxes, and supervision retarded what could have been a more extensive commerce. There was little intercolonial trade, though it was not altogether absent owing to legal exceptions in the trade policy and a certain amount of contraband, but the mercantilistic policy of maintaining the American kingdoms as colonies which were permitted to trade only with the mother country obstructed the growth of greater interdependence between Central America and colonies in North and South America. Early development of commercial routes between Central America and Peru on the Pacific and with Havana and Santo Domingo on the Caribbean diminished in the seventeenth century as Spain tightened its commercial monopoly in an effort to thwart European rivals who were challenging Iberian hegemony in America.

Communications difficulties also retarded commerce. Combined with imperial restrictions, this meant a continual isolation of the several provinces. Both imperial and local officials regularly recognized the need for roads and ports, but few did anything about it. A stream of royal decrees ordered civil, clerical, military, and commercial leaders to develop and care for a system of roads, including a carriageway from Chiapas to Panama. Sections of this *camino real* were built during the colonial period, and some impressive bridges still remain from the old route, but it was never operational in its entirety. Greater effort went into building roads to get major export commodities to market. A better communications network might have served to unite the kingdom more fully and to provide opportunities for the outlying reaches of the kingdom, but it never developed. Such a system is, in fact, only becoming a reality in the present decade! What few muddy roads there were served only the narrow interests of the principal merchants of the capital or the planters with whom they dealt. Carriageways were rare; for the most part both goods and passengers were carried on the backs of mules or Indians over muddy and steep trails or in narrow and dangerous pirogues on swollen streams. More than anything else, the surface communications reflected the underdeveloped state of this colony. The poor roads inhibited any sense of unity which might have developed. Intercourse among the provinces, difficult at best, was often virtually impossible. Chiapas become more closely tied commercially to Mexico than to Guatemala; Costa Rica developed ties with Chiriquí in Panama. Nicaragua and Honduras remained isolated, and what communication there was between El Salvador and Guatemala only heightened the resentment of Salvadorans against the preferential treatment given the people of the capital. A similar resentful, separatist attitude developed in the Los Altos districts of Quezaltenango, Totonicapán, and Sololá.

The ports were not much better than the roads. The tropical, lowland climate and terrain seriously retarded establishment and maintenance of adequate deep-water ports on the Caribbean, and Veracruz continued to be the major outlet for Central American goods. Disease, the jungle, the climate, floods, and landslides all worked against repeated efforts to develop the Caribbean ports during the colonial regime. Trujillo and Puerto Caballos lost their early importance once the gold played out, and only a small amount of trade trickled through the Gulf of Honduras.

The easier accessibility and more healthful climate of the Pacific shores, despite the dearth of natural harbors, caused early and continuous interest in port construction there. These concerns had contributed to the shift of focus from the Darién colony to Panama City in 1519. In 1535 a royal order permitted the construction of ships on the Pacific coast as a means of encouraging industry and commerce, and Pedro de Alvarado promoted the opening of ports and shipyards at Iztapa and Realejo. Other ports developed later at Acajutla, Nicoya, and Puntarenas. But as imperial restrictions discouraged intercolonial or overseas trade, these ports languished, until they amounted to no more than a few grass huts serving an occasional vessel.

Interest in a transisthmian route dated from Alvarado's time, and Carlos I issued encouraging decrees. Except for the mule and river route across Panama, however, the dream remained unrealized during Hispanic rule and commerce on the Pacific did not prosper.

The small amount of commerce limited the importance of the export-import merchants. Economic and social power in the kingdom lay in landholding, agricultural production, and control of Indians. Merchants were, of course, essential to the landholders to handle exports and provide the imports they needed or wanted. The most important merchants were closely allied with or part of the landholding families. The principal merchant houses were clustered near the central plaza in the capital. They had connections with merchants in Seville and Mexico. Locally, their interests were best represented in the ayuntamiento, in which several frequently held membership. The ayuntamiento's edicts reflect the merchants' genuine concern for the welfare of commerce, roads and ports, agricultural production, price regulation, and other, related issues. The establishment of a merchant guild (consulado de comercio) in Mexico in 1549 did little to provide greater representation for the Central American merchants, other than to offer a commercial tribunal where litigation might be taken. It nevertheless set the model for an institution which Guatemalan merchants, at least as early as 1649, wished to duplicate in their own kingdom. As with other colonial commercial centers below the level of viceregal capital, however, this was not permitted until the end of the eighteenth century. The Crown thus denied the Central American merchants the privilege of their own private court, or *fuero,* forcing them to depend upon civil officials and ordinary courts.

Wealth was limited to a very few, and the economy of the seventeenth century failed to provide adequate opportunities for expansion of even that limited prosperity. A handful of merchants and planters lived in the capital, where they created an imitation aristocracy. Similar elites could be found in the provincial capitals, although they paled in comparison with that of Guatemala, which in turn failed to reach the grandeur of its counterparts in Mexico City or Lima.

There was sufficient affluence, however, to permit considerable beautification of Santiago de Guatemala. Magnificent homes and large commercial houses filled with imported goods lined the principal streets near the center of the city, but the grandeur of the metropolis was most reflected in the opulence of the ecclesiastical establishment, as great churches, monasteries, convents, and seminaries abounded. An architectural style developed in Santiago which smaller towns throughout Central America imitated.

From the beginning, manufactured goods commanded high prices which only the well-to-do could afford, while the vast majority of the population used local, crudely made merchandise. Controls over markets and prices provided some check against runaway inflation for scarce goods, while an exploitive labor system kept wages low. Most of the people were poor. There was a shortage of currency to such an extent that barter was widespread. Credit was difficult to get and interest rates were high. The clergy often played the role of bankers, although merchants extended credit to planters against their future crops.

Spain's involvement in European wars drained American resources. In general, colonials were exempted from military service in these struggles, except when Spain's enemies struck at America itself, but the Crown called upon them unceasingly for financial support. A steady rise in taxes, forced loans, and other assessments increased the burden on an already strained economy. Creoles sought relief, and in

1604 the Crown turned over collection of the *alcabala*, or sales tax, to the Ayuntamiento of Guatemala. This permitted a reduction in the amounts most citizens paid, but soon there were new increases in the tax rates. The rates rose throughout the seventeenth century, and tax evasion and corruption came to be a major part of colonial economic life, a situation which persists to this day.

Supervision over every aspect of the economy was detailed and restrictive, but not necessarily inflexible. Bribery and other forms of corruption were the creoles' answers to restrictive legislation or unpopular policies. Depression and currency depreciation contributed to a real decline in living standards in the latter part of the seventeenth century, but government officials supplemented their salaries with illicit activities and bribes, and they frequently ignored royal prohibitions against engaging in commerce or other private remunerative activities.

The restrictive commercial system and inadequate facilities for commerce in the sixteenth and seventeenth centuries inevitably opened the way for illegal trade in Central America, just as they did in other parts of the empire. Spain's rivals—France, Holland, England—carried on a brisk trade with creole planters and merchants in cacao, tobacco, indigo, and other plantation crops, and provided goods to the creoles at prices considerably below the official rates. Spain strictly forbade foreigners from engaging in such trade, but the laxness of enforcement and the willingness of royal officials to accept bribes or other pay-offs permitted smuggling to flourish. On the Caribbean coast the independent Mosquito Indians, often supported by the British, became active middlemen in the trade. Such commerce was not always peaceful: Indians and foreign interlopers, particularly in Costa Rica and Nicaragua, often simply attacked the settlers and carried off their crops and treasure.

The maritime expansion by Spain's rivals exposed both Caribbean and Pacific shore settlements to devastating raids, which retarded the colonization of the tropical coasts. The transit route for Peruvian treasure across Panama was especially tempting to the freebooters, but the coastal settlements from Darién to the Golfo Dulce all suffered repeated attacks. Forced to increase expenditures for coastguard and shore fortifications, the Spanish government inevitably added to the already heavy tax load on commerce. In the seventeenth century the establishment of rival colonies in the Caribbean provided markets and bases for buccaneers to continue their marauding activities along Central American coasts. In 1642 the British captured and held Roatán Island, in the Bay of Honduras. With this toehold, the British began to control much of the Caribbean coast of Central America. A year later a Dutch force captured and virtually destroyed Trujillo, and the Spanish abandoned that port until 1789. In response to these attacks, the Spanish built large fortresses along the Caribbean coasts and along the rivers leading into the interior. Fort San Felipe, on the Río Dulce in Guatemala, and Castillo Viejo, on the Río San Juan in Nicaragua, stand today as reminders of those swashbuckling days.

But the forts failed to stop the incursions. In the 1660's British woodcutters settled at the mouth of the Belize River. ("Belize" is a corruption of the name of Peter Wallace, a buccaneer.) Belize became an important buccaneering base; it was the seed of modern British Honduras. Although Spain refused to recognize British sovereignty in Belize and occasionally succeeded in ousting the intruders, the settlement operated as a British colony most of the time thereafter. In 1665 and again in 1670 English buccaneers penetrated the isthmus in Nicaragua as far as Granada. Henry Morgan, buccaneer of buccaneers, crossed the isthmus and sacked Panama City in 1671, causing the Spanish to abandon the city for a new site a few miles up the coast. Other buccaneers crossed Panama repeatedly in the 1680's. Between 1665 and 1680 the Matina Valley cacao region of Costa Rica was virtually in English hands. The decade of the 1680's witnessed an increase in British domination of the Mosquito coast, and slave hunting was added to the list of foreign atrocities in the region.

One of the most daring and bizarre chapters in the history of international rivalry in the region was the effort of William Paterson to plant a Scottish colony at Darién. Paterson projected an agricultural and commercial colony which could trade on both oceans. Launched with the backing of the British Crown, the expedition of 1200 settlers landed on November 4, 1698, at a place they named New Saint An-

GUATEMALA AND BELIZE

drew, near the abandoned Spanish settlement of Acla. Although the
settlers expressed friendly inclinations toward all and advocated free
trade, their colony was actually a threat not only to the Spanish and
the Indians of the region, but also to the English commercial companies with which it would compete. For that reason the colony received neither supplies nor aid from British commercial colonies in the
Caribbean. In the end, the tropical climate and severe hardships led to
ruin. The colonists abandoned the place in June of 1699, several
months before the Spanish ever got around to making any formal
protest. Although this colonial adventure failed miserably, the fact that
the Spaniards had been able to do nothing to prevent its establishment
suggests the weakness of the empire at that time.

Political, economic, and ecclesiastical organization created a social
structure which became thoroughly entrenched in Guatemala during
Hapsburg rule. It was a society in which there were three clearly rec-
ognizable social classes, plus a number of other, somewhat mobile sectors. Most of the inhabitants were Indians, particularly in Guatemala,
Honduras and El Salvador, and, to a lesser extent, in Nicaragua. African slaves were fewer in numbers there than they were in the Caribbean islands, but nonetheless they were an important additional
laboring group, first in Honduras to work the mines, but later in
Nicaragua and Guatemala to work in cane fields and sugar mills. As
serfs or slaves this class provided the bulk of the work force throughout the colonial period, tilling the fields, working the mines, and providing personal service. Their masters comprised the other two identifiable social classes. The first of these, the Spanish bureaucracy, resided
principally in Guatemala City. Mostly Spanish-born and, except for
the *oidores* of the Audiencia, short-term residents who carried out their
duties in service to the Crown and themselves, they seldom had any
sincere interest in the long-range prosperity of the Kingdom of Guatemala. The other social class was composed chiefly of large landholders,
most of whom had been born in the colony. They were united as an
untitled, colonial aristocracy. Denied easy access to the principal political, administrative, and economic offices or control of the powerful in-

stitutions because of the monopolization of these institutions by the bureaucrats, this ever-expanding creole class found strength in its economic control of production and commerce. It also exercised an increasing influence in the colony through evasion of laws, corruption, and illegal trading and smuggling. Some peninsular bureaucrats, of course, became founders of creole families, and new settlers arrived throughout the colonial period, so that there were almost always some Spanish-born among the "creole aristocracy" just as there were some creoles among the "peninsular bureaucracy."

In the Caribbean the Spaniards had pursued a merciless policy of slavery in their efforts to create a labor force for the mines and plantations. The results there had been disastrous, as the entire native race was exterminated and had to be replaced by expensive slaves imported from Africa. In Central America the conquerors sought to avoid a repetition of this circumstance, although there were enough cases of cruelty and brutality to suggest that many Spaniards did not learn the lesson. In Costa Rica and in much of Nicaragua and Panama, where the Indians did not live in sedentary society and fled or resisted, much of the Indian population was annihilated. But in Guatemala, and, to a lesser extent, throughout the isthmus, the conquering Spaniards—few in number and aware of that fact—treated the natives more humanely. They sought the aid of Indian caciques to control and exploit Indian labor. Pedro de Alvarado, as harsh as he had shown himself to be in military conquest and in the repression of Indian rebellion, recognized the danger of extermination, and in 1530 he issued orders which reflected his desire to preserve the Indian population. Seventeen ordinances prohibited the Spaniards from removing Indians from the kingdom (slave raiding from the Caribbean was a problem) or making excessive demands upon the Indians. Disease, too, had been a major killer of Indians, and Alvarado and subsequent governors took steps to preserve the health of the natives and to prevent the spread of epidemics. These efforts were not wholly successful, however, as dysentery, smallpox, and plague continued to decimate the population. The great epidemic of 1545-48 was especially deadly.

From the beginning, the key to social position in the colony rested in the ownership of land and control of Indians to work the land. Theoretically, all land belonged to the Crown, and, although it was physically taken by acts of the conquerors, it had to be granted formally by the King. Land was therefore an incentive and stimulant for the Conquest, and it attracted settlers. The vacant lands became an important source of income for the royal treasury, and the *composición*, introduced in 1591 essentially as a title tax, became the means by which the Crown either taxed or reclaimed land. Although the Crown from time to time issued decrees protecting Indian lands, it failed to forestall the emergence of a dominant class of creole landholders from which Indians, and, for the most part, ladinos, were excluded. Struggles for control of the land thus occupied much time and litigation in the colony. Family feuds and political intrigue were closely related to land disputes, as the descendants of the conquistadores and immigrant newcomers with influential connections in Spain or with the peninsular bureaucracy vied for ownership of the best lands and encomiendas.

In time, the combination of economic exploitation and the moral pressure of the Church created a paternalistic attitude in the landholding class. The Indians persisted in many of their pre-Conquest religious beliefs and practices as a kind of natural defense against the cultural imperialism of Spanish Christianity. Even today, manifestations of the pagan traditions are easily found among Guatemalan Indians. The Guatemalan creole attitude, one of the most deep-rooted prejudices of creole mentality, was that the Indian was living happily in poverty. They defended, for a longer time than did the leaders in most other parts of the empire, the repartimiento, arguing that the Indian was lazy and would not work unless obligated to do so. In creole eyes the Indian was inclined to vice, especially to drunkenness, and this would increase if they did not keep him occupied with obligatory labor. In a paternalistic and self-righteous manner, they convinced themselves that the Indians did not suffer poverty in their simple and tranquil life.

There was, of course, racial mixing from the beginning, and a growing number of ladinos began to fill the towns and countryside. The conquistadores had mated with Indian princesses, although such unions were rarely formalized into marriage and offspring did not gain ready acceptance into either creole or peninsular society. Unlike the situation in some other parts of the Spanish empire, Spanish women did immigrate to the isthmus, and there they formed the basis for a pure white aristocracy which set itself racially above the ladinos, even though by the eighteenth century some ladinos had gained limited acceptance among creoles. Particularly in Guatemala and Costa Rica, where white women were brought into the colony early in its existence, a white ruling class remained. But there were not nearly enough white women for all the Spaniards, and, inevitably, casual and forced relationships led to a large number of illegitimate, dislocated ladinos, people who were not easily absorbed into the established social classes. Some of these became wage laborers in the country. Many gained acceptance from their creole fathers, although they could not enjoy the full privileges and rights of their legitimate half brothers and sisters. But they could sometimes get small farms, or enter commerce or the professions. A much larger number formed a classless group in the major towns. They sought work where they could find it. From their ranks came most of the artisans, small merchants, peddlers, service personnel, etc., and, although they do not have all the attributes of a bourgeoisie, by the end of the colonial era they were a middle sector of considerable importance in Central American society.

There was some cooperation, a degree of social communication, and other relationships between the Spanish bureaucracy and the landholding elite in the colony, but it was the Audiencia that best represented the bureaucratic class interests. Creoles, whose major strength was in the ayuntamientos, resented not having better representation. Serious clashes over control of the wealth and Indians of the kingdom reflected the differences between those two bodies. Disputes over petty and personal differences punctuated the growing tension. They quarreled over substantive economic issues of tax collection, land grants, Indian repartimientos, and so forth, but also over formalities related to the prestige of their respective institutions. They jealously guarded their privileges and took great offense at departures from established procedure. The President and the Audiencia sometimes became involved in creole family feuds. The peninsulares feared too much autonomy for the creoles and at times seem to have resented their own exclusion from creole society.

Both classes feared the rootless and sometimes violent ladinos. Ordinances limited or prohibited the ladinos' rights to bear arms or own horses. There was also concern over the growing number of blacks in the country by the early seventeenth century, for escaped slaves sometimes rebelled and formed bandit gangs in remote areas that had not yet been pacified. Many succeeded in reaching the Caribbean coast, where they mixed with the natives. The resulting *zambos* eventually came to be known as "Caribs," though they were not at all related to the Caribbean Indians of the same name. Guatemalan landlords had earlier favored importing Africans to alleviate the labor shortage, but by the beginning of the seventeenth century they questioned the desirability of continued slave importation. A static society had developed in which there were enough Indians to fill out the laboring force, while there was a certain amount of unemployment among free elements and no effective means of putting them to work had been devised. The ayuntamiento of the capital urged the Audiencia to stop the slave importation, but the Audiencia, more representative of imperial interests and international commerce (including the slave trade), showed some reluctance. Nevertheless, it would appear that the creoles got their way, for few additional slaves were imported after 1620. Despite creole fears, the blacks were probably not the most oppressed group in the colony. As slaves they were worth more than the Indians. They could purchase their freedom, and in the seventeenth century a good number did this, so that a small but significant group of free blacks emerged. However, with the decline in importation of slaves, and with miscegenation, much of this racial group gradually assimilated into the ladino sectors.

Thomas Gage, an Englishman who traveled in Central America in 1648, described the differences between the two upper classes as "more opposite one to another than in Europe the Spaniard is opposite to the French, or to the Hollander, or to the Portugall." Gage, who had become a fervent Hispanophobe by the time he wrote this account for

Oliver Cromwell, reported that the hatred was so great that the creoles would welcome conquest by "any other nation," and that "the cause of this deadly hatred hath proceeded from a jealousie which the Spaniards have ever had of the criolios, that they would fain withdraw themselves first from the commerce with Spain, and secondly, from the Government which is laid upon them; which is such, that the Criolios must be always under, and a subject, always governed, but scarce any a Governor."

The privileged classes were not alone in their exploitation of the Indian masses. The urban middle and poorer classes also abused them. These classes included the principal middlemen who supplied foodstuffs and other goods for the towns and cities; they dealt harshly and brutally with the Indian suppliers and committed violence and intimidation upon them to get the supplies at the lowest possible prices. The Indian, at the bottom of the social order in spite of lengthy royal decrees offering protection and devout friars who championed his cause, was always subject to intimidation, harassment, and cheating.

By the end of the seventeenth century, notable changes had occurred. The creole class could not be easily characterized as the descendants of the conquistadores, although certainly it included some of these. But many creoles had come upon hard times because of economic failure or because they had been on the losing side of major litigation with other creoles, peninsular officials, or the occasional Indian or ladino who successfully brought his grievances to a tribunal. Competitive new settlers had joined older ones, and, through marriage, cunning, or talent, some had built up new estates of importance. Thus the creole aristocracy was not a static institution; it was continually changing in composition and leadership. Some creole families had become genteel poor, with small landholdings, or they had moved into towns and cities and become less prestigious elements of the population. The society could not be described as mobile in any very large sense, yet there was movement both from above and from below into a growing middle sector which one day would become important in these countries. By 1700 the creole class had become more clearly defined than it had been in the days following the Conquest, when relations with the officialdom had been closer. Class interests were now clearer and were reflected in clashes between the ayuntamiento and the Audiencia. The bureaucracy, from the Captain General down through the corps of short-term peninsulares sent out from Spain, had less and less to do with the creoles. What relations existed often were of an illicit or corrupt nature, as this was the principal manner by which the creoles defended their interests. The system had become less dynamic. There were no longer schools for Indians, as the clergy had become more interested in running their fincas and plantations and in administrating the monasteries and schools for Spaniards and creoles. They, too, had succumbed to a paternalistic view of the Indians and were even in large part responsible for it. The successful conquest of the Indian populations had resulted in the imposition of a severe economic and social exploitation of that class by the creoles, and the heritage of that conquest has died slowly in Central America.

Chapter 3 • Bourbon Central America

The accession to the Spanish throne of the Bourbon Felipe V plunged the empire into a costly war. In fact, the War of the Spanish Succession opened a century in which war and international rivalry seriously altered the course of isthmian history. Yet, as important to Central America as the intercolonial wars, the American Revolution, and the conflicts growing out of the French Revolution were, other contacts with foreigners produced even more profound challenges to the status quo in the eighteenth century. Thus, the Kingdom of Guatemala upon the eve of its independence was a substantially different society than it had been when authority over the colony passed from the Hapsburgs to the Bourbons in 1700. The revolution in mentality and approaches to economy, politics, and religion which transformed the western world in the eighteenth century had predictable ramifications in this peripheral corner of civilization. The Enlightenment, together with Spain's involvement in the military and economic decline of the empire, brought changes to Central America that persist to the present day.

The close relations between the Bourbon monarchs facilitated the entry of French ideas into the Spanish world. Although they never worked the same degree of social and intellectual change as they did in France, they nonetheless contributed to a profound change in mentality and brought Central America into the Age of Reason. Creoles, immigrants, merchants, clerics, and bureaucrats who had traveled and studied in France were responsible for part of this influence. Inevitably, a trickle of French works, even some which were banned, entered the colony. More important in spreading Enlightenment ideology in this remote kingdom, however, were works in Spanish which reflected French thought. Peninsular newspapers were notable, particularly those which carried the writings of Benito Jerónimo Feyjóo y Montenegro, Bernardo de Ulloa, Gerónimo de Uztáriz, Bernardo Ward, and, most popular among the Central American intelligentsia, Pedro Campomanes. Spanish translations of French and English works also found their way into the colony, and it is likely that they were read more than were the originals. In Central America, the Spanish language works were more readily accessible both from the standpoint of language and legality, and it is probable that most Central Americans who gave much thought to changes in the economic, social, or political structure took their inspiration from Spanish interpretations rather than directly from the works of Smith, Rousseau, Voltaire, Quesnay, Condillac, or other foreign philosophers. Colonial periodicals, notably the *Gazeta de Guatemala* (1729-31; 1793-1816), but also the *Gaceta de Méjico* (1732-39; 1784-1821), *Gaceta de la Havana* (1782-90), *Papel Periódico de la Havana* (1790-1805), *Diario de Lima* (1789-93), *Mercurio Peruano* (1791-94), and *El Pensador Mejicano* (1812-14) were also vehicles for the new ideas. Guatemala had its first printing press by 1660—in Latin America only Mexico City, Puebla, and Lima had presses earlier—but ecclesiastical publications accounted for most of the colony's printing until the end of the eighteenth century.

Throughout the eighteenth century similar intellectual influences on Spanish officials brought tangible changes in administration of the colony, which in turn stimulated and permitted creole thought and action. After experimenting in Spain with French-oriented modifications in governmental structure, new administrative organization was applied to colonial rule in an effort to increase productivity and efficiency.

The new policies eventually touched nearly all aspects of life in the colonies, but they can generally be divided into four categories: anti-clerical measures designed to reduce the size and temporal power of the clergy, commercial measures designed to increase production and trade between Spain and the Indies, administrative reforms designed to provide more responsive government and make tax collection more efficient, and military and naval measures to improve Spain's defensive posture and to protect her commerce. All of these measures had as their larger aim the restoration of Spanish prestige, prosperity, and authority in a century that found a once-great empire reduced to a second-rate position behind England and France.

These policies were by no means uniformly determined or enforced. Long debates among the Kings' ministers preceded decisions, and stormy changes at court precluded any consistent policy running throughout the century. Yet taken as a whole, the Bourbon reforms represented a genuine effort by the Spanish government to recoup lost ground, answer domestic and colonial grievances, and meet the foreign challenge. Few major changes came to the Kingdom of Guatemala before the reigns of Carlos III and Carlos IV in the final third of the eighteenth century. Some renovation had already begun, however.

Efforts to check clerical power clearly began during the first half of the century. Guatemala City had become one of the hemisphere's strongholds of clerical wealth and prestige. The Dominicans held large estates in the Verapaz and elsewhere and were reputedly the richest order on the isthmus. The Franciscans ranked an impressive second, with Augustinians, Bethlehemites, and Mercederians also important. The Jesuits also had some wealthy establishments, even though they were less conspicuous in Central America than they were in other parts of the empire.

Early in the eighteenth century the Crown began to issue royal decrees restricting these orders by limiting their right to construct new monasteries or to accept novices prior to their adulthood. Moreover, the Crown decreased or abolished certain taxes levied for the support of the Church, particularly those collected in Indian parishes. The aim, of course, was not to destroy the Church, nor even to deny it temporal power, but rather to arrest the alarming growth of the clerical population, which was becoming parasitic on the nation. These measures were directed primarily against the regular orders, although some limitations were placed on secular clergy as well. The Bourbons favored the secular clergy and wanted to promote what they considered to be legitimate functions of the Church; for that reason Felipe V elevated Guatemala to archdiocese status in 1742.

What in some ways was the strongest anticlerical measure of the eighteenth century, the expulsion from the empire of the Jesuit Order in 1767, had a relatively minor effect in Central America. Among the twenty Jesuits exiled from the kingdom, however, was one of Central America's greatest literary figures, the poet Rafael Landívar.

Competition from Spain's rivals, particularly Great Britain, stimulated some of the most important commercial and military modifications in the colony. Rivalry among the European powers had afflicted Central America since the sixteenth century, when French corsairs began to raid Caribbean port settlements. The Dutch had smuggled contraband into Central America in the seventeenth century, but from the mid-seventeenth century forward the British were the most menacing of the nations that vied for the wealth of the isthmus. They, or buccaneers operating with their tacit support, stole dyewoods and mahogany from the Honduran and Guatemalan coasts and established a base at Belize which eventually became the entrepôt for a large, illicit traffic with Spain's colony.

In the eighteenth century the Spanish Bourbons, with French aid, sought to remove the British from these shores. They built a string of forts stretching from Yucatán to Panama. Yet although the Spanish drove the Belize woodcutters away occasionally, they repeatedly returned. By 1741 British officials in Jamaica regularly appointed a superintendent for Belize, although for the most part local loggers and merchants managed their affairs autonomously. At the same time, British subjects cultivated relations with the Mosquito Indians and established what was virtually a satellite kingdom there. This Mosquito Kingdom provided bases from which the British conducted contraband trade, raided Spanish settlements in Nicaragua and Costa Rica, and generally weakened Spanish defenses on the Caribbean coast.

The War of Jenkins' Ear and the War of the Austrian Succession (1739-48) brought renewed British assaults to the Caribbean coasts. Before peace was concluded at Aix-la-Chapelle in 1748, the British had significant, if still vulnerable, settlements at Belize, Roatán, and on the Mosquito Coast at Black River, Cape Gracias a Dios, and Bluefields. Spain, taking cognizance of these incursions, increased its defense expenditures and appointed officials of higher rank and greater ability to the isthmus, but they were unable to oust the invaders. In fact, in 1754 250 Englishmen stopped an expedition of 1500 Spaniards through the Petén, and Belize remained British. British residents established a fort there the following year to resist subsequent attacks from either Yucatán or Guatemala.

The Seven Years' War brought further English victories. In 1756, Mosquito Indians, urged on by the British, captured and executed the Governor of Costa Rica and carried out devastating raids against Matina Valley cacao plantations. Meanwhile, British naval forces dealt catastrophic blows to Spanish shipping in Central American waters.

The Bourbon response was not purely military. Beginning with the reorganization of the Casa de Contratación in 1717, royal orders began to dismantle the Seville-Cádiz monopoly over colonial trade. Without discarding the principle of monopoly itself, the Bourbons opened participation in the closed commercial system to a wider circle of both Spaniards and colonists in an effort to provide alternatives to smuggling. Spain modified, then abandoned entirely, the fleet system. Efforts to establish trading companies which would trade directly between Spain and Honduras or Guatemala failed to prosper, but they did contribute to a spirit of freer commercial activity. Beginning in the 1760's the government of Carlos III launched a series of reforms culminating in the general Free Trade Act of 1778, which permitted greatly expanded Spanish-American trade. The lifting of trade restrictions widened the opportunities for Central Americans to engage directly in trade with both Spain and other colonies, thus lessening the economic dependence on Mexico. The roads and ports of the colony were ill suited for these new opportunities, but colonial governors urged the Church, the military, and other institutions to accelerate their road-building and communications activities, including navigation of the San Juan, Lempa, Motagua, and Polochic rivers. The volume of trade passing through the Bay of Honduras increased notably, as did trade through San Juan del Norte (Greytown) and the Pacific ports of Acajutla and Realejo. Sonsonate, as a center of the indigo-producing region of El Salvador, enjoyed the greatest growth; it regained the prominence it had once had as a cacao center. In 1803 the Pacific ports were allowed to receive re-exported Asian goods by sea from Acapulco. Meanwhile, regular mail ship service between Spain and the colony began.

Other Bourbon measures established state monopolies on liquor and tobacco in an effort not only to control or limit consumption, but more especially to keep these items out of the contraband trade and to increase government revenues from their sale. Efforts to promote mining included the establishment of a mint in 1733, the lowering of royalties, and currency reform. Export taxes were lowered, and that encouraged the planters to experiment with new crops.

Administrative reforms complemented the commercial reforms. The effects of the establishment of the secretariat system and the trend toward a modern ministerial cabinet and reorganization of the Council of the Indies in Spain cannot be said to have been immediately felt in Central America, yet the impact of these and other measures, which streamlined and made more efficient colonial administration, inevitably touched the lives of the colonists. The concept of a more well-defined separation of powers than had existed under Hapsburg rule was one feature of Bourbon reform which gradually found its way into the colonial mentality. Meanwhile, the Crown began to issue decrees and ordinances which provided for more efficient administration under existing laws and institutions, particularly in the collection and disbursement of revenue.

The latter part of the century brought welcomed salary increases for the Spanish bureaucracy; these were aimed at encouraging incentive and promoting more responsible officials. Although inflation canceled much of this increase, there was improvement both in the quality of personnel and in their services during the final third of the eighteenth century. Creoles began to find their way into the bureaucracy at a more rapid pace than before. Colonial governors and corregidores began to take greater interest not only in law enforcement and tax collection, but also in the general development of the colony. Officials conducted surveys, procured reports on economic development, established new towns, planned new roads, and concerned themselves more generally with the welfare of the inhabitants.

The most important administrative reform was the appointment of intendentes to oversee financial and military administration in the colony. Launched in Spain early in the century, the intendancy system was not introduced in the Indies until 1764, in Havana. Central America did not inaugurate the system until 1786, when it was established as part of a general application to the Viceroyalty of New Spain. Honduras, El Salvador, Nicaragua, and Chiapas became intendencies. Guatemala itself remained outside the system, under the direct administration of the Captain General in the capital. This action elevated El Salvador to equality with Honduras and Nicaragua, removing it from the immediate jurisdiction of Guatemala City.

As the intendentes held broad financial and military authority, this new organization of the kingdom increased provincial autonomy and thereby contributed to the separatist spirit of the several provinces in the last years of Hispanic rule. Salvadoran "nationalism" essentially dates from the start of the intendancy system. Although it was certainly not Spanish intention, in Central America it would appear that the system contributed to the disunity of the kingdom by raising the status of regional centers.

The establishment of the intendencies coincided generally with military reforms designed to improve the defenses of the kingdom. The new intendants received authority over military questions and orders to reinforce fortifications. A general reorganization of the imperial military establishment took place at about the same time. The number of regular Spanish troops stationed in Central America increased after the beginning of the American Revolution, when, in

1777, the regular detachment was doubled from 100 to 200. Additional artillery also arrived. Still, the regular establishment remained small compared with the militia units on which defensive needs rested.

There were also some minor reforms in education and health. In 1799 a government order was issued requiring all communities of more than a hundred taxpayers to provide elementary school facilities, but there is no evidence that it was implemented. More immediately successful was the beginning of vaccination in the kingdom in response to a smallpox epidemic in 1780. Although a regular program of vaccination was not in effect before 1850, the partial program of the government checked smallpox fairly effectively in the late colonial period.

The increase in commercial activity promoted the emergence of a larger and more vocal merchant community, principally in the capital, but to a lesser extent in other commercial centers as well. The interests of the merchants had been expressed principally through the ayuntamiento of the capital, but landlord interests were dominant there. The commercial deputation, established first in 1729 to supervise collection of the *alcabala,* or sales tax, began to evolve as a separate institution which voiced the interests of the merchants of the capital. Guatemalan merchants had requested their own *consulado* as early as 1649, but not until the eighteenth century did the Crown receive such petitions seriously. Consistent with the Bourbon commercial reforms, the powers of the Mexican and Sevillian merchants with respect to Central America had been gradually reduced, with greater jurisdiction assigned to consular deputations or ayuntamientos in the provinces. In the 1780's Madrid declared its intention to increase the number of overseas merchant guilds. Guatemala was the second of eight colonial commercial centers selected between 1792 and 1795 to enjoy such privilege, these eight being the only additions to the older institutions in Mexico and Lima made throughout the entire colonial period. The merchants thus gained their own fuero, a tribunal where judges sympathetic to merchant interests would hear commercial litigation and disputes. Royal edicts assured colonial merchants of their legal equality with peninsular counterparts. Although actual practice sometimes challenged the reality of the statements, they were reflections of official efforts to encourage colonial mercantile development.

The merchants' charter specifically charged them to protect and develop commerce and to promote "by all means possible the advancement of agriculture, the improvement of cultivation and the yield of its produce, the introduction of the most advantageous machines and tools, the facilitation of internal communication, and, in sum, whatever seems conducive to the greatest increase and extension of all the areas of cultivation and trade," including development of roads, ports, and river transport.

Exercising these judicial and developmental functions, and quickly assigning sixteen consular deputations from Ciudad Real to Cartago, the merchant guild became a major force on politics and the economy during the last years of the colonial period. It promoted economic development in Guatemala and El Salvador, but shunned improvement of ports and roads that might divert trade and production away from the capital's merchants. A company organized by the merchant guild to navigate the Río Motagua provided limited service for a few years. The merchants promoted, with partial success, plans to populate the Caribbean coast with colonists from Cuba and the eastern Guatemalan mountains. And the Guatemalan guild joined with the Veracruz Consulado in forming an insurance company in 1802.

Despite some increase in production and exports stimulated by the relaxing of trade restrictions, the economic picture by the close of the century had become bleak for many Central Americans, and many of them had grievances. Commercial export was still not the mainstay of most of the region's inhabitants. Even the landholding class was engaged more in subsistence farming and production for local markets than in plantation production for overseas markets. This was especially true in Costa Rica, but to some extent it was true for the colony as a whole. There was still little trade among the provinces that composed the kingdom, a condition that even the twentieth-century Central American common market has changed only slightly. Cacao exports had continued to decline, and by 1800 Central America was importing cacao. Sugar exports, never of primary importance, also suffered, for West Indian production was rising rapidly.

The growth of the European textile industry and the accompanying demand for colorful dyes gave Central America an opportunity to recover some of the ground lost in the cacao decline. Guatemala had produced cochineal since pre-Columbian times, although southern Mexico had been a more important producer and had discouraged Central American exports in the eighteenth century. In 1811, however, the Captain General promoted its redevelopment in Guatemala. In the meantime, Guatemala, El Salvador, and Nicaragua had become major exporters of indigo. The free trade decrees had favored indigo exports, which exceeded a value of two million pesos for some years of the late colonial period. The government encouraged production by promoting better roads and easier labor procurement. It directly aided the planters through fixing prices and permitting the planters to incorporate the Indigo Growers Society (*Montepío de Cosecheros de Añil*) in 1782. Although there were large planters involved in indigo production, the bulk of the production came from smaller producers. Guatemala City merchants financed this production and reaped usurous profits by loaning small farmers money against their crops. It was to combat this practice that the Indigo Growers Society formed a fund, established with a royal grant, from which crop loans could be made to members, thus relieving them of dependence on the merchants. It gave the indigo planters some independence in the late colonial period. This explains the bitter dispute between the Consulado, representing the merchants and large planters, and the Indigo Growers Society, representing the smaller or medium indigo planters. Later, after the decline of indigo, cochineal producers would return to the former dependence on the merchants for financing.

Spanish involvement in foreign wars and revolutions was costly and afflicted Central America with demands for higher taxes, increased defense expenditures within the kingdom, forced loans and so-called "patriotic donations" to the government, and alarming inflation. The costly process of moving the capital following disastrous earthquakes in 1773 also placed a continuing burden on the colony. Severe

locust invasions around the turn of the century, combined with competition from Venezuela, South Carolina, and the East Indies, contributed to a decline in indigo exports, although El Salvador continued to
export the dye until the late nineteenth century. Average annual exports through legitimate channels dropped from nearly a million
pounds during the decade 1791-1800 to less than half that amount in
1810-20. Reflecting the decline, the indebtedness of the Indigo Growers Society rose from $434,861 in 1800 to $662,250 by 1820. Thus the
colony found itself in difficult economic straits upon the close of Hispanic rule. It is even possible that, during the final half-century of
Spanish rule, the royal government spent more on the colony than she
received from it, despite the rise in taxation and forced loans. Given
the hard times and the growing presence of the British on the Caribbean shores, it is not surprising that there was a rise in smuggling and
contraband activities, both of which encouraged the notion that free
trade was advantageous and would bring lower prices for foreign goods.

The Treaty of Paris (1763) reflected British strength, but promised
the region peace and stability. By that treaty the British recognized
Spanish sovereignty throughout Central America and agreed to dismantle all their fortifications there, while the Spanish conceded to
English settlers the right to cut dyewood and to continue settlements
necessary for that purpose. In fact, the British did not dismantle the
fortifications. The English colonies remained, and soon after the 1763
treaty Sir William Burnaby drew up a code of laws for Belize residents which provided a structure of colonial government, including
provision for land titles. The Spanish tried to isolate these settlements
from their own subjects, but even so, such enclaves became centers
for the growing contraband trade. London encouraged this trade
through the establishment, beginning in 1766, of free ports in the
West Indies convenient to the Spanish colonies. Nor did the treaty
bring the expected peace, for, despite the absence of a state of war,
retaliatory raids by both sides continued to disrupt the shore settlements of both empires.

The outbreak of the American Revolution and Spanish cooperation
with the insurgent North Americans provided some opportunity for

Spain to recoup her losses. Although British-supported Mosquito Indians continued to harass the Matina Valley and other locations on the Caribbean watershed, in 1779 the Spanish succeeded in driving the English from Belize and Roatán. However, the English settlers simply moved to the Mosquito Coast. From there they launched a devastating expedition into the interior of Nicaragua. In that same year the English captured Omoa. Captain General Matías de Gálvez soon dislodged them, but not before they had destroyed the fortress and a million pesos' worth of merchandise. The British were destructive, but they failed in their plan to cut the kingdom in half at Nicaragua, and, as French and Dutch attacks on England increased after 1780, the British threat receded. The Peace of Paris (1783) reaffirmed the provisions of the treaty of 1763, permitting the British once more to cut dyewood and make settlements in Belize under Spanish sovereignty, but the British were to evacuate the Mosquito Coast. A clarification of the treaty came in 1786, in a Convention between Britain and Spain which gave the British the right to cut mahogany as well as dyewood (they had been doing so all along anyway) and reconfirmed Spanish sovereignty and British rights to settle. With immigration of settlers from the Mosquito Coast after 1787, Belize became a permanent, thriving port and the center for extensive trading with Central America.

There were a growing number of exceptions to the rules against trading with foreigners after Spain allied with England to suppress the French Revolution in 1793. Prices shot upward rapidly, reflecting the higher taxes and maritime losses as well as the general wartime inflation. After Spain switched sides under duress in 1796, trade between the peninsula and the isthmus became difficult, owing to British control of the Atlantic. This forced Spain in 1797 to turn to neutrals to carry much of her colonial trade. The United States, as the leading neutral, benefited greatly from this decision, and North American shipping flowed to the isthmus. Although Madrid rescinded the privilege in 1800, the expanded trade continued, either illicitly or by means of the large number of legal exceptions to the rules which the royal policy allowed. There was a notable increase in non-Spanish commerce along both coasts between 1793 and 1810, and discussion developed within the colony over the merits of the freer trade. J. B. Irisarri argued for greater freedom, but the merchants controlling the new Guatemalan Consulado, in concert with established Spanish mercantile interests, protested against the liberalization. They sought to defend their own interests within the closed commercial monopoly. Yet the inability of Spanish naval forces, particularly after their defeat at Trafalgar in 1805, to suppress the contraband trade or protect their shipping lanes meant that the flow of trade via Jamaica and Belize continued without hindrance.

The Bourbon commercial and administrative policies, changing fortunes in the international trade of Central American commodities, and the exigencies of war brought substantial economic transformation. The landholding aristocracy reacted in a variety of ways. Philosophically, the intellectual currents of the century made an impact, and there was a developing liberal element in the colony. Yet all could not agree that the changes were for the best, and inevitably there were those who believed that changes inaugurated for the general welfare of the empire did not necessarily improve the lot of the Kingdom of Guatemala. Moreover, the reforms which sought more efficient and direct administration challenged the accommodation of corruption and evasion which the creoles had developed with the bureaucracy. Riots greeted the inauguration of the liquor and tobacco controls in 1756 and 1766. Other outbreaks, not only in the capital but in Indian villages as well, punctuated the late colonial period. None could be regarded as a major threat to the stability of the regime, as the Tupac Amaru revolt in Peru, the Comunero revolt in New Granada, and, subsequently, the Hidalgo revolt in Mexico were, but they nevertheless reflected a growing restlessness and apprehension over the changes taking place.

The economic hard times and the tightening of Spanish administrative control at the end of the eighteenth century heightened longstanding differences between the bureaucracy and the local aristocracy, as well as between the interests of the capital and those of the provinces. The monopoly that the merchants and government officials exercised over the rest of the kingdom had long been a source of resentment. The destruction of the capital and the subsequent move to New Guatemala City, the wartime economic demands and pressures, and the growth of more liberal economic and political philosophies combined to accelerate basic social changes which were occurring in the eighteenth century. As a result, there was a more complex social structure at the close of the colonial period than that which had existed during Hapsburg rule.

The bureaucracy had become more efficient, more professional, and more detached than before. Although there had been a greater number of creoles admitted to the bureaucracy in the eighteenth century generally, this trend seems to have reversed itself late in the colonial period, and the creole complaint of exclusion from major offices appears to have been justified.

The creole aristocracy, which, as a result of both domestic expansion and immigration, was larger than it had ever been, was also changing in composition. This was a continuous process. It went on throughout the colonial period, but it became especially noticeable in Guatemala with the move to the new capital. New European immigration brought significant changes. Although the group of newcomers was small in number, it included persons of influence who moved into the creole establishment with success. This was most evident in Costa Rica and Guatemala. In Costa Rica, where a number of Galicians increased the Spanish population, an industrious class of small farmers developed a more egalitarian economic and social structure than found elsewhere on the isthmus, owing chiefly to the absence of a native labor force to exploit or sufficient exportable commodities to justify or finance importation of Africans. Immigrants often had the advantage of closer contacts with Spanish officials and privileged persons at court. Earlier settlers were, therefore, sometimes displaced by newcomers. The rise to prominence of the house of Aycinena is the best illustration of this phenomenon in Guatemala, although there are other examples.

Juan Fermín de Aycinena left Navarre and came to Guatemala via Mexico in the mid-eighteenth century. In Mexico he had expanded his modest wealth as owner of a string of mules, and he reinvested his profits in indigo and livestock in Guatemala and El Salvador. He also invested in Honduran silver mining, but indigo became his principal economic activity and he established an important exporting house in the new capital. In 1780 he purchased the title of Marquis from the government of Carlos III; he was the only resident holder of a noble title in the kingdom at that time. In Guatemala he soon became the leader of the aristocracy, a process probably facilitated by the disruption caused by the destruction of Antigua Guatemala as well as the other upsetting factors of the period. Fermín sired a large family, and their connections by marriage enlaced the principal members of the Guatemalan landholding and commercial elite. New immigration brought similar, if less spectacular, rises in fortune in Costa Rica and Nicaragua, while economic decline in Honduras led to the near disintegration of the landholding elite there.

The creole aristocracy had developed a dangerous mental attitude toward the mother country by the close of the eighteenth century. It embraced two views of Spain, one historical, the other immediate. They were quite different; indeed, they were in direct conflict. On the one hand, the creoles idealized a glorious Spanish past—Spain at the peak of its power, the Spain of the Conquest, with its elevated cultural and spiritual values. They saw themselves as defenders of this spirit in the New World. On the other hand, in their immediate view, they saw scheming and calculating royal officials threatening their economic and political positions with bothersome and misguided laws and ambitious immigrants challenging their share of the land and wealth of the colony. Against this Spain the creole aristocracy was developing an intuitive bitterness. It was also forming a conservative core which would survive to the present.

The Indians remained at the bottom of society. As a class they remained segregated, although the growth of the ladino population had resulted in encroachment into their lands and towns by that group, which, in the provinces southeast of Guatemala, had become a major element by 1821. The Hapsburg institutions of encomienda and repartimiento by which the aristocracy had controlled the Indians were giving way to other forms in the Bourbon century, even though they lasted here longer than in Mexico. Wage labor became more common than before, and it often resulted in debt slavery. Seasonal repartimientos, often requiring monthly obligations for work on indigo or cochineal plantations, replaced earlier arrangements. These repartimientos have modern counterparts in several parts of Central America, where Indian workers are brought from their highland villages to lowland plantations at harvest time. Indian caciques continued to collaborate with the creoles in exploiting the Indians. A harsh policy on the part of the bureaucracy and the landholders, one designed to "keep the Indian in his place," accompanied the breakdown of the repartimiento system and assured that the Indian would continue to provide needed labor. Local priests helped to control the Indians. Few Indians became priests. The priests, usually ladinos or creoles, were often the real authority in Indian communities, exercising not only spiritual guidance, but considerable economic and political authority as well.

Indian revolts were cruelly suppressed, and the creoles and ladinos accepted this as necessary and proper to their own interests. In the creole mentality, the Indian was a beast of burden who could be treated with animal brutality in order to preserve society. In much of the kingdom, the Indian had been so totally oppressed that he ceased to exist as a separate entity. He blended in with the ladino in order to survive. Only in highland Guatemala did authentic Indian civilization really persist extensively. There, Indians continued to speak native Maya dialects and to live outside the mainstream of the colony's development.

Probably the most significant change in the eighteenth century was the growth and emergence of the ladino sector. Although not clearly identifiable as a social class, ladinos provided the growth of the middle sectors which were playing an ever larger role in Central American society and would provide important impetus for change after independence. Indians left their pueblos and were drawn either to live in towns, sometimes becoming ladinos in culture and customs, or to the fincas as hired serfs. The shift to seasonal rather than monthly repartimientos was significant in this, as they allowed the landholder to use and pay for the Indians only when their labor was most needed. Landlords rejected efforts made to end this practice in 1810. They increasingly hired ladinos to do the normal labor and used the Indians only when the need was greatest. This, of course, often coincided with the time that the Indian's own fields needed him most; thus Indian production declined for lack of labor. The market became more tied to creole and ladino production, and less to Indian pueblo production, and many of the pueblos were absorbed into new towns.

Rural ladinos were not well off economically, but they enjoyed greater freedom than Indians and they began to encroach on Indian lands, markets, and opportunities. Although the ladinos had few legal rights and commanded less authority than the creoles, their numbers and ambition made them a formidable threat to the Indians. Ladino farmers became important producers and, in fact, produced the largest part of the indigo. They were exploited by the merchants, who often came from the same families as the large landholders. When the ladino farmers banded together in the Indigo Growers Society, they received support from the bureaucracy, particularly from Captain General Matías de Gálvez and Baron Héctor de Carondelet, Intendente of El Salvador. Notwithstanding exploitation by the creoles, the industry and aggressiveness of the rural ladinos made them an element of importance by the close of the colonial period.

But the ladinos occupied an even greater role as the backbone of emerging middle sectors in the cities and towns. Ladinos were in the majority in most of the larger towns and cities of the kingdom at the close of the colonial period, although creoles still governed the economic and social life of most. Guatemala City, as well as San Salvador and Léon, had developed middle sectors of considerable importance. Lacking the attributes or awareness of a true middle class, these people nevertheless represented an emergent middle group—racially, economically, and socially—which would play major political roles in the nineteenth and twentieth centuries. Composed principally of ladinos, without firm roots either in the creole or Indian classes, it also included certain of those formerly of the creole class who, through ill fortune, had descended to lower status. Some Indians, too, took on European manners, dress, and culture and entered this group. There were institutions where social mobility occurred, most notably the Church, the military, and the university. These urban middle sectors embraced a wide range of groups, from the numerous, impoverished rabble of the larger cities to the professionals who served the aristocracy and the bureaucracy. Between was an important, if relatively powerless, group of artisans and provisioners.

The artisans, skilled laborers manufacturing by hand nearly everything used in the daily life of the cities, had organized themselves into guilds which had gained some recognition by the end of the colonial era. These guilds were more in the tradition of medieval craft guilds than modern labor unions, and they served principally as a means of control of the artisans by the ruling classes. They protected the artisan only to the extent that they limited entrance into the crafts, yet this rarely served to permit increased profits because of short demand, for the ayuntamiento, which was controlled by the creoles, fixed prices on most commodities. In fact, although there were some notable exceptions of wealthy artisans, in general this group was poorly paid and had only a low standard of living. Moreover, it was not a homogeneous class; it simply provided goods and services for the elite, and it had little notion of separate class interests.

In the same manner, there was no sense of common interest among members of the upper middle sector, composed of merchants, lawyers, physicians, minor public officials, university professors, clerics, and other professionals. Rather, they served and aspired to join the creole aristocracy or peninsular bureaucracy which paid their wages, salaries, and fees.

The large unemployed or underemployed rabble in the capital was composed of members of the middle sector who had failed to hold employment or who had drifted in from the countryside in hopes of finding more lucrative employment. Many performed menial, underpaid tasks, but principally they lived by begging or crime and eked out a living as best they could. Some were peddlers, and they often served as middlemen in the trade of goods between rural pueblos and the capital. Thus they were one more group of exploiters the Indians had to confront. This urban rabble also existed in some of the larger provincial cities, and it was growing in size at the close of the colonial period. It was a group that could be rallied easily to riot or demonstration, a role which the group continues to play to the present. Among this unruly population, vice and crime were high. Inhabiting the slums of the cities, these people lacked sufficient opportunity to move upward economically. The hard times of the end of the period caused them to become more restless, and crimes of violence became so frequent as to worry the authorities.

The elite attempted to protect themselves against these middle sectors by insisting upon enforcement of laws prohibiting ladinos and Indians from bearing arms. On this the Audiencia and the ayuntamientos were in agreement. Repeated ordinances and decrees prohibited all but the ruling classes from carrying firearms and sabres. Yet such decrees failed to arrest the crime wave, so, in 1806, another decree was promulgated, this one denying even knives and daggers to the rabble, under penalty of 200 lashes and six years at hard labor.

The rough statistics available for the close of the colonial period reflect the growth of the ladino population. Although the Indians remained in the majority in Guatemala and Chiapas, the ladino had become the predominant element in the remainder of the kingdom, excepting Costa Rica, which was always predominantly European. Yet even Guatemala and Costa Rica both had significant ladino groups. For the kingdom as a whole, Indians represented 65 per cent of the total, ladinos 31 per cent, and Spaniards and Creoles but 4 per cent. In Nicaragua the ladinos, including all of the various racial mixtures, amounted to 84 per cent of the population. In El Salvador, where less than 1 per cent of the population were Spaniards and only 2 per cent were Creoles, some 54 per cent were classified as ladinos and 43 per cent as Indians.

Small numbers of blacks lived on the Caribbean coasts, but the earlier black concentrations in the interior had diminished or disappeared as separate minorities, they having been assimilated into the ladino population. Black slavery had declined in the eighteenth century because of the more ready availability of cheap Indian or ladino labor. The blacks on the Caribbean coasts were more closely related to the British colonial enterprise than to the Spanish.

Some differences can be seen in the attitude of the two ruling classes toward the emerging middle sectors. The bureaucracy, representing the Spanish government, was officially sympathetic to their needs and demands, perhaps even using them to check creole pretensions. It recognized the value of a larger economic base than the tiny creole aristocracy provided, and it promoted, through more liberal economic programs, the growth and initiative of this sector. Thus, the bureaucracy encouraged the Indigo Growers Society and supported provincials in their disputes with Guatemala City. Although the Guatemala aristocracy continued to dominate the society, Spanish policy mitigated its abuses somewhat, but, more significantly, it abetted the rising antagonism on the part of the provincials toward the creole aristocracy centered in the capital, thereby contributing to the separatist movements in the post-independence years. The creole class, on the other hand, feared the growth of the middle sectors and guarded its social and economic privileges against ladino ambition. This effort was more successful in the capital, where the creoles had real power, than in provincial centers, where the ladino was comparatively more powerful. While creoles had respect, admiration, and affection for certain individual artisans and professionals, just as they did for faithful servants, no such admiration extended to the middle sectors as a group or class. Toward the lower middle sector, creole indifference became disdain and fear of mutinies and rioting, particularly after the French Revolution convinced them of the capacity of the rabble for mischief.

Set against this social structure, the growing debates over economic and political policy which the Enlightenment stimulated reached their climax as Spain's colonial empire began to disintegrate. The Napoleonic Wars provided the opportunity for new British imperialism. Although Trujillo repulsed a British attack in 1797, the British had retaken the Bay Islands in the preceding year and begun to transport large numbers of black slaves there from the eastern Caribbean. The

British successfully repulsed a Spanish effort against Belize in 1798. Skirmishes continued into the first decade of the new century as the British extended their armed support of the Mosquito Indians and the contraband trading. A growing United States commerce also found its way into Central America, despite British measures against it.

The Treaty of London (1809) made England and Spain allies against the French and permitted more amicable relations between their Central American colonists. Trade expanded rapidly, and Belize, although its inhabitants numbered fewer than 5000, took on a more prosperous appearance as new construction sprang up. In 1810 the Magistrates' Council of the town responded to this growth—they ordered two fire engines. By then the British had successfully established bases that facilitated extensive illicit trade. It had damaged not only the Spanish trade monopoly, but also the limited manufacturing industry, particularly of textiles, permitted in Central America under Spanish mercantilism. It had exposed the Central Americans to an ever-increasing supply of comparatively inexpensive British goods and, as a by-product, to British ideas on economics and politics.

By the close of the eighteenth century, foreign ideas had challenged the order which had been so deeply established during the Hapsburg centuries. Members of both the bureaucracy and the creole elite had begun to think in terms of freer economic institutions, representative government, and a more open political process, and they had begun to question the wisdom of monopolies, special privilege, and the role of the Church. Traditionalist institutions, such as the University of San Carlos, resisted these ideas, understandably. But by the end of the century there were a number of men throughout the kingdom who represented an enlightened sector of the Guatemalan elite. Leading this group were a Costa Rican friar, José Antonio Liendo y Goicoechea, who championed curriculum reform in the University; a Honduran lawyer, José Cecilio del Valle, who promoted the study of political economy in the colony; two dynamic editors of the liberal and sometimes controversial *Gazeta de Guatemala*, Alejandro Ramírez and Simón Bergaño y Villegas; the publisher of the *Gazeta*, Ignacio Beteta; a Salvadoran planter-merchant, Juan Bautista Irisarri, who advocated

freer trade and road and port construction on the Pacific coast; and
the Dean of the Cabildo Eclesiástico, Antonio García, who argued for
greater economic opportunity for ladinos as a means of increasing
agricultural production.

These men formed the nucleus of the Economic Society, a representative Enlightenment institution which had originated in Switzer-
land and had quickly spread to France, into Spain, and, in the 1790's,
to the Indies. Chartered in 1794 and established the following year,
the Guatemalan Society promoted ways to improve the economy, the
arts, education, and industry. It supported the *Gazeta de Guatemala*
and sponsored classes in political economy, bookkeeping, mathematics,
foreign languages, and drafting when the University failed to offer
such subjects. Its liberalism led to its suppression from 1800 to 1811.
No precise evaluation of the impact of these men on the thinking of
the population in general is possible, but what is overwhelmingly
clear is that by 1800 the mentality of the elite had changed notably.
There now existed a significant number of people who looked forward
to change and progress.

The furor created over the Spanish Constitution of 1812 focused
on liberal-conservative differences which had been brewing for at
least a half-century, and it established the dialogue for the half-century to follow. Among the immediate results in Central America of
the liberal Spanish Cortes of 1810-14 were the restoration of the
Economic Society, the creation of three *Diputaciones Provinciales* (in
Guatemala, León, and Ciudad Real), the election of ayuntamientos,
the establishment of a new university in León, and the liberalization
of trading privileges. Central Americans participated in the Cortes,
and representatives from each of the six provinces were among the
signers of the 1812 Constitution. In 1813 Guatemalan creole aristocrat
José de Aycinena became a Councilor of State in the Cádiz government.

With Spanish trade thoroughly disrupted by the Napoleonic Wars,
the new British alliance with the Cádiz government and the availability of Belize's aggressive merchant houses provided the opportunity for
expansion of Central America's foreign trade. Although more imagined

than real, the threat of Napoleonic invasion of the isthmus brought
forth the first official discussion of the free trade issue in the kingdom.
The Ayuntamiento, representing the landholding aristocracy, proposed
formation of a trading company to engage in foreign commerce, so
that a tax levied on the profits of the company could provide revenue
for the defense of the kingdom. The Ayuntamiento cited the exigencies of war and hard times as justifications for violating the royal
legislation against such commerce. The merchants' reply, strongly
negative, questioned the magnitude of the threat and pointed out other
sources of wealth in the kingdom—such as the Church—which might
be taxed and which could meet the need more quickly were the danger
truly imminent. For the merchants, the crisis was insufficient justification for upsetting the established channels of Guatemala's commerce
with Cádiz. The merchants must have realized, further, that such a
company as the Ayuntamiento proposed, calling for a capitalization of
600,000 pesos, would have been dominated by the Aycinena clan,
which alone had the capital to establish and carry it forward. The
company would simply be more unwanted competition. From this
point forward through independence, the Consulado consistently
echoed the peninsular point of view on commercial questions.

Freedom of trade was not the only issue to emerge while Napoleon
held Fernando VII captive in France. The liberal trends reflected in
the 1812 document divided the creoles and upper middle sector in
Central America into opposing political factions. Elements of each
group hoped that representative political institutions would gain them
a stronger voice in their own government and economic affairs.

The conflict between the landholding aristocracy and the official
bureaucracy became intense during the second decade of the nineteenth century. José María Peinado's *Instructions* on behalf of the
Ayuntamiento of Guatemala City to Antonio Larrazábal, Guatemalan
delegate to the Cortes of Cádiz, reflect vividly the Spanish-American
liberalism of 1811. In Central America it would not become evident
until a decade later that most of its supporters were not guided by
true progressive spirit, but by self-interest. For the moment, however,
they championed political liberalism, including elective and represent-

ative offices, relaxation of commercial restrictions, a conscious effort to stimulate production and to develop intellectual as well as economic resources, a freer press, and the emergence of incipient political parties. The aristocrats maintained their control of the municipal government and of the newly created provincial deputation, but Larrazábal had no sooner departed for Spain than a change of command led to a reactionary turn in the political climate of the kingdom.

Captain General José de Bustamante arrived on March 14, 1811, fresh from a successful command at Montevideo, where he had effectively resisted the creole aristocracy of Buenos Aires. A man of singular dedication to duty and unswerving in his loyalty to the Crown as well as to the principles of authority and absolutism, Bustamante had little sympathy with the liberal Cortes or the Constitution which it soon promulgated, much less with the ambitious colonial aristocracy headed by the Aycinenas. While carrying out the letter of the liberal laws of the Cortes, he displayed a notable lack of compliance with their spirit. He ended freedom of the press and stifled the creole ayuntamientos and provincial deputations. He curtailed foreign trade, and he was obviously elated when the restored Fernando VII suppressed not only the Constitution but all of the decrees of the Cádiz government with a single stroke of his pen.

The fortunes of the Aycinenas, who had been vocal in their support of the Cádiz government and its liberal policies, now took a serious turn downward. Their control of the Ayuntamiento was impaired when a royal order removed from public office those who had endorsed Peinado's *Instructions* to Larrazábal (who now found himself in a Spanish jail). The Aycinenas had not been associated with the independence movements which had flared in San Salvador and Nicaragua; indeed, José de Aycinena had directed the suppression of the 1811 rebellion in San Salvador and had succeeded a peninsular as Intendente there. Nevertheless, from 1814 forward Bustamante clearly suspected these creole leaders of revolutionary designs; he guarded against any Central American imitation of the kind of uprising Miguel Hidalgo had led in Mexico. The merchants of the capital now gained the ascendancy in the advisory councils of the Captain General.

Bustamante sought ways to increase productivity and thereby reverse the declining economic trends and spreading poverty. To this end he proposed land distribution and salaried labor, giving landless Indians and ladinos small plots to work. Such plans further alienated the creole aristocracy against the Captain General, whose projects they saw as a threat to their own land and labor. The economic welfare of members of the aristocracy deteriorated in direct relation to their political status. Bustamante refused them positions of high office, pressed a suit for back taxes against the Aycinena family, and denied them the government protection and advantage they had formerly enjoyed. Some turned to contraband trade. A few involved themselves in the abortive Belén conspiracy against Bustamante in December 1813. A few months later a new plot in San Salvador also failed dismally.

Between 1811 and 1818, while Bustamante suppressed the outward manifestations of political partisanship, political factions became crystallized. The differences among the factions were political, social, economic, regional, even religious, but they were not particularly nationalist or anti-Spanish. There was little sentiment for independence, and the government easily put down the few isolated insurrections. Supported by the pro-peninsular mercantile community in the capital, the textile producers, and the small landholders throughout the Kingdom, the government party sought to prevent all breaches in the protected commercial system. Inexpensive British cottons were the principal object of its policies, as cotton imports were damaging the native weaving industry and cutting into profits normally reserved for the capital's merchants. Meanwhile, the steady decline in indigo profits forced many of the planters to come to terms with the merchants.

The government's protection of the bloc of merchants, weavers, and indigo producers left the creole aristocracy in a difficult position. Many of them were denied office because of their support of the Constitution of 1812 and, more specifically, of Peinado's *Instructions,* until a general amnesty in 1817 restored their citizenship privileges. But their economic position further deteriorated with the indigo decline. The rains in 1816 were heavier than usual, and they damaged the crops; at the same time, a new tax was placed on overseas trade to help

defray expenses of the Pablo Morillo expedition against Simón Bolívar
in South America. Without the official laxity that had formerly permitted freer trade, the creoles faced serious financial problems. In
Guatemala they found allies only among those who shared their hatred
of Bustamante—mainly those who favored independence or restoration
of the Constitution of 1812. It proved a strange alliance of the "best
families" with social outcasts, an inordinate number of whom were
upper middle sector professional men of illegitimate parentage. This
alliance, born of expediency, was doomed to disintegrate once the
common foe was gone in the 1820's. So long as Bustamante remained,
the alliance had to be a discreet one, if indeed it could be manifested at
all. But the aristocracy had allies elsewhere, persons whom it could call
upon more readily. The letters that flowed from the Aycinenas and
others of the "family" to influential friends in Spain reflect their desire
to see Bustamante ousted.

When Bustamante was finally removed in 1818, the "family" lost no
time in restoring its former position in the colonial government and
society. Even before Carlos Urrutia y Montoya arrived from his previous post in Santo Domingo, members of the creole aristocracy surrounded this elderly, mild-mannered officer. They won his confidence
and regained the upper hand. Regardless of the capabilities Urrutia
had displayed in earlier positions, by the time he came to Guatemala
he was in the twilight of his competence as an administrator. It was,
in part, his easygoing attitude which permitted the relatively peaceful
transition to independence in Central America. While Urrutia ha-
rangued against contraband, his decrees made foreign trade easier,
for they attempted to replace smuggling with legitimate commerce on
which the government could collect taxes. Thus, in 1819 Urrutia
authorized trade with Belize, and merchants associated with the "family" were quick to take advantage of the decree.

Yet Urrutia failed to end contraband trade. His relaxation of Bustamante's coast defense measures encouraged smugglers, while privateers
flying the ensign of Latin American republican governments drove
Spanish shipping from the seas. By closing the port of Izabal and removing the heavy garrison from the fortress at San Felipe, Urrutia per-

mitted illicit trade to flow easily through the Río Dulce and into the country via either the Río Polochic or the road from Izabal to Guatemala. After privateers—notably Louis Aury, flying first the flag of Buenos Aires and later that of Colombia—made several forays against the Central American coast, even the Ayuntamiento joined the Consulado in calling for regarrisoning of San Felipe.

Restoration of the Constitution, the result of the revolt led by Rafael Riego in Spain (1820), permitted open political discussion, and for the first time labeled political factions appeared in Central America. The interests of the Aycinena oligarchy were taken up by Dr. Pedro Molina in his newspaper, *El Editor Constitucional,* which began publication in July 1820. Molina, of illegitimate birth, was most assuredly not a member of the "family," nor were most of his close associates. The alliance born out of opposition to Bustamante, nevertheless, now carried the opposition further, to the closed economic system. Free trade became a leading issue, although Molina himself championed independence as well, for even the liberal Spanish government offered little promise of adequate colonial representation. The more moderate sector responded with its own newspaper, *El Amigo de la Patria,* edited by José Cecilio del Valle, noted for his liberalism in the late colonial period, but now opposing radical change. Del Valle, from a Honduran cattle-ranching family, had come to the capital in the 1790's and had subsequently made his mark as a successful attorney and government official. Never accepted into the society of the "family," del Valle, as a leading adviser to Bustamante, had become closely associated with the merchants who opposed the Aycinenas and their relatives. Thus, these two early political factions found members of the upper middle sector as their principal spokesmen. Neither truly represented the middle sectors; rather, they stood for different wings of the creole aristocracy, both reflecting influence of personal interest and Enlightenment thought.

The campaign of these two factions centered on the elections at the end of 1820 for seats on the Guatemalan Ayuntamiento and the Provincial Deputation. They waged the campaign passionately in private homes, on street corners, at public meetings, and in the newspapers.

The chief issue was freedom of trade, but many other topics, largely revolving around personalities and qualifications, found their way into the argument. The radicals charged the moderates with corruption, outdated economic views, and self-interest, and they said the moderates were lackeys of the "hated Bustamante." The moderates retorted with an attack on the privileges of the aristocracy; a cry against the dangers of free trade to the jobs of the working class, especially those engaged in textile production; and a defense of gradual, orderly, social and economic reforms consistent with the traditions of the country. In general, the newer members of the aristocracy and the lowest classes supported the radicals, while the middle sectors and older aristocracy favored the moderates.

There was no clear-cut victory for either side, as several candidates elected by the small electorate were not clearly associated with either faction. The moderates gained a delicate advantage in the Ayuntamiento by virtue of the election of José del Valle as First Alcalde, while the radicals gained a narrow margin in the more powerful Provincial Deputation. Jealousies between the two institutions, which had overlapping functions, added to the difficulties brought on by the partisan differences.

Augustin de Iturbide's Plan de Iguala in Mexico forced the issue of independence into Guatemalan politics in mid-1821. Molina pressed the issue and found growing support. The Aycinenas had become convinced that their best interests—they were inherently conservative, even though on the trade issue they had been liberal—lay in a break with the now liberal-controlled peninsula. The moderates, in the main, held to a loyalist position throughout the summer, and the issue became foremost in the pages of *El Editor* and *El Amigo*. In March of 1821 Sub-Inspector Gabino Gaínza, recently arrived from Chile, had assumed temporary command from the feeble Urrutia with the backing of the Provincial Deputation. Gaínza pursued a middle course. On the one hand, he issued strongly worded public statements against independence; on the other, he worked privately with the radicals and tolerated, if he did not actively encourage, independence sentiment.

The success of Iturbide's Plan and indications that a Mexican army might be forthcoming to "liberate" Central America had much to do with Guatemala's decision to declare the kingdom independent on September 15, 1821. The decision was by no means unanimous, but by this time several moderates had reluctantly accepted independence as an alternative to possible civil war. None of the "family" delegates opposed the declaration, which was adopted by a vote of 23 to 7 in a stormy junta of the leading personages in the capital. It changed practically nothing except political sovereignty. The government remained virtually the same. Moderate leader José del Valle, who had cautioned against any hasty declaration of independence, was instrumental in drafting the document and in organizing the provisional government, and Gabino Gaínza continued as chief executive.

The immediate issue became not independence from Spain, but rather the alternatives of being an independent republic versus being annexed to the Mexican Empire. The threat of armed intervention from Mexico influenced the decision, but in the weeks between September and January the nature of the alliance betwen Molina's pro-independence party and the "family" can be seen vividly. The "family" rapidly consolidated its position and captured key offices. None of the principal positions were filled by Molina or his close associates. The transitory nature of the party became evident on this issue; it forced a realignment of factional loyalties along more logical class lines. Molina, perhaps somewhat naïvely, favored complete independence. The aristocracy, now led by Mariano Aycinena and his nephew, Juan José, Marquis of Aycinena, ardently championed annexation to royalist Mexico. With the support of Gaínza, the kingdom formally proclaimed annexation on Jaunary 5, 1822.

In the province there were mixed reactions to the decisions made by the central government in Guatemala. Establishment of three *comandancias,* with seats of power at Ciudad Real (with jurisdiction over Chiapas and Los Altos), Guatemala (Guatemala and El Salvador), and León (Honduras, Nicaragua, and Costa Rica), followed the precedent of the provincial deputations, but challenged more traditional provincial loyalties. While the majority of the ayuntamientos of the kingdom approved of annexation, there was notable opposition in San Salvador, which had become the leader of the attack on the hegemony of the capital. Mexican troops finally had to conquer El Salvador.

With the question of sovereignty and form of government apparently settled, politics in Guatemala focused again on the issue of commercial policy. Central Americans, within generous limits set by the imperial government, were now free to trade with anyone, and the Belize commerce flourished. British cottons and manufactures flowed into the country at a level theretofore unseen, and in 1822 Guatemalan merchants legally exported cochineal in quantity to Britain for the first time.

A few of the merchants who had staunchly opposed free trade in the colonial period were able to move into the new trade patterns, but the majority refused to abandon hope of continuing their traditional relations with Cádiz under a protected system. The Consulado expressed this viewpoint vociferously in its reports on the state of the economy. Attributing the ruin of a once-thriving domestic cotton industry to free trade, the merchants called for an end to British trade, or at least the passage of a high protective tariff. The merchants failed to win their case, however, and freedom of trade with a low revenue duty prevailed.

New political labels replaced the old tags which the new alignments had made outmoded. Those who were liberal, who favored free trade, economic liberalization, republicanism, and clerical reform, were branded as *Fiebres,* or hotheads. Those who were conservative, who were accused of desiring continuance or royalist institutions and of opposing reforms, were dubbed *Serviles.* Membership and support of these parties first tended to follow the lines established by Molina and del Valle, but as the new economic forces developed—notably free trade and the rise of the cochineal industry—they also reflected the cleavage between Guatemala and the rest of the provinces. The resentment of El Salvador was strongest, and it became the liberal stronghold, but protests against the economic advantages of the capital came from all of the provinces. Events in Mexico again forced action, and the abdication of Iturbide in March 1823 led to a declaration of absolute Central American independence on July 1 of the same year. Only Chiapas elected to remain with Mexico. The other states became the United Provinces of Central America.

A provisional junta with little authority took over, and it succeeded in launching a new government and suppressing two insurgencies in September. Despite repeated efforts by pro-Spanish elements to overthrow the government, commercial relations with the former mother country and its Cuban colony gradually improved, although Spain withheld formal recognition of the Central American states until after 1850.

Central American independence thus began with political parties which had long-standing economic differences struggling for control. That economic self-interest and jealousies played important roles in the political activities of both the "family" and the merchant monopoly is obvious. The question of free trade became not just an economic issue, but a political and social one as well, as it threatened the position of the merchants, artisans, and producers who had been protected under the Spanish system. At the same time it offered new opportunities for that portion of the creole aristocracy which had held economic, social, and political power and prestige in the days before Bustamante, but which at the hour of independence found itself struggling in the face of a declining indigo market. To this economic conflict was added political idealism and philosophies stemming from the Enlightenment, still in many ways foreign to the traditions of the region. As a result, the Central American federation had a turbulent and unstable beginning.

The century preceding independence was a time of enormous intellectual, economic, and political change. The class structure of Central America reflected these changes as new elements took over leadership of the creole aristocracy and potentially important middle sectors emerged. Spanish political hegemony ended, but already Great Britain was achieving commercial dominance on the isthmus. By the time of independence the earlier promise of prosperity had evaporated, and poverty and economic decline faced the new nation. This set the stage for many of the difficulties of the nineteenth and twentieth centuries.

Chapter 4 • Expectations and Achievements of Independence

Though the Central Americans were spared a war against Spain or Mexico, they engaged in stormy debate and bloody internal strife throughout the first decades of independence, for the class antagonisms which had begun to emerge at the close of the colonial era erupted in the new republic. They came to blows over Church-State relations, fiscal policies, officeholding, economic planning, trade policy, and general philosophy of government, but few issues arose after independence that had not already been brought up during the tumultous years between 1808 and 1823. Two political parties which were to vie for control of all the Central American states throughout the remainder of the century, and in much of the twentieth century as well, became clearly established during these bloodstained years of the United Provinces. The Conservatives pleaded for moderation, order, and the stability of traditional, familiar institutions. The Liberals argued for a continuation of the reforms already begun under the Spanish Bourbons. The Liberal Party, never very well defined across Central America, had many factions. Often idealistic, they sought to make Central America a modern, progressive state, casting off the burden of Iberian heritage, and to absorb eagerly republican innovations from France, England, and the United States. This meant, in general, that Liberals stood for restrictions of clerical power and privilege; abolition of slavery; abolition of burdensome taxes on commerce; elimination of privileged and exclusive fueros and guilds; more egalitarian political and judicial institutions; public education, and economic development, especially road, port, and immigration projects. The Constitution of 1824, largely fashioned by the Liberals and patterned somewhat after the United States model of 1789 but also very much after the Spanish model of 1812, embodied these ideals.

The Constitution established the structure of the federation. It provided for a single-chamber Congress and reserved considerable autonomy to the states. Yet it offered an adequate framework for a strong union, and it was not constitutional deficiencies, but the failure or inability of the federal leaders to enforce its provisions which allowed the states to continue their drift toward absolute sovereignty. Plagued from the outset by political and economic difficulties, in the two decades of their existence the United Provinces never achieved nationhood. The seeds of their disunity were already present in the provincial jealousies and ideological differences of the late colonial period.

The political parties, initially very fluid in composition, never fully reflected classlines. Yet in the 1820's, as interests became crystallized, the Liberals came to represent more clearly the middle sectors, particularly the upper middle ladinos in the professions, whom the white creoles had denied control of the principal institutions. Competition for the positions of the departed Spanish bureaucracy provided political rewards and fostered opportunism in the political life of the country. The scramble for spoils sometimes obscured ideological issues, but the economy remained an important determinant of political affiliation. As Central America had been more closely tied than many of the colonies to the Spanish monopolistic trading system, independence hurt those dependent on the trade considerably. Advocates of free trade had argued with glowing idealism the economic advantages of independence, yet the rapid introduction of British goods crippled local industry and threatened local merchants. As these economic realities became evident,

leading members of the aristocracy defected from liberalism and assumed what was their more natural, conservative posture.

When Central America seceded from the Mexican Empire, there
was general agreement upon the ideal of unification of the kingdom
into a single republic. The form the new government should take,
however, led to bitter differences. The Conservatives, particularly in
Guatemala, where that faction was strongest, wanted a unitary system
reminiscent of the colonial regime. The Liberals, on the other hand,
favored a confederation on the North American model. The Liberals
represented the provinces, which, because of their geographic isolation
and economic and social resentment toward the capital, had already
gone far toward developing local provincial autonomy. The concepts
of home rule which had developed since 1810 had made deep impressions and could not be easily discarded. As early as 1815 Simón Bolívar,
the South American patriot, had projected the ideal of a prosperous
and progressive confederation on the isthmus. In his famous "Jamaica
Letter," he had written:

> The States of the Isthmus from Panama to Guatemala will perhaps
> form a confederation. This magnificent location between the two
> great oceans could in time become the emporium of the world. Its
> canals will shorten the distances throughout the world, strengthen
> commercial ties with Europe, America, and Asia, and bring that happy
> region tribute from the four quarters of the globe. Perhaps some day
> the capital of the world may be located there, just as Constantine
> claimed Byzantium was the capital of the ancient world.

Central American Liberals echoed this infectious if unrealistic optimism as they organized society and government after they won, by
the barest of margins and amid cries of fraud, the election of 1825.
They had controlled the government since July 1823, and even before the election they had abolished slavery and noble titles, limited
the monopolies, enacted a generous immigration law, and adopted the
federal Constitution of 1824. Now, under the leadership of Manuel
José Arce, they embarked on a bold revolutionary program which
alarmed the Conservatives, who were led by Mariano Aycinena and
José del Valle. Tax reform eliminated unpopular Spanish levies, but

left little revenue to cover the debt assumed from the colonial and imperial governments or to pay for expensive new projects. Arce's government turned to foreign capitalists to meet the financial crisis, but a large loan from the London firm of Barclay, Herring & Richardson actually produced only a small amount of cash for the federation. Since the government repaid practically none of it, the loan did not place an immediate burden on the federation's finances, but the indebtedness remained to trouble British–Central American relations for years afterward.

Recognizing the impossibility of immediate transformation of the economy and society, and facing the reality of considerable Conservative strength, moderates led by President Arce himeslf soon defected from the Liberals. This resulted in Conservative control of the federal and Guatemalan government in 1826, but it also sparked a bloody civil war. The Liberals found a leader in Francisco Morazán, the Honduran son of a creole from the French Caribbean, and they regained control three years later. Violence had already flared between Liberal and Conservative factions in Nicaragua. El Salvador was near rebellion over the efforts of Ramón Casaus y Torres, the Conservative Archbishop of Guatemala, to block appointment of Liberal José Matías Delgado as Bishop of El Salvador. By 1827 bitter fighting raged around the Guatemalan-Salvadoran border, and elsewhere, from Los Altos to Costa Rica, skirmishes and revolts brought anarchy and chaos to the isthmus.

Following their victory in 1829, the Liberals dealt vindictively with their enemies. They imprisoned or exiled the Conservative leaders and granted the state governments extraordinary powers to deal with all who opposed the Liberal regimes. In the years following, federal President Morazán used the full powers of his office—and more—to attain order and stability in the republic, but in this he failed, for turmoil characterized the period even after he moved the federal capital from Guatemala to the more sympathetic San Salvador.

Moderate José del Valle won the presidential election of 1834, but he died before taking office. Had he lived, he might have brought conciliation and harmony to the opposing forces and thereby preserved

the Central American union. In his place the Congress reelected
Morazán, who had apparently been willing to step aside for del Valle,
and the Liberal regime continued.

In Nicaragua the rivalry between the two ancient cities of Granada
(more conservative) and León (more liberal) continued to breed violence. Newspapers began to appear throughout the isthmus. Although
many had only brief lives, taken together they document the bitter
and passionate hatreds of the protagonists as they added the press to
their arsenal of weapons. Their ferocity was as violent as the enormous
explosion of Nicaragua's Volcán Cosigüín, in January 1835, which
sent earthquakes throughout the isthmus, changed the courses of
rivers, and sprinkled ashes as far away as Colombia, Jamaica, and
Oaxaca.

Costa Rica, also ruled by Liberals during most of the early period,
virtually ignored the federal establishment, continuing in the remote
position which it had occupied throughout the colonial period. Costa
Rica successfully asserted its independence from Nicaragua and became more closely involved economically with Colombia and Panama.
In the 1830's it began to develop coffee production as a major export.
It was the first Central American state to do so. Costa Rica was not
immune to the turbulence of the rest of the country, however, and
several violent uprisings there punctuated the 1830's.

In Guatemala, after 1831, Governor Mariano Gálvez pursued with
temporary success a policy of conciliation. He restored a measure of
harmony to Guatemalan society through compromise and an economic program which courted middle sector Conservative groups in the
capital. An ambitious program to increase production, expand transportation, and colonize the lowland areas of the Caribbean coast, for
example, promised tangible benefits to commercial interests, while steps
toward protective tariffs appealed to weavers whose markets had been
captured by British textiles. Although political passions still ran high
in the state—which accounted for more than half the population of the
republic—and there were separatist rumblings from Quezaltenango,
where the inhabitants resented the fact that their voice was small in
both state and federal government, by 1834 Gálvez had achieved rela-

tive peace in the state. Peace and growing trade, largely owing to the British promotion of Belize as the major entrepôt for Central American exports of dyes and mahogany, had arrested the economic decline. Protective tariffs had prompted some revival of the textile industry. A serious debt, shortage of currency, and accompanying high interest rates still plagued the economy, but cochineal exports, which rose dramatically in the 1830's, gave both planters in the countryside and merchants in the capital a sense of prosperity. In retrospect, however, Gálvez's first administration appears as a calm before the storm which soon swept across the state.

Governing most aspects of Guatemalan life were the Europeanized residents of the capital, which by 1833 was a city of no more than 40,000. The political and economic disturbances that began during the Bustamante administration, the decline of indigo exports, and the disintegration of the Kingdom of Guatemala following independence all contributed to an erosion of the collective importance of the white, creole elite dominated by the Aycinenas, several of whom were now in exile. Contrary to the popular opinion of the time, this "aristocracy" was no longer united politically, although it is true that most were Conservatives. Members of both parties came from its ranks. Not included in the "aristocracy," but closely associated with the creole ruling class, were ladinos from the upper middle sectors whose political power had been inaugurated by the Cortes of Cádiz. Most of the leaders of the Liberal Party and the Gálvez administration came from this group. Not the least of its interests was the acquisition of more land, still the key to greater economic and social prestige in the country.

The production and commerce of the state rested in the hands of these two groups, and although there was considerable political gain to be made by branding individuals as "aristocrats" between 1821 and 1839, in all probability the line between these groups had become blurred by the political differences between Liberal and Conservative. Changing circumstances had reduced the favorable economic position which the Aycinena clan had held at the close of the reign of Carlos IV, but this elite was still the most durable element of the Guatemalan upper class in the transition from colony to republic. It was a period of considerable dislocation for the elite, with many Spaniards leaving the country upon independence—there was a notable decrease in the number of Basque names among economic and social leaders in the country after 1821, for example. Meanwhile, there was a small flow of newcomers which enlarged the European resident class in the capital.

This relatively small group of Europeanized residents in Guatemala City dominated the politics of the era. Although there was some class mobility, largely along economic-cultural lines, the remainder of the population in the 1830's still had little or no voice in any of the states.

Throughout the isthmus, the ladinos were the most volatile group in the society, and they succeeded in asserting themselves most notably in El Salvador and Honduras, where the whites were fewest. Ladinos were in the majority nearly everywhere between white Costa Rica and Indian Los Altos. Many of these small farmers, merchants, and artisans had suffered greatly from economic disruption, and the rural ladinos came to blame the Liberal regimes for the economic failures. The Indians, still a large majority of the population in Guatemala, were more isolated and generally less involved with the European community than were the ladinos. Many still did not speak Spanish. They continued in their traditional way of life, little aware of or interested in the possibilities of modern economic and social advance.

In 1837 a major revolt shattered the delicate atmosphere of conciliation and incipient prosperity. Unlike earlier civil wars, this one did not involve the creoles and upper middle sectors; it erupted among peasant populations throughout Central America. It was most violent in the eastern mountain region of Guatemala, the area known as *la montaña*, where a peasant hero, Rafael Carrera, emerged to command the movement. A natural *caudillo*, with intuitive military and political perception, Carrera dramatically altered the course of Central American history and destroyed Liberal aspirations for more than a quarter-century. Carrera's revolt was not merely another quarrel between Liberals and Conservatives for control of the government; rather, it was a popular rebellion engendered by a growing sense of grievance against the governments of Morazán and Gálvez, and it was aggravated by a catastrophic cholera epidemic. The grassroots reaction against the Liberals was especially violent against foreign elements and against efforts to change traditional life-styles and patterns of rural life.

At the heart of the difficulty lay the Liberals' reform program—the rational extension of changes inspired by Enlightenment philosophers, initiated by Spanish Bourbon ministers, accelerated by liberal Spaniards in Napoleonic times, and continued by creoles after independence. The creoles added a new dimension, however, when they made a conscious effort to emulate the rapidly advancing English-speaking world. Direct contact with English and North American merchants and diplomats in Central America was responsible for part of this, but probably more important were the readings and travels of Central Americans. Morazán and Gávez believed that enlightened legislation could transform Central America into a modern, progressive republic. Convinced that their nation's underdevelopment was the result of Spanish colonialism, they sought to destroy Hispanic institutions and laws and to create new ones modeled upon the successful experience of Great Britain and the United States. In practice, however, although they made substantial headway in gaining the acceptance of the elite, they found the changes unwelcome among the lower classes. Gálvez promoted what he believed to be a rational program to improve the state's economy, judicial system, bureaucracy, educational opportunities, communications, and general welfare. The federal government and the other states pursued similar, if somewhat less extensive, policies. But the Guatemalan Liberals displayed exceptional ineptitude in converting a population accustomed to paternalism to their well-intentioned reforms.

Although Gálvez's program claimed to promote prosperity, many remained unconvinced. The dislocation occasioned by the shift to cochineal production could not easily be absorbed. Gálvez's tariff policy favored the weavers, but heavy imports of British textiles had already ruined many of them, and they continued to be apprehensive of Liberal talk of economic freedom. Cotton production had also dropped, and for the same reasons. Gálvez's tariff adjustments were too little, too late.

More directly responsible for the popular reaction was the reestablishment of a direct head tax, reminiscent of the tribute once collected by the Spaniards which had been abolished shortly after independence. After 1829 the government had forced loans from wealthy citizens, but this income proved inadequate for the ambitious Liberal program. Gálvez established the head tax at two pesos per capita, an amount which was large enough to be a burden to the Guatemalan peasant of the 1830's. In El Salvador the tax resulted in widespread rioting, forcing suspension of the levy there, but Gálvez maintained the tax in Guatemala.

Plans for an extensive network of roads and ports required a labor force, and the government frequently reminded local officials of the obligation of all residents to work on the roads three days out of every month. One could substitute a wage payment, but for the masses it meant unwelcome forced labor. The practice was not new, but Gálvez enforced it more rigorously than it had been in the initial days of the republic.

Still another aspect of the Liberal economic program contributing to rural unrest was the land policy of the government. Since 1825 it had promoted private acquisition of public land as a means of increasing production, and Morazán accelerated these efforts. It seems likely that the real result of this reform was to allow those with some capital to increase their holdings. Individual ownership had no great appeal to the Indians, but Gálvez tried to encourage it as a civilizing force. In the end, lands which local inhabitants had formerly used in common passed into the hands of *latifundistas,* as peasants became sharecroppers or debt peons. More important, a number of large grants to foreigners stirred unrest in eastern Guatemala.

An integral part of Gálvez's vision of a prosperous state was his program of foreign colonization in the more sparsely inhabited reaches, as a means of stimulating their development and attracting a more industrious citizenry into the state. Such plans dated from the eighteenth century, but Gálvez's emphasis on northern Europeans was new. The growing British commercial activity out of Belize had intensified traditional suspicion of foreigners. The Spanish colonial administrations had dealt harshly with foreign interlopers, but since independence the Liberals had welcomed them, and this caused apprehension among those who believed themselves to be victims of foreign competition. Foreign influence was evident in many aspects of the Central American federation, but the concessions made to mahogany loggers, and the projects to colonize the northern and eastern portions of the country with Englishmen, especially antagonized the residents of those regions. They came to regard the government as more favorable to foreign than to national interests. Not only in Guatemala, but also in Costa Rica, such colonization schemes were crucial in turning large numbers of the population toward more traditionalist political leaders and in creating the conservative reaction which swept over the isthmus. Tangible evidence of the dangers of such colonization policies were the expanding British presence in Belize, the Mosquito Coast, and the Bay Islands, and the secession from Mexico of Texas by Anglo-American colonizers there.

Yet the Gálvez government ignored or suppressed petitions against colonization contracts from residents of the region, and the anti-foreign movement spread. The reformers considered ridiculous the idea that they were betraying their country to Europeans. They attributed the eastern towns' opposition entirely to the self-interest of native woodcutters. A rebellion in Chiquimula in the fall of 1835, probably linked with uprisings in El Salvador against Morazán's federal government, focused on the foreign issue, just as anti-English propaganda inflamed the residents of the east. Government troops suppressed the rebellion, and levies to pay the military's expenses were imposed on the towns involved. Such levies were standard practice, but they could only have increased the townspeople's resentment. The federal government, alarmed by these uprisings, pressured Gálvez into issuing a conciliatory decree guaranteeing Guatemalan citizens full rights, but it failed to pacify the inhabitants, whose resentment flared again when the first English colonists arrived in mid-1836.

Central to the Liberal program was the removal of the clergy from its traditional role in politics, the economy, and education. Anticlericalism had firm roots in the Bourbon century, but after independence the attack on clerical privilege accelerated. It was greatest in Guatemala and Nicaragua, where the Church had been strongest. Anticlericalism intensified after the Church backed the Guatemalan Conservative regime of 1826-29. Liberal victory in 1829 brought swift retaliation, with implementation of earlier measures. Far from separating Church and State, the government established close control over the Church. Morazán began the systematic removal of anti-Liberal clergymen, including the Archbishop. Following suppression of monastic orders, exile of prominent Conservative clerics, and enactment of religious liberty in the republic, the federal government prevailed upon state governments to continue the assault on clerical privilege. They censored ecclesiastical correspondence, seized Church funds and property, ceased collection of the tithe, abolished many religious holidays, decreed the right of individual clergy to write their wills as they wished, legitimized inheritance of parents' property by children of the clergy, authorized civil marriage, and legalized divorce, among other things.

Priests did not take lightly challenges to the traditional authority of the Church, especially in the countryside, where parishioners were already disenchanted with the Gálvez government on other grounds. In Indian and ladino villages the priests were more than spiritual leaders. They were the most trusted members of the community, and they served as principal advisers to the civil authorities. They were often the bankers as well. Given this status, village curates could inflame parishioners against a government which attacked their sacred institution, brought Protestant foreigners into the country, and threatened the very bases of society. These village priests were in the vanguard of the uprising that rocked Guatemala in 1837.

None of Gálvez's reforms were closer to his heart than his plan to remove education from the traditionalist hands of the Church and to set up secular schools open to all Guatemalans. An ambitious program called for the establishment of public schools throughout the state. Through a broad range of cultural plans, Gálvez attempted to westernize the Guatemalan Indian. One program permitted uneducated children to be taken from their parents and assigned to "Protectors" who would provide for their education. In practice, however, this provided inexpensive personal service for the wealthy, and the poorer classes viewed it unfavorably. Understandably, attempts to change long-established customs and prejudices exposed the Gálvez administration to criticism from the illiterate masses as well as from members of the elite who felt threatened by mass education.

Probably no part of the Liberal program proved quite so objectionable to so many as the effort to revise the judicial system of the country. Nor is any other aspect of the program quite so representative of the philosophical changes underway. Thoroughly convinced that the Spanish system of private fueros and multiple courts was unjust and out of step with enlightened nineteenth-century jurisprudence, the Liberals—chiefly through the endeavors of José Francisco Barrundia—adopted the Livingston Codes for Guatemala in late 1836. Written by Edward Livingston for Louisiana in 1826, but rejected there, this system of penal law struck the Central American Liberals as a good replacement for the system they had been abolishing piecemeal. Trial by jury had already been inaugurated in El Salvador in 1832 and in Nicaragua and Guatemala in 1835. Almost immediately, however, problems had arisen in the countryside. In states where illiteracy was general and a class system well established, trial by jury proved impracticable, and anecdotes quickly circulated ridiculing the decisions of Indian juries. The requirements of Livingston's penal code proved to be equally impracticable, as jails with separate cells for prisoners did not exist, and their construction with forced labor added to the irritation of the populace, who identified the codes much more with centralized rule from Guatemala City, foreign influence, and anticlericalism than with social justice.

Ruthless enforcement measures seemed to belie the Liberal claims about liberty and freedom. Harsh and totalitarian tactics had been escalating in Guatemala ever since the strong-arm rule of Bustamante, and the Liberals who came back to power in 1829 were vengeful against the Conservatives who had preceded them. Gálvez divided the state into four *comandancias* in 1832, with a general over each, and thereafter military government was characteristic. Both Morazán and

Gálvez resorted to martial solutions in regulating the morality of the inhabitants, suppressing criticism of their own policies, and persecuting their enemies through exile and confiscation of property. The barbaric conduct of government troops further inflamed country people.

Into this atmosphere of bitterness came the terrible scourge of cholera. The epidemic that struck Central America in 1837 had been anticipated. In 1833 cholera had broken out in Mexico, and Gálvez had warned of the danger to his state then. He opened new water and sewage facilities and prohibited burials inside the churches. Despite these precautions, late in 1836 or early 1837 cholera entered the country, probably via Belize. The government responded with quarantines of infected areas, enforced by sanitary cordons. These measures were undoubtedly sound, but they were poorly understood and did not succeed. The masses, already alienated from the Gálvez government, feared vaccines, and they believed the priests who told them that the medicine which the government's health officers put into the water was poison. Panic resulted and violence broke out, particularly in the hard-hit montaña region.

Irate over the government's reforms, and having watched cholera spread over the land like a divine retribution (which the priests said it was!), the peasants rebelled in various places, beginning in March 1837. Although the first insurgency occurred at San Juan Ostuncalco, in Los Altos, other uprisings followed in the montaña, which was more ladino than Indian and traditionally more restless, while at the same time more generally dominated by parish priests.

José Rafael Carrera (1814-65), born in the run-down Candelaria neighborhood of Guatemala City, was a ladino; he was representative of the lower middle sector. Receiving no formal education, he drifted about, working at various menial jobs. By the time he was fourteen he was a drummer in the Guatemalan army, fighting against the forces of Morazán. By 1834 he had become a swineherd in the montaña district of Mita. There his fortunes began to improve. He had a friendly relationship with the village priest in Mataquescuintla, and this led him to make a favorable marriage and to gain a position of some local importance. When trouble broke out in 1837 Carrera commanded a platoon of government troops enforcing the cholera quarantines. In June of that year he abandoned his post, responding to a call for aid from peasants resisting government forces in near-by Santa Rosa. Carrera converted a mob of untrained peasants into a ferocious guerrilla army which soon struck panic into the hearts of the elite. Frequently wounded, this violent man repeatedly displayed exceptional physical courage and determination. Fearlessly leading his forces in fanatical charges against troops with better arms and training, he inspired the enraged peasantry to courage, sacrifice, slaughter, and victory.

Popular uprisings against the Liberal reforms stretched from Costa Rica to Quezaltenango during the first half of 1837, but the nucleus of the War of la Montaña developed around Rafael Carrera, in the district of Mita. Carrera's forces grew from a small band into a raiding army which forced the government to escalate its efforts at suppression. Atrocities and vindictive retaliations occurred with increasing frequency as the war widened throughout the remainder of the year. The cholera added to the suffering of the people. Revolts in Honduras and Nicaragua weakened federal authority there. In late June Carrera issued a manifesto which suggested the prinicpal grievances of his followers: (1) abolition of the Livingston Codes; (2) protection of life and property; (3) return of the Archbishop and restoration of the religious orders; (4) abolition of the head tax; (5) amnesty for all those exiled in 1829; and (6) respect for Carrera's orders, under pain of death to violators. Though Carrera was often defeated by government forces, he always eluded capture, finding refuge among the peasants of the mountainous country, where his legendary image grew steadily.

Even in the face of popular insurgency, the Guatemalan Liberals bickered among themselves as to what course to follow. Gálvez, in a misguided search for unity, became more conciliatory toward the Conservatives, only to alienate the more extreme Liberals headed by Barrundia and Pedro Molina. With increasing invective the Barrundia faction assailed the government in the press and in the legislature, accusing Gálvez of suppressing freedom throughout the state in order to quell a local rebellion. In December Gálvez appointed two Conservatives, Juan José Aycinena and Marcial Zebadúa, to his key ministerial posts, further antagonizing the Barrundia faction. Confronted by a spreading peasant revolt and with growing dissension within the Guatemalan state government, Morazán began to harbor doubts about Gálvez, and he failed to send the assistance from the federal capital in San Salvador which might have saved the Guatemalan Governor.

As the war raged on, Gálvez's reforms were one by one sacrificed for lack of funds—funds which had to be spent for the military. The state budget put into effect in September 1837 revealed that, of a total of just under 300,000 pesos, 110,000 pesos were appropriated for the Department of War, 57,000 for the Department of Justice, and only 12,000 for Public Education. Having placed too much faith in advanced laws and too little in the sentiments of the people, Gálvez was paying the price. Without enough troops to occupy the entire country, Gálvez sought to defeat and capture the caudillo and thereby arrest the rebellion. But the raiding and looting continued. The war was becoming a race war, with rural Indians, ladinos, mulattoes, and zambos joining together against the urban white creoles and foreigners. Violence was widespread, and the countryside became thoroughly unsafe. Commerce and communications came to a standstill. Without federal reinforcements, Gálvez's days in office were numbered.

Barrundia determined to form an alliance with Carrera as an opportunistic means of ousting Gálvez—he was confident that he could dominate the supposedly illiterate guerrilla leader. It was a fatal miscalculation. In late 1837 Barrundia's initial efforts at negotiation with Carrera were rebuffed by the priests who advised Carrera. But the priests changed their minds when Barrundia formed an opposition government at Antigua and Aycinena and Zebadúa resigned from Gálvez's government. Left alone, Gálvez bravely refused to surrender. He tried to raise a larger army and threatened the rebels with attack, but it was a futile gesture, for by late January there was general dissatisfaction with his government even within the capital. The municipal government dissolved itself in protest. In return for Carrera's military alliance, Barrundia's agents agreed to nullification of the Livingston Codes, relaxation of the anticlericalism, and, dangerously, recognition of Carrera as commander of all the insurgent forces. The agreement succeeded in bringing down Gálvez, but it spelled eventual disaster for Barrundia's cause.

Carrera's peasants poured into the city on January 31, 1838. In spite of some inevitable brutality and vengeance by the rural forces, order soon prevailed. Carrera himself was obedient to the new government, and he maintained his troops under command, evacuating most of them within a few days. He had succeeded in toppling the government. He had been assured that the Liberal excesses would be discontinued. He returned victorious to the montaña, encouraged, according to some sources, by an $11,000 bribe to hasten his departure from the capital.

The Barrundia faction appeared to have triumphed. Gálvez had resigned in favor of Lieutenant Governor Pedro Valenzuela, who was more acceptable to Barrundia. Pedro Molina became president of the legislature. Carrera, commissioned a lieutenant colonel and given military command of his home district of Mita, was out of the capital, along with his dreaded peasant army.

The real situation was otherwise, however, for the coalition which sustained the government was exceedingly fragile and all feared a return of the caudillo. Although Gálvez was out of power, he still had support in the legislature, and, in addition to the Barrundia faction, the Conservatives now made an important resurgence, having gained first from their alliance with Gálvez and later from the proclerical attitude of Carrera. Despite their proclerical sentiments, however, they were not yet ready to court the feared guerilla leader. Thus they vacillated between coalition with moderate Liberals and formation of a new Conservative faction. In the meantime, the departments of Los Altos took advantage of the situation, seceded from Guatemala, and declared their allegiance to Morazán.

The events of the next few weeks reveal the real power structure in the state. By February 20 the government was addressing Carrera as "General" and processing with kid gloves the complaints of landlords against Carrera's peasants on their lands. Pedro Molina resigned as president of the legislature, which body then restored the Church to its former position, removed the military governments, and called for return to constitutional rule. These decrees reflected the popular will, as voiced by the guerilla caudillo. The preamble of a decree of March 12, which terminated all nonelective officeholders, illustrated the attention the legislature gave to this will when it acknowledged that "a great majority of the population of the State have armed themselves to resist the administration that violated their guarantees and the fundamental pact." It justified Carrera's revolution as "directed to reestablishing law and liberty . . . and demanded by self-preservation against tyranny, [as] not only legitimate but consecrated by reason and justice." The liberal language of this decree probably reflected the continuing influence of Barrundia, but the repeal of the Livingston Codes soon thereafter revealed his declining power.

Barrundia was slow to recognize the growing Conservative strength, and he doubted the ability of Carrera to bring sufficient force against a united government. Carrera, on the other hand, dissatisfied with the government's progress toward his demands, prodded by growing anti-government sentiment from rural property holders, and persuaded by the priests that he was being used by the Liberals, renewed the guerrilla warfare. Valenzuela, urged on by Barrundia, responded with repression. But the election of a new Representative Council, clearly reflecting Conservative gains in public opinion and headed by Conservative Mariano Rivera Paz, put Barrundia in an untenable position. Conservative strength was rising, and it was drifting reluctantly toward alliance with the masses. In the end, Barrundia had to fall back on his Liberal ally, Francisco Morazán, and the re-entry of the federal President into the state with 1000 Salvadoran troops in mid-March marked a new phase of the struggle.

The Guatemalan government had cautioned Morazán against marching into the state, for he would upset the recent understanding with Carrera, who had returned to the montaña in peace. Yet the resumption of warfare by Carrera in March forced state officials to look to the federal government for help. After negotiators rejected Carrera's demands, Morazán launched a campaign to crush the rebellion. The guerrillas responded with new ferocity, especially, although not exclusively, against foreign-owned properties. Often losing skirmishes, but never decisively defeated, the guerrillas harried the government

in an ever-extending area, one which finally stretched from the Caribbean to the Pacific and from El Salvador into the Verapaz and Sacatepéquez. Morazán absorbed the machinery of the state government,
pushing aside the Conservatives, and, as Gálvez had done earlier, he
escalated the repression. Both sides committed atrocities. With Morazán in control of the capital, the Liberals reinstituted part of the program which they had sacrificed to appease Carrera.

In the meantime, the federation over which Morazán presided was
becoming a fiction. Nicaragua seceded on April 30, and a month later
the federal Congress in San Salvador formally allowed the states to go
their separate ways. When, on July 7, the Congress went even further
and declared the states to be "sovereign, free and independent political bodies," Morazán decided it was time to return to San Salvador
and put his government in order. He believed, incorrectly, that he had
greatly weakened the Carrera revolt in Guatemala. He would be
equally ineffectual in restoring the now shattered Central American
union. Honduras and Costa Rica followed Nicaragua out of the federation before the end of the year.

In less than a month following Morazán's departure the Conservatives, supported by popular demonstrations calling for action to forestall a new invasion of the capital from the montaña, had gained control of the government of Guatemala. On July 22, 1838, Valenzuela
turned over the executive power to the Conservative Rivera Paz. Three
days later the legislature decreed a general amnesty for all political acts
in the state since 1821, welcomed back exiles, and declared all civil
rights and guarantees reestablished. There followed a stream of legislation dismantling the Liberal program and beginning the restoration
of the institutions of the colonial era. In rapid succession the legislature provided for State support of the Church, formally declared national sovereignty, reduced by half the direct head tax, repealed civil
marriage and divorce, revoked Gálvez's municipal organization system,
and generally reversed the direction of Guatemala's government.

Despite Conservative ascendancy in the government, no accord had
yet been reached with Carrera and there were still important Liberal
officers in the army. The government therefore continued the military

efforts to suppress the guerrillas, but with Morazán's troops gone Carrera made notable gains. By early September he had occupied Antigua and once more threatened the capital. A sudden counteroffensive by the Liberal General Carlos Salazar, however, dealt Carrera a stunning defeat at Villa Nueva in September, although Carrera himself escaped into the hills and soon resumed the resistance. He bought time to reorganize his haggard forces in December when he signed a treaty at El Rinconcito agreeing to lay down his arms and recognize the government of Guatemala in return for his restoration as military commander of Mita. The country enjoyed a breath of peace.

The respite was short, however, for, encouraged by the apparent collapse of the Carrera movement, the Liberals attempted to recoup their position. On January 30, 1839, Morazán deposed Rivera Paz and in his place put General Salazar, the hero of Villa Nueva. Meanwhile, Conservatives had gained power in Honduras and Nicaragua, and they joined forces against the Liberals in El Salvador. Carrera was in league with those Conservative leaders, particularly Francisco Ferrera of Honduras, and the new Liberal thrust by Morazán convinced Carrera that there could be no peace until Morazán was defeated once and for all. Morazán's term as President of the federation expired on February 1, and his opponents now claimed that he was the true rebel, for he was in office illegally after that date. Morazán's technical resignation in favor of Vice President Diego Vijil impressed virtually no one. No election had been held, and in truth the federation had ceased to exist. The cause of the Conservatives and of Carrera had finally become one: the elimination of Morazán. Carrera swore to restore Rivera Paz and to join with the Conservatives of Honduras and Nicaragua in ousting Morazán.

Three weeks later Carrera entered Guatemala City unopposed at the head of a large and orderly army. He promptly restored Rivera Paz as Chief of State. He spent the remainder of the year mopping up Liberal resistance in Guatemala and supporting Conservative forces in El Salvador and Honduras. In January 1840, he moved swiftly into Los Altos and crushed the Liberal stronghold in Quezaltenango, an event evidently welcomed by the majority there. In a "Farewell Address" to the inhabitants, he assured them of his continued protection now that he had put the province back on the "road to progress." He promised lower taxes and immediately abolished the head tax. In fact, however, residents of Los Altos were to learn that under Carrera the country would be run largely for the benefit of the economic interests of the capital and the central region of the state, and that the creole aristocracy would jealously guard and narrowly define national development according to its own interests, just as it had in the colonial period.

A showdown between Morazán and Carrera remained inevitable. Morazán refused to abandon the federation idea, even though with the fall of Los Altos he held only El Salvador. In March 1840 he took the initiative and invaded Guatemala, outmaneuvering Carrera's forces and entering the capital city on March 18. On the following day, however, Carrera's troops stormed into the city, completely routing the Liberals. Morazán and a few of his officers escaped by sea to Panama. Two years later he returned to Central America for the last time. He briefly usurped power from the moderate Conservatives who had established themselves in Costa Rica under Braulio Carrillo, but another popular uprising cut short his aspirations of reunification, and he died before a firing squad in San José on September 15, 1842.

Carrera's decisive defeat of Morazán in 1840 was not only the culmination of the guerrilla leader's surge to power in his own state; it was also a major step toward the establishment of a new power structure throughout the isthmus. Carrera had already formed an alliance with Francisco Ferrera, the Honduran Conservative. Now he dictated terms to the defeated Salvadorans and imposed one of his own lieutenants, Francisco Malespín, as caudillo in El Salvador until 1846. From 1840 to 1844 Carrera held the military power but not the presidency in Guatemala. Both Liberal and Conservative factions vied for power and Carrera successfully played one off against the other. The period witnessed the definitive establishment of the five Central American states as independent entities, usually under Conservative rule. While they sometimes paid lip service to reunification, in fact they increased their sovereignty. With Conservatives gaining power in all

five states, perhaps Carrera might have followed up his victory over
Morazán by uniting the isthmus under his own leadership. Yet federation had become too closely associated with Morazán and the Liberals for the Conservatives to embrace it easily. Strong provincial loyalties in each state, each with its own respective caudillo, had developed,
and Carrera had no real ambition to reunify the isthmus. Content to
dominate the neighboring states, he permitted Costa Rica and Nicaragua to go their own ways. Indeed, despite Conservative sympathies,
it is doubtful that those two states would again have accepted the political hegemony of Guatemala without bitter resistance. In 1842 all of
the states except Costa Rica entered into a defensive pact dedicated to
maintaining their individual sovereignty and preventing restoration of
the Constitution of 1824. Although Costa Rica remained aloof from
the alliance, her government formally denounced Morazán and the
Liberal program in the same year.

Carrera's Guatemala was built upon the ruins of Morazán's federation, but the Conservatives soon found they could not control the caudillo. The first decade of his rule was a period of political adjustment
to caudillismo. Carrera's enormous ego grew with his age, and he demanded strict obedience and adulation from all. Once he saw a portrait
of Napolean Bonaparte. He commented, "Another me!" Carrera's will
was law, and his insistence from time to time on the priority of peasant
interests sometimes made life uncomfortable for the elite with whom
he shared power. He was an astute politician, with a capacity for manipulation. He checked Conservative efforts to dominate the government by giving occasional support to the Liberals. Yet his own interests gradually shifted to the more traditional conservatism of the
oligarchy. The growth of his estate probably contributed to this. At the
beginning, he controlled his wife's property. As he prospered militarily,
his holdings increased, and by the time he formally became President
in 1844 he and his family had amassed a considerable fortune.

A study of the legislation of the Conservative years in Central America makes it clear that a very substantial reaction against Liberalism
took place, especially in Guatemala, but in all five states without ex-

ception, as Conservatives restored much of the institutional structure of the colonial period. In Guatemala, however, the Conservative elite paid a price. What had already begun to happen in Honduras and Nicaragua through the process of *mestisaje* (*miscegenation*), but which had been largely resisted in Guatemala, where the European population was larger, now took place there. Some Indians, but more especially ladinos, began to play a part in Guatemalan political life. The hold of the white elite over government was clearly broken, even if their social dominance had been restored in the State of Guatemala. Although government leaders often paid lip service to the federation, strong regional loyalties outweighed any spirit of unification.

The new legislature, installed in Guatemala in May 1839, dismantled the remains of the Liberal program. Under the direction of Rivera Paz—in reality, under the guns of Rafael Carrera—a disciplined state with restored Hispanic institutions emerged. The Assembly moved expeditiously. It began by restoring the religious orders and inviting the exiled Archbishop to return. It confirmed a slate of appointments acceptable to the Conservatives—including Carrera as Commanding General of the Army—began a process of consolidating the customs service, and put the treasury in order. Municipal elections in July gave the Conservatives control of the capital. In August the legislature reestablished the national mint and the merchant guild, turning over responsibility for road and port development to the latter's supervision. Later it revived the office of corregidor—a reflection of the re-centralization of control over the country—reestablished education under Church auspices, established a national bank, and revived the *residencia* examination, carried out at the conclusion of the term of office for all public officials in the state. The legislators reduced taxes on foodstuffs in another response to popular opinion, but reinstituted the former alcoholic beverages controls. They abolished the head tax altogether, as did all the other Central American governments, but they restored the tithe tax. They decreed a new Declaration of the Rights of the State and its Inhabitants, which, although maintaining in print many civil liberties, clearly turned the direction of the state toward authoritarianism.

Roman Catholicism once more became the official religion, and the Church regained its fuero and *cabildo eclesiástico*. The session then adjourned, having definitively terminated the Liberal revolution.

In 1840 the reaction continued. The Guatemalan government, in an effort to balance the budget in the face of Carrera's continued military expenditures and a sizable debt, slashed the salaries of public and military officials substantially. Reestablishment of the tobacco monopoly increased government revenues. With Carrera's cooperation, the government sought to end military abuses against local populations. It also tried to develop the economy through promotion of new crops and subsidies and reestablished the Economic Society—another colonial institution—to aid promotions. Carrera himself proposed protective tariffs for local industries and division of lands by municipalities to promote production of cochineal and silk. Meanwhile, the Church regained more of its confiscated property, although Carrera refused to sanction restoration of all it had lost. The Conservatives restored the colonial land institutions that the Liberals had sought to destroy. In so doing, they tied the Guatemalan economy to a relatively small group of wealthy landowners and merchants and established a major obstacle to movement toward a generally more dynamic economy. The restoration of the University of San Carlos, with Father Juan Aycinena as rector until 1854, represented well the aristocratic, proclerical, and reactionary philosophy that regained control.

These measures had the effect of restoring the stability of the Hispanic regime. A stifling dictatorship settled over the country, for Carrera was one of the classic Conservative caudillos in mid-nineteenth-century Latin America and his was an iron rule. The regime had the same distrust of non-Spanish foreigners that had characterized the colonial era. The return to Hispanic tradition stopped short of actual reversion to imperial status, as did happen briefly, in the Dominican Republic, but in 1851 Carrera restored the Spanish red and gold to the Guatemalan national flag, where they remained symbolically for twenty years. Though suspicious of foreign colonization schemes, the government nevertheless continued to entertain such projects. But, significantly, Guatemala turned from the Protestant English to a company of Belgian Catholics for north coast development. The Belgians had no more success than the English, however.

Threatening the Liberals with death in popular slogans not unlike those of Argentina's Juan Manuel Rosas, Carrera made it clear that their residence in Guatemala depended on their cooperation with him. Such periodic coalitions as occurred during the first decade of his domination ended after the Liberals briefly unseated the caudillo in 1848. Carrera was back in power as chief of the armed forces within a few months. He was unforgiving, and he proceeded to establish absolute Conservative rule. He resumed the presidency in 1851, and his term was extended for life three years later. The dictatorship was total from that time until his death in 1865. From his deathbed he named as his successor a trusted general, Vicente Cerna, under whom the Conservative regime survived for six more years.

The Conservatives' attitude toward the Indian reflected their reactionary philosophy of looking back to the Hispanic period. The Guatemalan legislature in 1839, recognizing that Indians were a majority of the state's population and that it was in the public interest "not only to protect this numerous class, but also to develop and improve its customs and civilization," decreed an Indian Code. Noting that the Liberal program had mistreated and exploited the Indians under the pretext of equal treatment for all, the committee reporting the bill said that the system of the colonial era was really better. That system "compelled them to work, to provide public service on certain projects, and to pay taxes," the committee admitted, "but it also gave them protection against the influential and the powerful in their land claims." It provided for their care and welfare and for their self-respect, the committee added, whereas the system of the Liberals abolished all that and the Indians had lost their respect for authority and order. Thus the new code reversed Gálvez's idea of incorporating the Indian into western civilization. It even called for reestablishment of the office of Indian interpreter and, realistically, ordered local officials to translate decrees into indigenous languages. Gálvez's program had aimed at assimilating the Indians. The Conservatives claimed that this meant exploitation, with the danger of rebellion and violence. Instead, they offered paternalism and protection. Such a policy ensured the continuance of a large segment of the Guatemalan population as a separate Indian nation, segregated from the mainstream of the national life, and this situation continued well into the twentieth century.

The same Conservative reaction which had put a peasant leader in command of Guatemala took place throughout Central America. The reaction was less intense in the other states, but the issues were much the same as they were in Guatemala. More political freedom remained, at least at times, in the other states, where Conservative rule was less absolute. Caudillos in those states failed to maintain their power for so long a period as the Guatemalan leader did—Honduras was particularly unstable—but between 1840 and 1870 Conservatives held office more than Liberals in all of the states. Thus, strengthening of clerical power, restoration of regular orders and Hispanic institutions, and consolidation of political and social power by the aristocratic landholders occurred everywhere in the isthmus. Reestablishment of the University of San Carlos in Guatemala and the foundation of new universities in Costa Rica (1843), El Salvador (1847), and Honduras (1847) were representative of the Conservatives' approach. In Nicaragua, too, the colonial university, established in León, gained new life during the Conservative years. Rejecting the more modern academies and lyceums of the Liberals, the Conservatives turned back to the traditional Spanish university.

Relations among the states were slightly improved over the previous period, but communications were still abysmally poor. By 1850 it still took a letter normally two weeks, and sometimes up to two months, to reach Costa Rica from Guatemala. Efforts were made to establish free trade among the five states, but poor communications and the fact that all produced the same commodities and had little to sell to each other meant that little trade or interdependence actually evolved.

Although Liberal historians of Central America have criticized the Conservative regimes, their impact was not entirely negative on the region. It is true that Conservatives broke apart the Central American Federation, depriving the isthmus of badly needed unity, but much of the cause for that may be blamed on the Liberals' poor governance, strong regional jealousies, and fear of central government. The Conservative regimes discarded the idealism of their predecessors for the romanticism which glorified a brighter past and emphasized their common Spanish-Catholic heritage. The Church regained its old position, and fueros returned—along with the class privilege they represented. The paternalistic concern for the welfare, if not the advancement, of the peasant and Indian was restored. Governments revived some old taxes, but kept their expenses at modest levels. They left most development to the private sector, but under government supervision. Insofar as powerful foreign interests—notably the British— would permit, they abandoned free trade. Declining indigo markets created severe economic problems for El Salvador, but the other states expanded their exports modestly, establishing favorable trade balances which contributed to improvement in their debt problems. Where the Liberals had been eager to adopt foreign innovation, the trend now turned anti-foreign and nationalistic. Foreigners continued to play the dominant role in overseas trade, but now Spanish as well as British merchants received favors. Culturally, the period was one of stagnation, but Conservative rule nevertheless achieved greater economic growth than had been made in the early years of independence, even though it was less than the more advanced nations of the western world experienced in the mid-nineteenth century. The relative peace and stability of most of the period permitted this growth along traditional lines. But most economic activity remained at the subsistence level and exports still represented only a tiny part of total Central American economy. The xenophobic tone of the Conservative years imposed a certain isolation on the isthmus, allowing the individual states some of the national characteristics which so distinguish each of them from the others today. To be sure, foreign interest in a transisthmian route, a topic we will explore in the next chapter, prevented that isolation from becoming complete or permanent.

Socially, the adjustment by local aristocracies to ladino participation, even leadership, was difficult, but it characterized this period also.

Carrera's accession to power forced this adjustment in Guatemala. Elsewhere it had been occurring, more gradually, since the eighteenth century. In Costa Rica it did not take place, and whites remained in the ascendancy there. In Guatemala especially, therefore, a degree of social revolution came about. Inevitably, Carrera's concern for the peasant caused the elite to distrust him. His guerrilla warfare had been aimed at the wealthy, and he had abstained generally from attacking the persons or property of the poorer classes. As he allied with the Guatemalan aristocracy his attitude may have changed somewhat, but it was several years before the oligarchy felt secure. While Carrera retained veto power, he gradually allowed the elite to run the country again. Although his concern for the poor may have waned as his own riches increased, there is little doubt that, through charity and paternalism, the government he dominated provided a better life for the masses than had the progressivism of the Gálvez Liberals. It was no improvement over the colonial period, yet the Liberals' claim that general prosperity would be the inevitable, if long-term, result of their programs would not soon get another test.

Rafael Carrera and his allies represented a popular reaction against the Liberals' efforts, from 1823 to 1837, to impose economic, political, and social systems which challenged three centuries of tradition and culture. Carrera's reaction was essentially negative and emotional, but in finally allying himself with the Conservatives he also supported positive elements. The Conservatives supported a strong Church; an elite of educated landholders and merchants to run the society and economy with a paternalistic concern for the rural masses; a healthy suspicion of foreigners, combined with a respect for the Hispanic heritage of the country; and expansion of the economy along sound, proven methods with benefits reinvested at home. Particularly from 1850 forward, Carrera promoted these programs for Guatemala and worked to establish caudillos—Guatemalans, whenever possible—who would pursue similar policies in the other states. For Carrera, Morazán had proven the impracticability of federation and liberalism, and the two had become synonymous. Better to develop each state separately, he believed, maintaining peace and order, creating an environment where there might be economic growth along trusted lines.

Nearly all the Conservative policies were to fall to liberalism later in the century, but Carrera's emphasis on state nationalism and autonomous government survives to the present day, the one great victory of nineteenth-century Conservatism. Nearly everyone agreed that Central American union was a desirable objective. Carrera himself thought so. Yet Carrera and the Conservatives, far more clearly than the Liberals, recognized the realities of mid-nineteenth-century Central America. They believed they could best serve their peoples by developing strong individual states and defending themselves against foreign pretensions. In acting on their beliefs, they laid the foundations for the nationalism of the modern states of Central America.

Chapter 5 • Central America and the World

While the Conservatives preserved a certain self-imposed isolation on Central America, the industrial expansion of the major nations of the world inevitably reached the isthmus. External forces thus had as much to do with the development of Central America in the nineteenth century as did internal turmoil. The growth of production and commerce in export staples moved the isthmus closer to monocultural dependency on the industrial world. Major improvements in transportation encouraged this growth and also led to the shift of commerce from Caribbean to Pacific coast ports.

The Central American Liberals' glowing expectations that their new republic would soon rank among the world's major nations were to a large measure predicated on exaggerated notions of the geographic importance of the isthmus and of the Central Americans' ability to capitalize on that location through construction of an interoceanic canal. Such speculation was the product of both foreign encouragement and long-standing local interest. Hopes for a canal date from the sixteenth century, although the seventeenth-century plan of a Franciscan friar, Martín Lobo, was the first to receive serious consideration. Lobo died in Trujillo upon returning from Spain, where he had presented his project to the Crown. No one followed up his efforts with specific action, yet the idea remained alive throughout the colonial period and was given wide publicity by Alexander von Humboldt, who recommended a canal through Honduras in 1805.

Many Central Americans associated the concept of an interoceanic canal with prosperity, and the project was an important part of the unrealistic optimism of the first decade of independence. Believing that such a transit route would make the isthmus of central importance to world trade, Central American leaders eagerly sought the advice and support of interested foreigners. For the rest of the century, English, Dutch, French, and North American agents encouraged and negotiated plans to construct a canal, usually through Nicaragua. In fact, much of the diplomatic history of the isthmus in the nineteenth century revolves around these efforts to provide for sea communication between the Atlantic and the Pacific.

Not surprisingly, the British played the dominant role in nineteenth-century Central America. As the leading maritime nation, Britain, quite naturally, sought to extend the commercial foothold she had established in the last years of Spanish rule. A transisthmian canal would directly benefit British commercial and imperial designs in a much greater area than just Central America. The British presence on the isthmus took several forms. In some instances it was an intentional manifestation of imperial policy. In others, however, it reflected the overzealousness of local British agents, who at times exceeded rather considerably their instructions and authority. Still other actions came from private British subjects, resident in the area, acting with no authority from—nor in connivance with—the British government. These distinctions also characterized North American activities, which as the century progressed began to rival those of the British. Understandably, many Central Americans did not recognize such distinctions. For them the specter of imperialist conspiracy by the English-speaking powers offered a facile but plausible explanation for all manner of foreign activities in Central America.

As early as May 1825 the National Constituent Assembly of the United Provinces asked the state governments to initiate navigation of the principal rivers of the country, suggesting that private companies of either natives or foreigners be formed for the purpose. Clearly, the assembly had an interoceanic route in mind. And a month later the federal government ordered negotiations opened for the construction of a canal. The leading Central American historian of the era, Alejandro Marure, wrote that, "by means of the canal, the republic would be transformed within a few years into the richest, most populous and happiest nation on the globe." Federal decrees sought to expand trade and commerce with Europe, the Americas, and Asia. The government soon contracted for canal construction, first with the firm of Aaron H. Palmer of New York in 1826 and then with a Dutch group, but nothing more than a few surveys came of these agreements.

Meanwhile, the English government sent George Alexander Thompson to investigate the situation, especially in Nicaragua. His visit resulted in no immediate canal agreements, but it initiated the close relationships between British diplomats and Central American leaders, especially those of the Conservative Party. In 1837-38 an English engineer, John Baily, surveyed a route for the Nicaraguan government, and shortly thereafter United States agent John Lloyd Stephens prepared a detailed report on Nicaraguan canal potential. Publication of both reports greatly stimulated foreign interest in the project. A memorial from a group of New York and Philadelphia businessmen had prompted Congress to commission Stephens's report on the canal. North American commerce in the Pacific was growing, for fast clipper ships which could reach beyond the Atlantic now dominated the Yankee merchant fleet.

The French were also interested. Efforts to negotiate an agreement with the government of Nicaragua failed to materialize in 1844, but in 1858 Felix Belly and his Paris associates received a concession for construction of a canal. Belly made another detailed reconnaissance, but in the end his concession lapsed without action; he could not organize the necessary financial support for the enterprise.

These early efforts reflected an interest which was not sufficiently attractive to the capital available for such projects. However exciting the possibilities of interoceanic transit, the actual amount of trade involved was not yet sufficient to warrant heavy capitalization, for most of the western nations still had ample opportunities for investment in railroads and canals in their own territories or in areas of more promising economic growth. Moreover, the chaotic political scene in Central America made potential investors wary of the region. During this period European investors looked more favorably toward the rapidly developing Mississippi Valley of the United States for internal improvement investments. Nevertheless, commercial expansion and interest in an isthmian route during the first half of the century created an intense rivalry between the two English-speaking nations, and that rivalry played a significant role in the development of modern Central America.

The British had long been interested in the eastern coast of Central America and had encouraged log cutters and smugglers to develop the port of Belize. Upon the restoration of Fernando VII in 1814, old treaties were renewed. They guaranteed Spanish sovereignty over the area and continued the British rights to cut wood and maintain a settlement. British settlers and diplomats vigorously expanded that settlement, revived their earlier interest in the Mosquito shore, and exploited opportunities for contraband trade with the colonists of the Kingdom of Guatemala. In 1816 they returned to their earlier practice of crowning the Mosquito King, in this case George Frederick II. They set up a puppet state and ran it from Belize. The principal British activity was commercial, but territorial expansion was not absent from their minds, and, as the independence of Central America developed, British sovereignty over the eastern coast came closer to reality. After Central America and Mexico declared their independence from Spain, Britain effectively maintained Belize as a colony. Blacks from the West Indies swelled the population, but trouble resulted when slaves convicted of insurrection in Barbadoes were brought in, as they contributed to a violent tendency at the settlement. There was little work for slaves in the colony, however, and, although the black population grew during these years, the number of slaves declined. Census records show a total population increase from 3824 in 1816 to 4107 ten years later. During the same decade, the slave population, through manumission, death,

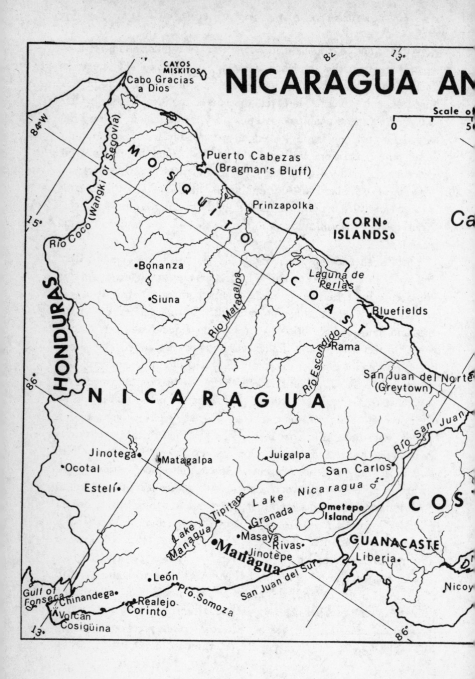

and escape, dropped from 2742 to 2468. Thereafter the population grew only slightly, with a small white community of less than three hundred managing the affairs of the settlement and controlling the commerce. Efforts to turn it into an agricultural colony failed. The British Crown regarded it as a commercial station, an entrepôt for the Central American trade, but showed little desire to develop it further.

Immediately after Central American independence, a Scottish adventurer, Gregor MacGregor, attempted to plant a settlement called Poyais on the Mosquito Coast. MacGregor had operated along the Central American coast in league with Louis Aury and other privateers flying Latin American republican flags. In April 1819 MacGregor took Portobelo, and he held it for nearly three weeks before the Spanish dislodged him. The following year he paid the Mosquito King a trivial amount in liquor and other items for a land grant of roughly 70,000 square miles in the region of the present-day province of Olancho, Honduras. Backed by London financiers, but without government sanction, MacGregor returned to Scotland and promoted a major colonization enterprise. Forty-three colonists arrived at a deserted site they named Saint Joseph's in February 1823; a month later 160 more followed. From the start, hardship, violence, and disease doomed the colony. By June all the survivors had deserted to Belize. Additional colonists sent by MacGregor arrived later, and they, too, went to Belize where the authorities attempted to establish them at Stann Creek, about forty miles south of Belize. By the end of 1824 this settlement, although founded under more favorable arrangements than Saint Joseph's, had also been abandoned. MacGregor eventually served prison terms in both England and France, but this could not restore the hundreds of lives lost nor dampen the resentment against British imperialism which was growing among Central Americans. Other Britons, with less fanfare, continued a close relationship with the Mosquito kings, and British influence expanded along that coast.

The slavery question further troubled relations between Belize and Central America. Central America quickly abolished slavery after independence, and Belize slaves sought refuge in the free territory of the Petén. It was difficult for either the federal government or the governments of the states to enforce their wishes in the remote jungles of northern Guatemala, but irritation developed when Belizeans pursued fugitive slaves into the region. British pretensions in the region challenged the new republic's sovereignty and promoted nationalist sentiments which had little to do with the fugitive slave issue itself. The British levied a 5 per cent duty on Central American goods passing through Belize in retaliation against the emancipation policy, and this intensified the feeling, particularly in Guatemala. Despite the close trade relations developing between Britain and the isthmus, Liberal disillusionment with Great Britain began. By the time Conservatives came to power, Britain herself had abolished slavery in the Caribbean colonies.

British imperialism became more overt after 1830, when they established a garrison and colonists on the Honduran Bay Islands. Central American troops recovered the islands shortly thereafter, but the British, taking advantage of the collapse of the United Provinces and the subsequent Honduran impotence, attacked again in 1839 and reoccupied them in 1841. The British frequently backed up their policies and the activities of their subjects in Central America with gunboats. Nevertheless, the mid-century Conservative governments successfully resisted most of the British territorial ambitions and defended national independence better than their Liberal predecessors had.

Meanwhile, the commercial incursion was more thorough. The Belize commercial firm headed by Marshal Bennet and John Wright took advantage of Belize's role as the principal port for Central America's exports and imports. Lacking satisfactory deep-water ports of its own, and with the population and production centers in the highlands or on the Pacific slopes, Central America turned to the Belize merchants' natural outlet via the Caribbean for their goods. British merchants did not generally establish themselves in Central America, as they did in several Latin American states that had major ports on the coast, but there were a few notable exceptions. Of these the most important was Bennet, who established, as a branch of his Belize firm, the Guatemalan house of William Hall and Carlos Meany in the 1820's. In the same decade George Skinner and Charles Klee established mercantile families which continue to be important in Guatemala to the present day. Among the other foreigners who served British mercantile interests during the first thirty years of independence were John Foster, Thomas Manning, Walter Bridge, and Jonas Glenton in Nicaragua; William Barchard, Richard McNally, Frederick Lesperance, William Kilgour, and Robert Parker in El Salvador, who operated with less permanent success; and Peter and Samuel Shepherd on the Mosquito Coast. The Shepherds received a massive land grant from the Mosquito King in return for a few cases of whiskey and bolts of cotton chintz.

Important as these British merchants were in arranging and managing commerce with Britain, her diplomats were probably more important in encouraging such trade. British consuls, led by Frederick Chatfield, made extraordinary efforts to promote the interests of their compatriots. From 1825 forward, Britain steadily reduced her duties on nearly all Central American export produce. Cochineal and indigo from Guatemala, El Salvador, and Nicaragua became Central America's principal items of foreign exchange as the British textile industry expanded the market for these dyes. Hides and tortoiseshells from Honduras enjoyed similar favors. By 1846 all Central American products except coffee entered Britain duty free. Coffee, which was becoming important for Costa Rica, soon received preferential treatment as well.

Belize remained the only port on the eastern coast of Central America of any importance, despite repeated Central American efforts to develop their own outlets. Such ports as the Central Americans did maintain—Izabal, Omoa, Trujillo, Gracias a Dios, San Juan del Norte —seldom harbored ships trading directly with the outside world, but rather served simply as transfer wharfs for the small skiffs and schooners that sailed between Belize and the Central American coast. Efforts to provide a second British entrepôt at San Juan del Norte (Greytown), to serve Nicaragua and Costa Rica, generally failed during the first half of the century. Before 1850, most Nicaraguan and Costa Rican produce was shipped from the Pacific ports of Corinto, in Nicaragua, which gradually replaced the colonial port of Realejo in importance in that state, or Puntarenas, in Costa Rica. After 1850 Central American commerce shifted dramatically to the Pacific.

Loans furthered the British domination of the Central American international economy, adding the bond of debt to that of commerce between the two nations. The fiasco of the Barclay, Herring & Richardson loan of 1825 did restrain many investors from rushing to Central America with capital offerings. Nonetheless, a series of loans from British firms to the Central American states created a maze of debt problems which was not unraveled until the twentieth century. The Liberal governments of the 1820's encouraged such arrangements, and, although Conservative governments were more wary, such transactions did not end altogether. The Carrera government, in negotiating a loan with the London firm of Isaac & Samuel in 1856 to pay off its earlier debt, for instance, had to pledge 50 per cent of its customs receipts to service on the debt. Such arrangements involved British nationals in the internal finance of the Central American governments to the extent of compromising their national sovereignty.

Efforts to stimulate mineral exploitation resulted in concessions to English mining companies, particularly in Guatemala and Honduras, but, undercapitalized and lacking adequate transportation development, without exception they failed to increase significantly Central American mineral production during the early years of independence.

Still another area of British influence was in colonization projects, through which the Liberals had sought to illuminate Central American society and economy. From Guatemala to Panama, governments designed projects to attract European emigrants. The results were disappointing. There was a trickle of Englishmen, but most of them either died or returned home, although a few drifted into the urban centers and became influential in commerce or agriculture. The most notable efforts were those begun in Guatemala under the administration of Mariano Gálvez. Gálvez hoped to colonize the sparsely populated northern regions of his state. Small individual grants to foreigners were followed by a massive concession to the Eastern Coast of Central America Commercial and Agricultural Company, a group whose origins were suspiciously linked to Gregor MacGregor's Poyais enterprise. The company agreed to develop the entire eastern zone of the state, from Izabal and the Verapaz into the Petén. The results were poor, and they contributed to the low esteem in which the Gálvez government was held. A motley crew of Englishmen established a temporary colony at Abbotsville, near the Río Polochic, which failed to prosper. Unfortunately, the English were more interested in exploiting mahogany resources than in agricultural colonization, and the colony disintegrated. Over-all, the project only heightened anti-British sentiment among residents of eastern Guatemala.

A similar arrangement, made with a Belgian company to develop the port and region of Santo Tomás, eventually superseded the English grant. Carrera and the Conservatives had grave doubts about the wisdom of such colonization projects, although, through bribery and intimidation, the government approved the Belgian contract and did its best to ensure its success. It, too, collapsed in the end, and the lowland region remained undeveloped.

A by-product of the colonization projects was the improvement in shipping service from the Caribbean. The English company's steamer, the *Vera Paz*, linked the Golfo Dulce with Belize, thereby increasing the commercial dependence of Guatemala on the British port. The Belgian company later provided service with Belgium on an irregular basis. By 1850 there was regular, if sometimes unreliable, steamship service on the Caribbean coast. In 1851 the five states joined together to subsidize two sailing vessels in regular service along the Pacific coast.

Central American exports, especially of Guatemalan cochineal, increased after 1840, when the political scene became somewhat more stable. For lack of adequate transportation or ports, El Salvador and Nicaragua enjoyed less growth than Guatemala, while Honduras remained unimportant. Costa Rica, which largely depended on her Pacific port, began to gain importance as a coffee exporter in the 1840's and rapidly increased her exports of that commodity after completion of the Panama Railway in 1855. The government of Braulio Carrillo finally stopped the raids by Mosquito Indians into the Matina Valley, bringing an end to the tributary payments the residents of that region had been making to the Mosquito.

Guatemalan produce dominated the exports of Central America at mid-century. The British textile industry provided the major market for cochineal, and it also encouraged cotton production. In 1856 the discovery of coal-tar dyes threatened the natural dye industry and eventually led to the ruin of the cochineal trade. Expanded cotton production quickly enabled some Guatemalan planters to make an easier transition from cochineal to coffee production, which took several years to develop. The British consul promoted cotton cultivation by distributing seed and instructional booklets provided by a Manchester textile manufacturers' association. The Civil War in the United States allowed Central America temporarily to gain a larger share of the international cotton market. Nicaragua and El Salvador also expanded their exports of cotton during that conflict.

LEADING GUATEMALAN EXPORTS AS PERCENTAGES OF TOTAL EXPORTS, 1840-1871

Years	Cochineal %	Cotton %	Coffee %	Total exports (millions of pesos)
1840-50[a]	93	—	—	0.7[b]
1851-55	79	—	—	1.2[b]
1856-60	81	—	1	1.5[b]
1861	71	—	5	1.1
1862	61	—	9	1.4
1863	57	1	13	1.5
1864	44	15	12	1.6
1865	53	19	17	1.8
1866	57	5	23	1.7
1867	57	6	22	1.9
1868	41	1	36	2.2
1869	51	—	32	2.5
1870	34	—	44	2.6
1871	33	—	50	2.7

[a] Figures for 1840-50 partially based on estimates.
[b] Annual averages.

Central American commerce was also closely tied to the British in terms of import trade. Again using the Guatemalan example, which accounted for most of the trade of Central America during the nineteenth century, we find that by 1840 nearly 60 per cent of Guatemala's imports came via the Belize settlement, while another 20 per cent came directly from Britain and 15 per cent came from Spanish ports, accounting for nearly all the imports. England remained the most important supplier after 1850, even though the importance of Belize declined drastically with the development of Pacific trade after 1855. From 1850 through 1870, imports into Guatemala, as valued by customs, came from abroad in the following percentages: Great Britain, 61; Belize, 6; France, 17; Germany, 5; Spain and Cuba, 4; U.S.A., 3; Belgium, 2; and others, 2.

As the dependency of the Central American states on overseas areas, rather than on each other, grew, the trade among them continued to be insignificant. Transportation trends and foreign development of trade intensified this situation, creating in each state colonial enclaves which had little or no economic relations with each other. The best roads ran from the capitals and producing areas to the ports, while interstate routes remained impassable. Instead of developing an interdependence which might have contributed to more sincere unionist sentiment, the states actually became more separatistic.

The British were not the only foreigners who played important roles in Central American development in the mid-nineteenth century, although their commercial dominance accurately reflects their general position there. The Liberals' promotion of immigration in the 1820's failed to achieve its optimistic goals in terms of numbers, although a smattering of Frenchmen, Italians, Germans, and Belgians did join the few English residents. Several foreigners came to pursue careers in the military. Trading opportunities and possibilities of developing the canal route attracted others. The five states signed treaties of friendship, navigation, and commerce with most of the major European nations before 1850, and the consuls to the states promoted the interests of their resident nationals.

Although Spain refused to give official recognition to the independent status of Central America until 1863, she moved quickly to ensure the continuance of Spanish commerce with the former colony. The Spanish government was in no position to pursue this aim with the aggressiveness of the British, but it did permit continued Central American trade with Cuba and the Iberian peninsula. At the same time Spain permitted trade with the newly independent nations, she did not give up hope of reasserting her authority there. Faced with the Liberals' policies, some Central American Conservatives looked favorably toward reconquest by Spain and requested aid from the Governor of Cuba. Guatemala, Nicaragua, and Costa Rica all experienced pro-Spanish insurrections during the first decade of independence, and in 1832 Central American royalist forces succeeded in taking the fortress at Omoa, Honduras. Morazán's troops quickly dislodged and captured them, but later, when the Conservatives came to power, Spaniards were welcomed in Central America.

Despite their importance in international and even domestic commerce and finance, these foreigners represented only a tiny minority of the population, and they failed to give any Central American city the more cosmopolitan flavor that coastal centers such as Buenos Aires, Valparaíso, Lima, Havana, or Veracruz took on in these years.

The United States, although she was destined eventually to play the major role in the isthmus, had little contact with the region before 1850, her major energies being turned toward her own internal development and her expansion into Mexican territory. A few diplomats and travelers—most notably, John Lloyd Stephens—recorded their impressions, and this developed some North American interest in the isthmus, but trade remained a minor consideration until later in the century. The United States, in accordance with James Monroe's sympathetic Latin American policy, was prompt in recognizing the independence of Central America, but she made no overt effort to check British expansionism there until the end of the Mexican War. To be sure, a number of North Americans recognized the significance of an interoceanic canal, but not until the United States acquired Oregon and California were positive steps taken to ensure North American interests on the isthmus. The Bidlack Treaty, signed in 1846 and ratified in 1848, guaranteed the United States the right of transit across Panama, and under its terms a U.S. company constructed the Panama Railway between 1850 and 1855.

Anglo-American rivalry on the isthmus became intense as diplomats Frederick Chatfield of Great Britain and E. George Squier of the United States sought to extract guarantees and concessions for their respective nations and nationals. Chatfield tended to line up behind Conservative forces, and he thereby became associated with the breakup of the federation, while Squier became a champion of the Liberals. While this was in part ideological, it was also directly related to the growing commercial dominance which the British had developed there and their desire for stable government to further those ends. At the same time, there may be some truth to the charge that the British were not particularly interested in a united federation which might challenge more effectively their hegemony on the isthmus.

After 1839 the British efforts to gain control of the entire eastern coast of Central America once more accelerated, and Queen Victoria's gunboat diplomacy became commonplace along that shore. This, combined with a series of agreements between the Central American states and Great Britain, guaranteed British commercial interests. The seizure in 1848 of the settlement at the mouth of the Río San Juan, however, resulted in strong Central American opposition. The United States, now interested in a canal route to connect her eastern states with her newly acquired Pacific territories, protested forcefully, despite serious internal conflicts at home.

The resultant Clayton-Bulwer Treaty of 1850 provided for joint United States–British control of any transisthmian route. It ambiguously declared that neither nation would fortify, colonize, or exercise dominion over any part of Central America. Although the treaty apparently guaranteed the United States equality on the isthmus, the British regarded it as applying only to future activities and refused to relinquish their establishments on the Caribbean coast. Two years later they tested the resolve of the United States: they declared the Bay Islands a British colony. Honduras protested vigorously, with United States support; negotiations ensued; and the British finally agreed to withdraw in 1859. To the present day, however, the black residents of the islands have a British culture. By a treaty made in 1860 with Nicaragua, the British agreed to abandon the Mosquito Coast. They were slow to abide by the terms—the question of sovereignty was not finally settled until 1906—but the British wave had crested.

British sovereignty in Belize, which the Central Americans had never recognized, was also dealt with in 1859, by a treaty with Guatemala. Guatemala agreed to recognize British sovereignty over the colony in return for a British promise to construct a road from the Caribbean to the Guatemalan capital. Hoping to turn the road into a means of restoring Belize's lost commercial importance, the British began surveys, but costs, difficulties, and other, higher priorities delayed the project. The Guatemalans wished the road to terminate at their own Caribbean port, whereas the British intended to channel trade directly to Belize over the road. Finally, the Guatemalans abrogated the treaty and proceeded to construct a railroad on their own, leaving the Belize question smouldering to the present.

Problems with neighbors added to the foreign difficulties of Central America. Mexico attempted to expand the frontiers of Chiapas into Soconusco, while Colombia pressed claims to the eastern coast as far as Gracias a Dios. Rafael Carrera, cultivating friendly relations with Santa Anna, whom he admired, successfully resisted the Mexicans, although the issue was to come up again after his death. The Costa Ricans effectively contested the Colombian claim, except that they had to give up their claims to the San Andrés and Providence islands. Further tension in the border regions resulted from the Caste War in Yucatán (1847-55). Yucatán, never reconciled to Mexican rule, had actually seceded in 1838, and the peninsula remained unstable after its incorporation into the Mexican Republic in 1845. The bloody revolt of the Santa Cruz Maya, who were nearly successful in driving the Indians' white and ladino masters from Yucatán, caused widespread disruption in southern Yucatán and created apprehension in Guatemala as well. Many Yucatecans fled into British Honduras and Guatemala, causing a crisis of law and order in the former, although, in the long run, providing badly needed population to develop the economy.

Within Central America, disputes were more serious. The continued differences between Liberals and Conservatives manifested themselves in both internal civil wars and wars between states. The harboring by one state of exiles and plotters from other states became a practice which repeatedly led to bloodshed. The meddling of strong leaders in the affairs of neighboring states and the sponsoring of exile forces in revolutions became commonplace following independence, and those activities have come to characterize Central America. Notwithstanding sincere efforts that have been made to eradicate this practice in the twentieth century, exiles continue to play an important political role in the region. Such political behavior was and is a major obstacle to Central American unification, and it has been compounded by the participation of foreign governments as well as foreign private interests.

Internal difficulties and political factionalization provided the opportunity and justification for a still more serious threat to the independence of Central America.

The William Walker episode is related directly to the Liberal-Conservative struggle throughout the Central American states as well as to "Manifest Destiny" and the Anglo-American rivalry for control of an interoceanic transit route. The aggressive British blockades and landings of forces in Nicaragua throughout the 1840's helped to discredit the Conservatives who had overcome Liberal elements there by 1840. Much of the time there were virtually two governments operating in the state, one in León and the other in Granada, but the Liberals were gaining a broader base of support because of the alleged Conservative connections with the British. The principal military leader after 1845, General Trinidad Muñoz, who was more opportunistic than committed to political principles, sought to form a coalition with Liberals and even agreed to removal of the capital from Granada to León. Granadian forces, supported by Conservatives from Costa Rica and Honduras, defeated Muñoz in 1851, and the following year they moved the capital to Managua, which was destined to become the compromise site between ancient Granada and León. Many years would elapse before they settled the issue, however, and fighting between the two factions erupted again in 1853.

Economically and socially, the long civil disturbances had taken their toll, and Nicaragua had declined in relative importance since the colonial period. Ripe for foreign exploitation, as the British had already recognized, it remained the most logical place for an interoceanic canal. Discovery of gold in California in 1848 suddenly placed Nicaragua at the center of the principal route to San Francisco and the gold fields. The Clayton-Bulwer Treaty of 1850 opened the way for both British and American exploitation of the canal route, but by late 1849 Cornelius Vanderbilt and his associates had already succeeded in getting concessions to establish a transit route across the isthmus via the Río San Juan and Lake Nicaragua. Colonel O. W. Childs of Philadelphia made a thorough survey in 1850-51, and Vanderbilt's American Atlantic & Pacific Ship Canal Company received the full cooperation of the Nicaraguan government for construction of the route.

The question quickly became embroiled in international politics when Costa Rica claimed the territory around the eastern terminus of the proposed canal. Chatfield assured the Costa Ricans that Britain supported Costa Rica's claim to Greytown (at the mouth of the San Juan) and the Mosquito Coast, while the United States supported Nicaragua's claim. Costa Rican insistence that she shared the Río San Juan continued to be a source of irritation between the two states for more than half a century.

Meanwhile, the Costa Ricans pursued transisthmian schemes of their own. In particular, they promoted development of the Golfo Dulce region along their Pacific coast. A French colonization company agreed to open an interoceanic route from the Golfo Dulce to Bocas del Toro on the Caribbean, making the region an entrepôt for commerce across the isthmus. This idea, less feasible than either the Nicaragua or the Panama schemes, never bore fruit, but it diverted Costa Rican interest from the San Juan to some degree. At the same time, it involved Costa Rica in a new boundary dispute with Colombia over the Chiriquí border. That dispute extended into the twentieth century and became part of the quarrel over the boundary on both coasts between Panama and Costa Rica, where hostilities erupted briefly in 1921, arousing the interest of the League of Nations. The United States attempted to mediate, adding new arbitrations and treaties to the several already discarded. The two republics did not finally settle their boundary until 1944. At that time, Panama retained the Bocas del Toro region, while yielding to Costa Rican claims elsewhere.

The thousands who were eager to get to the gold fields after 1848, however, would not wait for a canal or railway to be built. The alternative routes to California, one through the uncharted and arid Indian territory of western North America, the other around Cape Horn, were dangerous and expensive. Recognizing this, Vanderbilt formed the Accessory Transit Company to offer immediate passenger service across the isthmus. Still another Vanderbilt company, the Nicaragua Line, provided rapid steamship service from New York to Greytown and from San Juan del Sur or Corinto to San Francisco. Accessory Transit operated smaller steamers on the Río San Juan and Lake Nicaragua. A short stagecoach line between the lake and the Pacific completed the route, which was operating fully by mid-1851. Failing to find sufficient financial support in his own country, Vanderbilt turned to British financiers, thus pitting himself against United States financial interests, headed by George Law, who were backing the Panama Railway. British opposition to an American-controlled route thwarted Vanderbilt's efforts to develop the canal. A rate war between the two firms resulted in bargain prices. Passage on Vanderbilt's Nicaragua route, for example, dropped from $400 to $150 first class and to $45 steerage, New York to San Francisco. Since the Panama route was longer and less comfortable, at least until the railroad was completed in 1855, Vanderbilt won most of the passengers and Accessory Transit returned good profits in its early years, despite the problem of continued civil strife in Nicaragua. Greytown flourished as a port and began to take on commercial importance beyond its role as a passenger terminal.

While Vanderbilt was in England, his San Francisco manager, Cornelius Garrison, conspired with New York financier Charles Morgan to wrest control of Accessory Transit from the Commodore. A major financial struggle for control of the company ensued, and soon Vanderbilt overcame his adversaries. But in 1855 the flooding Río San Juan changed its course, causing great destruction in Greytown and ruining the port there. In any case, the Accessory Transit Company was doomed once the Panama Railway was completed, as it was in the same year. Vanderbilt skillfully divested himself of most of his Accessory Transit interests and bought into the Panama route at the right time. This complicated financial intrigue led to the entrance of William Walker on the scene.

Walker was the son of an austere, frontier-fundamentalist family in Tennessee. Of gifted intelligence, Walker completed college in Nashville at age fourteen. In the next years he obtained a medical degree at the University of Pennsylvania and continued his medical studies in Paris, Heidelberg, and Edinburgh. Then he gave up medicine and went to New Orleans to study law. It was 1845, and he was only twenty-one years old. After two years of study and a brief practice, he turned to journalism. He became a vigorous and controversial editor of the New Orleans *Crescent,* reflecting a youthful idealism which included an antislavery position. In New Orleans he fell in love with an enchanting and talented young woman, Ellen Martin, and they were going to be married, but fever took her life. Embittered, he emigrated to California via Panama. In California he was unsuccessful in either gaining great wealth or finding a position which satisfied his aspirations. Then, in 1853, he participated in a filibustering expedition into Sonora which, although abortive, provided him with the experience and contacts which led to his Central American venture.

Within Nicaragua, Liberal gains in 1854 had evaporated when Guatemalan aid from Carrera reached the Conservatives. The Liberals turned to North American private assistance to counter this setback. They offered Byron Cole, a San Francisco associate of Walker, a large land grant in Nicaragua in return for help in ousting the Conservatives. Cole persuaded Walker and Cornelius Garrison to support the Liberal cause in return for additional land grants. By this time both Cole and Walker were thoroughly imbued with the mentality of "Manifest Destiny," and they looked upon Nicaragua as a field for expansion of democratic ideals as well as land development.

Under contract with the León Liberals, in June, 1855, Walker and fifty-seven other Californians landed at Realejo. In the initial encoun-

ter, at Rivas, Conservatives led by the Honduran Santos Guardiola defeated the Californians. Retreating to Chinandega, Walker awaited
reinforcements from Cole before engaging the government forces
again. Other Liberal forces also suffered setbacks, however, allowing
Walker to emerge as commanding general. He took Granada in October, reversing the Liberals' fortunes. Conservative leaders, fearing for
the lives of their families there, agreed to peace, even though their
forces were not totally defeated.

A coalition government headed by a Conservative, Patricio Rivas,
resulted, with Walker as armed forces chief. Rivas was never any more
than a figurehead for Walker's designs. Liberal constitutional reform
followed and the Conservative army disbanded. The Tennessean consolidated his control by executing or exiling those who opposed him.
He reached an early understanding with the Church to dispel its fear
of Liberal anticlericalism. Later, however, the Church became a powerful force in rallying the people to support the Conservative ground-
swell against Liberalism, just as it had in Guatemala in 1837.

The United States Minister in Nicaragua, John Wheeler, compounded Central American fears of Washington's expansionist complicity in the intervention when he recognized Rivas's puppet regime
on November 10. Officially, the Department of State did not sponsor
Walker, but, despite its protestations of neutrality in the affair, hind-
sight makes it clear that the Pierce administration did nothing to discourage Walker. Such feeble efforts to restrict recruiting as were made
did little to offset the strong pro-Walker stance taken by Pierce's minister in Nicaragua. And the United States, ignoring protests from the
other Central American governments, formally recognized the Rivas
government on May 14, 1856.

New York and San Francisco interests of Morgan and Garrison
aided Walker in his drive for power. They sent arms, money, and vol-
unteers as part of their effort to undercut Vanderbilt's control of the
transit route. As veterans of the Mexican War and Southerners flocked
to Nicaragua to join in the spoils, Walker's army grew to more than
2500 men. Walker provided large land grants and other concessions,
and, although Central America had outlawed slavery a quarter-century

earlier, the belief grew that the United States might soon annex Nicaragua as a slave state. Walker himself, a man of expedience, departed from his earlier antislavery views when he welcomed these new arrivals. Those who opposed Walker looked abroad for help.

It was not long in coming. United States and British naval forces had clashed in 1854 over control of the transit route, and feeling was running high in both governments. The British had opposed Walker's intervention all along, and, although they took no immediate action, they encouraged Costa Rican, Honduran, and Guatemalan apprehensions. Fear of North American invasion spread throughout the isthmus, but Central Americans still regarded the conflict as basically a continuation of the Liberal-Conservative struggle. Although the Liberals were, generally, out of power throughout Central America, they praised and defended Walker's intervention; Walker's efforts to bring the Jacksonian Revolution to the isthmus coincided with their own political ideologies of reform and development. They agreed with him that Central America needed a renaissance of republican and democratic values, destruction of the aristocratic party, development of public education, and increased production and trade. From Guatemala, Carrera had denounced the intervention in July 1855, and Costa Rican President Juan Rafael Mora had pronounced against Walker on November 1. By February 1856, the Conservative governments of all four of the other states had agreed to cooperate in sending troops to aid the "Legitimist" government of Nicaragua against the filibusters. Costa Rica led the way with a formal declaration of war on March 1, and the British supplied arms, munitions, and equipment to her forces.

By May the tide began to turn against Walker. Cholera broke out among his forces just as new Guatemalan troops arrived to aid the Hondurans and Salvadorans who had already joined the Costa Rican troops. Both sides suffered heavy losses in the bitter fighting, but the Conservative forces continued to receive reinforcements and arms in greater numbers than the Liberals did. Vanderbilt's agents were successfully sowing discontent among the Liberals, and Rivas, finally disgusted with his puppet role, deserted. An election in June made Walker President. He assumed office in July, and he desperately tried

EL SALVADOR AND HONDURAS

Scale of miles

0   50   100

to rally and enlarge his American fighting force by offering large land grants, making English the official language of the state, and legalizing slavery. Through a crash program he sought to Americanize the republic, and through a forced-labor vagrancy law he attempted to provide a peasant work force for the landholders. He attracted a few more adventurers to his army, but in the process alienated thousands more Central Americans as the southern U.S. slaveholders' designs to annex Nicaragua became overt.

By November a large, united Central American force was operating against Walker in Nicaragua. Carrera, as the leading Conservative on the isthmus, had been urged to take leadership of this "national" army. He declined, pleading that he could more successfully serve the cause by remaining in Guatemala to raise men and money. It was Mora, therefore, who emerged as the principal Central American hero in what became known as the "National War." The fighting dragged on, in terrible destructiveness. Granada was burned, and it has not to this day fully recovered its former importance or architectural beauty. At the end of the year the British began a blockade which prevented additional reinforcements from reaching Walker. The Peruvian government loaned $100,000 to the Costa Ricans, and additional help and encouragement came from other South American states.

The end came in April 1857, when Walker's beleaguered and disease-ridden forces repelled an attack of some 2000 Guatemalans. The battle inflicted very heavy losses on the attackers, but it exhausted the defenders. When Mora promised Americans who surrendered medical aid, food, liquor, and free passage home, most of them deserted, leaving Walker with less than 200 soldiers. President Buchanan of the United States mercifully intervened, sending Commander Charles N. Davis to arrange a truce, and on May 1, 1857, Walker surrendered. With his staff he boarded Davis's vessel, and the remaining troops soon followed in another United States warship.

Walker received an enthusiastic welcome when he arrived in New Orleans, and the "hero" soon tried to organize a new expedition. He found it easy enough to recruit men, but money was more difficult to attract, for the transit route was no longer an issue. The Panama Railway was now firmly established. A recession was restricting the United States economy, and the lusty gold rush fever for California had subsided. Federal officials harassed Walker, but he still reached Greytown with another expedition before United States naval forces stopped him and brought him back to New Orleans, where he successfully conducted his own defense against charges of violating neutrality law. Walker remained obsessed with the idea of returning to Central America and he raised a third expedition, but once more federal officers checked him. He received a final chance in 1860, when British residents in the Bay Islands, bitter over London's agreement to turn the islands over to Honduras, approached him with a plan to set up an independent government there. Walker accepted, for he secretly harbored the ambitious plan of again allying with Central American Liberals to seize Honduras and, ultimately, to reestablish the federation. An old Honduran Morazanista, Trinidad Cabañas, was leading a new Liberal uprising in Honduras at the time, and Walker hoped to ally with him. Walker and his hastily formed expedition sailed to Roatán in June 1860. Finding the British still in command there, he crossed to the mainland and captured Trujillo. Soon after, however, a regiment of British Marines landed and captured Walker. They turned him over to the Hondurans, who promptly tried, sentenced and executed the "grey-eyed man of destiny."

Walker's intervention left a permanent mark on Central America. Although the unity it engendered against the common enemy soon faded and Central American federation remained an illusive dream, the earlier champions of such union, the Liberals, were thoroughly discredited. Significantly, the eventual return of the Liberals to power in Central America was led by men who, for the most part, were not connected with those Liberal leaders who had supported Walker. Younger men now had to emerge to the leadership of the Liberal Party, and they brought with them new concepts of progress and development. The Conservative victory thus permitted an extension of Conservative power for a longer period than might otherwise have occurred. This was, of course, most obvious in Nicaragua, where the Conservatives were able to hold on against their discredited, demoralized, and "traitorous" Liberal opposition until 1893. Beginning under General Tomás Martínez, this long period of stable government, following so much turbulence in Nicaragua, gave the republic a chance to develop again.

Another result of the "National War" was the discrediting of the United States. The great interest the North Americans had shown in the 1850's waned rapidly as they became embroiled in their own bloodbath of the 1860's. Central American governments were cool toward an effort made by President Lincoln to settle former slaves in Central America, although some ex-slaves, as well as some Confederate landowners, did settle in Belize. After the Civil War, concern with Reconstruction and western settlement occupied North American energies and capital. Completion of the Union Pacific Railroad in 1869 diminished the need for a transisthmian route. At the same time, anti-United States feeling opened the way for the French. Felix Belly succeeded in getting a contract to build a canal through Nicaragua in 1858—in part because he promised protection against the United States. Lack of capital and the Costa Rican claim to the Río San Juan contributed to the failure of this project, and the French looked elsewhere. They signed a contract with Colombia in 1878 to dig a canal through Panama under the direction of Ferdinand de Lesseps, the Suez Canal builder. By the time that enterprise failed, the United States had once more developed a strategic interest in the region, and she moved aggressively to take over the operation, which culminated in the opening of the Panama Canal in 1914.

Completion of the Panama Railway had important effects on the development of Central America, as commerce shifted from the Caribbean to the more accessible Pacific coast, nearer the centers of population and production and with less lowland jungle and marshland to traverse. With the exception of Puntarenas, Central America lacked natural deep-water ports on the Pacific coast. Unprotected wharfs simply extended over sand beaches into the ocean, and small launches or barges transferred produce, merchandise, and passengers between the wharfs and the oceangoing vessels which anchored in deep water off shore. Although Iztapa, Acajutla, Amapala, Corinto, and Puntarenas were less than ideal ports, the shift of commerce to the Pacific was dramatic and rapid. In particular, it allowed El Salvador and Nicaragua, whose commerce had languished since the end of the Hispanic period, to return to the world economy. Coffee became the vehicle for this return. Guatemala and Costa Rica also benefited greatly from the Pacific coast trade, as their freight costs dropped rapidly. Cart roads were built from the producing regions down to the ports, and beginnings were made on railroads. Regular steamship service connected these ports with Panama and opened the Atlantic to them. The shift in Guatemala from Caribbean to Pacific ports in these years is representative of what happened in all the states.

VALUE OF IMPORTS (IN U.S. DOLLARS)

Years	via Caribbean Ports	via Pacific Ports
1853-58	$4,231,642	$2,100,994
1859-64	1,720,659	5,549,598

Conversely, the Caribbean coast, now neglected, sank into a gloomy despair. At Belize, the entrepôt for the region since independence, the volume of trade dropped by more than half between 1854 and 1856 and continued to decline thereafter. This helps to explain the British willingness to build a road from Guatemala City to the north coast. They hoped to build the road to Belize, but Guatemalan insistence that the route should terminate at Santo Tomás rather than Belize caused the British to be reluctant to honor their commitment.

Belize began a long period of depression from which it has not yet recovered. It endeavored to promote immigration and to develop a stronger agricultural base, but, except for a few displaced U.S. Southerners after the Civil War, and a few Mexicans, not many colonists came. Involvement in the Caste War of Yucatán had not helped the development of the colony either. It became a backwater, gradually tied more closely to New Orleans than to Jamaica by virtue of the shipping routes. A shipping line organized in New Orleans in 1866 first developed closer economic relations between the two ports. In spite of an over-all decline in the colony's commerce, trade with the United States increased. Politically, there was also stagnation. The limited self-government which the settlement had early enjoyed diminished when Belize formally became a Crown Colony in 1862 and then voted a virtual end to self-government in 1870. The decline of Belize symbolized the decline of the Caribbean coast and rise of the Pacific ports as Central America's doorways to the world, all of which was the result of effective exploitation of a transisthmian route.

The mid-nineteenth century was a tumultuous period on the isthmus. Foreign economic imperialism challenged Central America's new-found political independence. Interest in an interoceanic canal intensified the foreign interest. The British took the lead, but North Americans eventually began to challenge them as both sought advantage on the isthmus. The foreigners penetrated the Conservative isolationism of the period, forcing colonial aspects of the industrial revolution onto the region. The result was greater economic activity, better roads, ports, and a shift of commerce and shipping from the Caribbean to the Pacific watershed. Production of and dependence upon agricultural staples increased, as did the desire for foreign manufactured goods. Added to the breakup of the United Provinces and the rise of caudillos, foreign encouragement of separate state sovereignty dimmed hopes for reunion of the federation. Yet the Conservatives succeeded in maintaining their territorial integrity. By 1865 the separate national identity of the five states was firmly established, although union still remained an important part of Liberal rhetoric.

New ideas were a predictable by-product of the foreign contacts. Central Americans became aware of how far their society lagged behind the developing nations of the North Atlantic, and Liberal resurgence was the inevitable result.

Chapter 6 • Coffee Republics

The decline of the natural dye markets, occasioned by discovery of aniline dyes, left the indigo and cochineal industries of Central America in trouble. Yet Central America still had a valuable agricultural product, for the loose, volcanic soil, the constant, year-round temperature, and the single rainy season made the land ideally suited for coffee production. Transportation and port development had not progressed sufficiently to permit large-scale exploitation of coffee until the mid-nineteenth century. Costa Rica led the way in the 1830's, but all five republics eventually went into production of the crop. The Conservative caudillos promoted coffee exports, but it was under the Liberal dictatorships of the latter part of the century that coffee reached its position of preeminence among exports. Coffee best represents the most successful aspects of the Liberals' approach to economic development. Yet coffee production and export could not alone provide all the modernization and economic growth that Liberal rhetoric promised.

Many of the characteristics of the coffee industry developed first in Costa Rica, setting the pattern for other Central American states and Colombia. Colonial Central America grew small amounts of coffee, although the principal producers of the eighteenth century were Cuba and Haiti. In 1805, as a part of the Bourbon effort to promote agricultural development and diversification, the Spanish government relieved all coffee produced in the kingdom of certain taxes, and in Costa Rica Governor Tomás de Acosta introduced coffee plants and encouraged their cultivation. Immediately upon independence, the town councils of Cartago and San José began to encourage coffee cultivation, and by 1834 Costa Rican production had reached 50,000 pounds annually. In the same year a few Guatemalans began cultivating the crop. Except for occasional exports, transportation obstacles prevented the Costa Ricans from developing much of an overseas market via the Caribbean, but in the 1830's they made sizable shipments of coffee beans from Puntarenas to Chile, where Valparaíso had become an important Pacific coast entrepôt for British and European trade. Larger amounts began to flow toward European markets in the 1840's. Completion of the Panama Railway facilitated more exports. The coffee boom in Costa Rica contributed to the emergence of a strong landed class, but it also permitted the state to modernize somewhat more rapidly than other Central American states. Although foreigners assumed important production and marketing roles, most of the coffee lands remained in Costa Rican hands.

As early as 1845 Guatemalan merchants and planters noted changes in the Costa Rican economy with interest, and their government began to promote coffee cultivation more actively. By 1855 coffee fincas were springing up around Cobán, Antigua, and Amatitlán, and coffee replaced nopal-cochineal cultivation in the last two areas. From there, coffee spread southward to the Pacific coastal slopes. The value of coffee among all Guatemalan exports rose from 1 per cent in 1860 to 44 per cent in 1870, when it became the largest single export commodity, a position it has held ever since.

Development of Pacific coast shipping permitted El Salvador to join in the production in the 1870's. Nicaragua and Honduras followed in the 1880's, although coffee did not become a major crop in Honduras until after World War II. The total production of these small republics has never been large in volume—it has never accounted for more than 15 per cent of the world total—but Central American coffee has consistently been noted for its high quality and special blending uses. Tax relief, subsidies, transportation development, and legislation providing inexpensive land and labor encouraged the coffee expansion. These incentives began under the Conservative caudillos, but Liberal government intensified them. Sugar production received similar promotion and also expanded, but much less so than coffee because of the competition of Caribbean, Louisiana, and Hawaiian sugar producers, who had more favorable transportation facilities.

The transfer of power from the Conservatives to the Liberals which occurred in the latter third of the nineteenth century all across Central America, and which caused an acceleration in the tendency toward modernization, with increased dependence on coffee and other export commodities, was part of a larger phenomenon occurring throughout much of the western world. Politically, it took the form of a resurgence of Liberalism, in a strong reaction against the Conservative caudillos who had held sway over much of the mid-nineteenth century. The Liberals of the latter part of the century, although they shared the utilitarian idealism of earlier Liberals, were now taken with at least the superficial aspects of positivism. In general, they believed themselves to be more practical men. They were certainly more concerned with economic progress than with achievement of political utopias. The coincidence of the rise of coffee production with their political domination reflects the strong emphasis they placed on productivity for foreign exchange and comparative advantage. Dictatorship continued to be the principal form of government in Central America, but with important differences from the caudillo governments of the mid-nineteenth century. Mexican President Porfirio Díaz became the prototype new Liberal dictator with whom Central American chieftains such as Justo Rufino Barrios, Marco Aurelio Soto, José Santos Zelaya, and Manuel Estrada Cabrera could be compared.

There were several reasons why the Liberals were finally able to overcome the Conservative regimes in the isthmus. Although specific problems varied from one state to another, the economic shifts and dislocations had put severe strains on the Central American governments.

Unemployment had risen in some areas, and even many planters had become disillusioned with governments which had been unable to find adequate solutions to the problems of declining markets for their commodities or to changing world trade conditions. The outlying districts were alienated by tendency of the Conservative governments to operate principally for the benefit of a select group in the capital. Meanwhile, the increasingly available foreign capital made the Liberals' dreams of material advancement appear attainable, and foreign agents and diplomats encouraged such dreams.

The Walker episode had discredited many of the older Liberals, but younger professionals, army officers, or planters—several of whom had formerly cooperated with the Conservatives—took their places as leaders of the opposition. A core of Positivist-oriented intellectuals flourished at the University of San Carlos in Guatemala during the 1860's, and, as a result, a new generation of Liberal leaders for Guatemala, Honduras, and El Salvador was created.

The series of revolts that transferred power from Conservatives to new Liberals in Central America began in El Salvador, where Gerardo Barrios rose briefly to power. General Barrios had been loyal to Carrera, and he had been a leader in the National War against Walker, but, as an avid reader and francophile, he had inevitably gravitated toward Liberal-Positivist doctrines and rejected the intellectual suffocation of Carrera's Guatemalan regime. In 1858, as head of the provisional government of his state, he returned the capital from Cojutepeque, where it had been established after a destructive earthquake in 1854, to the Liberal stronghold of San Salvador. He soon announced the need for educational, political, and economic reforms. Then he defiantly ordered the remains of Francisco Morazán brought to San Salvador, where they were reburied with state honors. Immediately thereafter he returned the government to the legitimate President, Miguel de Santín, but in 1859 he reassumed power. He was formally elected to the presidency the following year.

Carrera watched suspiciously as Barrios began his reforms. He assured Barrios of his continued friendship, but at the same time he assembled an army near the Salvadoran frontier. When Barrios began to restrict clerical power in 1863, Carrera invaded, even though Barrios toned down his anticlericalism and agreed upon a new concordat with the Vatican. Barrios soundly defeated Carrera at Cojutepeque, but he failed to follow up his victory. Carrera successfully reorganized and launched a new offensive. Before the year ended he had replaced Barrios with Conservative Francisco Dueñas. Barrios attempted to return two years later, but he floundered on the Nicaraguan coast, and Nicaraguan authorities turned him over to Dueñas, who imprisoned him. Three years later a Salvadoran firing squad ended the Barrios threat. Although the Liberal threat in El Salvador had stalled, Dueñas did not reverse all of Barrios's program. Particularly after Carrera's death in 1865, a less reactionary regime prevailed.

The death of Carrera signaled revolt in both Guatemala and Honduras. Carrera's chosen successor, Vicente Cerna, initially succeeded in suppressing these uprisings, and at the same time he moderated the reactionary tone of the government. In Honduras, however, Liberals succeeded in establishing a shaky government, and they provided a refuge for Guatemalan exiles. These Guatemalans joined with Honduran forces in an effort to "liberate" El Salvador, and in April 1871 they defeated Dueñas and installed Field Marshal Santiago González. Subsequent Salvadoran refusal to indemnify Honduras for her aid in ousting the Conservatives launched a long, sordid history of irresponsible meddling in the internal affairs of each state by the others. Such activities became all too common in the late nineteenth century, and they served as a background for the joint United States–Mexican attempts to bring stability there during the first decade of the twentieth century. González returned fully to the policies of Gerardo Barrios with a program of educational reforms, public works, and anticlericalism. Instability reigned in Honduras until Marco Aurelio Soto, a dedicated Liberal, gained the presidency in 1876.

The key to stability in Honduras and El Salvador, of course, was Guatemala, for so long as a strong Conservative government held sway there, no Liberal government was safe in the smaller, neighboring states. Early Liberal revolts against Cerna failed, but in June 1871 the Liberal revolutionaries, under the leadership of Miguel García Granados, a member of one of Guatemala's leading families and a military officer who had been important in planting coffee in Los Altos, and Justo Rufino Barrios (no relation to the Salvadoran general), with aid from Mexican Liberal Benito Juárez, succeeded in overthrowing the government. In 1873, after a brief regime under the well-meaning and democratic but inept García Granados, Barrios assumed full power. He directed the prototype new Liberal dictatorship of Central America. Developing a professional military as his political base, he ruled with a strong arm. It was he who was principally responsible for establishing Soto in power in Honduras and supporting a series of Liberal regimes in El Salvador. Ambitions of realizing Morazán's dream of a united federation, however, brought him into conflict with his neighbors and resulted in his defeat and death on the battlefield at Chalchuapa, El Salvador, in 1885.

Meanwhile, in Costa Rica, modernizing trends had been noticeable already under the moderate conservatism of Juan Rafael Mora. Challenging Mora's accession to a third term in the presidency, and capitalizing on economic dissatisfaction, the military ousted the hero and put in his place Dr. José María Montealegre. Mora attempted an invasion through the port of Puntarenas a year later, but he was captured and executed.

Montealegre was the son of a Guatemalan creole who had come to Costa Rica in the late colonial period as a tobacco monopoly official and had subsequently been important in the development of coffee cultivation in the state. His family dominated the government of Costa Rica for a decade, but they achieved considerable democratization of the process of government during the period. While Montealegre began some of the educational and economic reforms associated with the new group, his government provided an orderly transition to the classical new Liberal dictatorship of Tomás Guardia. Guardia, an army officer, took power in 1870 and ruled the state, either as President or as chief of the armed forces, for the next twelve years, thoroughly establishing the Liberal Revolution in Costa Rica.

In Nicaragua, where the Liberals were tainted more than elsewhere by their association with Walker, the Conservatives were able to hold on much longer. Their solid oligarchy maintained power even as it was itself gradually attracted to some of the Liberal economic reforms and approaches to material development. Even so, growing difficulties with Liberal Costa Rica and Honduras and an emerging domestic middle group with strong foreign ties diminished the Conservative strength. When, in 1893, Granadans balked at continued rule by Roberto Sacasa, one of the few Conservatives from León, Liberals took advantage of the division and, under the leadership of José Santos Zelaya, established the Liberal Reform there. Zelaya represented the rising middle sector in Managua and he espoused the Liberal reforms already inaugurated elsewhere in Central America. His iron dictatorship antagonized even some of the Liberals, and new coalitions formed which included traditional Conservatives from Granada, who still hated the León group. Nonetheless, once Zelaya was in power, Liberal support from Honduras helped him maintain himself against opposition for sixteen years.

Similar revolutions occurred throughout Latin America, and Central America's experience may at least in a sense be seen as following the trend of the Mexican "Reforma" and Porfiriato. Panama, too, after breaking away from Colombian rule with United States assistance, underwent a Liberal Revolution. It succeeded in bringing in Positivist-oriented governments from 1908 forward.

The distinguishing characteristics of the Liberal regimes that dominated Central America from about 1870 into the mid-twentieth century were not uniformly present in every state. Some of the changes, it is true, were already beginning under Conservative rule. The differences between the Conservative caudillos and the new Liberal dictators is in part one of style and tone, but these differences reflect basic disagreements in theoretical philosophy and vested interests. Although the Liberal Revolution was incomplete, it clearly created new elites, destroyed old oligarchies, and permitted the rise of new middle sectors which would inevitably play larger roles in the economy, society, and government.

The Positivist orientation of the new Liberals is evident from their speeches, their legislation, and their action. To these men the rapid advances made by the United States and western Europe in the nineteenth century were impressive. The scientific emphasis of the "sociocracy" called for by Auguste Comte and other Frenchmen and the application of Darwinian evolutionary theory to society as proclaimed by Herbert Spencer appealed to this new group of Central American rulers. Costa Ricans had developed rather close economic and cultural ties with Chile, where by the 1850's Positivist thought had already made a serious impact. In Guatemala a group at the University of San Carlos emerged. The most notable of them was the Honduran Ramón Rosa, but future new Liberal dictators Justo Rufino Barrios and Marco Aurelio Soto were also members. From 1860 forward, newspapers of Costa Rica and El Salvador began to reflect the new emphasis on material progress and scientific development of society.

These new leaders were less idealistic than their predecessors of the Morazán days. While they did not formally abandon democratic political philosophy, they now believed that economic growth and prosperity were necessary before true political democracy could be established. Seeing themselves as scientific realists, they believed that order and progress were the two goals worthy of greatest emphasis. To be sure, personal and family allegiances still played a vital part of Central America's political and social structure, obscuring the importance of the new philosophy at times. But, over the half-century that followed, clear patterns emerged which reflected their obsession with material development; their anticlericalism; their faith in scientific and technical education; their rejection of the metaphysical; their willingness to postpone political democracy through what Comte called "republican dictatorships"; their emulation and imitation of northern European and North American values, capital, and leadership; and their insensitivity to the desires and needs of the working classes (which is, perhaps, understandable, given the political support those classes had provided to the Conservative caudillos).

The development of the export economies by the Central American states reflects their emphasis on material progress. With legislation fa-

voring export crops and the entrance of foreign capital, they increased
the flow of raw materials—chiefly agricultural, but some mineral—out
of the country, while at the same time they enlarged the region's dependency on foreign markets and capital. Guatemala, Honduras, and
Belize, seeking to popularize their products, participated in the World's
Industrial and Cotton Centennial Exposition in New Orleans in 1884–
85. This and subsequent international expositions served to develop
closer trade relations between Central and North America. From 1880
forward, the Mexican, Central American & South American Commercial Exchange and the New Orleans Board of Trade actively promoted
greater maritime trade with Central America. That promotion helped
give the port of New Orleans its preeminent position in commerce with
Central America.

Coffee production, already important as the replacement for earlier
export commodities, received the most attention in the late nineteenth
century. The planters, encouraged by the subsidies, tax exemptions,
and the promise of large profits, brought new land into cultivation.
Government-sponsored publications provided the latest agro-technical
information. Everything possible was done to expand production. Foreigners played an important role in this expansion, although the industry remained in native hands to a substantial degree. Even where
foreigners did enter the business in large numbers, as in Guatemala,
they were immigrant settlers who usually remained in the country and
became a part of the local social scene, whereas the foreigners involved
in the exploitation of bananas, who came later, were not.

The foreign role was proportionately greatest in Nicaragua, where
Germans, Frenchmen, and North Americans together produced more
coffee than the Nicaraguan producers, and in Guatemala, where a
relatively small number of Germans produced an extraordinarily large
percentage of the state's coffee. Englishmen were important in Costa
Rica. Cooperating with both foreign and native planters were the governments, eager to expand their revenues; import-export taxes were the
principal source of income of every Central American government.
Their legislatures and courts cooperated, their laws and judicial deci-

sions making it easy for the planters to get cheap and available labor; at the same time, they either ignored or suppressed working-class interests.

The peak of emphasis on coffee production was reached in the decade of the 1880's, although it has continued to be the principal export of the region to the present day. By 1883 it accounted for 82 per cent of Costa Rican exports. The world demand for coffee accelerated greatly in that decade, and while production more than doubled, prices tripled, producing vast increases in profits and revenues. In this coffee decade there arose a number of important foreign and Central American family fortunes through which new oligarchies were established. Foreigners led the way in technology and processing of the coffee, and, most important, through their contacts and the assistance of their consuls they tapped new markets in Europe and North America. The European markets were especially important from 1870 to 1890. European merchants financed much of the rapid expansion by extending credit to their nationals in the producing areas. United States coffee importers were more reluctant to agree to such arrangements, but by 1913 they had also become major purchasers of Central American coffee, as the table on exports shows. The outbreak of World War I changed trading patterns significantly, and thereafter the United States share was greater.

CENTRAL AMERICAN COFFEE EXPORTS, 1913
in quintales (100 pounds)

Shipped to:		Shipped from:			
	Guatemala	El Salvador	Nicaragua	Costa Rica	Total
Germany	432,329	121,201	75,634	25,451	654,615
United Kingdom	106,666	34,151	32,854	231,382	405,053
United States	211,886	107,796	36,753	16,032	372,467
France	—	159,559	103,012	—	262,571
Italy	—	95,389	—	—	95,389
Austria-Hungary	42,054	35,574	—	—	77,628

The Liberals, aware of the dangers of monoculture, and desirous of economic growth on a wide front, sought to diversify and expand production in other commodities. Governments collected statistics regarding production and potential of other products, and, although there was often a lack of the sustained effort necessary to get these projects well launched, some progress was made. Sugar, bananas, cotton, chicle, cacao, rubber, timber, and zarzaparilla were among the principal products that joined coffee as the exports of these states. In 1884, at the New Orleans exposition, the Guatemalans exhibited more than a thousand separate varieties of their produce. The governments provided land free or on easy terms for those who would develop new crops. Some commodities which were encouraged, such as livestock and wheat, became more important for local consumption than for export; nevertheless, they contributed to economic growth. That Central America did not become a land of great prosperity as its leaders had promised cannot obscure the fact that there was considerable expansion of production. Significantly, their advances were much greater than were those of Belize. Even Honduras, the poorest of the independent Central American states, was more progressive than British Honduras, and by 1882 programs for encouragement of agriculture in Honduras were attracting immigrants from the British colony.

Mineral development stimulated high hopes among many Central Americans as they prospected for gold, silver, and less precious metals. Foreign capitalists and miners received generous concessions to develop mining in all five states. New silver mines in south and central Honduras actively revived interest in old colonial ventures. The center of economic activity shifted the area of greater population density, helping to promote and justify Tegucigalpa as the capital city. Nicaraguan gold mines developed in the mountains near Puerto Cabezas (Bragman's Bluff), and North American companies worked them sporadically. Gold was the country's leading export between 1938 and 1949, El Salvador and Costa Rica also exploited small mineral deposits, but Guatemalan efforts generally failed. The greatest mineral resources appear to have been depleted, although mineral extraction continues to be important for both Honduras and Nicaragua. In most cases the companies which tried to exploit the Central American minerals found the costs to be higher than their available capital, and they could not develop long-term successful operations.

By the time of the outbreak of World War I, coffee was by far the most important export of Central America. It accounted for 85.2 per cent of Guatemala's exports, 80.4 per cent of El Salvador's, 63.3 per cent of Nicaragua's, and 35.2 per cent of Costa Rica's. Bananas, which accounted for slightly over half of the exports of Honduras and Costa Rica, occupied a distant second place in isthmian exports. Although Central America had achieved a degree of export diversification by 1913, few other products had much economic significance. Monoculture remained characteristic.

Essential to the growth in the export economy were improved roads and ports. All of the Central American governments made concerted efforts to build roads, railroads, and new deep-water ports on both coasts and to improve communications. The obstacles were great and the costs were very high, but these works comprised one of the real achievements of the era. Ministries of Development, established to promote all aspects of the economy, generally supervised these efforts, although much that was accomplished came through private enterprise. Foreign and internal loans provided the capital for the projects, but they rarely brought the expected returns and thus contributed to the financial problems of the republics. Corruption bled away much of Central America's energy and funds, as dictators built roads to favor their own particular interests at the expense of national development. Despite the Liberals' attacks on class privilege, more often than not they simply replaced an older privileged elite with a new group. Critics of Justo Rufino Barrios accused him of doing this when he promoted the development of the western departments of Guatemala (Los Altos), which had long been neglected by Guatemalan governments.

Railroad development was painfully slow, despite enormous expenditures. Concessions were repeatedly given to foreign companies, but for the most part they could not raise sufficient capital to see the projects to fruition. The torrential rains, steep terrain, and dense vegetation created problems which were virtually unknown to the foreign engineers who had built the railroads of North America and Europe, but before 1900 they had completed several important lines on the Pacific slopes. Almost nothing had been done to connect the capitals and producing areas to the more inaccessible Caribbean coast, however.

In 1854 Costa Rica had opened the first rail line, a fourteen-mile stretch between Puntarenas and Esparta, but it was near the end of the century before railroads carried much freight in Central America. El Salvador, with a smaller area, and limited to the Pacific slope, made the most progress. The British-owned El Salvador Railway Company, opened in 1882, provided the basic line, and there were trunks off it. Barrios promoted a line from the Pacific port of San José to Guatemala. It was completed in 1884, and other spurs followed. His plans for a railway to the north coast were less successful. As with most of the rest of Central America, that region had to wait until a giant foreign firm, the United Fruit Company, did the job in the twentieth century. Nicaragua also had an excellent railway system connecting the principal cities and Pacific coast ports by 1900, but had nothing linking the Caribbean with the population or producing centers except the steamers on Lake Nicaragua and the Río San Juan. Those steamers, however, were unprofitable, and for that reason they were abandoned by the private interests. The government took over the ships, and it provided minimal—and deteriorating—service to San Juan del Norte.

The governments also constructed good carriageways on the Pacific slopes; these connected Guatemala, Tegucigalpa, San Salvador, Managua, and San José with their respective ports. Little advance was made toward the Atlantic. Stagecoach lines preceded the railways all along the Pacific coast. El Salvador took the lead in road and bridge building; she was first in Central America to pave her highways with asphalt. These paved roads were often without solid foundations, and they suffered from potholes and washouts rather frequently, yet the network of roads gave the El Salvador of the 1920's the appearance of being the most progressive of the Central American states. Forced labor provided much of the manpower for highway construction. In Guatemala, for example, the law required every male to contribute four days or two pesos annually toward road works.

Inadequate deep-water ports continued to handicap Central American commerce on both coasts. The Pacific ports flourished in the late nineteenth century; while the older roadsteads of Ocos, San José, Acajutla, Corinto, Puntarenas, and Amapala all expanded, new ports opened at Champerico, La Unión, and La Libertad. On the Caribbean, the Guatemalans first developed Livingston, reviving the interest in that place which had begun during the Gálvez administration, and then Puerto Barrios. Hondurans developed La Ceiba and Puerto Cortés. Bluefields, Nicaragua, which was largely developed by British and North American interests, grew as Greytown (San Juan del Norte) declined, the harbor of the latter filling with silt as the dream of an interoceanic canal slowly died. Limón served the small Costa Rican Caribbean commerce. Most of these Caribbean ports, well described by O. Henry in his *Cabbages and Kings*, were hot, stinking, dreary clutters of wooden shacks and warehouses with rusting metal roofs. They would later develop into the principal banana ports of the country. However, regular steamship service did connect them with the major North American and European ports, as it had not in earlier days.

Expansion of international trade inevitably revived interest in interoceanic canals. Following the French failure to develop the Nicaragua route, the Nicaraguan government gave a canal concession to a North American concern. The Nicaraguan Canal Company made extensive surveys and began to dig, but then the Panic of 1893 forced it to quit, and it left millions of dollars' worth of equipment to rust at Greytown. A similar fate befell the French company which, in 1878, had undertaken to build a canal through Panama. The hopes for greater prosperity from such canals in Nicaragua and Panama encouraged much of the unrealistic thinking and planning regarding economic development on the isthmus. Undercapitalization, for example, was a serious problem for the canal schemes, as it was for most major public works projects in nineteenth-century Central America.

Communications improved, although more slowly than in most of the rest of the world. Telegraph lines went up along the principal routes. A marine cable to Guatemala was completed in 1880, and it provided direct communication with major cities of the world. Telephone service began in government offices in Guatemala and Quezaltenango in 1884, and soon thereafter there were phones in the other major cities, although both the quality and the quantity of service leave much to be desired even today. Honduras led the way in intercity service; that state used existing telegraph lines several hours per day for telephone transmissions.

The positivists believed that expanded productivity and exports would spark an industrial revolution which would lead them into the same sort of sophisticated economies enjoyed by western Europe and the United States. With the greater revenue from exports, they expected the general standard of living to rise and secondary industries to spring up to satisfy the needs of the people. In fact, little of this sort of chain reaction took place. Although the governments ostensibly encouraged the organization of manufacturing and industry, the economic growth was insufficient to stimulate adequate domestic markets, nor was there technology, skilled labor, or capital in sufficient quantity. To be sure, a few textile mills opened, along with some other shops and small factories, but it cannot be said that any sort of "industrial revolution" occurred.

What the increase in exports did achieve was a great increase in commerce. Between 1870 and 1900, for example, Guatemala's volume of trade increased by more than twenty times. Instead of contributing to industrial development within Central America, however, the export profits were simply spent on imports of manufactured goods. The increase in consumption was uneven, as most of the population remained at the subsistence level, but there was clearly a great increase in imports which could be paid for with the exchange gained in export staples. However, the fact that all of these countries maintained a favorable balance of trade throughout the period does not necessarily indicate an increase in national prosperity, for significant amounts of the profits which came to coffee planters and merchants were reinvested abroad. This capital flight was rarely reflected in official import-export figures. Most of the imports came from the United States, Great Britain, Germany, and France. Foreigners played a major role in this trade, as they were the principal merchants handling it. The Central American governments gave generous concessions to foreigners for all sorts of distributorships and marketing of foreign manufactures, and the number of foreign commercial firms increased greatly. Many failed, but the stronger of them became powerful elements in the Central American economy. Because of the shortage of currency and financial facilities, some of them also became financial agents, carrying on a brisk banking business. Their commercial paper was often substituted for negotiable currency and facilitated credit operations.

Banks also proliferated, both foreign and domestic. Efforts to establish banks dated from the first decade of independence, but there had been little success until the volume of international trade provided the business for enlarged banking services. Each country formed its own national bank, often with the aid of substantial foreign loans. These banks served as the vehicles for government financing of public works projects, either through direct loans or through the sale of bonds to domestic and foreign investors. Tariffs accounted for more than 50 per cent of total government income in all five states, and with the increasing trade and rising import duties, government revenue grew. Nicaraguan government revenue, for example, from all sources rose from little more than $100,000 in 1850 to nearly $3,000,000 in 1890. Government officials believed that future increases would be even larger. Personal taxes were contrary to Liberal philosophy, and they were staunchly opposed. Other sources of income for the governments were state monopolies, such as liquor and tobacco; sales taxes; other taxes and licenses; and charges for services, such as the telegraph, post office, or mint. Unfortunately, despite the increased revenues, the regimes were not efficient; they were hindered by corruption, poorly organized or faulty fiscal systems, and poorly trained personnel.

Although foreigners played key roles in the Liberals' program of reconstructing and revitalizing the Central American economy, few outsiders were brought to the isthmus as immigrants. As in the early

years of independence, the intent of the Liberal immigration laws of
the last third of the nineteenth century was to interest and attract large
numbers of industrious foreigners to come and join in the agricultural
and industrial development. These laws, intended to lure a large, exemplary working class, resulted instead in the entry of a small but
experienced class of entrepreneurs who took advantage of the Liberals'
laws to create an arrogant class of merchants and planters who determined the direction of the Central American economy for several
decades. Central America lacked the open territories, direct shipping
lines, expanding urban opportunities, and labor shortages of nations
such as Argentina, Brazil, and the United States, which, with similar
laws, attracted millions of Europeans during the period, and so the
isthmus received only a trickle of working-class immigrants.

Despite the failure to industrialize or to develop highly diversified
and prosperous economies, the capital cities of the Central American
states did take on a more modern appearance during the late nineteenth
and early twentieth centuries. After years of warfare and economic
stagnation, during which their populations had remained relatively
constant, the cities of the isthmus began to experience rapid growth.
Medical advances cut the mortality rate, and opportunities for employment attracted rural people into the cities. More active government
participation in the economy expanded the bureaucracy. Through
public works projects the streets were paved and lighted; grand public
buildings, theaters, and stadiums were erected; and parks, racetracks,
monuments, and aqueducts were laid out. The cities took on an appearance of modernity, even elegance. Street railways, first mule-drawn
and later electrified, were installed, and public services in general
were expanded. Even the smaller cities enjoyed this growth. Managua and Tegucigalpa, which had been little more than villages, joined
in the modernizing trend and became bustling, minor metropolises.
The influx of foreigners and travelers stimulated brisk increases in the
numbers and quality of hotels and restaurants, which had virtually not
existed before the Liberal resurgence. In this business, as in others,
foreigners dominated, and German, French, English, and Italian names
were often seen on the signboards and advertisements of these hostel-

ries, lending a superficial air of cosmopolitanism to the backwater capitals. Inevitably, increases in vice, prostitution, and crime also accompanied the population growth.

Provincial towns, on the other hand, declined, intensifying the startling contrast between the capitals and the rural areas of each country —a process which has continued to the present. Towns which had been important, such as León, Granada, Comayagua, Cartago, and Totonicapán, languished, while the national capitals became the showplaces of the elites who controlled the society and economy.

The urgency of material development required strong executive leadership and planning and an inherent lack of faith in popular democracy, both of which contributed to the formation of military dictatorships. In fact, Central American historians have referred to the period as the "Age of Dictatorship." New constitutions paid lip service to the republican principles of earlier Liberals, but in fact the institutions that evolved provided for centralized, executive-run governments, with the military as the real arbiter of public affairs. Not surprisingly, military men tended to dominate the presidencies of these states. The *personalismo* which had characterized the mid-nineteenth-century caudillos remained a factor, but now support rested upon a more professional military force rather than upon the rabble or upon personal armies.

The most typical of these "republican dictatorships" were those led by Justo Rufino Barrios, Manuel Estrada Cabrera, and Jorge Ubico of Guatemala; Tomás Guardia of Costa Rica; José Santos Zelaya and Anastasio Somoza of Nicaragua; Marco Aurelio Soto, Luis Bográn (a Barrios protégé), Policarpo Bonilla (a Zelaya protégé), and Tiburcio Carías Andino of Honduras; and Santiago González and Maximiliano Hernández Martínez of El Salvador. All created political machines in which they centralized authority, and all depended heavily upon the military, rigged political institutions, and a social structure which replaced the old oligarchies that had supported the Conservative caudillos with a new elite of coffee producers and foreign interests served by a military bureaucracy.

The dictators maintained judicial and one-house legislative branches subservient to their wishes. They remained in office beyond expiration of their terms, subverting popular elections or constitutional restrictions and thus undermining what little lip service they did pay to democratic and republican processes. Only in Costa Rica, where the opposition won a national election for the first time in 1889, did elections mean anything, and even there they were not always free.

Officials appointed and regulated by the President exercised control over local areas. With police power, these *jefes políticos* maintained order and a climate favorable to the foreign and native planters and entrepreneurs who benefitted from the system. The methods of the dictators were such that some critics have observed that there was little difference between Carrera's Conservatism and Barrios's Liberalism. There were some actual differences in the manner in which these dictators controlled, but they were minor compared with the institutional changes that occurred and the social revolution that accompanied the Liberal takeover. For the first time, large, permanent bureaucracies developed to carry on national administration. The improved communications and more professional military forces enabled the bureaucracy to rule the rural hinterlands of these countries to a degree never before attained.

The Central American Liberals who came to power in the latter third of the nineteenth century represented—as had their predecessors in the 1820's—those members of the landed aristocracy and urban middle sectors whose interests Conservative governments had failed to serve. The narrow cliques of families who had monopolized Central America's economy through privileged institutions and personal relationships were thrown out in nearly every country, although there were exceptions, and some families survived the transition from "Conservative" oligarchy to "Liberal" oligarchy. The Liberal Revolution cut off the political power of the Conservative interests, thus depriving them of the positions through which they had amassed wealth, controlled labor, and continued their predominance. Some Conservatives were killed in the revolutions themselves, but more were forced into exile or chose it voluntarily. Strong-arm dictators, or legislatures and courts which provided a legal excuse, often confiscated their lands. These lands became the property of a new landed aristocracy composed of the Liberals and their friends.

In almost every case, the new Liberal dictators and their associates became wealthy and powerful at the expense of the former rulers and their supporters. The breakup of the power of the old families was most complete in Guatemala, Costa Rica, and Nicaragua; in Honduras and El Salvador, where the line between Liberals and Conservatives was less clearly marked, there was greater survival of older families. In El Salvador, of course, the most important of the Conservative families had been eliminated in the time of Morazán, and in Honduras the absence of any great landed wealth blurred the lines between Liberals and Conservatives. Rather quickly, the new oligarchy became as inbred and aristocratic as their Conservative predecessors had been, and, indeed, by twentieth-century standards they themselves became conservatives, particularly in their reluctance to accept political liberalism and in their refusal to make economic and social reforms which would have distributed the nation's resources more widely.

There was, nevertheless, a substantial institutional restructuring, one which clearly characterizes the Liberal Revolution, and it accommodated the new dominant class. The Liberal rulers abolished or reduced in importance Hispanic institutions which had served the Conservative interests. This was most evident in Guatemala, where the Carrera regime had gone furthest in restoring Hispanic institutions. They suppressed the privileged merchant guild; its development functions were absorbed by the new National Ministry of Development, and its judicial privileges were incorporated into the ordinary civil and criminal court system. Later, the Economic Society, which was often regarded as a "Liberal" institution but smacked of the privileged, elite character of the Conservative regime, was also suppressed. The Liberals ended other vestiges of the Spanish colonial regime throughout Central America. The most important institutions, the Church and the army, both underwent substantial change. The Church, on which the Conservatives had depended to cement their alliance with the masses, lost its former wealth and position. Although specific restrictions varied from state to state, all five states confiscated Church lands and nationalized the endowments of religious orders. They removed some orders from the country altogether, forbade clerics to wear clerical garb except in discharge of their religious functions, banned or restricted religious processions, permitted civil birth registration, first legalized and then made compulsory civil marriage, established religious toleration and welcomed Protestant immigration, abolished compulsory tithe taxes and the clerical fuero, once more removed the Church's monopoly on education, and restrained the moral censorship which the Church had been allowed to impose. In addition, other concerns of the Church, such as hospitals, charity, and care of orphans and the aged, began to be taken over by the state. Reductions in the number of clergy left many rural areas without priests, thereby diminishing the Church's influence over the peasant population.

The Church fought back, particularly in Guatemala, where it was strongest. There it excommunicated President Barrios and other officials. Barrios responded by exiling the Archbishop and Bishops, and in the end the Liberals succeeded in reducing the Church in power and prestige. While it remained the refuge of Conservative upperclass elements, the Church lost the strong authority it had once held over the masses. Although not totally ended even today, the major role the clergy had played in rural Central America became minor. This was one of the most important changes ever to take place in Central America.

The armies of Central America had been the caudillo's personal militia, composed of ill-disciplined and low-paid rabble who enjoyed privilege and prestige of a sort, but also evoked universal disdain and fear. The Liberal regimes turned them into professional organizations of a permanent, institutional nature. The enlisted troops, it is true, for the most part remained poorly paid, ragged, barefoot, and not very "professional," but the officers corps was institutionalized through national military schools. In this El Salvador took the lead, but the Escuela Politécnica of Guatemala eventually became the model. The Liberals hired foreign instructors, and a few of their own officers went abroad to study in European military schools. The military became a more respected profession. It also served as one of the few institutions in the country to provide social mobility. Few persons of the lower classes were actually able to rise into the middle and upper strata of society. For the emerging middle class, however, the army became an important avenue to prestige and power.

The military included more than just the army, as several states established Civil Guards, or National Police forces, which also took on professional status. These forces became the means by which dictators controlled their countries and suppressed political and social disorder as well as ordinary crime, making their states safe for the development they were so eager to effect. Compulsory military service enabled the army to become a means of providing some education to the masses, especially along lines which would promote support for the modernization policies and nationalize *esprit* and support behind the government. Moreover, the military began to provide useful services to the society. The Military Hospital, for example, offered the best medical care available in Guatemala. By 1900 the military had been made responsible for construction and maintenance of roads and bridges throughout Central America and was also active in educational and other public-service programs.

However, the military, while it became the principal defender of Liberal governments, at the same time it also became the arbiter and destroyer of such governments. The stability which was so much a part of the ideal of the Positivists who justified the dictatorships was less characteristic of Central America than it was of Porfirio Díaz's Mexico. In fact, revolts became common in Central America, and the region became notorious for its frequent civil disturbances, not for stability. Factionalism, political and personal, within the military became intense, and it resulted in continual intrigue. With no check on their power, the armies removed governments at will as military chieftains jockeyed for power and position and alliances among commanding officers shifted. These personal relationships, which were tied to economic and family interests outside the army, often obscured the ideological differences of political parties. In any case, by 1900, except in Nicaragua, the old Conservative Party was gone and politics had become factional struggles within the Liberty Party.

The peculiar problem of Central America was the constant meddling of governments in the affairs of their neighbors, meddling which contributed to the almost continual turmoil on the isthmus. Only the most ruthless of dictators, such as Zelaya or Estrada Cabrera, were capable of withstanding these forces for more than a few years. Any President who completed his constitutional term of office without being assassinated or forcibly removed had achieved the extraordinary. The influx of arms into the countries, and their political instability, contributed to a rise in crime and lawlessness, in sharp contrast to the situation in Mexico in the same period. Nevertheless, the same protection and courting of the foreigner which characterized Mexico at the time could also be found in Central America.

The greatest stability developed in El Salvador, where, through a well-trained police force and the agreement of about fourteen families, peace was maintained from 1898 through 1931. During much of the period (from 1913 to 1927) the country was dominated by the Meléndez family, under whose rule the coffee industry flourished and El Salvador became known among foreigners as the most progressive of the Central American republics. The Great Depression brought financial disaster and the reincorporation of a strong military dictatorship under General Maximiliano Hernández Martínez.

Costa Rican progress, although somewhat unnoticed at the time, was, in the long run, more sound. Its educational reforms were among the most successful in Latin America, and literacy was gradually extended to nearly all citizens. The state would eventually boast more teachers than soldiers, yet military revolts continued and Costa Rica became involved, at times belligerently, over continuing boundary disputes with Nicaragua and Panama. Honduras and Guatemala, meanwhile, frequently experienced military coups, although the Estrada Cabrera dictatorship (1898-1920) succeeded in holding continuous power longer than any other government in Central American history, this despite repeated revolts and assassination attempts. Nicaragua's experience, examined more fully in the following chapter, was unique, since United States intervention there permitted the Conservatives to rule again under North American military occupation.

The internal instability and bickering among the states emphasized once more the need for union and establishment of a central government which might bring the internecine quarrels to a halt. Union had remained a political goal of the Liberals, even though local jealousies had retarded its achievement. Barrios and Zelaya attempted to unify the isthmus again through their own military power. Both failed, yet other men, undiscouraged, made reunification efforts thereafter. Treaties recognizing the desirability of union had failed to bear tangible results. A movement led by Nicaraguan Salvador Mendieta developed; it aimed at peaceful political union. After failing in several attempts between 1895 and 1898, Mendieta and his followers organized the Central American Unionist Party (September 1899). Its goal was to elect party members to office in each state. Once elected, they would lead their respective states into a new federation of twenty departments which would cut across old state boundaries and regions, breaking down the traditional regional loyalties, but following more natural geographic divisions. In Positivist fashion, Mendieta's influential *Enfermedad de Centro América* pointed out the ills of Central America and prescribed scientific approaches to their elimination. Disdainful of the cultural heritage of his own land, he saw union as the key to its regeneration.

Upon the overthrow of Estrada Cabrera in 1920, the Guatemalan Unionist Party gained power, but its tenure was short-lived owing to the intervention in 1921 of the military, who were concerned over "subversive influences." Since then, although the unionist spirit has continued to persist among many intellectuals and a few political leaders, it has failed to gain power in any of the Central American states.

Noteworthy cultural changes accompanied the Liberal revolutions, in large part as the result of the decline of Church authority and removal of education from its domination, as well as the increasing foreign influence in the country. The goal of mass education enunciated by Liberal intellectuals came nowhere near achievement except in Costa Rica, where literacy rose from 11 per cent in 1864 to 31 per cent in 1892, 76 per cent in 1927 and 85 per cent in 1963. In the other republics gains were much less impressive, but throughout Central America there was a drive to establish more schools, at least for the urban middle class. Kindergartens were begun during the period, but the most notable expansion took place at the secondary level. Foreign teachers came, and they developed a widening range of intellectual contacts. National libraries and museums, academies, professional schools, and universities opened. They particularly emphasized scientific and technical studies, and they gave less attention to, and even opposed, the more traditional humanities. Expenditures for public education totaled nearly as much as that spent on the military, only service on the public debt ranking ahead of these two items in most of the annual budgets of the states. That the state of education remained lamentably poor cannot be denied, but in relative terms the period witnessed great progress.

Except in Costa Rica, however, teachers were less valued than soldiers, and intellectuals in general were not allowed to play significant roles in the development of their state's destiny. Before World War II, with rare exceptions, going into the teaching profession was more often a step down than a step up, socially and economically. Central America produced few great intellectuals or writers. Nicaragua's Rubén Darío was the most noted of them, but he created his greatest works outside of Central America. Nor were there great jurists or statesmen. The society was a shallow imitation of more developed areas, and it was notably lacking in indigenous creativity or imagination. National governments built large theaters, but then spent little or nothing to encourage the performing arts. Least of all was there any appreciation of the native cultures, even though the period saw the development of considerable foreign interest in Central American archaeology.

Newspapers, magazines, and book shops became more common. By 1895 Guatemala alone had thirty-three newspapers, including five dailies in the capital. Freedom of the press, if it did not become an absolute reality, at least became a political slogan which discouraged censorship or suppression of anti-government publications.

The Indians and rural peasants gained little from the new Liberals, who rejected the paternalism of the Conservatives while using the empoverished masses as the manpower to provide the material advances of their regimes. Through forced labor, vagrancy laws, and legalized debt peonage the poor were put to work on the plantations or roads. In Guatemala, where the *mandamiento* virtually restored the colonial *repartimiento,* Indian villages provided labor for both private and public works. Much Indian land was alienated when residents could not produce legal title documents. Such land became available at low cost for planters, while its inhabitants were forced to seek wage employment on the fincas. The Guatemalan *mandamiento* formally ended with the Labor Code of 1894, but that law, far from protecting labor, was designed to "stimulate work" and "discourage vagrancy." It gave the planters, under a contract system, extensive authority over workers, and it tacitly endorsed debt peonage.

The laws which in theory emphasized the equality of all men actually went much further in protecting the employer than the employee. These governments ruthlessly worked the rural people and provided them with few benefits. The people were virtual slaves to a system which worshipped material progress for a selected few. Both on the farms and in urban establishments, six-day workweeks and ten- and twelve-hour workdays were common. That such labor was inefficient and characterized by low productivity and absenteeism sustained the notion that the Indians were lazy and shiftless. The landholders and bureaucrats who relentlessly exploited the helpless peasants had little comprehension of the necessity of providing adequate incentives and rewards and of providing channels by which the workers might improve their status through hard work. Currency inflation further deteriorated labor's standard of living during the period. Alcoholism became a major problem among the poor, if employer and government reports may be believed. Forced to provide for an expanding economy which provided economic and social benefits only for the middle and upper classes, cheap alcohol undoubtedly offered the working-class people one of the few pleasures they could afford.

Whenever the Indians or workers made any effort to organize or strike they were ruthlessly repressed by armed troops. Local planters and employers, as well as local officials, had substantial police authority, and they imprisoned and punished workers who got out of line. The 1894 Guatemalan law, for instance, dealt in detail with the obligations of workers, defined as *colonos* (those residing permanently on a finca), or *jornaleros* (day laborers who hired out for specified periods). In both cases, the obligations of the worker to the owner effectively kept the worker tied to the land. In essence, the system created a new class of landholders who lived off the exploited labor of serfs. It remained in force until the overthrow of Jorge Ubico in 1944.

Meanwhile, the governments continued to grant land to planters so they could enlarge and develop coffee fincas and other plantations. All of the states but El Salvador had considerable public land for development, but in addition to this land there was the communal land of the Indians, which was steadily encroached upon. The government provided surveying either free or at very low cost and protected privately held titles at the expense of communally held lands.

The Liberal revolutions set out to bring about rapid material progress and thereby establish prosperity in the Central American states, and, in large measure, they achieved their limited goal. They built roads, ports, and bridges, and they expanded agricultural production and exports. Yet they failed to promote the general prosperity. One landed oligarchy dedicated to traditional values simply gave way to another which, in concert with foreign investors, reserved the advantages of modern civilization for itself. The social costs of this were very high. By the early twentieth century it was evident that the oligarchies had turned over control of their countries in large measure to foreign planters, merchants, financiers, diplomats, and, in the case of Nicaragua at least, even to foreign armed forces. In order to attract investment and development to an area which had yet to prove its worth, they had made exceedingly generous concessions. Foreign consuls had encouraged and helped work out the details of such arrangements. Ever since the adoption of limited liability laws in the mid-nineteenth century, it had been possible for small companies to amass greater amounts of capital and to look abroad for lucrative possibilities. Central America received such investment, but all too often the capitalization was insufficient to overcome the enormous obstacles to development in the region, and failure resulted. The instability of the governments was one of the major obstacles, but natural obstacles were also important. Large national debts grew, and they became the subject of unpleasant relations with the major powers. Sometimes intervention resulted. In Central America, the British in particular practiced gunboat diplomacy through the end of the nineteenth century, but the United States was fast challenging British hegemony.

Within each country the foreign domination of major extractive and commercial enterprises inevitably created growing popular resentment. The Germans were especially resented in the coffee country of Guatemala, while the English and the North Americans were gaining disfavor because of their involvement in transportation and commerce.

The nineteenth century had seen the region break from Spain amid glowing hopes for prosperity and development; the twentieth century found it still divided and becoming part of a new colonial empire. Little advancement had been made by most of the people. Central America had not learned that general economic improvement depended on the growth of a larger market and general improvement of wages and services. A new oligarchy, based principally on producing and selling coffee to the wealthy nations, had political control, but it was a control that depended upon and had to be shared with the foreign interests, which increasingly came to be typified by the great banana company.

Chapter 7 • Banana Republics

Of all the projects that the new Liberal dictators fervently promoted to develop their states, railroads ranked first. The leaders could not conceivably bring about the sort of economic advantages they envisioned without the advantages of the rapid and large volume transportation which railroads could provide. All of the states made generous concessions, to foreigners and natives alike, toward this end, and by 1880 their efforts had produced notable successes on the Pacific slopes. The Caribbean watershed proved more difficult, however, and repeated failures by both public and private enterprises all along that coast were general. Success there required either massive capitalization or enough available cargo to make the railroad return profits quickly, even before it was completed.

For those reasons, the Costa Rican government of Tomás Guardia turned to one of the greatest of the nineteenth-century railroad builders, Henry Meiggs. In 1871, in return for land grants along the line, Meiggs agreed to construct a railroad from San José to Puerto Limón, on the Caribbean coast. Meiggs turned the contract over to two nephews, Minor Cooper Keith and Henry Meiggs Keith, and work soon began. Until it was completed, the line was of little use to the established coffee economy of Costa Rica. The coffee grew in the central valley and Pacific slopes and was thus shipped more easily from Puntarenas than from Limón. The Carribbean route was not completed until 1890, but in 1878 Minor Keith began to ship small quantities of bananas from Limón to New Orleans. This traffic showed losses initially, but the railroad soon began to profit from the banana trade. By 1885 Costa Rica was exporting more than half a million bunches annually, and the volume grew rapidly thereafter, for the railroad built trunk lines into banana-producing areas even before the main line reached San José. Keith formed the Tropical Trading and Transport Company, acquired more land and ships, and developed a large trade in bananas between Costa Rica and the Gulf coast of the United States.

Meanwhile, from the 1860's forward, as steam navigation had grown, ships had begun to pick up bananas along the Caribbean coast as sometimes-profitable cargoes to the Gulf coast. In most cases they simply bought from native producers with little regularity, but bananas were becoming a recognizably important product, and the Central American governments began to encourage their production with export-tax exemptions. Although the volume of this trade was initially small, it promised growth.

In 1870, a Boston ship captain named Lorenzo Baker began to transport bananas up from Jamaica to Boston. At first this only amounted to an occasional cargo, but by 1885 Baker had built it into a profitable trade. He formed the Boston Fruit Company, which developed a brisk business in the tropical fruit in the Boston area, much as Keith and others had done in the lower Mississippi valley. By 1890 both Boston Fruit and Tropical Trading and Transport were prospering and had acquired much coastal land. They expanded rapidly and absorbed smaller operators. In 1899 the two merged, forming the United Fruit Company, with Andrew Preston, Baker's successor in the Boston Fruit Company, as president and Minor Keith as first vice president. The company soon become one of the giant North American corporations. It extended its operations into the other Central American countries and soon dominated the isthmian banana industry.

In the Antilles the company moved into other fruits, and into sugar, but in Central America the operation for some years remained principally a banana operation. The company continued its interest in railroads and moved into Pacific coast regions as well as the Caribbean. It completed the transcontinental route in Guatemala in 1908. In the meantime, UFCO went into production on the Honduran coast and began a railroad there. Later, it built railroads in Nicaragua, Panama, and El Salvador. Honduras eventually became the major banana producer in Central America and the only country from which bananas became the principal export. But the company failed to live up to its promise to connect Tegucigalpa with the coast by rail, and the Honduran railroads did little more for the economy than serve the banana trade, extending inland no further than San Pedro Sula. By 1912 UFCO had a railroad network in Central America under its control through its International Railways of Central America (IRCA). In addition to the railroads, United Fruit Company had steamships. "The Great White Fleet," which dominated service between Central American shores and the United States, an important part of the process by which North American economic interests replaced the British in the region. UFCO steamers became just about the only vessels serving the eastern coast, and the company dominated the ports from Limón to Puerto Barrios.

The company extended its activities to make its primary operations more efficient. It inaugurated radio communications between Central America and the United States in 1910, which led to formation of a subsidiary, Tropical Radio Telegraph Company, in 1913. UFCO controlled and enlarged the distribution process in the United States, which by 1950 consumed approximately 50 per cent of the world export of bananas, creating a near vertical monopoly on bananas and a large portion of the trade in other tropical fruits as well. Later, it expanded into food processing within Central America.

The company's success inspired imitators and competitors. Small companies sprung up along the coast. The Vacarro Brothers came from New Orleans to La Ceiba in 1899 and developed a thriving trade. This led to the formation of the Standard Fruit and Steamship Company in

1924, when the Vacarros merged with other small companies to become UFCO's largest competitor, contributing to the substantial growth of La Ceiba and the north coast of Honduras. A more aggressive competitor emerged from the energetic labors of a Bessarabian immigrant, Samuel Zemurray of Mobile, after he acquired the concession to build a railroad on the same coast between Cuyamel annd Veracruz, near the Guatemalan border. Zemurray built his concession into a major banana exporting firm out of Puerto Cortés, forming the Cuyamel Fruit Company in 1911. United Fruit aided and financed the early efforts of both the Vacarros and Zemurray. It held a half-interest in the Vacarro Brothers firm and 60 per cent of the Hubbard-Zemurray Steamship Company, but later it sold those interests to develop Honduran banana plantations of its own around Tela and Trujillo. Even after UFCO sold its interests in these companies, however, friendly relations existed between them, and they cooperated in expanding banana production and marketing. In the 1920's, however, Cuyamel and United became fiercely competitive, particularly over land concessions in the area of the Nicaraguan-Honduran disputed border. Agents of the banana companies lobbied with the governments, and, through intrigue and manipulation, even to the extent of sponsoring revolutions and civil war in these states, they obtained favorable concessions. The rivalrly ended in 1929 when United purchased Cuyamel for some $32 million, but soon thereafter Zemurray became chairman of the UFCO board.

The banana trade brought the Caribbean coast of Central America much closer to the United States. The failure of Honduran mining to produce the rich rewards that had been contemplated left bananas as the major export of that republic. The ports and towns of the north coast became more closely tied to New Orleans than to Tegucigalpa, which declined in importance while La Ceiba, San Pedro Sula, and Puerto Cortés grew. These places, and those on the Nicaraguan coast as well, were closer in terms of transportation to New Orleans than they were to their own capitals, and the enclave nature of their economies increased when there should have been more even national growth.

The banana industry, unlike that of coffee, which was to a large degree developed by individual producers on small fincas, became in effect a giant foreign-controlled plantation. It needed large acreages, which it usually got by concessions from the governments. The Positivist-oriented regimes wanted economic development badly and were willing to make large grants of land to get production, railroads, shipping, and port facilities. United Fruit not only marketed the produce of its own plantations; it also purchased bananas from smaller, independent producers. Since it controlled the market, producers had little choice but to sell to the company at its price. This amounted to a virtual monopoly over production.

There had long been a desire in Central America to find ways to improve the hot, eastern lowlands and to develop easier communications and transportation with the Caribbean and beyond. The fruit companies fulfilled that dream, providing Central America with many of the things which Liberals since had been proposing for the isthmus since the 1820's. Land was supplied by the willing governments, but in the sparsely populated lowlands there was a labor shortage, and few laborers from the highlands could be enticed to the hot, disease-ridden coastal plains. Thus, the fruit companies imported Jamaican and other West Indian blacks to provide a work force for the plantations, railroad construction, the docks, and other port facilities. This gave the eastern coast a substantially different racial composition from the highlands and Pacific coast of these states and thereby produced serious social tensions later.

Disease was a major obstacle, and the United Fruit Company took a lead in efforts to rid Central America of yellow fever, malaria, and other diseases of the tropics, as well as taking measures against hookworm and other debilitating parasites. It set up clinics, inaugurated innoculation programs, and cooperated with international agencies and foundations in these efforts. Solution of these health problems was essential to the growth of the tropical settlements. Plant diseases and fungi were a further obstacle to development. Panama disease hit the banana plantations early in the century, and, beginning in 1935, a leaf spot disease called Sigatoka plagued the banana lands. Diseases and insects required a heavy investment in spraying, plant culture, and research. Moreover, hurricanes frequently devastated the banana plantations. Such natural catastrophies emphasized the fact that anyone who was interested in the successful exploitation of tropical fruits had to have the ability to absorb heavy losses from time to time and also had to have large amounts of reserve land for development. More recently, however, the fruit company has turned to the practice of purchasing bananas from small producers, this in response to demands for agrarian reform which challenged the company's vast acreage. This practice relieved the company of the necessity of holding such large blocks of land in reserve, but it meant that the company had to provide extensive research and technical assistance to the small producers.

UFCO also had a near monopoly on transportation. Railroad rates became high and service poor, but Central American complaints accomplished little. Steamship rates were the same, with lower rates from the United States to Central America than from Central America to the United States. Moreover, the improvement in international transportation failed to stimulate the hoped-for internal growth. Steamships, for example, connected Central American ports with the United States and Europe, but often they did not connect those ports with each other. Before World War I German, Dutch, English, and Italian freighters shared the trade with the United States, but after 1914 North American shipping dominated the sea-lanes of Central America, particularly from the Caribbean shores, which had languished since the completion of the Panama Railway. The fruit company favored its shipping lines in a variety of ways. For example, in Guatemala IRCA rates for hauling coffee were proportionately higher to the Pacific port of San José than to Puerto Barrios on the Carribbean, where UFCO ships could carry the cargo.

The banana industry accomplished many of the Liberals' objectives, albeit at the price of national sovereignty and economic independence. Among the benefits were development of transportation and ports; valuable foreign exchange, which financed further (if modest) economic development; substantial tax revenues; exploitation of lowland regions; and eradication of deadly diseases endemic to the tropics.

After World War II, the UFCO made a concerted effort to improve its image in Central America and contributed generously to the educational, social, and cultural progress of the isthmus.

While UFCO was the most obvious and most important of those who poured North American capital into Central America as the twentieth century began, it was by no means the only figure in the picture. In fact, a three-way struggle for economic control of Central America had begun in which both the United States and Germany—two latecomers in the imperialist race—challenged the hegemony of Great Britain. The North Americans had obvious geographical advantages, yet German individual initiative in the coffee industry, the growth of German shipping and manufacturing, and an aggressive diplomacy combined to make the Europeans formidable competitors.

Despite the importance of North Americans in bananas and Germans in coffee production, native Central Americans retained control of much of the agriculture of their countries, and the new class of landlords that arose in cooperation with the Liberal governments and foreign investors lived comfortably. They depended, of course, on foreign markets, merchants, factors, and bankers. Moreover, foreigners took the lead in scientific farming, and foreign-owned plantations generally produced higher yields than the native-owned plantations did. Foreigners often financed the native-owned crops, and this resulted in mortgages and eventual foreclosures in some cases. The native landholders, then, were at one and the same time in league with and controlled by the foreigners.

In commerce and trade the foreign control was even stronger. Although Central Americans continued to manage most of their own local trade, foreign resident merchants and agents managed international trade and even large-scale internal trade. By the twentieth century there were British, German, Dutch, North American, French, and Middle Eastern merchants operating in Central America in significant numbers. Since 1960 the Japanese have also become influential, most especially but not exclusively in El Salvador, where other foreigners had been relatively less important. In Costa Rica the foreigners integrated relatively easily into the society, but in the rest of Central

America they tended to remain a class apart, a foreign community. Their presence was felt least in El Salvador, but it was important everywhere. In Costa Rica the foreign-born portion of the total population rose from 2.4 per cent in 1883 to 9.4 per cent in 1927. International trade was almost totally in the hands of foreigners, and in this trade we can easily see the growth of German and United States competition for what was once almost exclusively a British domain. Before World War I the United States took the lead in the trade, while Great Britain fell behind Germany. German trade in the isthmus was temporarily displaced by that war, but it recovered during the decade following. The most consistent trend during the decades between World War I and World War II, however, was the increasing share of the trade that the United States enjoyed.

PERCENTAGES OF CENTRAL AMERICAN COMMERCE WITH
GREAT BRITAIN, GERMANY, AND THE UNITED STATES

Year	Great Britain	Germany	United States
1913	17.6	21.0	44.6
1929	13.0	17.5	53.4
1938	6.7	18.4	55.8

In processing and manufacturing industries, which, since most finished goods were imported, were few and relatively unimportant, foreigners, who had both capital and technical experience, also came to play an important role. Monopolies on tobacco and alcohol, which the state once controlled, were now sold to private individuals or companies, and foreigners, particularly the British, gained control of these industries in Nicaragua and elsewhere.

In transportation there was substantial foreign rivalry. The British had an early lead and accomplished much of the early railroad building in Central America, but later the North Americans came to be dominant. As for shipping, Central American-owned ships were insignificant and the British had built up a predominant position in the nineteenth century. They continued, with the Pacific Mail Steamship Navigation Company, to dominate Pacific coast shipping, particularly after World War I forced the German Kosmos Line out. On the Caribbean coast, however, the British were clearly supplanted by the United Fruit Company and the Hamburg-American Line. Even British Honduras became more closely tied to New Orleans than to Jamaica or Britain. Belize's location on the Central America–New Orleans banana route stimulated new investment in the tiny colony and resulted in some new economic activity, although in general Belize remained depressingly poor.

Later, in the 1930's, Honduras took the lead in aviation, providing air service between its principal centers to make up for its inadequate land transport. Transportes Aéreos Centro-Americanos (TACA), organized in Tegucigalpa in 1932, was later incorporated in El Salvador, but it, too, eventually came to be controlled from New Orleans. Real domination of the air industry, however, fell to a better-capitalized foreign corporation, Pan American Airways, which became, with United Fruit, one of the most important of foreign operations in Central America.

Foreign control of internal transportation, which was principally dedicated to convoying export commodities to deep-water ports, pointed to one of the real obstacles to Central American development and national integration. Guatemala and El Salvador are the only Central American states connected to each other by rail, and this only as a result of the line connecting San Salvador with Puerto Barrios via Zacapa. Likewise, while steamer service connected all of the states with the United States and Europe—even if that service was sometimes irregular—it was often difficult, if not impossible, to get service from one Central American country to another, or between ports along the coast. Government-owned or -subsidized steamers sometimes provided such service, but the foreign companies were reluctant to promote this apparently unprofitable traffic. Thus, modern transportation improvements, which might have brought the states closer together, instead seemed to emphasize their separateness. Only in recent years has there been inexpensive bus service between the states.

Across the board, foreign investments rose steadily during the first half of the twentieth century, but most of the increase was North American. Before World War I, United States investment in Central

America was probably less than $30 million, while British investment represented more than $188 million. By 1930 United States investments had climbed to $227,239,000, compared to the British $131,769,000.

After World War I United States investment and activity in Central America increased rapidly. The war had largely eliminated German and British competition. During the 1920's the new foreign-dominated oligarchies solidified themselves as a clear-cut conservative core. The crash of 1929 was a serious blow to these oligarchies, and in all but Costa Rica the response was a rise of strong dictatorships which could reestablish "order and progress" and restrain the rising demand for reform from the working classes. The governments of Ubico, Hernández Martínez, Carías, and Somoza reaffirmed their faith in foreign capital, and they clamped an iron rule over the isthmus from Guatemala through Nicaragua.

The closer relations with foreigners had mixed results for Central America. It completed the Liberal Revolution and destroyed vestiges of Hispanic feudalism and colonialism, but it established an oligarchy of foreign domination, leaving the majority of the population to face many of the same social and economic problems they had suffered under before. Foreign soldiers of fortune or adventurers, who would have been disciplined in their own countries had they behaved there as they did in Central America, were encouraged to sow revolution and corruption in the Central American states. They contributed heavily to the growing reservoir of hatred which was building against the German and North American *gringo*. Foreign companies justified unscrupulous business practices in crass Darwinian terms of survival of the fittest long after it would have been impossible for them to use such arguments at home. These companies contributed to a certain kind of development, it is true, but the benefits went mostly to foreigners. Even natives who were in on the take banked their money abroad—in New Orleans, New York, Geneva, London.

While private commercial interests were extending North American economic control over Central America, the United States government supported the process with an expanded military and diplomatic presence in the Caribbean region. Whether this was by direct design—by "dollar diplomacy"—or coincidental to strategic defense interests has long been debated, but the fact remains that military intervention and diplomatic pressure accompanied the economic expansion and ensured the replacement of British dominance by United States hegemony. Expanding British interests elsewhere in the world, rivalry with Germany and France, involvement in the Boer War, and the strategic necessity of cultivating closer relations with the United States all contributed to the British decision to tread more softly in the Central American area in the face of North American expansion. President Grover Cleveland's diplomatic intervention in the Venezuelan–British Guiana boundary dispute in 1895 has often been cited as the point at which the British turned over their sphere of influence in the Caribbean to the United States, but a year earlier the strong United States protest against British intervention on the Mosquito Coast had been a force instrumental in securing British withdrawal there. The British made a last effort at gunboat diplomacy in Central America with a blockade of Corinto in 1895. United States efforts achieved a settlement, and, in return for the payment of an indemnity, Nicaragua finally gained British recognition of her sovereignty and territorial integrity. Shortly thereafter, Cleveland assigned former Confederate General Edward Porter Alexander to arbitrate the Nicaragua–Costa Rica boundary dispute, beginning close involvement of the United States government in Central America's internal affairs.

Official United States interest in the Caribbean region was more obviously demonstrated by its entry into the Cuban war for independence. But the acquisition of Puerto Rico, a naval base in Cuba, and a Pacific island empire as a direct result of that intervention spawned new interest in an isthmian canal, as the strategic necessity of moving naval forces from one ocean to the other became apparent. North American support for a canal had waned following completion of the transcontinental railroad, but interest had never disappeared entirely. Discussion of an interoceanic canal surfaced again in the 1880's, particularly after the Colombian government conceded rights in Panama to a French company in 1878. The Universal Inter-Oceanic Company, under the direction of Ferdinand de Lesseps, began digging in 1882. Meanwhile, Washington pursued a new treaty with Nicaragua to secure rights to a canal there. The United States Senate rejected a treaty in December 1884, but in 1887 the government of Nicaragua conceded rights to the Nicaraguan Canal Association, which sponsored surveys and promoted the creation of the Maritime Canal Company, formed in the United States in 1889, to supervise construction. It brought equipment to Greytown and began dredging there, but soon ran out of capital as a result of the world-wide depression of the 1890's. As the French were learning in Panama, exceptional engineering requirements were enormous and costly obstacles, as was yellow fever. Operations had all but ceased in Nicaragua by 1895. The French company went bankrupt in 1889, after having spent $260 million on its project. The company's chief engineer, Philippe Bunau-Varilla, returned to France to organize a new venture, but his New Panama Canal Company could not attract the needed capital.

Because of the restored United States interest in the Caribbean, Bunau-Varilla had the chance to recoup his losses by selling the French concession to the United States. The United States Navy Department strongly supported reestablishment of a canal venture. Since at least 1894 Assistant Secretary of the Navy Theodore Roosevelt had been advocating renewed efforts in Nicaragua. Bunau-Varilla was instrumental in shifting interest to Panama. A congressional committee headed by Admiral John G. Walker, after one of the most thorough investigations ever made of Central American canal routes, recommended the feasibility of the Nicaraguan route. Nevertheless, the French interests, led by Bunau-Varilla and New York attorney William N. Cromwell, worked frantically at persuading the Congress to authorize the Panama route and acquire the French concession. In the meantime, ratification of the second Hay-Pauncefote Treaty with Britain, which removed the Clayton-Bulwer prohibition of fortification, cleared the way for United States domination of a canal. The Nicaraguan government made clear demands regarding its sovereignty rights and control over any interoceanic canal that the United States might build there, making the Panama route still more attractive to United States interests. Finally, Roosevelt, who had become President in 1901, persuaded the Walker Commission to change its recommendation to Panama. Negotiations between the United States and Colombia began in March 1902, even before the Congress had passed the Spooner Act, which authorized the President to purchase concessions and property of the New Panama Canal Company at up to $40 million.

The United States presence in Panama had been growing ever since the Bidlack Treaty, under which the Panama Railway had been completed in 1855. Panama's somewhat isolated location in relation to the remainder of Colombia had contributed to lax government and to a varying degree of autonomy for the isthmus. Shortly after independence from Spain, several attempts at secession were made. They all failed, but Panama enjoyed thirteen months of independence in 1840-41 and self-government under a federal constitution from 1853 to 1863. The isthmus remained virtually autonomous until Colombian President Rafael Núñez reestablished a centralist regime in 1885. Thereafter, instability in Bogotá was often reflected in the streets of Panama City, and civil disorder became as frequent in Panama as in the rest of Central America. Before 1885 the United States, in order to protect North American interests on the railroad, had sent troops into Panama on numerous occasions, always with the consent of authorities in Panama. After the establishment of a strong Colombian rule the United States refrained from direct intervention, in spite of several violent outbreaks. Serious disorders, uprisings which were connected with the Thousand Days' War in Colombia, began in 1899, however. In September 1902, without the consent of any Colombian or Panamanian official, United States troops landed on the isthmus, touching off a strong protest from Bogotá which strained relations between the United States and Colombia. Diplomats reached a canal agreement, the Hay-Herrán Treaty, in January 1903, and the United States Congress ratified it in March, but the Colombian Congress, which opposed any surrender of Colombian sovereignty over the canal zone and was angered by the intervention, refused to ratify. The North Americans threatened to proceed with the Nicaragua route, but the Colombians remained adamant.

Bunau-Varilla and Cromwell, in league with Panamanian politician Dr. Manuel Amador, now promoted the insurrection which led to Panamanian independence later in the year. With the full knowledge of President Roosevelt, they plotted the overthrow of Colombian authority in Panama. As the uprising began, United States warships moved to the scene, and in the end they prevented Colombian troops from crossing the isthmus from Colón to Panama City. Washington promptly recognized the new government and within two weeks negotiated a treaty for the canal construction, acquiring the French concession and providing for United States control of a ten-mile-wide canal route. Under United States administration the canal opened in 1914. Probably more important than the engineering feat, in which more than 400 million cubic yards of earth were moved, was the eradication of yellow fever and malaria, which permitted the labor force of Panamanians, West Indians, and Chinese to survive where their predecessors had succumbed to disease. Following completion of the work many of these laborers were left without employment, and their presence created serious social problems for the government of Panama, problems which neither the canal company nor the United States did much about for several decades.

The canal greatly improved the potential for world trade of Latin America, but most of the benefits went to those nations which were already developed—and their shippers—as the canal facilitated the flow of trade which they controlled. Just as monocultural production dominated the economic life of other Central American nations and stunted their growth, so also did Panama place too great a reliance on direct and indirect revenues from the canal at the expense of more diversified national development.

In 1911 Theodore Roosevelt openly admitted that he had had an active role in "taking" the isthmus. By that year the United States had become considerably more involved in Caribbean affairs. Its military forces had occupied Cuba, and its Congress had made the island a protectorate under the Platt Amendment. The treaty of 1903 between the United States and Panama included provision for a similar arrangement. Fiscal intervention in Santo Domingo began in 1904, and it escalated to military occupation in 1916. A similar fate befell Haiti in 1915. Within the states of Central America, it was in Nicaragua where the new North American colonial empire became most evident.

As a prelude to intervention in Nicaragua, the United States joined with the Porfirio Díaz government of Mexico in an effort to establish order and peace on the isthmus. United States officials since the time of John Lloyd Stephens had stated their support of Central American union, urging those states to put aside their internecine quarrels. Development of the Panama Canal had given the United States government a much closer interest in the isthmus, just as the growth of commerce had increased North American businessmen's attention to the region. Beginning with Secretary of State James G. Blaine, the United States government had professed its interest not only in inter-American cooperation, but specifically in Central American unification. The State Department had applauded the efforts made in the 1890's to establish union, and it had endorsed the 1902 Corinto Convention, by which all of the Central American states except Guatemala agreed to submit to a tribunal of Central American arbitrators any disputes that might arise between them.

Yet in practice the Central Americans failed to solve their differences amicably. Exiles from one country conspired against their homeland's government from the asylum of a neighboring state. And foreign adventurers and soldiers of fortune, sometimes serving foreign commercial interests, contributed to the disorder, despite official pronouncements by their governments deploring such behavior.

Efforts to unseat the dictator Manuel Estrada Cabrera, who was generally friendly to North American business interests, led to the joint United States–Mexican diplomatic venture of 1906. El Salvador was supporting the Guatemalan revolutionaries, and war between the two states resulted. When Honduras joined El Salvador in the conflict, Roosevelt attempted to bring a cessation of hostilities through diplomatic means. When this effort failed, Roosevelt invited Díaz into a joint peace-keeping effort. Costa Rica joined with the two northern republics in sponsoring a meeting aboard the U.S.S. *Marblehead*, and all of the Central American states sent representatives. By the Marblehead Pact, signed in July 1906, all of the Central American states agreed to end hostilities, to stop abusing asylum, and to meet within two months in Costa Rica to work out a plan under which they would submit future disagreements to the joint arbitration of the presidents of Mexico and the United States.

At San José, four of the states, with Nicaragua absent (Zelaya refused to recognize the right of the United States to interfere in Central American affairs), reached accords which formed the basis for closer Central American cooperation. They agreed that the presidents of Mexico and the United States would arbitrate all differences arising from the recent war, and that a central American tribunal would deal with future disputes. They also agreed to bar political exiles from other states from the border regions of their homelands and to refuse to allow their territories to be used as bases for revolutionary movements against their neighbors. Finally, they agreed to establish a Central American Bureau in Guatemala City and a pedagogical institute in San José. In a spirit of optimism, the meeting closed.

Less than four months later Honduran troops invaded Nicaragua. The invasion was a response to Nicaragua's giving aid to Honduran rebels who were operating against President Policarpo Bonilla. Zelaya denied any complicity and agreed to submit the matter to a tribunal formed under provisions of the Corinto Treaty of 1902, but both states refused to cease fighting, and on February 8, 1907, the tribunal announced failure. The Nicaraguan forces defeated the invaders, and Miguel Dávila succeeded Bonilla as Honduran chief of state. Guatemala and El Salvador then agreed to intervene and to replace Dávila with former Honduran President Terencio Sierra. Nicaragua accepted the proposal that Sierra should be President, but would not acquiesce to the intervention. At this point, before Guatemala and El Salvador could actually carry out their threats, Díaz and Roosevelt persuaded the states to meet in Washington.

Representatives of all five states met there from November 14 through December 20, and they agreed to an extensive and optimistic program of cooperation and international tribunals. Efforts to reestablish the Central American confederation failed, but the delegates signed eight conventions which they hoped would move the isthmus toward that goal and, more immediately, put an end to the disorder. Incorporating a principle declared by the Ecuadorean diplomat Carlos R. Tobar, they agreed that they would not recognize governments which came into existence by revolts against constitutional regimes until free elections had reestablished constitutional rule. Moreover, they agreed not to intervene in the internal disputes of their neighbors, while also recommending that each country prohibit reelection of presidents, thus ensuring "alternation in power." They barred political exiles who lived in states adjacent to their own from living near the border, and they agreed that revolutionists would be brought to trial in the country in which they staged their revolts. Further agreements provided for extradition of criminals, future conferences, an assortment of commissions, and the establishment of a Central American Teachers' College in Costa Rica. They set up the Central American Bureau to promote the reunification of Central America and to gather and distribute information. The Bureau was to assist the various commissions in the promotion of a system of education with an essentially Central American character; the development of commerce, agriculture, industry, and transportation; and the standardization of civil, commercial, and criminal legislation as well as of customs duties, currency, and weights and measures. The most ambitious effort of the Conference, however, was the establishment of the Central American Court of Justice to resolve all disputes among the several states. The Court was composed of five justices, one from each state, who were to be free of all other public and private obligations and were to serve five-year terms. The Court was to convene at Cartago, Costa Rica.

The new Central American peace-keeping machinery received its first test during the following summer, when Zelaya complained that Guatemala and El Salvador had instigated a revolutionary movement in Honduras. The Court investigated the situation and ordered all three governments to reduce their military forces and not to intervene.

All three obeyed and peace was preserved. Although there was some criticism of the manner in which it settled the dispute, the Court had made a successful beginning, and for several years it succeeded in averting war among the Central American states. Mexican participation ended with the overthrow of Díaz and the onset of the Mexican Revolution in 1910. United States prestige in the region diminished after the invasion of Nicaragua in 1912. Yet the Court continued to exercise some influence until it had to face directly a case involving the United States.

The Central American states' policy of rapid material development, and their friendly attitude toward foreign capital, exposed them to several dangers. In tying their economies closer to the international capitalist system they ran the risk of involvement in the sometimes catastrophic market fluctuations, and they linked themselves to international monetary problems and foreign markets over which they had virtually no control. The instability and civil disorder that plagued most of the states, moreover, often endangered the foreign economic interests, leading to armed interventions by governments dedicated to protecting the interests of their nationals. Destruction of property, threats to the lives of foreigners, and irresponsible governments which defaulted on or even repudiated debts jeopardized Central America's foreign relations. In the face of aggressive European policies which sometimes used debt or damage collections as an excuse to expand colonial or commercial empires. President Roosevelt evolved his corollary to the Monroe Doctrine. In effect, the United States justified its interventions as necessary to forestall European aggression. The result in Central America was the completion of the Liberal revolutions under the dominant influence of the United States.

By the end of the nineteenth century, all of the Central American states had indebted themselves heavily to foreign creditors. Even El Salvador, which had the best record, was heavily in debt. Service on the national debt was the major item in the budgets of every state at the turn of the century. New loans were contracted to pay off old ones; interest rates and service charges were abominably high and contributed to the Central Americans' growing feeling of frustration and exploitation. The problem was not unique to the Caribbean republics, but these small states were more vulnerable to foreign intervention than were larger countries.

As early as 1868, Carlos Calvo, the Argentine jurist, had argued persuasively on behalf of nonintervention, declaring the "absolute equality of sovereign states." He had said that national courts are not subject to appeal in cases where the rights of foreign nationals are involved, and that when foreigners invest in Latin America they take a risk for which they are compensated by the exceedingly high interest rates and charges. They should not have the protection of their own government. Eventually, most Latin American nations included in their contracts the so-called "Calvo clause," which required the foreigner to accept the ruling of the national courts and forbade his recourse to his own government for defense of his rights.

Another Argentine diplomat, Luis María Drago, later promoted the same idea; it evolved into the nonintervention doctrine which was accepted in limited form by the United States at the Hague Convention of 1907 but not fully endorsed until the Inter-American Conference at Buenos Aires in 1936. During the first two decades of the twentieth century, the United States, with a variety of specific justifications, intervened frequently in the internal affairs of the Caribbean nations.

United States intervention in Nicaragua eventually resulted in military occupation and the establishment of a puppet regime. The intervention had been caused by the debt problem, in combination with the growing internal opposition to the Zelaya dictatorship. Zelaya recognized the dangers of heavy indebtedness to foreign creditors, and he sought to minimize Nicaragua's commitments. Unlike many of the leaders of the new Liberal governments, although Zelaya favored material development through foreign capital and technological investment, he was often harsh on foreigners who failed to observe Nicaraguan regulations. He recognized the hazard of selling out his country to foreigners. His protective policy had been instrumental in the United States decision to build the canal in Panama, where the government was less jealous of its own rights and territory. Foreigners anxious to finance Nicaraguan development and debt found Zelaya difficult, and segments of the foreign community, particularly British interests who had been allied with the Conservatives, connived to overthrow him. Since many North Americans had associated themselves with some of the British elements, particularly on the Mosquito Coast, they also became involved in the revolts. The revolution of 1909 began in Bluefields, the foreign and Conservative stronghold on that coast. Earlier uprisings at Bluefields had failed, but now the Taft administration exhibited open sympathy for the rebels who supported the local governor, Juan Estrada, against the national government. When Washington broke diplomatic relations with Zelaya after his government executed two United States officers in the rebel force, Zelaya resigned in favor of Dr. José Madriz. Not satisfied, however, the United States continued to withhold recognition, and Estrada's revolt continued. In August 1910 the rebels captured Managua, and Estrada became Provisional President.

The confusion surrounding the collapse of Zelaya's sixteen-year dictatorship produced financial chaos. Government irresponsibility furthered this, as Estrada secretly authorized the printing of large amounts of paper money. In November a Conservative government, organized with the mediation and counsel of special United States Envoy Thomas Dawson, achieved some order. The Dawson Agreement provided that Estrada would continue as President, but it established a United States–Nicaraguan commission to rule on claims against the government arising from the revolution and cancellation of concessions granted by Zelaya. It also promised negotiation of a loan treaty with the United States. When disorder continued, it seemed likely that the United States might try to impose the sort of fiscal controls it had applied in Santo Domingo. An election confirmed Estrada's presidency, but in May 1911, threatened with military revolt by General Luis Mena, Estrada resigned in favor of another Conservative, Vice President Adolfo Díaz. Díaz inaugurated a conservative constitution, restored the privileged position of the Roman Catholic Church (although he preserved religious liberty), and placed the country under the protection of the United States.

The Knox-Castrillo Treaty, signed in June 1911, was never ratified, but it nevertheless served as a basis for the relationship that followed between the United States and Nicaragua. It provided for loans totalling $15 million to Nicaragua and in return it gave the United States the right to protect its interests in that country and to arbitrate any dispute in which Nicaragua became involved. Under its provisions, private loans began to flow from the United States to Nicaragua, and these bound the Díaz government to North American interests even more closely. Meanwhile, the Liberals, who were by no means defeated, continued their assault on the government.

Faced with violence and insurgency both from the Liberals and from dissatisfied Conservatives led by General Emiliano Chamorro Vargas, Díaz asked the United States to send military aid to protect North American interests and to "extend its protection to all the inhabitants of the republic." Taft responded by sending in Marines. They seized the railroad connecting Corinto with the interior and then took over the principal cities. Pressured by the United States Minister, George T. Weitzel, Chamorro withdrew his opposition to Díaz and received as a reward the Nicaraguan Ambassadorship to Washington. With the Marines occupying the country, and with the electorate limited to a few thousand, an election in November 1912 confirmed Díaz, the only candidate on the ballot, in the presidency until 1917. A contingent of Marines remained to guarantee Díaz's security, while United States financial agents took over collection of the country's customs duties and managed the National Bank and railways.

A series of agreements culminating in the Bryan-Chamorro Treaty of 1916 cemented the protectorate status of Nicaragua, while at the same time sabotaging the incipient Central American unification movement. These agreements gave the United States exclusive and perpetual right to construct and operate an interoceanic canal via the San Juan River and Lake Nicaragua and ninety-nine year leases to the Caribbean Corn Islands and to a naval base on the Gulf of Fonseca. In return, Nicaragua received $3 million to be applied against its foreign debt.

The United States Senate had repeatedly refused to ratify treaty recognition of the protectorate status of Nicaragua. Provisions recognizing the United States' right to intervene to maintain Nicaraguan independence or to protect life and property and forbidding Nicaragua to make treaties which jeopardized her independence or territorial integrity, to declare war without United States consent, or to contract public debts beyond her ability to pay had to be deleted from the Bryan-Chamorro Treaty to secure ratification in 1916. The treaty included American supervision over and disbursement of the $3 million, however, and, in effect, Woodrow Wilson and the State Department proceeded as if the protectorate status existed.

Costa Rica, El Salvador, and Honduras all protested against the Bryan-Chamorro Treaty as a violation of their territorial rights and of Central American treaties. The Central American Court of Justice heard the complaints of Costa Rica and El Salvador and ruled in their favor in 1916 and 1917, but Nicaragua and the United States refused to accept the Court's decision. Instead, Nicaragua withdrew from the Central American Court, and, there being no effective way to enforce the ruling, the Court collapsed. A second Washington Conference in 1923 attempted to revive it by establishing a new tribunal of arbitration, but the spirit of 1907 had been destroyed. Although a certain cooperative attitude returned in the 1930's, when the 1923 agreements expired there was no strong sentiment to renew them.

In 1916, with the backing of the United States and a substantial amount of popular support, Emiliano Chamorro won election to the presidency of Nicaragua. The Liberals were prevented from campaigning and the United States officials prevailed upon Díaz's candidate, Dr. Carlos Cuadra Pasos, to withdraw before the election. A relative of the new president, Diego Manuel Chamorro, succeeded Emiliano to the presidency in 1921, again with United States support.

United States military control of Nicaragua during the years 1912-25 was much less total than that exercised in Santo Domingo or Haiti during the period. The Marines were sufficient to maintain the government in power and to protect North American economic interests, but they did not act as the general police of the country. When the government reduced the size of the Nicaraguan Army as a fiscal econ-

omy, banditry and civil strife increased. The United States commitment to reform in Nicaragua was never so complete as it was in the
islands, and a large part of public administration remained with Nicaraguan officials. By 1924, with United States financial interests
healthy and the Nicaraguan debt reduced to a manageable amount
for her economy, there was pressure within the United States to withdraw the Marines. Following the election of 1925, in which the Conservative Party retained control, the Marines withdrew and the new
President, Carlos Solórzano, took office.

New revolutions broke out immediately, however, and United States
interests became alarmed that the Mexican government was supplying
arms to the Nicaraguan revolutionaries. The Marines returned in
1926. Emiliano Chamorro ousted Solórzano from the presidency, but
he himself now faced severe Liberal opposition led by Vice President
Juan Bautista Sacasa. The State Department negotiated a settlement
which brought Adolfo Díaz back to the presidency, but this hardly satisfied the Liberals; warfare resumed, with a growing number of United
States troops and aircraft involved. Nicaragua began to take on some
of the guerrilla aspects of the Mexican Revolution. Guatemala and
Costa Rica offered mediation, but Díaz refused. In May 1927, at Tipitapa, State Department official Henry Stimson succeeded in negotiating a temporary compromise agreement; Díaz would remain President through 1928, when an election would be held under United
States supervision. In the meantime, the United States would participate actively in pacification of the country and help form a National
Guard to police the state. Liberal army chief José María Moncada
agreed to this settlement, perhaps to gain favor with the Americans; at
least it would appear that some kind of a deal was made. Moncada won
the presidency in the 1928 election.

Augusto César Sandino, one of Moncada's lieutenants, refused to accept the agreement, however, and he continued the guerrilla warfare.
Operating in the rugged terrain from Matagalpa northeastward, Sandino proved too elusive for either Nicaraguan or United States forces.

While both Moncada and the Marines struggled against Sandino,
Moncada worked actively to terminate the protectorate. Unlike Díaz,

he was not willing to be simply a puppet. But the North Americans controlled his regime from a number of points: the American Embassy; the Marines, who occupied the state as a conquered territory; the Guardia Nacional, with its United States Army officers; the High Commissioner of Customs; the Director of the Railway; and the National Bank. While Moncada collaborated with these foreign managers of his country, he also worked to bring a peaceful end to the United States occupation. His efforts were responsible for the transfer of the unpopular United States Minister, Charles C. Eberhardt, to Costa Rica early in 1930, but troop withdrawals did not come quickly enough to satisfy the more radical elements. Sandino attracted leftist sympathizers, although he publicly rejected the support of the Communist International. Yet his connections with Mexican leftists and his anti-Yankee movement made him the natural hero of Marxists everywhere.

In 1932 the North Americans supervised another election, probably as fair a one as any ever held in the state. The Liberals again won, Juan Bautista Sacasa gaining the presidency in a campaign in which he called for United States withdrawal. Herbert Hoover accepted the verdict willingly, and in January 1933 the last of the North American troops left Nicaragua. The military intervention was over, but the United States economic and commercial domination remained strong, as it did throughout the isthmus by this time. Aside from removal of the United States military occupation forces, the Liberals made no real break from United States domination. On the contrary, as elsewhere in Central America, the Liberal leaders collaborated willingly and profitably with North American interests, both private and government.

Although Nicaragua was the only Central American state actually to suffer a long-term United States occupation, intervention threatened the others as well. From 1911 through 1924 the United States was instrumental in mediating differences among political leaders in Honduras, and military intervention was always a possibility there. Woodrow Wilson abandoned his dedication to the preservation of constitutional governments in the case of Guatemala when it became apparent that the Estrada Cabrera government was no longer the best protector of United States interests. The United States State Department's intimation that it would not oppose the overthrow of Estrada was a major factor in his ouster in 1920.

The policy of the United States government in the early decades of the twentieth century clearly agreed with the process of economic domination by North American capital interests. By 1930 Central America was intimately tied to the North American economy by its dependence on North American markets, loans, customs regulations, and military missions, and the threat of armed intervention hung over any state that challenged the North American hegemony. The reaction against neocolonialism and the retreat from active intervention that had taken place within the United States beginning with the Republican administrations of the 1920's were not fully understood in Central America. Not until the election of Franklin Roosevelt and the declaration of the "Good Neighbor Policy" was there a willingness in Central America to believe that United States imperialism was on the wane. Nevertheless, by his foreign policy Roosevelt was highly successful in establishing friendly relations with the governments which emerged in the 1930's, so that all of the Central American governments were virtual satellites of the United States by the time World War II began. This process was completed by military, educational, economic, and cultural missions which had their roots in wartime policy. New forces were at work, however, that would challenge Central America's colonial status and the continued social injustice and economic inequality in its states.

The Liberals who dominated the late nineteenth century and early twentieth century had promised both political freedom and material progress. For most Central Americans they had sacrificed the former to achieve the latter for a select few. The order which the Positivists had said should accompany the progress was notably lacking on the isthmus. Yet the strong grip of the elite, who had control of the military and cooperation of powerful foreign elements, made change difficult, if not impossible. The Liberals had taken Central America out of its economic isolation and placed it unequivocally in the mainstream

of neo-colonialism. The accompanying economic growth and modernization of the capitals achieved some of their goals, but it also hastened
the growth of larger middle sectors who would not forever accept exclusion from power. Inevitably, as these sectors began to share the
crumbs of the economic growth, they demanded larger political and
social privileges as well.

Chapter 8 • The Challenge to Liberalism

The reforms and policies of the New Liberals and their alliances with foreign economic interests contributed to the rapid growth of urban centers in Central America. Efforts to modernize and develop the national capitals—and, occasionally, other towns—vastly widened the gap between city and country, making the cities attractive and providing the lure of employment and economic advancement to the people of the rural areas. Thus, along with modern buildings, wide boulevards, monuments and parks, factories and airports, there grew poverty pockets that mushroomed into huge slums around the outskirts and even within older sections of every Central American capital. Control of epidemic diseases, improved medical care, and a corresponding drop in infant mortality led to startling increases in population in all of the states. Caught in the revolution of rising expectations, these new urban dwellers became active participants in political and social movements. Since they were denied adequate opportunities to achieve their expectations, they were open to persuasion by skilled political leaders and demagogues at political rallies and demonstrations. They were omnipresent reminders of the failure of the Positivist development program to provide a general base of prosperity and progress.

Central American cities and the societies they encompass have changed radically since the mid-nineteenth century, when they were primitive and remote from most of the conveniences and pleasures of western civilization. Originally the centers of administrative activity, they became the social and economic centers for each state as well. They emerged as minor imitations of New York and Paris, although in appearance they were more like New Orleans or Miami.

Only Tegucigalpa, capital of Honduras, departed from this pattern. As the mining boom subsided and the banana and shipping industry concentrated on the Caribbean coast, which was still not well connected to the interior of the country, that area developed a more cosmopolitan flavor, while Tegucigalpa slipped backward into the role of a sleepy, provincial capital. It retained that picturesque old charm which became submerged in the other Central American capitals. Not until the 1970's did the city begin to take on a "modern" appearance. La Ceiba and, eventually, San Pedro Sula, more properly reflected the social and economic changes brought on by Positivism in Honduras.

None of the Central American countries, with the possible exception of Costa Rica, had a dominant middle class, yet during the first half of the twentieth century middle sectors emerged in the capital cities as important, identifiable elements in the population. New and rapid modes of transportation—streetcars, later replaced by buses and mini-buses, supplemented by private motorcycles and automobiles—gave the middle-class workers and the professionals new mobility and freedom. Living patterns changed perceptibly. The indoor bathroom became one of the major differences between rural and city living, between the middle and lower classes. The upper classes provided a thin veneer of culture and refinement in more traditional European terms. The emerging middle class worshipped the material culture which so characterized the Positivist dream, often in imitation of the more garish aspects of North American life. Through expanding educational systems and communications, the children of peasants who had never been beyond the horizons of Sacatepéquez or Matagalpa now became aware of a larger world, of events in Europe and North Amer-

ica, of a glossy paradise to the north—at least as it was presented by
Hollywood film-makers. Daily newspapers sprang up in profusion
from the 1890's forward, many lasting only a short time, but some
achieving a degree of popularity and respectability. Their circulations
were small by the rest of the world's standards, but they had a major
impact on Central American thought. By the mid-1920's the leader was
La Prensa of San Salvador, with a circulation of about 5000. Close
behind were *Nuestro Diario* of Guatemala and *El Diario de Costa
Rica*, each with about 4000 daily, although the newly formed *El Imparcial* would soon surpass *Nuestro Diario* in Guatemala. In Tegucigalpa and Managua, *El Cronista* and *El Comercio,* respectively, served
about 3000 readers each. All these papers had several competitors.
Even today, the quality of most Central American journalism has not
achieved a very high standard of credibility or professionalism, but
newspapers nevertheless played an important role in informing the
public and in stimulating its interest in political and economic affairs,
as well as in social and cultural activities.

The growth of leisure time activities among blue-collar and white-
collar workers reflected the improved economic conditions. Bicycling,
already important as a means of transportation, became a popular
sport. Cyclists raced both in enclosed parks and cross-country over
Central America's spectacular topography. European and North American cultural influence was increasingly evident. Tennis and polo developed some popularity among the upper and upper-middle classes,
as did golf, eventually, although soccer was much more popular among
middle groups, both as a spectator and participant sport. Interest in
bullfighting diminished in popularity, and the Plaza de Toros in Guatemala, destroyed by the great earthquakes of 1917-18, has never been
rebuilt. There are occasional bullfights at major fairs or celebrations,
but the activity has lost the popularity it still commands in Spain,
Colombia, or Mexico. Baseball, introduced into Central America as
early as 1880, grew rapidly after 1900. Actively promoted by recrea-
tional programs of the United Fruit Company and by individuals of
the North American business and diplomatic colony, it was taken up
by amateurs, and, eventually, professional baseball leagues were or-

ganized. Basketball and boxing also gained adherents, although the Central Americans, most of whom are small in stature, did not achieve much notice when they entered international contests. More recently, automobile racing has become popular. The more traditional Central American sport of cockfighting diminished, although the gambling on which it had thrived continued as an important pastime for many.

Newspapers and magazines, later, the radio, and, still later, television contributed to a revolution in marketing and consumption. Advertising, as well as news and sports features, created appetites for a wider range of products. Most were imports from the United States or Europe, but the growing market created opportunities for a range of small, local manufactures. The expansion of cigarette smoking is an obvious example. Central American men and even some women had long smoked cigars. The early twentieth century, however, witnessed a massive increase in cigarette consumption, particularly among women. Advertisements and motion pictures popularized this and other North American customs and gradually broke down more traditional Hispanic and Indian taboos regarding freedom of movement, sex, and morals. More employment opportunities became available to Central America's daughters, especially in government offices and, subsequently, in private businesses. Notwithstanding these changes, the women of Central America failed to achieve the rights and privileges that women in more developed nations gained at this time.

Wider extension of credit was another aspect of the change taking place. Although Central America lagged far behind the United States in adopting wide-open credit plans, there was growing acceptance of installment buying, with both merchant and bank credit permitting greater consumption, particularly of larger appliances and housing. This in turn stimulated growth in construction industries, which helped to answer the problems of the burgeoning urban populations. Suburban housing at a wide range of prices developed in all the capitals. Tegucigalpa again was somewhat the exception, but San Pedro Sula followed the trend. Automobiles and traffic jams, accompanied this centrifugal imitation of North American cities, particularly after

World War II. Some Central American cities, notably Guatemala and San José, have also acquired serious air pollution.

By no means, however, did all Central Americans enjoy the new affluence accompanying the emergence of larger middle sectors, and thus the economic and social change was less pronounced than that produced, for example, in the United States in the 1920's or in Argentina in the 1940's. Not only did severe economic and social ills persist, they increased. In the urban slums, which lacked the moral restraints of the rural communities, crime, illegitimacy, venereal disease, and desperate poverty became serious problems. Health services failed to meet either their physiological or their psychological needs. No Central American government has yet dealt realistically with these problems to any great degree.

The small upper classes, spread over five provincial capitals and spending much of their time abroad anyway, could not patronize a tradition of artistic or cultural development comparable to that of the larger capitals of Latin America. Twentieth-century Central American theater, painting, and literature are not very impressive. Rubén Darío (Félix Rubén García y Sarmiento) and Miguel Ángel Asturias are obvious exceptions, but, although they both employed Central American subjects in their works, they spent most of their lives away from their native lands. There are virtually no Central American playwrights. The motion picture industry and, more recently, television have enjoyed great popularity among all classes, and through their foreign fare they have done much to shape the desires and expectations of the Central American people.

The institutions of government served the interests of those who controlled the economy, often through harsh dictatorships, but always through a system which contradicted the constitutional phrases and campaign rhetoric about democracy and liberty. Political bosses held the keys to the system, and the principal political bosses were the chiefs of state. This was so even in Costa Rica, where democracy had made the most progress. Corrupt judges, government bureaucrats, and political appointees managed the government to suit the wishes of the estab-

lishment, and those who wished to get ahead learned to play the game
of bribery, influence, and family contacts. The excess of lawyers and
law students reflected the willingness of the middle sectors to prepare
themselves to play that game. Rigged elections or intimidation of the
opposition secured the positions of the bosses. The army was and continues to be the arbiter, for it alone has the power to change the bosses.
A positivistic professionalism in the military has not extended to non-
interference in government. In fact, the military remains one of the
principal routes for middle-class—and, occasionally, lower-class—elements to rise to higher position in the country.

Newer groups or institutions of the developing middle class have
become stronger than they were, however, and toward the middle of
the twentieth century they began to challenge more effectively the
domination of the oligarchies' Liberal governments. Two groups, products of Liberal reforms, have been especially noteworthy: organized
urban labor and the university students and intellectuals.

Urban growth made inevitable the development of labor organizations. Because of relatively slight industrialization, the comparatively
small size of Central American cities, and the tiny numbers of working-
class immigrants from areas of strong labor organization, this movement developed more slowly than in Europe, the United States, or
Latin American cities such as Buenos Aires, Mexico, Valparaíso, and
Havana. Dictators such as Estrada Cabrera and Zelaya viewed labor
organization as subversive to the interests of capital growth and to
peace and order. They suppressed strikes and labor demonstrations
with armed force. At most, they tolerated state-controlled mutual aid
societies. Legislation which was progressive in the eyes of merchants,
manufacturers, foreign investors, and other employers overlooked or actually repressed the rights of labor in the early twentieth century.
Most industrial establishments were small shops run by family interests. Workers had little opportunity to organize on either an industry-
wide or a company basis. Even textile manufacture was on a small
scale, and government and management alike frowned on unionization.
Paternalism was the rule.

Less than 10 per cent of the active working force of Central America resided and worked in the five capitals, yet they represented a potentially important force because of their concentration at the centers of political power and their ready availability for organization. As they gained economically and became educated, they began to participate more actively as political and social forces. Prior to 1920 the feeble labor organizations in Central America exercised slight influence, but after that date a freer political atmosphere in several states permitted labor's proponents to begin more effectual activity.

Labor organization in Central America became identified with Marxism early. Shortly after Estrada Cabrera's overthrow, a small, radical group of Guatemalan arsenal workers and students formed the nucleus for Central America's first Communist Party, which joined the Comintern in 1924. The government periodically suppressed its publications and discouraged its activities, but it nevertheless spearheaded the organization of a Central American Labor Council (COCA), which served as a headquarters for promoting trade union organization and communist propaganda from 1925 to 1930. It helped communists in Honduras and El Salvador make similar beginnings, although violent repression in the latter state in 1925 retarded the labor movement there. By 1928 trade union membership in Central America had reached some 5000. Pro-labor periodicals had appeared in Guatemala, Nicaragua, and Costa Rica.

Throughout Central America, labor made legislative advances, to some degree because of pressure from local labor organizations, but probably more because of the pressure from the League of Nations and the International Labor Organization, which was trying to establish minimum world labor standards. Guatemala ratified the I.L.O.'s 1919 standards in 1926. Certainly the example of the Mexican Revolution, in which, by the 1920's, organized labor had come to play a major role, must have intimidated some Central American politicians into supporting minimum labor benefits, such as laws limiting the industrial workweek to forty-eight hours, extra pay for overtime, workman's compensation laws, low-cost housing projects for workers, laws limiting the number of alien workers, and so forth. Legislation, of course, did not necessarily mean enforcement or implementation, and the workers' actual standards of living improved only slightly. But by the time of the Great Depression, urban labor constituted an incipient institutional force, one rather closely identified with international Marxism. The movement still represented only a tiny minority of Central American working people, but it had great potential strength.

The university students and intellectuals became a force as the natural result of the emphasis which the Liberals had placed on education. As I have already said, the sort of education they promoted did not stimulate much creative thinking in arts, humanities, or even the social sciences, but it did promote the development of more universities and more schooling in general for the emerging middle sectors. The availability of education offered the middle class the opportunity for advancement in the society, and the universities became essentially middle-class institutions in the twentieth century. A few of the students were sons of the urban working class, although most of them came from the professional and landholding classes; the wealthier members of society usually sent their children abroad for higher education. University education vastly accelerated the expectations of the middle class. Many young people studied law in order to have a profession, in order to establish themselves along traditional lines, but their studies also brought home to them the glaring deficiencies, inequalities, and injustices in Central American society. The Mexican and Russian revolutions, moreover, presented ideological alternatives to students who were searching for answers to their countries' problems. The university reforms which had begun in Córdoba, Argentina, in 1917 had had a major effect on the Central American universities. These reforms brought students into university administration, and they soon demanded recognition of university autonomy. As a result, the universities ultimately became highly politicized; they became not only forums for national politics, but—literally—battlegrounds at times.

The Mexican and Russian constitutions of 1917, as well as subsequent influences from those countries, suggested goals for many Central Americans who wished to throw off the North American domination. Once having been graduated, most students moderated their radical views as they became involved in making a living and advancing within the established system of Central America, but a nucleus of lawyers, teachers, and other professional men formed a cadre of leadership for more progressive development. From their ranks eventually would come new political and labor leaders, influential journalists, and diplomats to champion social revolution on the isthmus.

They were not all leftist radicals, for fascism appealed to some. But they tended to agree that their states needed government planning and direction of the economy, whether under a socialist system or one of controlled capitalism. The world-wide rise of nationalism coincided with a growing consciousness among Central Americans of the isthmus' status as an area of developing nations. Intent upon identifying their own cultural and political heritage, they assumed hostile attitudes toward the foreigners who dominated the region. Their nationalism, often rooted in resentment, fear, frustration, and a sense of inferiority, was frequently angry and violent. It had a contagious effect on other elements of the population.

Despite the growth of university communities and considerable building of schools between 1870 and 1930, Central American education lagged woefully. Salvador Mendieta estimated that by 1926 no more than 150,000 of the 5,500,000 Central Americans could read and write. His estimate may have been low, but even official statistics of the governments, when compared with those of other Latin American states, do not suggest great advancement. Moreover, pedagogy lagged. Memorization was about the only intellectual activity most Central Americans engaged in from childhood. Shortages of books and other materials accounted for part of the reliance on rote memory as the principal teaching device, but unimaginative teacher training and little contact with international intellectual circles explain it better. A few preparatory schools, such as the Liceo Centroamericano in Granada, were somewhat respectable, but the schools run by the foreign diplomatic and business colonies generally offered the best education, and children whose parents could afford them went to those schools.

Costa Rica easily led the way in educational development. Compulsory school attendance laws date from 1828, but real efforts at implementation of the goals implied by early Liberal legislation did not begin until the late nineteenth century. Education was regularly the largest single item in the Costa Rican budget in the twentieth century. In 1940 the University of Costa Rica was organized. It was made up of existing professional schools to which were added additional faculties, and it was the most advanced institution of higher education in Central America. It was the first to employ full-time faculties, build a central library, and integrate university expansion with national economic and social goals. In the 1960's the university served as the nucleus for expanded research and publication and gave great impetus to the arts. It became the seat of a united publishing program (EDUCA) for all the Central American national universities. Establishment of a second national university in 1972 in Heredia promised continuation of Costa Rican innovative leadership in higher education.

The Church, once so important in education, had a greatly diminished role, but one which did not disappear altogether. It continued to be an important moral force in some rural communities and among the wealthier classes in the cities. In Guatemala, Indian *cofradías* (lay fraternities) continued to be important governing and social elements locally, but their ties to the Church grew tenuous as priests became scarce. To some degree, returning to the Church became a status symbol among the rising middle class. Protestant missions provided practical educational and health benefits in some area, but their influence was local and could not bring general change. More recently, Roman Catholic missions have begun to restore the Church's influence. However, the progressive attitude of some foreign missionaries—Maryknollers and Jesuits, for example—has created friction with the local, more traditional clergy. In the 1960's the Church began to play a renewed role in higher education, and it was notably important in organizing the Universidad Centroamericana in Managua and the Universidad Rafael Landívar in Guatemala.

While change in the capitals was obvious, rural life in early twentieth-century Central America remained much as it had been a century earlier. The wide gulf in living conditions between city and country encouraged the migration of rural people to the cities. Methods of cultivation changed little except in the areas of export commodity plantations, where coffee or bananas received scientific attention. The cooperation of the government with the landlords in maintaining an inexpensive and docile labor force succeeded in checking most efforts at social change before the 1940's, and agricultural workers were exploited in all of the Central American states. Exploitation was worst in Guatemala, but it was nearly as bad in El Salvador and Nicaragua. Honduras remained more paternalistic and at the same time was more widely characterized by subsistence farming and minifundia. Costa Rica, where the coffee farms were often small, differed in that its government began early to pay attention to the welfare of all of its people. Illiteracy was high among peasants everywhere, including Costa Rica. Whereas a middle class was clearly emerging in the cities, no such phenomenon occurred in rural areas, where there were lords and peasants. The few day laborers, artisans, and merchants did not amount to a separate class.

Costa Rica, however, was politically and socially unique among the Central American states as the twentieth century opened. Historically, this uniqueness was the product of her relative remoteness from the remainder of Central America, her slight economic importance to Spain, and her lack of a non-white subservient class and corresponding lack of a class of large landholders to exploit its labors. Hispanic institutions were never as heavily fastened on Costa Rica's sparse population as on the rest of Central America.

The economy of Costa Rica permitted wider popular participation in politics and the development of more egalitarian political institutions than elsewhere. While it is true that Costa Rica led the way in the development of both native-owned coffee production and foreign-owned banana production, along with foreign domination of various aspects of the transportation industry, social and economic patterns of ownership and control did not create the small, wealthy oligarchies which were typical of the other four states. This was in part because of the absence of an Indian or Negro working force. Whites comprised about 80 per cent of the state's population by 1925; Negroes made up roughly 4 per cent, and most of them were West Indian banana workers, concentrated on the coasts. Mestizos amounted to 14 per cent of the population, while Indians were less than 1 per cent. The coffee industry developed on family-sized farms, permitting a wide distribution of wealth. It is true that certain families acquired greater wealth than others, and a coffee elite did develop, but it was not to the exclusion of an agrarian middle sector, which virtually did not exist in the other states. There was no significant landless class in the countryside, and new lands were being sold as the population expanded beyond the Central Valley. This agrarian middle sector, together with a more literate and democratically oriented urban population than that found elsewhere in Central America, was responsible for checks being placed on foreign domination of the economic life of the country. These checks were absent in the other Central American states. The Liberals did not dominate the period, so they could not sell out the country to the foreigners.

As early as 1909 the Costa Rican government began to tax the banana industry. Subsequent legislation increased this tax, placed restraints on the UFCO, and required further railroad construction and other benefits to the state. Costa Rican success in getting railroads built in return for exploitation of its banana lands stand in marked contrast to the Honduran experience. The fruit company's enterprise did result in a reemphasis on the Caribbean coast in Costa Rica, however, just as it did in the rest of the isthmus. The development of the railway and trade via Limón reduced the importance of the Pacific port of Puntarenas in the twentieth century. Limón grew as Puntarenas declined.

During the first third of the twentieth century, Costa Rican governments, regardless of their political affiliation, were more responsive to popular needs and moved to enact more advanced social legislation than did those of the other states. The state, or private and religious institutions with state assistance, built hospitals and other institutions to care for the sick, the aged, orphans, and the unfortunate. A state lottery supported these services. The government established a National Insurance Company. Health and sanitation provisions made Costa Rica the healthiest state in Central America, and, in cooperation with the United Fruit Company, the government waged major campaigns against malaria, hookworm, yellow fever, and other tropical diseases. By the 1950's there was one physician for every 2700 inhabitants in Costa Rica, as compared with one per 6300 in Guatemala (the worst of any Latin American country except Haiti), 5400 in El Salvador, 4800 in Honduras, 3300 in Panama, and 2900 in Nicaragua.

Constitutional government in Costa Rica gradually came to have greater success than elsewhere on the isthmus. In 1889 the Liberals had accepted electoral defeat. Conservative return to power ushered in a period of instability during which political allegiances sometimes became confused and opportunistic. The Liberals regained the upper hand for brief periods, but moderate Conservatives Cleto González Víquez (1906-10 and 1928-32) and Richardo Jiménez Oreamuno (1910-14, 1924-28, and 1932-36) dominated the early twentieth century. They did much, not only to restore peace to the state, but also to move it forward politically toward more democratic processes.

Elsewhere in Central America, barely discernible tendencies toward democratic process in the 1920's met a sharp reaction as a result of the hardships accompanying the Great Depression. The military dictators who emerged in Guatemala, El Salvador, Honduras, and Nicaragua had many of the characteristics of the New Liberals of a half-century earlier, but in the mid-twentieth century they seemed conservative to the rest of the world. Branding all attempts toward social reform as "communist," they dealt firmly, even brutally, with all who challenged existing conditions. In retrospect, these dictatorships appear to have been desperate, rear-guard efforts to save the New Liberal oligarchies and foreign investments from the growing popular force of working people and youth.

The collapse of the western capitalist economy in 1929 brought swift repercussions to the Central American oligarchies, for they depended upon exports for which markets and prices now declined rapidly. As in Europe and America, workers responded to the hard times with demonstrations, and they often resorted to violence. The utter inability of the existing governments to cope with the problem led to greater faith in more authoritarian regimes, and many of the people felt the lure of the fascist example of Italy or the socialist example of the Soviet Union. The questioning of democratic liberalism was widespread among the leading political figures in Central America, and fear of communist agitation reached a high pitch, enabling strong-arm dictators to seize power in four of the five Central American republics. Even in Costa Rica there were riots and worker uprisings, and these led to a suppression of civil guarantees early in 1932. Costa Rica's National Republican Party rose to power on the strength of its promises of reform and alternatives to communism to solve the social issues. Other Central American states produced no such effective alternatives. In those states, where more powerful oligarchies feared the masses and where the middle classes had not yet gained control of the political system, right-wing dictatorship resulted.

General Jorge Ubico emerged as Guatemala's dictator. Elected freely in 1931, Ubico moved swiftly to establish peace and order. To solidify his position, he absorbed most of the authority of the government into the executive branch. In 1932 he launched a vigorous war on the communists. He ordered ten of them executed, including Juan Pablo Wainwright, the Honduran communist organizer. Refugees from the unsuccessful leftist revolt in El Salvador of the same year suffered imprisonment. The purge reached its peak in 1934, when Ubico uncovered and crushed unmercifully a conspiracy against himself. A wave of assassinations, executions, long prison terms, and exiles removed all opposition. *Time* magazine quoted Ubico as saying, after the purge, "I have no friends, only domesticated enemies." The campaign destroyed the Communist Party in Guatemala. Those leaders who were not killed or exiled fled the country or stayed out of sight. Other opposition parties were neutralized as effectively. Labor organizations suffered a similar fate; the government disbanded unions and executed or exiled their leaders. Only closely controlled mutual aid societies and skilled craft guilds survived. A leftist organization continued to operate underground, but by 1940 it was no more than a skeleton organization, with most of its leaders in Mexico or El Salvador.

All opposition silenced, Ubico stabilized the nation's economy. His government was efficient, and it greatly improved Guatemala's credit, chiefly by granting favorable concessions to foreign enterprises, particularly United States business interests. Although Ubico's policies built up the national treasury and credit abroad, they did little for the average worker, as most of the benefits went to foreign capitalists or local managers. Extensive public works projects employed forced labor, while foreigners enjoyed privileges which were barred to most nationals. Significantly, in 1934 Ubico transferred the Department of Labor from the Development Ministry to the supervision of the National Police. Working conditions deteriorated as inflation forced prices up while wages either remained constant or declined.

Through demagoguery and patronage Ubico cultivated support among the agrarian working class. His political machine relied on occasional popular support among Guatemala's Indian masses. He reduced the power of the landlords over the peasants by abolishing debt slavery, while at the same time he increased government control over labor. A vagrancy law assured a supply of labor to the coffee planters, but Ubico's political bosses were able to control that labor force so that it might be used for government projects or, more to the point, as a means of government control of the landowners. Growing pressure from international organizations finally prompted a minimum wage law in Guatemala in July 1943, but it is doubtful that it made much difference. The real standard of living for rural Guatemalans remained deplorably low. Their labor provided them with only the barest essentials for survival.

Ubico, a few Guatemalans, and the foreigners profited handsomely, and they banked their money in New Orleans, New York, or Europe. A garrison of ragged, barefoot National Police kept order in each village under the orders of the local intendente or provincial governor. Crimes against foreigners earned swift and harsh punishment. An efficient secret service under the direction of Roderico Anzueto kept the dictator informed of nascent plots of organized resistance. Anti-intellectual and fearful of innovation, Ubico permitted no discussion of Guatemala's problems or social structure. The material improvements, the hundreds of miles of new roads, the diplomatic victories in disputes over sparsely populated border areas which he made were relatively minor gains when so few enjoyed their advantages.

El Salvador's development through World War II closely paralleled that of Guatemala. As coffee prices plummeted owing to the Great Depression, democratic tendencies in the tiny republic on the Pacific abruptly ended. The military ousted mildly socialistic Arturo Araujo in December 1931 and installed Vice President Maximiliano Hernández Martínez in the presidency. Hernández quickly reversed the leftist trend. A peasant uprising in January 1932 resulted in the murder of several landlords. The peasants then started to set up a collective regime, and government troops massacred thousands in response. Hernández, who was sympathetic to fascist solutions, was among the first to recognize Francisco Franco's Spanish Falangist government in 1936. Hernández ended whatever earlier threats there had been to the coffee barons' power. Not until 1942 were there serious protests against the government, and then they came from the military and students. These people were younger members of the middle class who had grown restless under the dictatorship and were demanding a change.

The Depression dictator of Honduras, Tiburcio Carías Andino, was less ruthless than his counterparts in Guatemala or El Salvador, but otherwise he had many of the same characteristics. Carías had developed the popular National Party in opposition to the Liberals in the 1920's and had himself received a plurality of the votes cast for president in 1923. His opponents had prevented him from taking office then, but when violence resulted the United States mediated the quarrel. In a new election Carías's choice, Miguel Paz Baraona, won, and he served until 1929. The Liberals recovered the presidency in the 1928 elections, although Carías's National Party retained control of

Congress. In 1932 Carías won the presidency, and this time he overcame Liberal efforts to deny him the victory. Then he, as had Ubico and Hernández, successfully consolidated his power into a dictatorship and managed to remain in power without standing another election until 1948. Carías suppressed the frequent Liberal revolts, though with less brutality than that displayed by his neighbors of the same period. His administration was not as spectacular in achievement as those of his neighbors were, although he pursued a program of public works and road construction which slightly improved the economic situation of this poorest of Central American republics. He promoted coffee production, especially in the northwestern department of Santa Bárbara, but also in Comayagua, Yoro, Olancho, and El Paraíso, and Honduras joined the other states of the isthmus as a major coffee exporter. Bananas remained the primary export, however.

Having experienced United States intervention most of the time between 1912 and 1933, Nicaragua developed somewhat differently than any of the other Central American states. North American capital flowed heavily into the state following World War I, and United States economic interests became dominant in the country. Under Conservative rule Nicaragua's progress toward democratic government was negligible, despite United States efforts to ensure free elections. Fear of leftist elements among the backers of Sandino, who had communists with him and was recognized by the Comintern as a progressive force, contributed to a desire on the part of the United States to provide greater political freedom for moderate parties as a check against communist gains, but the victory of the anti-interventionist Liberals in 1932 was, nevertheless, a blow to United States prestige. Hoover withdrew United States forces gracefully after the Sandino threat appeared to have been checked.

In February 1934, President Juan Bautista Sacasa met with Sandino in an effort to reach a peace agreement. After their dinner, however, National Guardsmen treacherously assassinated the guerrilla leader. Sacasa himself may have been innocent of any murderous intent, but his nephew, General Anastasio Somoza García, head of the National Guard, effectively thwarted all efforts to punish the guilty parties. In effect, Somoza became the master of Nicaragua from that moment forward, although he did not technically become President until after his election in December 1936, an election in which the only other candidate was in exile.

In subsequent years "Tacho" Somoza built the strongest and most durable family dynasty in Latin American history. Ruthlessly crushing all opposition—particularly that from the left, where Marxists had been trying to organize labor and students—he concentrated all authority in his own hands and shared it only with members of his political family. A neo-Positivist, he emphasized material progress, public works, and production and minimized political liberty and the rights of labor. He improved public education and health services. He was anticlerical and completed the efforts of earlier Liberals in Nicaragua to disestablish the Roman Catholic Church. He controlled the press and prevented serious opposition from gaining platforms. In time, he reached an accommodation with the Conservative Party, permitting it to function and exist, but only as a loyal opposition. Even though Conservative editors and politicians might occasionally become vehement in their attacks, and riots or other violence might occasionally disturb the peace and order, Somoza and his successors saw to it that the Conservatives remained a minority.

Somoza abandoned the anti-United States posture of the Liberals and accepted Franklin Roosevelt's offers of friendship. He received increasingly large amounts of United States economic and military assistance thereafter. Symbolic of the close relationship that developed between the governments of Nicaragua and the United States, first as a result of the intervention and later as a result of Somoza's policies, was the location of the United States Embassy: it was virtually on the grounds of the Presidential Palace.

Somoza himself did not remain continuously in the presidential office, but there was never any doubt as to who ruled. At the close of World War II, when revolutions were ending the dictatorships in other Central American states, Somoza successfully tightened his hold. In 1947 "Tacho" stepped aside to allow the election of Leonardo Argüello. When Argüello proved to be an unwilling puppet and attempted to remove his mentor, however, Somoza's Congress quickly declared him incapacitated, removed him from office, and sent him into exile. Provisional President Benjamín Lacayo Sacasa convened a Constituent Assembly which produced a Constitution to Somoza's liking and then elected seventy-five-year-old Manuel Román Reyes as President. However, Román Reyes died a few months later and the Congress then elected Somoza to finish the term. In 1950 he won another new Constitution that gave him dictatorial powers.

The key to Somoza's power in Nicaragua was not solely his command of the National Guard, which did provide muscle when needed. He also created a broadly based empire. He acquired land and commercial establishments and became the largest property holder in the state. Since the Somoza family often operated through associates, it is impossible to know the precise size of their economic empire, but it has been estimated that by 1970 they owned more than half of the agricultural production of the republic and had vast financial resources invested in industry, mining, and commerce both in Nicaragua and abroad. This economic control easily enabled the Somozas to eliminate serious competition and neutralize opposition even while they pointed with pride to statistical gains in Nicaraguan production, per capita wealth, health services, literacy, and economic conditions.

One effect of the Somozas' concentration of wealth was the growth of Managua, which had been largely destroyed by earthquake and fire in 1931. It became a bustling and modern city, while the traditional centers of León and Granada decayed and declined in importance. In numerous ways, the Somozas concentrated economic, political, social, and cultural power in the capital city at the expense of the old rival centers. (The 1972 earthquake, of course, demolished most of Managua, but the regime moved deliberately toward its reconstruction.)

In the early 1950s opposition to Somoza's political rule grew. The strongest discontent developed in traditionally Conservative Granada, for Somoza closed the university there and transferred its operation to León. As Somoza's large economic interests became more evident, there was opposition to the unequal landholding system in the country. Somoza responded to attacks on his regime with more repression, particularly after he narrowly escaped assassination in April 1954, but he also made some efforts toward more liberal social legislation. A social security system was established, women were given the right to vote, and an advanced Labor Code went into effect. Somoza was clearly learning fascist lessons: he attempted to create a block of labor support through a state-controlled trade union organization. Following Somoza's nomination by the Liberals in 1956 for yet another term, an assassin shot him. President Eisenhower sent his personal surgeon to attend the dictator, but on September 29 Somoza died in a Canal Zone hospital.

A discernible trend toward political liberalization followed the assassination of Anastasio Somoza, but there was no real progress toward restructuring the society. The elder of Somoza's two sons, Luis Somoza Debayle, succeeded his father. The other son, Anastasio, Jr. ("Tachito"), commanded the National Guard. Under their direction the Somoza political and economic empire continued to grow, to such a degree that some observers have referred to Nicaragua as a family fief. In an election held in 1957, Luis received 89 per cent of the votes cast. A long-time Somoza associate, René Schick, succeeded him to the presidency in 1963. The Conservative candidate, Diego Manuel Chamorro, Jr., declared that he had not been allowed to campaign freely, and many Conservatives boycotted the election or voted blank ballots. The Somozas remained firmly in charge, however. In 1967 a heart attack took the life of Luis Somoza, leaving Tachito in sole control.

Interestingly, the Somozas cultivated closer relations with the Mexican government, in part because they hoped for expanding trade and cultural exchanges, but also, it appears, because they wished to imitate the one-party political structure which has been so successful for the Mexican Revolutionary Institutional Party (PRI). That the PRI has stood for substantial structural reforms and socialist institutions seems not to have deterred the Nicaraguan interest. During the Schick administration several opposition parties were politically active, but Tachito Somoza won the 1967 presidential election easily. He agreed to include Conservatives in the government in 1972, but the devastating earthquake of December of that year led to reestablishment of a tight military rule, which Somoza justified on the ground of the need for unity during the economic and social reconstruction of the country. As in Honduras, national disaster was used as an excuse for a return to militarist rule. Nicaragua's forty years of relative political peace, however, permitted modest increases in per capita income, health services, education, and public works. Nevertheless, most of Nicaragua remained underdeveloped and poor.

The Liberal parties and the oligarchies they represented remained strong in most of Central America through the first half of the twentieth century. They achieved considerable modernization of their countries, although most still lagged behind much of the rest of Latin America in social and economic development by the criteria of the United States and western Europe. Yet the middle and working classes had been awakened and were beginning to challenge the exclusive domination of politics by these oligarchies. The oligarchies thus turned more and more to the military to protect their privileged status. This allowed the military to become a powerful institutional power in its own right. The latter half of the twentieth century would see these challenges take increasingly revolutionary forms as they further eroded the old order.

Chapter 9 • Central America in the Age of Social Revolution

Significant changes had begun to occur in all the Central American states before the end of World War II. The term "Social Revolution" may imply greater restructuring of society and economy than occurred in many areas, but the middle and working classes had begun to participate in the society, effecting permanent alterations in ruling patterns on the isthmus. Efforts to retain or restore the prewar dictatorships required significant concessions to popular needs and demands.

As impressive as Costa Rican progress had been compared to that of the rest of Central America, there was pressure there also for more radical approaches to development. The growth of the labor movement and education contributed to larger leftist organizations. As the old Conservative and Liberal party labels became meaningless, a major party realignment shaped up in the country. The moderate National Republican Party won a clear majority in 1936 with León Cortés Castro and again in 1940 with Rafael Ángel Calderón Guardia. Calderón sought leftist support, and the National Republicans formed a coalition with the small but militant Popular Vanguard, which was formed in 1943 when the Communist Party dissolved in order to seek a wider base of support. This coalition brought an expanding program of social welfare and reform, including an advanced social security system and labor code, established in 1943. But polarization resulted. Conservatives attacked Calderón's program as "communistic" and formed the Democratic Party in opposition.

The leftist coalition succeeded in holding power in the hotly contested 1944 election, as Calderón's choice, Teodoro Picado Michalski, defeated Cortés Castro (now a Democrat) and the National Republicans won a majority of the Congress. Social reform continued under Picado, who enjoyed the cooperation of Vanguardia leader Manuel Mora Valverde.

In 1946 two new political factions emerged. Otilio Ulate Blanco, publisher of the *Diario de Costa Rica,* organized more moderate conservatives into the vehemently anticommunist National Union Party. In the meantime, a former Conservative politician, José Figueres Ferrer, an aggressive and sometimes demagogic planter whose parents had been Catalan immigrants, organized the moderate leftist, but also anticommunist, Social Democratic Party. Both of the new parties reflected the growing concern over the role of communists in Picado's government. The Social Democrats, ideologically aligned with Social Democratic and Christian Democratic parties in Europe and South America and with the liberal wing of the Democratic Party in the United States, called for establishment of a "Second Republic" in Costa Rica to achieve wider popular participation and benefits. Both parties gained considerable support from opposition to Picado's revolutionary new income tax law, passed in late 1946.

The campaign for the presidency in 1948 loomed as a major turning point in Costa Rican history. In an effort to bring down the National Republicans, the Democrats and Social Democrats agreed to support Ulate against Calderón.

Disputed election returns followed a violent campaign. Two members of the National Electoral Tribunal announced that Ulate had won, but a third member called for further investigation. Then, on March 1, the Calderón-controlled Congress voted to annul the elections. Government troops arrested Ulate and other political leaders.

Rebellion erupted in several quarters. Archbishop Victor Manuel Sanabria y Martínez attempted mediation and achieved the immediate release of Ulate, but fighting continued. The principal opposition was a group called the National Liberation, led by José Figueres, which harassed government forces in the Central Valley. Another group of Figueres's forces, calling themselves the Caribbean Legion, took the port of Limón on April 11 and moved inland quickly to take Cartago and surround the capital. On March 13 most fighting stopped and negotiations began, although communists led by Mora continued to fight until March 19. With assistance from Mexican and United States diplomats, the parties agreed upon Santos León Herrera as Chief of State, and Picado and Calderón went to Nicaragua in exile. Figueres, who soon became a member of Herrera's cabinet, was the man behind the government from that point on.

On May 8 the Junta of the Second Republic, headed by Figueres, formally assumed power. It governed the state until November 1949. The Junta succeeded in restoring order and in repelling an invasion of Calderón forces supported by Anastasio Somoza. (A series of violent but indecisive clashes between forces backed by Somoza against those of Figueres continued intermittently into the 1960's. Figueres became openly committed to the ouster of rightist dictatorships, and Somoza did not hide his disdain for Figueres; each supported exile groups against the other.) Elections in December 1948 revealed that Figueres still enjoyed little popular support, as Ulate's National Union Party (PUN) won thirty-three seats in the Constitutional Assembly. Allied parties won eight seats, while Figueres's Social Democrats took but four.

Despite his lack of a popular mandate, Figueres made notable changes in the structure of Costa Rican government during the period of the Junta. Most significantly, he began the process of dissolving the Costa Rican army, although he kept a reserve force to provide for national defense. It proved adequate to resist the Nicaraguan-based invasions. He also outlawed the communist Popular Vanguard, nationalized the Costa Rican banks, placed a 10 per cent tax on private capital to pay for administrative changes, established agencies to promote agricultural production and to control inflation, promoted development of power resources, and, finally, drafted a new Constitution for consideration by the Constituent Assembly.

Understandably, the more conservative Assembly rejected Figueres's Constitution (March 1949). Rejecting the concept of a "Second Republic," they adopted a Constitution which differed little from their existing document. Under its terms, Ulate took office on November 8, 1949.

Ulate slowed the pace of social reform, but he did not stop it. Because he wanted to stabilize the nation's finances and improve its foreign credit, he was more cautious than Figueres about expensive social measures and public works. "Economy" was his watchword, and economy was as much responsible for his completion of the move to abolish the army as were Figueres's more revolutionary motives. He reduced government expenses to the bone wherever possible—including cutting down his own salary by 23 per cent, to $250.00 per month—while raising taxes on exports. He improved the civil service system. The state-owned banking system he inaugurated provided Costa Rica with the best credit system in Central America. Against the communists Ulate was ruthless, suppressing all their efforts to organize working-class groups. Violence sometimes resulted, as his police dealt harshly with leftist agitators.

In 1952, following a noisy campaign, Figueres won the presidency rather easily. His National Liberation Party (PLN) promised a broad program of social and economic reform, and he initiated legislation that resumed his program of 1948-49. The government quickly raised income taxes. It revised the contracts with the UFCO to provide greater income to the state, to raise employees' salaries, and to provide for state ownership and management of the fruit company's social service program, which included hospitals, clinics, and schools. To protect and promote local small industries, it raised tariffs. A general improvement in labor benefits accompanied this, and unemployment dropped owing to an expanded public works program.

Against Figueres's administration came charges of graft, corruption, creeping socialism, and demagoguery, charges which split the PLN and permitted a return of the National Union (PUN) in 1958 with the election of Mario Echandi Jiménez, a conservative. The rotation in office between progressives and conservatives continued; PLN candidate Francisco José Orlich won in 1962 and PUN's José Joaquín Trejos

Fernández won in 1966. In 1970 the electorate returned Figueres to the presidency, but his administration faced rising violence from impatient students and labor.

Since 1948 Costa Rica has been an example of moderate social and economic reform carried out under political democracy. National Liberation has been the dominant party in Congress most of the time, but it has held the executive branch only about half the time. The result is a patchwork of legislation which has brought to Costa Rica a modern blend of socialist and capitalist institutions. Violence has erupted from time to time, and Figueres's last four years were especially stormy. The opposition won every presidential election from 1948 until 1974, when Daniel Oduber won election and continued the PLN in power to 1978. While this may suggest that no government has really been able to satisfy the public very well, it also reflects a healthy political process which enjoys popular confidence and works well. Serious social and economic problems remain in Costa Rica, however. Oduber's regime was beset with major problems resulting in large part from the worldwide energy crisis and by scandals involving the activities of North American financier Robert Vesco.

Yet the strength of the PLN could only be overcome with unified coalitions of most of the opposition parties. From 1966 forward, at the center of these opposition parties was first Calderón Guardia and later his son, Rafael Angel Calderón Fournier ("Junior" Calderón). The Unity Party coalition of 1978 brought together under the candidacy of Rodrigo Carazo an unlikely coalition of disenchanted PLN members, Calderonistas, and oligarchical interests. Carazo narrowly defeated the PLN candidate Luis Alberto Monge, but the real victor was "Junior" Calderón. Too young for the presidency in 1978, Calderón loomed as a major candidate for the future and, despite the fairly large number of parties across a broad political spectrum, emphasized the trend toward two-party government in Costa Rica.

Costa Rican democracy remained strong, albeit endangered by the sharp downward turn in the economy during the Carazo administration. At the heart of the problem lay Costa Rica's growing foreign debt, $2.6 billion by 1981, the result of excessive borrowing abroad to meet the difference between higher prices for oil and other imports and lower prices for coffee and other exports. Moreover, the government continued to subsidize heavily public services and utilities and maintain a high level of welfare programs beyond income. Inflation in excess of 40 per cent per year resulted. In 1980 Carazo devaluated the *colón* and allowed it to float freely against the dollar. It fell from its 1979 value of 8.6 to the dollar to slightly more than 40 to the dollar by the end of his administration, when the Costa Rican economy was nearly bankrupt.

Luis Alberto Monge, again the PLN candidate, was too firmly committed to social democracy to attack the philosophy of the welfare state in the 1982 campaign, but instead cited government mismanagement and corruption. He won handily, gaining 58.7 per cent of the popular vote to Calderón's 33.6 per cent. The PLN also took 33 seats in the legislature to the Unity coalition's eighteen, with only six going to other parties. Monge's election was as much an affirmation of Costa Rica's commitment to the democratic process even in the face of serious economic crisis as it was a vote of confidence for the PLN. Yet Monge benefited from the bottoming out of the worldwide economic recession, and he was able to secure substantial aid and support from the U.S. and the international banking community. By 1984 the *colón,* which some had feared would reach 100 to the dollar, appeared to have stabilized at about 44 to the dollar. Although serious economic problems remained, there was a feeling of optimism in the country. Both the PLN and Calderonistas were strongly committed to social democracy and both opposed either leftist or rightist radical solutions, for the Sandinistas in Nicaragua alarmed many Costa Ricans. Ideological differences between these two mainstreams of Costa Rican political life were not great, so that the election of 1986 loomed as another test of personality and circumstance. Although still vocal, Pepe Figueres had finally faded from the leadership of the PLN, as the party, still dominated by aging veterans of the 1948 revolution, searched for someone to meet the rising popularity of the young Calderón.

In Guatemala, active opposition to Ubico began in 1941, when university students cheered the lone member of the National Assembly who dared vote against extending Ubico's tenure until 1949. Later the students became bolder, and they began to demonstrate in support of demands for changes in university administration. A group composed primarily of law students calling themselves the Esquilaches (apparently in reference to the 1766 Madrid revolt) met secretly to plot against the regime. Led by Mario Méndez Montenegro, the Esquilaches included a number of men who would later play major roles in the state's leadership: José Manuel Fortuny, Jorge Luis Arriola, Manuel Galich, Julio César Méndez Montenegro, and Mario Efraín Nájera Farfán.

Ubico, despite his pro-German sentiments—Germans controlled nearly two-thirds of Guatemala's exports—had had little choice but to join Guatemala's neighbors in declaring war against the Axis. He cooperated with United States agents in reducing German influence and economic power in Central America to the extent of confiscating German property and removing suspected Nazis to detention camps in Texas. The antifascist propaganda—including the Atlantic Charter and the wartime alliance with the Soviet Union—which entered the country undermined Ubico's hold, especially in the capital. In 1942 Guatemalan workers and university students demonstrated in sympathy with a Salvadoran revolt against Hernández Martínez. When, two years later, Hernández fled El Salvador and sought exile in Guatemala, there were even larger demonstrations of protest. Here was the beginning of the alliance among students, military officers, and workers which finally ousted Ubico. Spontaneous acceptance of student leadership characterized labor's support against the dictator. Ubico's recognition of the rising cost of living was inadequate. The 1943 minimum wage law was a mere gesture, and it fell far short of winning support from the urban workers. They continued to demonstrate.

Ubico responded by giving salary increases of 15 per cent to all government employees earning $150 or less monthly. This measure may have ensured the loyalty of government workers, but it alienated others, who received no corresponding raise. On June 22, 1944, he accused the students of promoting Nazi-fascist ideas, withdrew constitutional guarantees, and tightened the military rule over the country. This action led immediately to the series of strikes which ended in Ubico's resignation.

While workers and students battled police in the streets, Mario Nájera Farfán led a few professional men in the secret formation of the National Renovation Party (PRN). They agreed to support exiled university professor Juan José Arévalo Bermejo for President. At about the same time a group of students formed the Popular Liberation Front (FPL) and joined the crusade against Ubico, claiming adherence of 85 per cent of the registered university students. A third party, the Social Democrats (PSD), later resulted from a factional split within the FPL. These political factions had in common their desire to end the dictatorship and to replace it with a more egalitarian government, one which would modernize the country's institutions, integrate the Indian, encourage the growth of labor and peasant movements, and promote advanced social legislation and economic growth.

When railroad workers halted the country's transportation on June 26, more workers joined the strike. Ubico capitulated on July 1. He turned over power to a triumvirate of officers headed by Federico Ponce Vaides and went to New Orleans in exile, where he died two years later.

Ponce was potentially as dictatorial as Ubico, but the force of public opinion compelled him to reestablish constitutional guarantees, promise a national election in November, and permit the existence of political parties and labor unions as a condition to restarting the economy. Ponce did not yield easily to further demands. He quartered a detachment of mounted, machete-brandishing Indians at the outskirts of the capital as "proof" that the Indians supported his government. These troops broke up demonstrations. The press had become bolder in its criticism of the government once Ubico was gone, but on October 1 Alejandro Córdova, the respected founder and director of Guatemala's leading daily, *El Imparcial*, was assassinated, reportedly on Ponce's orders. Violence and terror followed. Then, before dawn on October 20, seventy students and workers under the command of

Major Francisco Arána took the fortress of the Guardia de Honor, from which they dispensed arms to other students and workers. By sunrise revolutionaries were in command of the city except for the recently constructed and heavily defended national palace, which they threatened to bombard with artillery. The foreign diplomatic corps helped organize a new government, which was installed by five o'clock the same afternoon. The revolutionary junta, which consisted of Arana, Captain Jacobo Arbenz Guzmán, and Jorge Toriello Garrido, who was a prominent merchant, governed until March 15, 1945, when Dr. Arévalo, who had been elected in December 1944, took office.

Arévalo, who had been teaching philosophy at the University of Tucumán in Argentina, projected a political ideology he called "spiritual socialism." He did not ignore material aspects, but stressed the dignity of man, national independence, and freedom of spirit. "Our socialism does not aim at ingenious distribution of material goods," he declared soon after his return from Argentina. "Our socialism aims to liberate men psychologically, to return to all the psychological and spiritual integrity that has been denied them by conservatism and liberalism." This doctrine of psychological and moral liberation meant for Guatemala a reform program that would challenge its oligarchy and the foreign domination of the country. In his inaugural address Arévalo announced a policy of sympathy for the worker and the peasant. Moreover, schools would henceforth "carry not only hygiene and literacy," but also the "doctrine of revolution."

The fall of Ubico prompted the return of political exiles, many of whom were influential in organizing labor unions and political factions. Foreigners also came into the country, and they influenced the course of political development. With them came a stream of leftist books and pamphlets, mostly by Mexican, French, or Russian authors, with which they sought to develop a Marxist ideology among Guatemalan workers and political leaders.

The railroad workers were among the first to reorganize after the fall of Ubico, and they resisted communist control for several years. The teachers, under the leadership of the young and dynamic Victor Manuel Gutiérrez Garbín, also organized early. They became the key to communist domination of urban labor in Guatemala, and they led the organization of the Central Labor Federation (CTG). Formed in August 1944, the CTG immediately affiliated with the communist-controlled Confederation of Latin American Workers (CTAL). Communist infiltration of the urban labor movement in Guatemala continued, and by 1950 communist leaders were well established in organized labor.

The CTG headquarters became a meeting place for returning exiles and foreign labor leaders who supplied ideological leadership which had previously been lacking. A "Clarity School" provided Marxist training to Guatemalan labor leaders. The government suppressed it in 1946, but in 1950 the communists opened a similar school which they named for Jacobo Sánchez, one of the men executed by Ubico in 1934. Labor's lack of experience in organization and its inability to produce leaders of its own on a democratic basis left the incipient urban labor movement in Guatemala City vulnerable to infiltration by experienced organizers and intellectuals. The Clarity School produced communist-trained leaders for precisely this role.

By August 1944, the communists had formed the National Vanguard Party as a voice for radical labor action. Faced with vehement anti-communist opposition, the Party changed its name to the Democratic Vanguard and met clandestinely until 1949, when it publicly became the Communist Party of Guatemala (PCG).

That urban labor accepted communist leadership can hardly excite wonder. No serious domestic competition for labor support developed, as had the Aprista movement in Peru, the CROM in Mexico, or Peronismo in Argentina; and no opponents to the communists offered labor a comparable program. The average worker neither knew nor cared much about international communism or political and economic theory, but he could be persuaded that he had been economically and socially exploited and oppressed and that he had been prohibited from organizing effectively to support his own interests. Communist intellectuals, foreign and Guatemalan, seemed to present the worker with an opportunity to improve his position, and they had little opposition.

Evidence of labor's new status appeared in the Constitution of 1945, a liberal, modern document which was patterned closely after the Mexican Constitution. It guaranteed the right to organize and strike and provided for collective bargaining, minimum wages, and a long list of other tangible benefits. It required employers to provide proper housing, schooling, and medical care for workers, and to pay indemnities of a month's salary for each year's employment to any worker discharged without just cause. The code also defined responsibility for regulation of labor unions, development of cooperatives and inexpensive housing, and arbitration of labor disputes, including the establishment of special labor tribunals.

The urban labor force thus began to realize material improvement from the reforms. Industrial wages in Guatemala increased by more than 80 per cent from 1945 to 1950. Labor benefited from the establishment of the Production Development Institute (INFOP); the Institute of Social Security; new public works, hospitals, and schools; and electrification.

A political action group (CNUS) within the CTG succeeded in accelerating the rate of social reform by committing the government to the objectives of organized labor, rural as well as urban. It could do this because many of its members held positions in the Labor Ministry and other government departments. Labor tribunals' decisions came to be almost invariably decided in favor of labor on the basis of the clause in the labor code stating that "private interests must yield to the social or collective interests."

Backed by substantial portions of the urban middle class and the proletariat, Arévalo pursued a program that promised to restructure Guatemala. One major reform was the provision for much greater self-government at the local level, replacing the centralized control as practiced under Ubico. An expanded educational program attacked the country's staggering (75 per cent) illiteracy while the government, through improvements in health services and disease control, tried to cope with the immense physical problems. INFOP worked to expand productivity, particularly in small manufacturing and processing industries, by supplying credit and technical assistance. Discussion of agrarian reform followed the urban reforms, but Arévalo's government did not move very far in that area.

Arévalo's support of labor and peasant demands and his "softness" toward the communists brought him into direct conflict with the principal defenders of the old order—the planters and foreign investors who were fearful of losing the advantages secured under Ubico. Those men believed that the "welfare state," labor unions, higher wages, social insurance, and increased taxes would wreck the economy—or more precisely, their own interests. Many military officers believed that only a military administration could govern the country effectively. Arévalo weathered twenty-two military revolts during his five years in office. The regime faced its most serious military threat in late 1949, following the assassination of Amatitlán of Major Francisco Arana, Arévalo's chief army supporter. The government issued arms to some workers, and they aided significantly in the suppression of the revolt. (Arévalo's successor was to be unwilling to resort to this anti-military measure.)

At the other extreme, a small but militant group of students, editors, and other intellectuals wanted a more thoroughgoing social revolution. The communists feared that Arévalo's program, although it coincided with their own in some respects, could not be made to conform to their conceptual approach and that it might pose a threat to their own party's establishment as sole leader of the proletariat.

As the election of 1950 approached the communists campaigned more openly. Led by José Fortuny, seventeen communists withdrew from Arévalo's Revolutionary Action Party (PAR) and began to publish a pro-communist weekly, Octubre. Arévalo, to prevent loss of his moderate support, responded with a tougher line toward the communists, but communist infiltration of government information organs gave them a big advantage. Several worked in the government news bureau. Another had been manager of the board of directors of the government's radio station since 1946. The official government daily, Diario de Centroamérica, reflected leftist views increasingly, and in 1949 Alfredo Guerra Borges, one of the country's leading journalists and a member of the Communist Party's executive committee, became its editor. The semi-official *Nuestro Diario* also came under communist management about 1948.

Yet the communists actively supported the government candidate, thirty-six-year-old Jacobo Arbenz, Arévalo's defense minister and a member of the National Renovation Party. The PRN joined with other parties—the PAR (Arévalo's party), the FPL, and the Revolutionary Party of National Union (PRUN)—in presenting a united coalition (*Unidad Nacional*) of moderate and leftist parties. The principal opposition came from conservative parties, National Redemption and the Anti-Communist Union, supporting Ubico's former director of public works, Miguel Ydígoras Fuentes. The government hardly permitted free campaigning, even though Arbenz would likely have won a free election. A government arrest order forced Ydígoras into hiding. As it turned out, Arbenz won an overwhelming majority.

Under Arbenz, Guatemala moved sharply toward the left and into a close relationship with the Soviet Union. In an effort to widen their popular support and play down differences between Stalinists and Guatemalan nationalists, the communists reorganized in 1952 as the Labor Party (PGT). The party promoted large organizations which pressured the government on behalf of agrarian reform, collectivization, and a foreign policy which scored the United States intervention in Korea and praised the Soviet Union.

As opposition mounted during the last years of the Arbenz administration, urban labor was his primary source of strength. Labor unions and other mass organizations served as weapons against the opposition, first with propaganda, later with more violent tactics. Anti-communists suffered arrest, imprisonment, torture, and assassination. There was a startling increase of attacks against centers of anti-communist activity by groups of masked hoodlums.

The communists tried to undermine the position of the army, which remained mostly non-communist. Arévalo had armed some workers during the 1949 insurrection of the Guardia de Honor. In 1952, as tension surrounded the passing of the Agrarian Reform Law, leftists argued for formation of armed "defense brigades" within the labor movement. The government refused, but as fear of foreign intervention rose in 1954, labor leaders repeated the idea. Ernesto ("Che") Guevara, a recent Argentine arrival employed in the agrarian reform department, urged that the labor unions be armed at once, but Arbenz, himself a military officer, was reluctant. Yet the army's fear of such action was a principal cause of its early repudiation of Arbenz during the subsequent invasion. Arbenz reduced military spending to 10 per cent of the national budget. It had been 17 per cent under Ubico.

The communist labor unions also played a role beyond Guatemala's borders. The PGT was a center for propaganda and agitation in the neighboring states. *Octubre* reflected an identification of interests between Guatemalan and other Central American workers. In 1954 Guatemalan workers joined Hondurans in a strike against the United Fruit Company on the north coast of Honduras. Other interventions occurred in El Salvador.

The agrarian reform program began in earnest in 1952, as the Arbenz government moved to bring the peasants more fully into the Revolution. Although the government concentrated on the vast foreign banana holdings of the lowlands rather than on native-owned coffee fincas in the populous highlands, the concept of land redistribution struck fear into landlords all across Central America and caused intensification of the movement to terminate the Guatemalan regime.

Yet in 1954 Guatemala was not a communist state. Arbenz himself did not openly profess communism, although his Salvadoran wife, María Cristina Villanova, was an active member of the Party and communists had easy access to the President. They held key positions in all three branches of the government and had begun to expropriate large landholdings, particularly those of the United Fruit Company. Implementation of the Arévalo reforms had begun the restructuring of the Guatemalan economy, society, and political life, but it was far from completed.

Opposition was mounting, but it is unlikely that the Arbenz government would have fallen from power if all or part of the military had not defected. The position of the Guatemalan delegation to the United Nations as well as official statements of the Guatemalan government suggested that, insofar as foreign policy was concerned, Guatemala had become a virtual Soviet satellite by 1954. The shipment of arms to Guatemala from eastern Europe in May of that year caused sufficient alarm in the United States to strain seriously the relations between the two republics. When Guatemalan exiles from Honduras, assisted by the United States Marine Corps and CIA advisers, invaded the country, the Guatemalan army refused to defend the government, and the crisis ended quickly. Arbenz escaped to Mexico and later went to Cuba and Europe. He died in 1971, shortly after returning to Mexico City.

The United States cut short the Guatemala Revolution when it determined that Guatemala had fallen within the Soviet orbit and that the Revolution threatened the United Fruit Company holdings. Later, revolutionaries in Cuba and Nicaragua would learn from the Guatemalan experience the importance of checking the armed forces and restructuring the society as quickly as possible.

Guatemala showed the rest of Central America just how far a small Caribbean republic could go in deviating from adherence to United States foreign policy and in challenging the hegemony of North American economic interests. Although rightists—including the United States ambassador to Guatemala—had warned against the Marxist tendencies of the Arévalo government, the Truman administration did no more than keep a half-open eye on Central America. Meanwhile, United States investments and profits in the republic rose rapidly after World War II. Despite the activities of communists and other leftists, the actual practices of the Arévalo government had not seemed to threaten those interests seriously. Even during the first two years of the Arbenz regime there was little official United States concern expressed.

With the Eisenhower administration, however, and with John Foster Dulles as Secretary of State, Washington suddenly became more keenly aware of the Soviet challenge in Guatemala. Dulles had close connections with the United Fruit Company. Arbenz's pro-labor policies also threatened other business interests, notably Pan American World Airways. Eisenhower's ambassador to Guatemala, John E. Puerifoy, condemned Arbenz to Washington and participated in the conspiracy to unseat him. The pro-Soviet stance of Guatemala in the

United Nations was an embarrassment to the fanatically anti-communist Republicans around Dulles, and he chose to end the policy of nonintervention which Franklin Roosevelt had inaugurated twenty years
earlier.

In 1953 the United States government and press had begun to react
vigorously to the increasing pro-Soviet and anti-American statements
and actions of the Guatemalans. Extravagant eulogies from the Guatemalan press and Congress upon the death of Joseph Stalin prompted
a number of North Americans to launch virulent attacks on the Guatemalan government and to call for intervention to suppress communism there. The United States news media picked up the charges and
gave sensational and distorted coverage to the "red regime" in Guatemala.

Dulles attempted to get strong inter-American backing, but the
watered-down resolutions against international communism at Caracas
in March 1954 lacked the support of several major Latin American
states. Those nations hardly sanctioned the sort of unilateral intervention which the United States sponsored in June.

Growing internal opposition to Arbenz solidified when the Archbishop, Mariano Rossell y Arellano, on April 10 called for Guatemalans to rise up and throw out the communists.

Alarmed over the arrival of Czechoslovakian arms at Puerto Barrios
aboard the Swedish ship *Alfhem*, the United States Department of
State determined to act. Frank Wisner, deputy director of the CIA, was
directly responsible for the operation known as "El Diablo." Two Guatemalan exiles, Carlos Castillo Armas and Miguel Ydígoras, had already organized a plan for invasion. The United States, under hastily
signed Military Security treaties, airlifted arms into Honduras and
Nicaragua. Then the governments of those states cooperated in outfit-
ting the invasion force.

Conveniently for the United States, Henry Cabot Lodge, Jr., was
president of the United Nations Security Council for the month of
June. The invasion finally came on June 18. When Guatemala protested, Lodge put off calling a meeting until June 25 and then obstructed the placing of the Guatemalan case on the agenda, arguing
that the Organization of American States should take up the matter.

Meanwhile, in Guatemala, the army refused to resist the invasion, and Castillo soon controlled the country. Arbenz resigned on June 27. The delay of international organizations in responding to the intervention precluded effective action on their part. The Inter-American Peace Committee of the OAS did not even convene until two days after Arbenz's resignation, and it accomplished nothing.

An interim government attempted to salvage the Revolution, but two days later it turned over control to anti-communist Colonel Elfego Monzón. Monzón met with Castillo in San Salvador on the following day (June 30), and on July 8 Castillo became head of the junta they had established. Following a plebiscite in October, he ruled Guatemala as President until his assassination in 1957.

Castillo moved promptly to remove all communist influence from Guatemala. First, he set up a National Committee for Defense against Communism which supervised a repressive purge. On August 10 he disbanded all political parties. A "Political Statute" decreed on the following day replaced the Constitution of 1945 and authorized Castillo's military rule of the country, outlawed the Communist Party, and banned communist books and propaganda. A wave of arrests and exilings followed. In an effort to recover funds which Arbenz and other government officials had taken from the treasury upon their departure, Castillo confiscated the property of some eighty government officials.

Despite the reactionary character of the Castillo government and most of those which have succeeded it, the Guatemalan Revolution was not totally dismantled. Many of the institutions which the Arévalo government had inaugurated remained, even though their enthusiasm and impetus toward social restructuring were lessened. The popularity of leftist social and political reforms among workers, peasants, and intellectuals could not be ignored entirely, so an effort was made to maintain the appearance of reform and progressive legislation. Few acts of the Arévalo and Arbenz governments were repealed, but they were superseded or amended to prevent the intended restructuring.

Intervention in the labor movement ended the influence of that element as a major political factor. A "right to work" law checked organized labor further in 1956. The Constitution of 1956 reflected the anti-communism of the era when it forbade any "foreign intervention" in the labor movement. A new Agrarian Reform Law, passed in 1956, provided for expropriation and redistribution of idle land, but the specific terms of the act meant that the landed class and the foreign holders had little to fear. The Church also regained some of its lost privileges, the most important of which was the right to own property, which it had lost following the Revolution of 1871.

In short, the old Liberal oligarchy—the coffee planters and other landholders, as well as the foreign capitalists and their subsidiaries—were restored to power and protected under neo-conservative military regimes. Although voices of moderation sometimes prevailed, it was clear that interests antagonistic to the social revolution had recovered control. But they could not suppress all opposition. Students were particularly vocal in their opposition after 1954. The Guatemalan government frequently had to use force to suppress demonstrations and riots against government policies. The military was the real arbiter, as it had been before 1944. After Castillo's assassination, the state suffered a series of unstable governments, and widespread terrorism and suppression of more progressive candidates accompanied elections. Following Castillo's term, Ydígoras had expected to gain the presidency, as a reward for his part in the overthrow of Arbenz. When he did not get it, the army intervened, and in January 1958 it held new elections, which Ydígoras won.

Ydígoras made an effort to unify the country and to stifle the objections of moderate leftist elements, but these efforts only got him into trouble with his conservative allies. Whenever free elections were held at local levels in the capital, the electorate expressed strong preferences for leftist candidates, men such as Luis Fernando Galich, who was elected Mayor in 1959 after various attempts to deny him the office failed.

Violence flared in Guatemala City frequently in 1960, as Ydígoras, seeking to widen his popularity, was reluctant to resort to harsh measures against the opposition, while at the same time he supported maneuvers to deny his opponents access to power through democratic means. Then Fidel Castro established his regime in Cuba, and, in the 1961 Bay of Pigs invasion, Guatemala aided the United States, further polarizing political opinion in the state. In November 1960, Ydígoras succeeded in quelling a major revolt, led by Colonel Rafael Pereira, which began in the capital at Matamoros Barracks. Other rebels had succeeded in taking over the Caribbean region inland as far as Zacapa before Ydígoras, personally leading his forces and supported by his air force's B-26 bombers, turned the tide. Although Pereira's threat failed, it was the beginning of a new phase in Guatemalan revolutionary history, as survivors of the rebellion, led by Lieutenant Marcos Aurelio Yon Sosa, formed the Thirteenth of November Revolutionary Movement (MR-13) and began a guerrilla warfare campaign which continued throughout the subsequent decade. Another officer, Luis A. Turcios Lima, later formed a rival guerrilla organization, the Rebel Armed Forces (FAR) which collaborated with the outlawed, underground PGT.

These guerrillas kept Guatemala in a state of turmoil throughout the 1960's. Although they failed to take much territory, they created a sense of insecurity in the country and were aided by substantial support from middle-class youth in the university and even from within the army. A right-wing terror organization, the White Hand (*Mano Blanca*), arose in response, and assassination and terrorism spread. Later, another organization, known as the Eye for an Eye (*Ojo por Ojo*), replaced the Mano Blanca when that group's close relationship to the government and police became embarrassing. When Turcios died—he was killed in an automobile wreck—César Montes emerged as a new and more dynamic, popular leader of the FAR. Leftist exiles clandestinely reentered Guatemala. Among them were Arévalo, Fortuny, Gutiérrez and Pellecer, the last of whom later renounced communism and joined the anti-communist forces. Ydígoras's failure to pursue a hard enough line against these "agitators" led to his ouster by the military in March 1963.

Ydígoras's successor, Colonel Enrique Peralta Azurdia, immediately declared a state of siege and moved the country into a military dictatorship. Especially trained troops accompanied by United States advisers checked the insurgents, though they did not succeed in suppressing them entirely. Political leftists met with assassination, arrest, or exile. Victor Gutiérrcz reportedly was dropped from an airplane 20,000 feet over the Pacific. Mario Méndez Montenegro, leader of the Revolutionary Party (PR), legal successor to Arévalo's PAR, was shot to death in 1965.

Peralta succeeded in restoring considerable stability and order. He permitted free elections in 1966, and the PR candidate, Julio César Méndez Montenegro, brother of the murdered leader of the party, won and took office. Moderates hoped for a return to progressivism, but while the army permitted Méndez to remain in the presidency, it did not allow him to rule. Some men would have resigned, as the army continued to be the real master of the country and continued the repressive measures. Courageously, Méndez chose to make the best of a bad situation. He found he could achieve little of his program, however, and by the end of his term he was criticized as a puppet of the rightists and as a traitor to his brother's memory. The conservative military took no chances in 1970, and, in an election from which most leftist elements were excluded, Colonel Carlos Arana Osorio won election. In 1974 the military continued its disregard for free and open elections. Amid widespread cries of fraud, General Kjell Langerud García, the son of a Norwegian immigrant, became President. Arana and Langerud maintained peace and order with police-state methods. Business boomed, however, and the growing middle class enjoyed affluence despite debilitating inflation. The military elite began to enter the economy in a major way. Not only did the Generals receive enormous salaries when they served as President (Ydígoras reportedly received $650,000 per year), but they were able to use their positions to acquire private companies, large land holdings, and monopolistic concessions, amassing fortunes in the process. They established their own bank as a further institutional base for their economic interests. The corruption associated with this economic expansion and the wealth of these military officers reached obscene proportions in a country beset with staggering poverty among the majority of its population. An earthquake which devastated much of central Guatemala and western Honduras in February 1976 added to the misery.

The civil war continued, however, especially in the rugged, northern parts of the country where a limited road network made it more difficult for the army to succeed. By 1975 the FAR had suffered serious setbacks at the hands of the U.S.-supported, counterinsurgency forces, but a new rebel force, labeled the Guerrilla Army of the Poor (EGP), emerged in northern Quiché to continue the struggle. The FAR eventually reorganized and resumed active warfare in 1978.

In 1978 General Romeo Lucas García of the Democratic Institutional Party (PID) succeeded to the presidency in a patently fraudulent election marred by widespread voter abstention. Guatamala's economic problems during this period were somewhat less serious than Costa Rica's because of the development of small but significant petroleum resources in the Petén and considerably less attention to social welfare, but falling coffee, cotton, and sugar prices and the worldwide recession had some ill effects. Guatamala's trade deficit rose from $63 million in 1980 to $409 million in 1981. Lucas and the clandestine right-wing death squads launched a brutal policy of genocide against Indians suspected of supporting or joining the guerrillas. As the Generals continued to seize large tracts of land, substantial numbers of Indians fled into Chiapas. Their numbers, in 149 refugee camps, had reached 180,000 by mid-1984. Concern of the clergy and international human rights organizations over political oppression focused unfavorable attention on the country and damaged the tourist industry. Yet Jimmy Carter's human rights policy only hardened the resolve of the Guatemalan military and death squads to deal violently with the left and even moderate progressives such as the Christian Democrats. Guatemala simply replaced a partial cut-off of U.S. arms sales with arms and advisers from Israel. Terror and assassination took a horrifying toll among leaders of labor organization and at the University of San Carlos. In 1980 the civilian Vice President, Francisco Villagrán Kramer, resigned in protest over the continued human rights violations.

VOTER ABSTENTION IN GUATEMALAN ELECTIONS, 1944-78

Year	Eligible Voters	Votes	Percent Abstention	Votes for Winning Candidate	% of Eligible Vote for Winning Candidate
1944	310,000	296,200	4.5	255,700	82.5
1950	583,300	407,500	31.1	266,800	45.7
1958	736,400	492,300	33.1	191,000	25.9
1966	944,200	531,300	43.7	209,400	22.2
1970	1,190,500	640,700	53.6	251,100	21.1
1974	1,568,700	727,876	53.6	298,953	19.1
1978	1,785,876	651,817	63.5	269,979	15.1

SOURCE: Adapted from Julio Castellanos Cambranes, "Origins of the Crisis of the Established Order in Guatemala," in S. C. Ropp and J. A. Morris (eds.), *Central America, Crisis and Adaptation* (Albuquerque: University of New Mexico Press, 1984), p. 136.

INCOME DISTRIBUTION IN GUATEMALA, 1981

Per Cent of Population	Monthly Income (U.S.$)
51.3	Less than $150
27.6	$151 to $300
8.4	$301 to $400
5.9	$401 to $600
3.5	$601 to $900
2.0	$901 to $1,200
1.3	More than $1,200

SOURCE: Inforpress Centroamericano, *Centroamérica 1982, análisis económicos y políticos sobre la región* (Guatemala, 1982), p. 131.

There was dissension among the military, however, and following the rigged election of another PID general, Angel Aníbal Guevara, younger officers, supported by elements in both the right-wing MLN Party and the Christian Democrats, moved to prevent his inauguration in March 1982, ousting Lucas during the last days of his regime in favor of a junta headed by retired General Efraín Ríos Montt. Ríos, who assumed the presidency on 9 June, had been President Arana's Army Chief of Staff (1970-74), but he also had been the presidential candidate of the coalition of parties headed by the Christian Democrats which had claimed victory in 1974. Even more striking was his role as a minister of the born-again, California-based Christian Church of the Word. Evangelical Protestantism in Guatemala, mostly with U.S. missionary support, has grown remarkably since about 1960, to the extent that an estimated 20 per cent of Guatemala's population today claim Protestant affiliation. In contrast to the new Catholic evangelism in the country, however, which has been often associated with "liberation theology" and the political left, most of the Protestants are staunchly conservative and identify with pro-U.S. policies.

Ríos Montt's accession to power brought some change to the pattern of military rule. Superficially at least, there was a noticeable effort to curb the corruption and to encourage a higher degree of ethics in the conduct of government. More impressive was the decline of death-squad activities and the restoration of security and peace in the central highlands. Political assassinations virtually ceased, and the disastrous decline of tourism, to which the violence had contributed, was reversed for a time. Yet the economic and military power of the powerful generals who had ruled the country since 1954 could not be turned back, nor was Ríos Montt in any sense sympathetic to leftist interests. He, and the officers he represented, were principally concerned with preserving the privileged position of the military, and perceived that military abuses and corruption threatened the institution. Massacres of Indian communities continued, as did the flow of refugees into Mexico. His government inaugurated a system of civil patrols, requiring Indians to serve, usually without firearms, but as guardians against the guerrillas. Those who refused met death. Ríos also abolished the constitution, restricted labor unions, and prohibited the functioning of political parties in his effort to maintain order. In response, the leftists united in the Guatemalan National Revolutionary Unity (URNG), an umbrella organization for the PGT, FAR, EGP, and OPRA (Organization of the People in Arms).

Ríos's challenge to the military oligarchy, his constant evangelical and moralistic preaching, the excessively large role of North American Protestants in his advisory councils, imposition of a sales tax (IVA), and his meddling with powerful economic interests ensured that his regime was relatively short-lived. In August 1983 a new coup replaced him with Defense Minister General Oscar Humberto Mejías Victores.

The new President appeared to be merely a caretaker for the military oligarchy, simply keeping order until the next election when the military would decide on an appropriate candidate. Mejía's government was characterized by a return to the high degree of corruption mentioned earlier, efforts to check the guerrillas who were now largely confined to the Petén, and failure to do anything about the growing poverty and economic problems facing the majority of the population. Cynicism and anti-communism were the most conspicuous characteristics of the government, with commitment to the same neo-Liberal policies on behalf of an entrenched oligarchy that had characterized Guatemalan governments since 1954. Elections for a Constitutional Assembly to write a new Constitution for the country July 1, 1984, reflected widespread voter apathy in the political process, in which seventeen parties (nine of them new) vied for the 88 seats. Mejía warned that the Assembly was limited strictly to writing the constitution and electoral and habeas corpus laws. Elections for a new president were to be held upon completion of the new constitution. The moderate Christian Democratic and National Union Center parties led the polling, but the much-delayed official results denied them a majority, so that a right-wing coalition appeared destined to dominate the Assembly.

Guatemala's complex political structure reflected the growth and fragmentation of the elite, with planter, business, and military elements struggling among themselves for the spoils of political power. Middle- and working-class interests sometimes gained from the division among the elites, but the violence and repression that characterized the system precluded general participation, and the worsening economic situation and continued population growth made prospects for future development bleak.

Guatemala continued to claim Belize (formerly British Honduras), but found herself increasingly isolated as other Latin American states announced their support of independence for the tiny enclave of British colonialism on Guatemala's Caribbean shore. The economic decline of the late nineteenth century had continued, and the colony had become more of a liability than an asset to Great Britain. It produced a few bananas and some sugar for export, and there was some improvement in the mahogany market, but chicle and citrus fruit production became the principal economic activities. Except for a small section where the foreign company and diplomatic representatives lived alongside a tiny local aristocracy, Belize City remained an unsavory, tropical village, with unpainted wooden houses, dirty streets, and open sewers.

In 1949 economic pressures forced the devaluation of the British Honduras dollar from U.S. $1.00 to seventy cents. The economic difficulties that followed led to the first serious challenge to the status quo when, behind the leadership of George Price, a group desiring structural change formed the People's United Party (PUP). Price, who had been educated in the United States, had served as secretary for local multimillionaire Robert Sidney Turton. The party quickly became a force in local politics, representing leftist views and gaining wide support from the working population. Because it was anti-British, PUP received support from the Arbenz government in neighboring Guatemala, which hoped to garner PUP support of Guatemalan sovereignty over the colony.

In 1954 the PUP swept legislative elections, winning eight of nine seats. Although the party split over the question of friendship with Guatemala, it soundly defeated the newly formed Honduras Independence Party (HIP), which favored entry into the West Indian Federation. Price directed modest improvements in the economy and moved the colony closer to independence, winning reelection in 1961. Soon thereafter, Hurricane Hattie swept over the Caribbean port, causing massive destruction. This led to the decision to establish a new capital city inland, near Roaring Creek at a place to be named Belmopan. Considerable expenditure went into the new site. The new public buildings, inspired by Mayan architecture, somehow fell short of Mayan grandeur. A decade after the hurricane, although the governor and a few government officials had taken up residence in Belmopan, the greater part of the administration was still conducted in Belize City, while most of the workers' cottages were empty and falling into ruins at Belmopan. Nevertheless, the new capital grew as Belize became self-governing in 1963 and gradually moved toward a fully independent status. An expanding tourist trade, capitalizing on the excellent deep-sea fishing and scuba diving along Belize's coral reef, and new agricultural development by North American enterprises offered at least a slim possibility of a viable economy for Britain's Central American stepchild.

Guatemala severed diplomatic relations with Panama over the latter's support for Belizean independence in 1977, but soon after several other Latin American states also declared their support for Belize and in November the United Nations General Assembly adopted a resolution favoring independence by a vote of 126-4 (with 13 abstentions). Guatemala's purchase of ten short take-off and landing aircraft from Israel in the same year alarmed Belizeans. Negotiations that followed failed to produce complete agreement, but Guatemala begrudgingly agreed in March 1981 to accept Belizean independence, aware that British troops guaranteed its territorial integrity. Although subsequent talks collapsed, Guatemala once more breaking relations with Britain and closing her Belizean consulates, on September 21, 1981, Belize officially became an independent constitutional monarchy within the British Commonwealth.

Although El Salvador had no Revolution comparable to Guatemala's, many of the same forces were at work and there were some parallels of development. Hernández succeeded in overcoming a military revolt on April 4, 1944, but four days later there was a general strike, called by middle-class professionals as well as workers, and he then resigned. The success of student and labor elements in pulling down Hernández was important in encouraging similar groups in Guatemala against Ubico, but the power of students and labor in El Salvador was slight. Salvadorans were universally tired of the dictator, and he accepted their view and stepped down peacefully rather than subject the country to more violence. Andrés I. Menéndez, a moderate military officer who was also a member of one of the principal families of the country, formed a provisional government, but in October a conservative faction, led by Osmín Aguirre Salinas, chief of police under Hernández, reestablished the dictatorship.

Aguirre and his chosen successor, Salvador Castañeda Castro, were elected in controlled balloting in January 1945. They dealt harshly with leftist elements such as those who succeeded in organizing labor in Guatemala. Since 1945 the military, in league with landholding interests, has run El Salvador most of the time. There are, however, both liberal and conservative factions within the military, and the pendulum has swung from side to side, providing for some movement toward social and economic reform. Whenever such movements have seemed radical, or when the conservatives have been frightened—as they were by the rise of Fidel Castro—there has been a reaction. The state for some thirty years enjoyed relative peace and order, with occasional military coups, some social progress, and freedom of expression. Clearly still within the New Liberal framework of government, El Salvador was, nonetheless, affected by some of the social reform movements around her. After the ouster of Castañeda in December 1948, Major Oscar Osorio presided over the country's first social security legislation, passed in 1949, and in 1950 a Constitution which provided public health programs, women's suffrage, and extended social security coverage was enacted.

Osorio's moderate Revolutionary Party of Democratic Union (PRUD) dominated the state for the next decade, with both leftists and rightists charging that elections were fraudulent. In 1960, however, Osorio lost control of the party, and he then formed the Social Democratic Party (PDS) in opposition. After growing disorder from both left and right, it appeared that he would attempt to overthrow the moderate, pro-United States President José María Lemus, and a small group of leftist officers moved in quickly and took over the government. The new regime lasted only a few months, and, in January 1961, right-wing military units installed a junta which broke relations with Cuba and instituted a more conservative regime, one similar to that which dominated Guatemala in the 1960's. Although a great number of civilian political parties operated in the country, Julio Rivera's conservative National Conciliation Party (PCN) and the army dominated the republic throughout the next decade. Despite its conservative base, the party sponsored moderate social reforms in an effort to stave off the demands of workers, peasants, and students. El Salvador's government, faced with a shortage of land and an expanding population, was forced to recognize the need for some social welfare programs.

The formation of the Christian Democratic Party (PDC) behind the leadership of the dynamic José Napoleón Duarte, mayor of San Salvador from 1964 to 1970, promised a more progressive, but strongly anti-communist, approach to El Salvador's social and economic problems. Duarte headed a coalition of opposition to the PCN in 1972. He campaigned tirelessly, despite violent harassment by the government. After a government "recount" overruled the National Electoral Committee which had declared Duarte the winner, he publicly counseled against the popular uprising on his behalf that seemed imminent. Duarte worked closely with labor leaders in an effort to consolidate organized labor behind him, but an attempted general strike failed when the government succeeded in maintaining the loyalty of transport workers. Amid rumours of a coup, the army tightened security over the country. Duarte denied complicity in the abortive coup that followed, but on March 25 police seized and beat him into unconsciousness. Diplomatic pressure gained his release from jail, and three days later he was quietly removed to Guatemala, where he was given asylum.

Meanwhile, the new President, Colonel Arturo Armando Molina, took office. He surprised many Salvadorans by resuming some social and economic reforms in a conciliatory effort to avert further bloodshed. The harsher aspects of the dictatorship abated, and Molina even began to adapt certain aspects of Duarte's platform, particularly those relating to administrative reform within the government. Beneath this veneer of conciliation, however, was a clear pattern of activity to prevent popular parties from challenging the oligarchy again, and in 1976 the PCN swept congressional and municipal elections as most opposition parties refused to participate. In the meantime, guerrillas of the People's Revolutionary Army (ERP) began to appear from along the Honduran border region. In the presidential election of 1977 the PCN's General Carlos Humberto Romero was the winner in another fraudulent election surrounded by rising political violence and repression.

Factions of the oligarchy now turned to military terror squads, as in Guatemala, while the left and center-left abandoned the electoral process. A civil war was under way by 1977. The Catholic clergy and newly formed Christian Base Communities began to speak out against the old order, supported by Archbishop Monsignor Oscar Romero, who boycotted the inauguration of President Romero and denounced the violence on both sides, calling for reform. Most of the opposition boycotted the 1978 legislative elections, won easily by the PCN. The growing repression and violence attracted international interest. The British cancelled arms sales and human rights organizations censured the Romero government.

The revolutionary junta that seized power on October 15, 1979, with subsequent reshufflings that eventually included Duarte as Chief-of-State, represented more centrist, but relatively impotent elements of the middle class after the conflict had already become polarized. It was primarily a move by younger and more progressive military officers, led by Colonels Adolfo Majano and Jaime Abdul Gutiérrez, to save the military's institutional privileges, which had been under fire because of military repression and corruption. These more moderate factions sought reforms that would preserve the legitimacy of military rule. Yet they failed to curb the human rights violations of the security forces and death squads. In January 1980 the leading civilian progressives on the junta, Guillermo Ungo and Román Mayorga, resigned and went into exile. Ungo, the vice-presidential candidate on Duarte's 1974 ticket, accepted the leadership of the Revolutionary Democratic Front (FDR), an umbrella organization of the three major leftist political organizations and their military wings established in April 1980. The FDR paved the way for union, in October, of most of the guerrilla organizations into the united Farabundo Martí Front for National Liberation (FMLN), named for the leader of the 1932 communist uprising. Large numbers of the politically active, including many Christian Democrats, had joined the guerrillas or their political organizations as the only means of dealing with a government that refused to recognize legitimate elections. Denied gradual reform and change as the Christian Democrats had advocated, a bloodbath enveloped the country, where more than 50,000 people have died, mostly at the hands of the government or its terrorists. Political assassinations have hit all classes and few families in El Salvador have been untouched by the violence. More than half a million Salvadorans have fled the country.

Moderates could not control the right wing military and, when the reformist Colonel Adolfo Majano was forced out of military command at the end of 1980, coinciding with the election of the Reagan government in Washington, Duarte simply became a captive of the old order, still believing he could do more within the government than outside. But he was ineffectual in stemming the atrocities of the military or in bringing peace. Duarte began an agrarian reform program designed to provide land for the peasants with just compensation to the large landholders, but it could not undo overnight the inequities of hundreds of years nor was it capable of bringing about the necessary expansion of the economy to solve the severe economic and social problems of the country. Reforms in the banking system and in the management of foreign commerce frightened private capital and failed to reverse the declining economic picture. His defeat in the 1982 elections ended that phase of the conflict with the election, under highly questionable circumstances, of a reactionary coalition dominated by Roberto D'Aubisson, widely believed to be associated with the death squads and accused by American Ambassador Robert White of being responsible for the March 1980 assassination of Archbishop Romero. While the February 1982 election reflected widespread exhaustion with the civil war, it also reflected consolidation of neo-Liberal forces to terminate the moderate coup of 1979. The new provisional president, Alvaro Magaña, although moderate in some respects, was dependent on this right-wing coalition, and was a compromise supported by the armed forces and the U.S. Embassy to stave off election of D'Aubisson, who for the moment served only as president of the Assembly. These political intrigues extended into the military and the shakeups in command and rivalries among the leading officers disrupted much of the effort against the guerrillas, who made substantial gains during 1983-84, but could not score a decisive victory. The civil war has cost Salvadoran economic development dearly. Capital flight has been extensive, production has declined, and real wages have dropped more than 25 per cent since 1972 in the face of spiraling inflation and a devaluation of the *colón* in 1982 from 2.5 to 3.5 to the dollar. An estimated 79 per cent increase in the value of exports in 1983, however, reversed the downward trend since 1979 and saved the economy from collapse.

The civil war dragged on, increasingly injected into an East-West struggle. The Reagan administration accused Nicaragua and Cuba of assisting the Salvadoran guerrillas while the U.S. poured more and more military aid to the government, despite U.S. Congressional objections after the murder of four U.S. Catholic women and two U.S. labor advisers in El Salvador. Congress limited the number of U.S. advisers in El Salvador to fifty-five, and balked at some of Reagan's requests for more military aid. One apparent response to this was Salvadoran agreements with Israel for anti-guerrilla security assistance. Israel already provided military assistance to Guatemala and Honduras. On the other side, Salvadoran guerrillas reportedly were receiving arms from the PLO and Libya.

The human rights record of the Salvadoran government remained abominable, but the Reagan administration certified that improvements were being made and put great emphasis on anti-communism and the democratic process as reflected in the 1982 and 1984 elections. In the latter election, a showdown between Duarte and D'Aubisson, Duarte won by a margin of about 54 per cent to 46 percent and took office in June, promising to curb the death squads, conduct a dialogue with the guerrillas, and continue the social and economic reforms he had begun in 1980-82. The key to his success would be whether or not he could bring the military under his control, and at this writing the answer to that question remains in doubt.

In 1948 the aging Honduran dictator, Carías, voluntarily stepped down in favor of his minister of defense, Juan Manuel Gálvez. Gálvez was then elected easily when the Liberal candidate, claiming that the government would not permit fair elections, withdrew. The National Party split in 1954 over Carías's desire to return to the helm.

When Carías was nominated to the presidency by the National Party, anti-Carías elements walked out. They formed the National Reformist Movement (MNR), naming as their candidate Abraham Williams Calderón. Williams had served as Carías's Vice President, but had left Carías's ranks after 1948, when Carías had passed him over for Gálvez.

The Liberals then chose Dr. Ramón Villeda Morales, a pediatrician who advocated civil rights, land reform, rights of organized labor, and revision of the government's United Fruit Company contracts. A hotly contested campaign ensued. Villeda's opponents accused him of being in league with the recently expelled communists of Guatemala. It was the first free election since 1932, and no candidate received a majority. The two conservatives, Carías and Williams, together polled nearly 52 per cent of the vote, 31 per cent and 21 per cent, respectively, while Villeda received 48 per cent. When the Carías-controlled Congress refused to elect Villeda, Gálvez's Vice President, Julio Lozano Díaz, seized power, establishing a new military dictatorship.

Lozano promised free elections in 1956, but he did everything he could to prevent a Liberal victory. Organized labor began to play a more active role in Honduran politics, and the workers attempted a general strike, but they failed to bring Lozano down. Lozano responded to the growing violence and disorder by exiling Villeda and other Liberal politicians and editors. He survived a military uprising on August 1, but his health was failing and the continued disorders disheartened him. On September 13 he accepted the advice of his physicians and flew to Miami for medical care, leaving the government to Gálvez, who was then serving as Chief Justice of the Supreme Court. Lozano returned, however, to supervise the October 7 election. In it his newly organized National Union Party (PUN), composed prin-

cipally of Williams's Reformists, won all the seats in the Constituent
Assembly. Violence characterized the election, and the Liberals, justi-
fiably, shouted fraud. A few days later Lozano indicated that he might
turn the presidency over to Williams after a year, but on October 21
military officers led by General Roque J. Rodríguez forced his immediate resignation. Rodríguez headed a junta composed principally of
younger officers—among them Juan Gálvez's son, Roberto Gálvez
Barnes—who favored restoration of popular civilian rule, but Honduras
became embroiled in a dispute with Nicaragua over the Gracias a Dios
region, and the junta delayed elections. Finally, in July 1957, the
younger members of the junta ousted Rodríguez and proceeded to supervise a fair election. The Liberals gained an absolute majority in
the Constituent Assembly, and in November that body elected Villeda
to the presidency, thus ending twenty-four years of conservative military dictatorship in Honduras.

Villeda promptly inaugurated a moderate social revolution, and he
became known as a responsible leader who cooperated closely with
John Kennedy and the Alliance for Progress. He suffered attacks from
both the right and the left, but the conservative opposition was
stronger, and after the rise of Fidel Castro in Cuba it became more
violent in its opposition to Villeda's alleged softness toward the Communists. Although his land and labor reforms were moderate, they
challenged the economic security of Honduras' traditional ruling class.
In October 1963, just before elections were to be held, military elements
forced the President into exile, postponed elections, and installed
Armed Forces Commander Oswaldo López Arellano as Provisional
President. It was a return of the Carías faction to power. A Constituent Assembly in 1965 adopted a new Constitution and confirmed
López as President through 1971. Meanwhile, economic pressures
worsened as industrious Salvadoran immigrants competed with Honduran workers and peasants for jobs. The dispute between Honduras
and El Salvador over immigrant labor remained unresolved, and in
1969 the two nations went to war. El Salvador quickly won the war,
but in one sense Honduras appeared to gain by it also. Because of the
crisis the two parties joined in a National Unity Pact (1971), and

this led to the election of Ramón Cruz as President, but López, as chief of the armed forces, really remained in control. The two parties had agreed to share the principal political offices while the state was recovering from defeat. Party differences soon surfaced again, however, and López resumed full authority in late 1972, ending the pact definitively. Early in 1975, after a scandal involving payment of $1.25 million in bribes to Honduran officials by United Brands Company (UFCO's successor) had discredited his government, the military toppled López. The new government, although militarist, appeared to have more progressive tendencies than its predecessor, but it in turn fell to a coup headed by General Policarpo Paz García in 1978.

Honduran experience had differed from that of Guatemala and El Salvador in that the Liberal Party, denied office effectively from 1925 forward except for two brief periods, 1929-33 and 1957-63, had made the transition to a more progressive position. Whereas the Liberals of Guatemala and El Salvador became, essentially, the conservatives of the twentieth century, in Honduras they developed a more modern position, although the party was split seriously into conservative (*Rodista*) and progressive (ALIPO) wings. The National Party, successor to the old Conservative Party, had greater strength in the military, which helps to account for a difference in the nature of the Honduran military when compared with its neighboring states. More to the point, the National Party accepted classical liberal economic philosophy and cooperated willingly with foreign economic development of the country. As with the neo-Liberal parties in the surrounding states, however, corruption and personalism were also strong characteristics of the party. Scandals involving bribes, drug traffic, and other forms of corruption brought widespread discredit to the Paz administration and there was growing unrest. Labor strife, sometimes violent, erupted in both urban and rural areas.

Yielding to pressure from the Carter administration, Paz took steps toward restoration of civilian, constitutional rule in Honduras. Congressional elections in April 1980 gave the Liberal Party a narrow edge over the Nationalists, and in the November 1981 presidential election Liberal Roberto Suazo Córdova defeated his Nationalist opponent decisively and promised democratic rule with social and economic reform. Suazo, a successful small-town physician for 25 years, had little government experience except for his service as president of the Constituent Assembly since April 1981, but he had been active in the Liberal Party, of which he had been General Coordinator since 1979.

The presence of thousands of Nicaraguan National Guardsmen, refugees from the Sandinista Revolution (dealt with below), and the development of a major counterrevolutionary force using Honduran territory for its attacks on Nicaragua with U.S. support, put serious strains on the Suazo government. The military imposed increasing controls on the country and the Army expanded to twenty thousand. Government deficits soared as military expenditures rose. Assassinations and mysterious disappearances became part of Honduran political life. The militarization led to vocal opposition from moderate and leftist groups, who accused the government of applying the "Argentine solution" to Honduras. Although less noticeable than in neighboring states, some guerrilla and terrorist activity in turn provided the military with justification for more repressive measures. Thousands of U.S. armed forces joined with Honduran troops in military maneuvers designed to intimidate leftists in neighboring Nicaragua and El Salvador, as well as within the country.

Army Chief-of-Staff Gustavo Alvarez Martínez appeared to be the real power in the country. He worked closely with U.S. Ambassador John Dimitri Negroponte, a diplomat experienced in CIA-backed operations in Southeast Asia. Alvarez was also linked to the local branch of the Reverend Sun Myung Moon's Unification Church, which supported the strongly anti-communist stance of the Honduran military, and he supported Ronald Reagan's open opposition to "liberation theology" in Central America. All this contributed to a growing rift between the government and the Catholic clergy. Alvarez's power grew when a heart ailment forced Suazo into hospital in July 1983, first in Honduras and then in the United States for twelve days in September.

Younger officers loyal to Suazo, however, forced Alvarez's resignation along with other top military officers in late March 1984 as anti-

American demonstrations erupted in the capital. American support of "democratization" appeared to be simply a cover for "militarization." Suazo made clear that he commanded the armed forces as he named a nephew of former President Oswaldo López, Walter López Reyes, as the new military chief, but he also pledged continued cooperation with the U.S. López, however, emphasized Honduras's geopolitical location and said Honduras should take advantage of it, threatening to expel anti-Sandinista *contras* from Honduras if more U.S. economic aid was not forthcoming. Outwardly, the remilitarization of Honduras had received a setback, but until the larger issues on the isthmus (discussed in the next chapter) are settled, Honduras's future remains uncertain. Major U.S. military presence, including the construction of airports and other military installations, has meant a substantial economic benefit for certain regions and groups, creating another form of dependency which in the long run is both unnatural and unhealthy for the development of the country.

UNITED STATES MILITARY AID TO HONDURAS, 1980-84
(Millions of U.S.$)

Year	MAP	FMS	IMET	Total
1980	—	3.53	0.45	3.98
1981	—	8.40	0.53	8.93
1982	11.00	19.00	1.30	31.30
1983	27.50	29.00	0.80	37.30
1984	40.00	—	1.00	41.00

MAP = Military Assistance Program (grants)
FMS = Foreign Military Sales (loans)
IMET = International Military Education and Training

US ECONOMIC SUPPORT FUNDS (ESF) TO HONDURAS 1982-84
(Millions of U.S.$)

1982	36.8
1983	48.0
1984	40.0

SOURCE: "Honduras: A Democracy in Demise," *Special Washington Update on Latin America* (Feb. 1984), p. 10.

In Nicaragua, under the Somozas, a close relationship had intensified between U.S. business and the Nicaraguan government, similar to that which had been developing with Liberal dictatorships elsewhere on the isthmus. The Conservative Party survived as the only important legal opposition party, but divided over the question of collaboration with the Somozas. Eventually, many Liberals also broke with the Somozas, as the regime became simply a family dynasty of economic and political power in the country. Nevertheless, the old Conservative and Liberal families continued to represent a privileged elite in a country that pursued modernization along nineteenth-century Liberal lines well into the late twentieth century. This meant great expansion of export-oriented agriculture, some industrialization, a growth of financial institutions, and emergence of a middle class in Managua. After the destruction of that city by the earthquake of 1972, however, misappropriation of reconstruction funds by Tachito Somoza contributed to widespread disenchantment with the regime even among former supporters.

The Somoza government was not entirely unmindful of the needs of the people, and like other Central American Liberal dictatorships, it succeeded in bringing about a degree of modernization and some improvements in education, medical care, and social services. Nicaragua continued to produce a larger share of its food consumption than any other Central American country, although the trend toward exports was making it more dependent on foreign food imports just as had happened in the other states. More and more land was devoted to coffee, cattle, cotton, or sugar instead of subsistence crops. Nicaragua's per capita annual income placed it behind Panama, Costa Rica, and Guatemala on the isthmus, and poverty was growing rather than declining as real wages lagged behind inflation and population growth. Indeed, one of the most discouraging realities for the Liberal modernization model of the last hundred years in Central America is the apparent decline in standard of living for most Central Americans. By the 1970's there was widespread poverty in the country and many of the undesirable benefits of the Liberal-capitalist development had fastened themselves on both rural and urban Nicaragua.

Although more modern political parties and labor unions appeared during the Somoza regime, none were allowed to play a major role in the politics of the country, as Somoza arranged with Conservative collaborators to divide all seats in the Congress between the two traditional parties. More radical opposition developed among university students and included the Sandinista Front for National Liberation (FSLN), formed about 1960 and always dedicated to a Marxist-oriented revolution. It gained few adherents until the late 1970's, when opposition grew against Tachito Somoza's efforts to frustrate all legal political expression.

As in the rest of Central America, after the Episcopal Conference at Medellín in 1968 the clergy began to speak out against the violations of human rights and lack of concern for the welfare of the poor. Radical Catholics supported the Sandinistas. More moderate elements led by Pedro Joaquín Chamoro, editor of the country's leading daily newspaper (the Conservative *La Prensa*), formed the Democratic Liberation Union (UDEL) in 1974. Meanwhile, twelve prominent Nicaraguans organized a broadly based campaign against the dictatorship that included praise of the Sandinistas. Jimmy Carter recognized that the dynasty's days were numbered, and his ambassadors in Managua encouraged local businessmen to organize to effect a peaceful transition to a more democratic regime.

The assassination of the popular Chamorro in January 1978 brought a dramatic upsurge in support for the FSLN. All segments of the population rallied against the dictatorship. A devastating civil war followed as Somoza clung tenaciously to power against both internal and international efforts to ease him out. United States indecision and bumbling appalled informed observers, as it seemed both to oppose and support the regime simultaneously. First halting military assistance to Somoza because of human rights violations, Carter later resumed aid and congratulated the tyrant on his progress in human rights after Somoza made two visits to the U.S. in May and June. Fear of communism remained an element in U.S. policy throughout the crisis and effectively limited both Carter's and Reagan's ability to react reasonably to the crisis in Nicaragua.

As the civil war destroyed town after town and killed thousands of Nicaraguans, international and domestic efforts to find a settlement proceeded slowly. Within Nicaragua, a Broad Opposition Front (FAO) succeeded UDEL in attempting to unify the diverse elements opposing Somoza, while several American nations attempted to mediate the conflict. Unrealistic efforts by the U.S. to exclude the Sandinistas from the process sabotaged these efforts. The U.S. was accused of attempting to establish *somocismo sin Somoza* (Somozism without Somoza). While the FAO and diplomatic corps failed in their efforts to bring a settlement, the Sandinistas broadened their own base of support. Their mass organizations, notably the United Peoples Movement (MPU) which in turn organized the National Patriotic Front (FPN) in February 1979, developed powerful grass-roots support for the FSLN, while Venezuela, Panama, and Costa Rica provided both moral and material assistance to their cause. By the end of 1978 Nicaragua was nearly bankrupt and serious capital flight had occurred. Production dropped 26 per cent during the year. Abroad only the governments of Honduras and Paraguay still supported the Somoza regime. The continued fighting would destroy Nicaragua's economy and intensify the suffering of its people.

Although the FSLN was itself divided into three factions ranging from Marxist-Leninists to Social Democrats, they maintained a unified front and launched a successful military offensive from Costa Rican territory at the end of May 1979. A general strike which closed 80 per cent of the businesses in the country coincided with the offensive. U.S. Secretary of State Cyrus Vance called openly for Somoza's resignation, stating what had been obvious for more than a year, that Somoza had lost the confidence of the Nicaraguan people. The Organization of American States also called for his removal in late June, but Somoza held out in his concrete bunker while house to house fighting against his National Guard laid waste much of Managua. Finally, on July 17, Somoza resigned and fled to Paraguay, where Argentine radicals later murdered him. His appointed successor fled on the following day to Guatemala, and the Sandinistas took over on the 19th, appointing a junta composed of three Sandinistas and two Conservatives. Real power in the country, however, as would soon become clear, resided in the Directorate of the FSLN and the Sandinista army. The non-

Sandinistas on the junta, Alfonso Robelo and Violeta Chamorro, resigned within a year and soon were supporting the opposition to the
government. Bourgeois elements originally dominated the Council of
State, established in May 1980, but the FSLN Directorate later added
14 delegates representing peasant and worker interests, giving the
Sandinistas a majority.

The collapse of the Somoza dynasty represented the demise of
nineteenth-century Liberalism in Nicaragua and the beginning of a
bold new experiment in which the interests of the masses would take
precedence over those of the traditional elites. As in Cuba, two decades
earlier, this conflict would be complicated by East-West confrontation.
That Nicaragua would move sharply toward socialism ahead of the
rest of Central America, after lagging behind it for so many years, is
historically a result of the Somozas' Liberal Party failing to allow more
moderate but progressive forces to develop and share in the political
process during the last half-century. As elsewhere on the isthmus, the
elite repressed middle- and working-class interests, leaving violence
and revolution as the only avenue for bringing about change. That a
tiny minority—the Sandinistas—were able to seize power and capture
the imagination of the majority of the population is not unique in the
history of revolution. The Sandinistas saw themselves as a vanguard
in the struggle to provide a better life for their compatriots. But the
new government faced an enormous challenge. The civil war had left
some 40,000 dead and half a million homeless. The economy was in
ruins. There was the nucleus of a counterrevolutionary force of some
7,000 National Guardsmen who had retreated into Honduras, while
other somocista exiles in Miami and elsewhere already were plotting
against the new government. All of the collaborators of the old regime
did not escape, however, and the government soon began trials of
about 7,000 political prisoners. New prisons had to be built to hold
them all, but the Sandinistas rejected the firing squads that had characterized the early days of the Cuban Revolution and instead outlawed
capital punishment as part of a 54-article bill of rights.

Many of the Sandinistas were convinced of the inevitability of
struggle against the United States, the champion of nineteenth-century

Liberalism and defender of the old order. They quickly mobilized much of the population into mass organizations of peasants, women, youth, part of the clergy, and neighborhood Committees for Defense of the Revolution. They created a militia that by 1984 brought Nicaragua's total armed forces to approximately 100,000, frightening their neighbors and putting a major burden on the economy. The MPU and FPN, on the other hand, were allowed to fade away since the Sandinistas did not have direct control of those popular revolutionary groups which had outlived their usefulness once Somoza was overthrown. They could have become rival political parties to the FSLN. How their authoritarian means, the intervention of Soviet and U.S. interests into the struggle, and the development of legitimate opposition to the radical Sandinista approach will affect the course of the Revolution and Nicaraguan history remains to be seen, but the first five years of the Sandinista Revolution have suggested the range of reforms.

The reforms began by providing new housing and health facilities for the poor, and sponsoring a literacy campaign that was a notable success, although their record of economic achievement was otherwise bleak. Expropriation of the vast Somoza family holdings provided the nucleus of a state-run economy, but the Sandinistas soon found that efficient management of these holdings was not automatic. Production declined notably even if better distribution of income was provided. Nicaraguan peasants received nearly 600,000 acres in an agrarian reform program between 1979 and mid-1983, as some 3000 cooperatives were established. Although an estimated 60 per cent of the economic activity of the country remained in private hands, there was a notable increase in government regulation. The Sandinista government inherited nearly $600 million of foreign debt, but managed to refinance it, with a severe austerity program and tight controls on currency. The bourgeoisie grumbled and some left Nicaragua, but the majority stayed, unwilling to abandon their country as their Cuban counterparts had done two decades before.

The Carter administration quickly recognized the new regime and approved a significant amount of economic assistance while expressing some concern over its leftward drift, but after Ronald Reagan took office, in January 1981, U.S. policy turned decidedly hostile. Accusing Nicaragua on April 1 of serving as a conduit for 200 tons of military equipment to the Salvadoran rebels, Reagan resumed military sales to Guatemala, sent military advisers to El Salvador, suspended AID programs to Nicaragua, and began CIA support of the anti-Sandinista National Democratic Front (FDN) operating near the Nicaraguan border in Honduras. A smaller opposition guerrilla group, Edén Pastora's Sandino Revolutionary Front (FRS), formed the nucleus of the Democratic Revolutionary Alliance (ARDE), which operated from Costa Rica and maintained an aloofness from both the U.S. and the somocista-tinged FDN. These forces, in addition to collaborating Mosquito Indian groups, put a substantial military burden on the Sandinista regime. In 1984 a move to unite the opposition forces appeared slowly to be making headway.

The Mosquitos and other Indians of the Caribbean coast became a serious embarrassment to the Sandinistas. Under the treaty with Great Britain by which Nicaragua had incorporated the Mosquito Kingdom, the Mosquitos were guaranteed autonomy. The Somoza dynasty had generally respected this provision. The Caribbean coast had always been well outside the mainstream of Nicaraguan life. Many of its inhabitants remained English-speaking, Protestant, their life style dependent on the wetlands of the tropical lowlands near the Caribbean. Primitive by some standards, they nevertheless had a strong sense of nationhood, which continued to thrive under the Somozas. The Sandinistas had ambitious plans to integrate the Caribbean Indians into the New Nicaragua, a concept that was incompatible with the independence that the Mosquitos had maintained against the rulers of Spanish-speaking Nicaragua since the sixteenth century. Moreover, the Mosquitos were located in the very area where the FDN was threatening Nicaragua and there was ample evidence that many Mosquitos and one of their principal leaders, Steadman Fagoth Muller, were conspiring with both the FDN and ARDE. The Sandinistas dealt with the situation by resettling thousands of Mosquitos away from the coast and border, forcing them to turn to agriculture in a hostile climate, after centuries of dependence on the sea.

Faced with U.S.-supported counterrevolutionary forces on both frontiers and with a vocal opposition within the country as well, in March 1982 the Sandinista government suspended the constitution and imposed stricter censorship, although it did not permanently shut down the opposition press, represented principally by *La Prensa*. A vigorous propaganda war between the U.S. and Nicaragua, with the guerrilla war in El Salvador hanging in the balance, undermined peace efforts by diplomats of Panama, Colombia, Venezuela, and Mexico, who began talks on Contadora Island, Panama, in January 1983. This "Contadora Group" sought to reduce foreign military presence in the Central American states. Their proposals received lip service approval from the United States and Nicaragua, but the rising tension and U.S.-supported disinformation, destabilization, and counterrevolutionary activities against the Sandinista regime, as well as the heavy presence of Cuban and eastern European advisers within Nicaragua, precluded an agreement under Contadora auspices.

Aside from ideological issues, the opposition accused the Sandinista leadership of profiteering, conspicuous consumption, corruption, and poor judgment. Moreover, they said the Sandinistas had polarized the Nicaraguan population instead of unifying it. Yet in response to U.S. policy, the Sandinistas, alarmed by the 1983 U.S. invasion of Grenada, made notable concessions. Expelling 1000 Cuban military advisers, releasing hundreds of Mosquito Indian prisoners, and offering amnesty to the *contras* were among the more notable of their conciliatory moves in 1983. The U.S., however, continued to insist that Nicaragua was a threat to peace in Central America and began to apply economic sanctions. The U.S. also engineered the resurrection of the Central American Defense Command (CONDECA) by Honduras, Guatemala, El Salvador, and Panama, with Nicaragua excluded and Costa Rican declining participation. This accompanied the U.S. arms buildup in Honduras already noted. Costa Rica emphasized its neutrality in the conflict, but was finding it difficult to resist the growing anti-Sandinista pressure from the U.S. because of its precarious economic situation which was dependent on U.S. support. Costa Rica found itself walking a tightrope between the Contadora and U.S. positions on Nicaragua. In early 1984 Costa Rica officially requested and received U.S. military equipment following border incidents between the Sandinista army and Costa Rican defense force.

When the Contadora Group presented its 21-point peace plan, in December 1983, the Nicaraguans declared that they would negotiate only with the U.S. "We don't talk to puppets," declared Foreign Minister Miguel D'Escoto, "only to puppeteers." Meanwhile, the U.S. had fleets operating off both Central American coasts while it conducted large-scale maneuvers in Honduras. Nicaraguan forces shot down a U.S. helicopter when it strayed across the border. Similar incidents occurred later in El Salvador when U.S. helicopters flew over guerrilla-held territory. In March 1984 there was an international outcry against the mining of Nicaraguan harbors by CIA-supported *contras* after several foreign ships, including a Soviet freighter, were damaged. Nicaragua brought charges against the U.S. for this activity before the World Court of Justice at The Hague, to which the Reagan administration arrogantly replied that it would ignore any judgment by that Court. Nevertheless, the mining ceased after the U.S. Senate passed a resolution (84-12) calling on the CIA to stop mine-laying operations.

The government announced elections for November 4, 1984, but the opposition protested that there could not be free elections without free press and assembly. The FSLN named Daniel Ortega Saavedra as its candidate and began a massive campaign for him in July. Most of the opposition united behind Arturo Cruz, an international banker who had been active in overthrowing Somoza but had broken early with the Sandinistas after serving briefly as their ambassador in Washington. Cruz refused to register for the election until guarantees were forthcoming, and was labeled a lackey of the U.S. by the Sandinistas as Ortega swept the election with only minor opposition.

Much of contemporary Central America reflects the persistence of nineteenth-century Liberalism—conservative by today's definitions—

among Central American elites, along with the inevitable rise of more modern, middle-class elements against it. While certain segments of the middle class have embraced neo-Liberalism, others, along with working-class representatives, have risen to challenge it, with the inevitable clashes of working class versus capitalist interests becoming important in Central American politics. The principal failure of Liberalism and capitalism in Central America has been their failure to reward labor with adequate wages so that prosperity could become more general and expand in a healthy manner. Especially in agriculture, but also in the capital intensive new industries promoted by the Common Market, labor has failed to receive a fair share of the gains, and this has retarded development of a stronger consumer-based economy. This continued repression of labor has deprived most Central Americans of better standards of living and a more participatory role in their governments. The close relationship of the United States to the old elites has been a major force in allowing the repressive policies to continue as long as they have.

The strength of the old oligarchies and their resistance to social and political modernization have failed, nevertheless, to block completely the trend toward social democracy. In all of the states, institutional change has occurred through the establishment of social security, public medical services, university expansion and innovation, national development ministries or corporations, labor departments, and agrarian reform. While Guatemala, El Salvador, and Honduras still resist the structural reform the left demands, the concessions which have been made reflect the pressure of the times, and they have sometimes shaken the intransigent position of rightist oligarchies. Yet these oligarchies and their allies remain a powerful force. Significant U.S. assistance and fear of Marxist revolution have helped to preserve military rule. But the old landholding oligarchies are being forced to share political and economic power with the larger middle classes, which have come into their own. These classes now play major roles in the economy and politics of every Central American state; it is no longer possible to say that Central America has no significant middle class. The emphasis of the neo-Positivist regimes of a decade ago on material development, production, and foreign investment has given way to concern for a broader distribution of wealth and popular participation in government, even though truly free elections are still rare outside of Costa Rica.

The recognition of middle-class and working-class voices, both in political decision-making and in the determination of national policy, is part of a trend toward corporatism which has changed the nature of twentieth-century Central America. This is why the middle class has begun to be effective in spite of the fact that elections are often rigged. As it has developed institutional strength—in labor unions, universities, political parties, the army, civic organizations, etc.—it has been able to exert pressures on national decision-making. Its strength in these institutions has forced concessions from traditionalists on a number of fronts.

At the same time, the military itself has become a powerful institution, as high ranking officers have gained economic power, challenging the traditional elites, while retaining the tradition of the *fuero militar*, or corporate privileges for the military. The result has been, especially in Guatemala, El Salvador, and Honduras, the development of various "mafia"-type, extended families often rivaling each other for control of regions, economic concessions, or privilege. These family-oriented power blocs cannot be ignored in analyzing modern Central America.

The old order remains strongest in Guatemala, where military domination on behalf of elite interests still prevails. Costa Rica, on the other hand, has reaffirmed its commitment to social democracy, while Nicaragua has launched a thoroughgoing socialist revolution while retaining considerable private enterprise. El Salvador and Honduras appear to be in transition to moderate social democracy, although in both countries there remains the threat of right-wing reaction.

Chapter 10 • The Failure of Reunification

The tradition of Central American unity was never really strong, even during the three centuries of the Kingdom of Guatemala. The Spanish rulers failed to develop close bonds between the provinces; instead, they created local loyalties and jealousies, particularly over the concentration of power in Guatemala City. The passionate and bitter struggles between the states of the United Provinces doomed hopes for unity after independence. Efforts toward unification made since 1847, both of good intention and of ulterior ambition, have rarely progressed beyond the stage of initial organization and planning. Salvador Mendieta's efforts early in the twentieth century emphasized the absence of real desire for Central American unity, and the total failure of his Unionist Party corroborated his pessimistic view.

Central Americans have often charged that foreign nations—Britain in the nineteenth century, the United States more recently—have sabotaged unity, following a "divide and conquer" policy. Certainly, there is some truth to the charge with regard to the activities of nationals and diplomats of both English-speaking countries. It was, for example, easier for the giant fruit companies to deal with small, unstable republics than with a larger, united nation. Yet had there not been substantial internal causes of disunity for foreigners to exploit, Central Americans might still have achieved union.

After World War II the development of foreign aid programs, particularly from the United States but also from international organizations, focused on the need for Central American unity and engendered a spirit of cooperation. Working either with the United States Agency for International Development or with United Nations organizations, the Central American nations developed a number of multilateral programs which promoted a spirit of unity, at least among the technicians and politicians associated with them. Cultural and ideological unity came more gradually with programs to eliminate unnecessary duplication in Central American universities and vocational schools.

The foreign assistance programs imposed a kind of unity over the region. Studies made by private corporations and foundations, by national and international governmental agencies, and by academicians in several disciplines encouraged the five states to face up to their common problems. The development of economic integration and its accompanying interstate organizations promoted cooperation and a sense of unity on the isthmus, as did the growth of intererstate investment and the development of easier transportation and communication among the states.

Nevertheless, aid programs were often ill-conceived and not applicable to the peculiar problems of Central America. The failure of the United States to support the revolutionary programs of Arévalo, the Sandinistas, and other more progressive forces has fastened an aura of reaction on U.S. programs and made them suspect to many Central Americans. At the same time the military establishments have expanded and become, often, the principal beneficiaries of aid programs. The refusal of most U.S. aid programs to recognize the need for basic restructuring of the society and economy of the region is at the heart of the failure of the programs to achieve real change. Thus, many Central Americans look at the programs simply as devices to maintain the peoples of the region in economic subservience to the capitalists.

Immediately after World War II, with more progressive governments in Guatemala, Costa Rica, and El Salvador—and even some spirit of the need for unity and change beginning to thrive in Honduras and Nicaragua—the movement for unity picked up. The Guatemalan and Salvadoran governments conducted some discussions toward the goal of union between 1945 and 1948, and these formed the background for a general meeting of Central American foreign ministers in October 1951. At that time they discussed possibilities for cooperation. From those meetings came plans for the Organization of Central American States (ODECA), formally founded in 1955. In 1952 economy ministers of the five states met in Tegucigalpa with the U.N. Economic Commission for Latin America. Subsequent meetings led to a treaty, in 1958, which aimed to establish Central American economic integration.

In a move toward the creation of a Central American Common Market (CACM), the states signed a series of trade agreements and planned new industries. This program expanded slowly throughout the 1960's. Costa Rica, already the most prosperous state, was reluctant to cooperate fully, fearing competition from countries with cheap labor and especially distrustful of Nicaragua. Thus, a true common market was never achieved, but substantial advance was made, particularly among the states of Guatemala, El Salvador, and Honduras, and new industries did develop.

Other results of the cooperation were evident. There was an acceleration in the program of road building, and the Inter-American Highway was completed as far as Panama in 1964; also, a vast improvement in the condition and number of paved or all-weather roads was made throughout Central America. These improvements facilitated the increased interstate trade and industry as well as promoting tourism, although continued political instability very much hampered that development. Tourism itself became an instrument for attracting potential investors. Costa Rica promoted immigration of North American retirees as another source of income and land development, although it was not sufficient to offset entirely Costa Rica's rather serious balance-of-payments deficit.

The common market idea did promote much new economic activity, and, combined with foreign investment, it brought some improvement

INTERSTATE CENTRAL AMERICAN TRADE AS A PERCENTAGE OF TOTAL
CENTRAL AMERICAN FOREIGN TRADE
(millions of U.S. dollars)

Year	All Foreign Trade	Interstate C. A. Trade	% Interstate
1950	518.00	17.30	3.34
1955	833.90	26.20	3.14
1960	954.20	65.40	6.85
1965	1650.50	271.00	16.42
1966	1773.90	349.50	19.70
1967	1886.90	427.90	22.68
1968	1997.50	516.60	25.86
1969	2037.60	498.00	24.44
1970	2331.98	585.43	25.10
1971	2411.30	552.90	22.93
1972	2718.20	611.50	22.50
1973	3534.00	776.90	21.98
1974	5092.00	1065.30	20.92
1975	5244.26	1055.48	20.13
1976	6319.66	1260.50	19.95
1977	8466.45	1505.14	17.78
1978	8598.80	1743.53	20.28
1979	9514.93	1776.63	18.67
1980	10399.37	2228.73	21.43
1981	9642.01	1909.22	19.80
1982	8073.00	1563.50	19.37
1983(e)	8400.10	1577.30	18.78

(e) = Estimate
SOURCES: Secretaría Permanente del Tratado General de Integración Económica
Centroamericana (SIECA), *Serie estadística seleccionada de Centroamérica y
Panamá* (Guatemala, 1973); SIECA, *Compendio estadístico Centroamericano*
(*Guatemala*, 1975); SIECA, *Estadísticas analíticas del comercio interamericano,*
No. 1 (Guatemala, 1983); SIECA, *Estadísticas Macroeconómicas de Centro-
américa 1979-1983* (Guatemala, 1984); *Statistical Abstract of Latin America,*
Vol. 22 (Los Angeles, 1983); and *Anuarios Estadísticos* of the five Central Amer-
ican republics. These figures do not include Belize or Panama.

in the standard of living of many Central Americans. This strength-
ened the larger middle classes, and they, in turn, demanded greater
participation in government. Yet the overall progress was disappointing.
Most of the industries tended to be capital intensive rather than labor
intensive and, thus, failed to provide a major source of employment
for the rapidly expanding population. Guatemala and El Salvador
gained the most from the greater interstate trade. Panama also joined
in, but, as with Costa Rica, her participation was minimal. By 1968

Honduras and Nicaragua were importing far more than they were selling to their Central American neighbors.

The two-week "futbol war" between El Salvador and Honduras in the summer of 1969 brought a halt to the growth of the CACM and pointed up the startling reality that, without stronger political cooperation, economic union was precarious. The Central American states had settled most disputes amicably since World War II, but the outbreak of this "war" brought back memories of the frequent civil wars and the meddling in each other's affairs which had characterized the isthmus in the nineteenth and early twentieth century.

Serious problems had been building for some time. To begin with, there was a grave demographic problem. El Salvador, the only Central American state without large amounts of public land, had a population density of nearly 400 persons per square mile, while Honduras had 55 per square mile. The traditional "fourteen families" (recently counted at 254 families) owned 95 per cent of the land in El Salvador, and for the most part they did not cultivate intensively. Their dominance of agriculture had, inevitably, created a serious land shortage. Because of that shortage, Salvadorans moved to Honduras, where they settled on the land or engaged in commerce or industry. The economic integration treaties signed in 1958 allowed free transit of inhabitants, facilitating the natural flow. In 1950 some 20,000 Salvadorans, 62 per cent of all foreigners, already lived in Honduras. By 1961 the number had increased to 38,000, or 74 per cent of all foreigners, and it continued to rise during the 1960's. Although the Salvadorans represented only 2 per cent of the total Honduran population in the 1961 census, their actual number was probably somewhat higher, because the figures do not include those who had become Honduran citizens. In some departments, notably Cortés and Valle, the Salvadoran population was as high as 5 per cent. These industrious and sometimes aggressive immigrants incurred the resentment and jealousy of the local peasants, workers, and shopkeepers, to whom they represented a real or imagined threat of economic displacement. By 1963 the Hondurans' anger had prompted the passage of legislation that limited the number of foreign workers in any enterprise to 10 per cent of the payroll.

More directly responsible for the conflict between the two states was the 1968 Honduran law prohibiting Salvadorans from owning land. Honduran large landholders had promoted this law, fearing that the land scarcity being created by the Salvadoran immigrants would cause Honduran peasants to demand land reform.

To the demographic problem of Salvadoran immigration into Honduras was added an economic reality—El Salvador had advanced economically much more than Honduras, particularly as a result of the common market. Interstate trade within Central America increased the trade of all of the states, but it did not bring equal benefits in the balance of payments. Honduras was negatively affected, especially during the mid to late 1960's. By contrast, El Salvador had benefited more than any other state by the integration agreements.

Boundary disputes had long embittered relations between the two states, but there had been little violence since the first decade of the twentieth century. Treaties settling the border questions, however, had never been ratified. In 1967 Salvadoran authorities arrested a Honduran in the disputed area, and the Hondurans responded by capturing forty Salvadoran troops in the area of their claim. El Salvador—admittedly, as a result of the incident—then sought to buy seven warplanes from the United States. The two Central American states broke diplomatic relations, and they were not resumed until President Lyndon Johnson's visit to El Salvador in July 1968 succeeded in temporarily restoring normal relations.

Tension remained, however, and the dispute came to the attention of an astonished world during World Cup soccer playoffs between teams representing the two states in the summer of 1969. Violence erupting around the games, which were played in each of their respective capitals, forced the teams to play the third and deciding game in Mexico, where El Salvador won. Meanwhile, Hondurans had savagely attacked Salvadoran residents in Honduras, forcing thousands to flee. In El Salvador the population retaliated by attacking the smaller Honduran population there. In late June El Salvador broke diplomatic relations and demanded reparations on behalf of her dispossessed nationals in Honduras. Honduras then made similar demands, and the two states carried their cases to the Organization of American States, which sent representatives of its Commission on Human Rights to investigate. On July 3, however, El Salvador claimed that a Honduran plane had bombed several points in the state. Sensational news reporting and unrestrained government propaganda inflamed popular opinion on both sides. Violent clashes multiplied along the frontier until, on July 14, Salvadoran forces invaded Honduras, advancing quickly to within seventy-five miles of Tegucigalpa. Honduras struck back with bombing raids on San Salvador and Acajutla. The war lasted only a few days, but neither country could afford the destruction and dislocation that occurred. Both states agreed to a cease-fire, arranged by the OAS on July 18, calling for an international observer team and safety guarantees for immigrants in both countries.

Landowners in El Salvador, fearing a return of the émigrés to El Salvador, where they would demand land, urged Salvadoran President Fidel Sánchez Hernández to fight on and not give up the territorial advantage already gained. Salvadoran troops remained in Honduras for several weeks before finally retreating. Peace was restored in August. The damage had been done, not only to physical facilities in both countries, but also to the common market concept and to the spirit of friendship among the states, which had seemed to be moving them closer to union. Bitterness has remained between the two nations, and solutions to the real demographic and economic problems are still wanting. Fighting broke out sporadically along the Salvadoran-Honduran frontier, requiring the continuance of the OAS force there. After futile negotiations, Honduras and El Salvador agreed to submit their dispute to arbitration in 1976 and reached agreement on a treaty formally ending the war in October 1980, although details regarding the border remained in dispute. Hundreds of thousands of refugees from the Salvadoran civil war caused relations to deteriorate in 1981, but Honduras resumed trade with El Salvador after 13 years in 1982.

The 1969 war had abruptly interrupted a decade of growth and economic diversification* although interstate trade soon reached pre-1969 levels and there was modest growth in the volume of trade

* See Chart, p. 277.

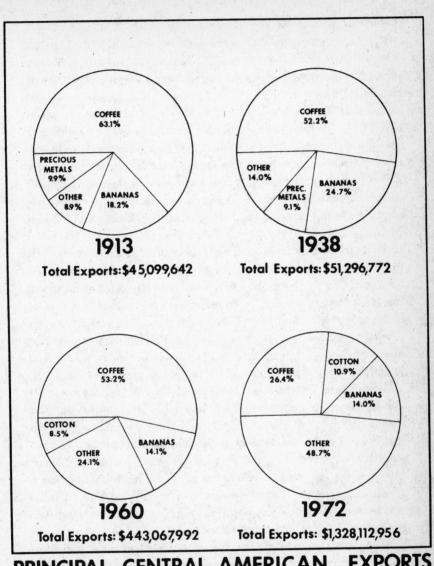

1913

Total Exports: $45,099,642

1938

Total Exports: $51,296,772

1960

Total Exports: $443,067,992

1972

Total Exports: $1,328,112,956

PRINCIPAL CENTRAL AMERICAN EXPORTS

throughout most of the 1970's. In the aftermath of that clash careful analysis revealed not only that economic union could go only so far without closer political confederation, but also that the CACM had not been uniformly beneficial for all five states. Indeed, the technocrats of SIECA, which included the best minds of Central America, concluded that if it was truly to benefit the entire region there would have to be provision for redistribution of the generated wealth that flowed from one region to another as a result of internal trade patterns. Political disunity hampered efforts to restart the integration movement. Although by 1972 a beginning had been made, the early 1970's will be remembered as a period of disillusion and frustration for the movement. Worsening economic and social conditions, however, stimulated by rampant inflation and the worldwide oil crisis, led to the formation of a High Level Committee which in March 1976 presented a draft treaty proposing sweeping modifications. If adopted, this treaty would have extended the integration movement to total trade liberalization, standardization of foreign investment rules, tax harmonization, free movement of labor and capital, a common agricultural policy, a coordinated system of basic industries, and a unified social policy that promoted health, nutrition, housing, support of labor unions, and harmonization of social security and minimum wages.

Official reaction to these recommendations was unenthusiastic. While admitting their theoretical desirability, no government was willing to relinquish the sovereignty and authority necessary to provide the sort of unified agencies to structure and administer these services. Defeat of the proposed treaty, which would have turned adversity into progress, was a watershed for the integration movement, which has been in decline ever since. The failure of the Central American elites to seize this opportunity was far more damaging than the "futbol war" for the future of the isthmus.

As we have already seen in reviewing the development of individual states in the last chapter, the economic recession and political turmoil of the late 1970's further fragmented the isthmus and made integration seem remote. The rise of the Sandinistas in Nicaragua and the guerrilla warfare in El Salvador curtailed trade on the Inter-American highway while the depression reduced exports for all the nations. A meeting of economic integration ministers in 1980 in Managua sought to revive the CACM. They agreed to draft a new treaty to replace the 1960 General Treaty and to establish a Maritime Transport Commission with headquarters in Managua, but little real progress had been achieved by 1985.

The political and economic crises made Central America the focus of a dangerous East-West confrontation and brought new manifestations of U.S. hegemony over the region. The pattern of military dictatorship in all of the states except Costa Rica had intensified in reaction to the rise of Fidel Castro after 1959. A military phase of the Central American integration movement was the formation of the Central American Defense Council (CONDECA) with strong US support in 1963 by the governments of Guatemala, Honduras, El Salvador, and Nicaragua. The 1969 war deflated this organization when Honduras pulled out, and in the 1970's it faded into near obscurity, with greater emphasis being placed on economic and social development. After the Medellín Episcopal Conference of 1968 the Church began to promote with some success greater attention to the plight of the poor and oppressed, contributing to a new awareness of the problem of human rights violations in Central America. International organizations began to focus on Guatemala, Nicaragua, and El Salvador, and they often scored the U.S. for its support of repressive regimes in those countries. When Secretary of State Henry Kissinger visited Costa Rica and Guatemala in February 1976 he was greeted with riots and outcries against U.S. support of reactionary regimes in Latin America.

United States policy took a dramatic turn under the administration of Jimmy Carter, as he sought to improve the U.S. image abroad and place his country in step with the march of reform and respect for human rights. His pro-human rights policy brought stiff opposition from elites in Guatemala and El Salvador, especially after the overthrow of Somoza in Nicaragua. Carter also pushed through successfully treaties under which the U.S. agreed to turn over the Panama Canal to Panama by the year 2000, easing the severely strained re-

lations between the U.S. and Panama and helping the government
of strong-man Omar Torrijos to reverse the ailing economic trends in
his country. Although the Carter government worked to prevent a
Sandinista victory in Nicaragua, it accepted their accession to power
gracefully and, after Sandinista leaders met with Carter at the White
House in late September 1979, the U.S. Congress approved a major
Nicaraguan aid package.

The election of Ronald Reagan brought a sharp reversal of these
policies. Reagan had opposed transfer of the Canal Zone, and his government obstructed implementation of the 1978 treaties, risking deteriorating relations with Panama in a period when that state was
undergoing political adjustments following the accidental death of
Torrijos. The Reagan administration cultivated better relations with
the Panamanian military, however. Soon after taking office Reagan
resumed military sales to Guatemala, sent US military advisers to El
Salvador, and suspended United States A.I.D. programs to Nicaragua.
On June 2, 1981, Secretary of State Alexander Haig condemned the
"large-scale shipments of Soviet military supplies" to Nicaragua. By
November 1981 Reagan has reportedly approved $19 million in aid for
covert operations against the Nicaraguan government. He also increased U.S. support against guerrilla opposition forces in El Salvador.
From the outset of his administration, it was clear that Reagan intended to roll back the revolutionary tide in Central America and to
make the isthmus a theater in the escalating confrontation with Soviet
power.

The new U.S. presence in Central America was most obvious in
Honduras, where a massive U.S. military and naval buildup supported
the militarization of Honduras and covert aid to the Nicaraguan
contras, intending to intimidate both the Sandinistas and the Salvadoran guerrillas. In 1983, with the strong backing of the Reagan
administration, Honduras, Guatemala, El Salvador, and Panama resurrected CONDECA, with Nicaragua excluded and Costa Rica, emphasizing its neutrality, declining to participate. But the Reagan government played on traditional Costa Rican fear of Nicaragua to
encourage a military build-up in that country as well. Major U.S.

maneuvers in Honduras highlighted the new organization, although the Ríos Montt government of Guatemala showed little interest, and Panama chose not to participate in these maneuvers. Moreover, training of Salvadoran troops in Honduras elicited a strong anti-military and anti-American reaction among Hondurans. The ouster of military chieftain Gustavo Alvarez was a blow to this policy, but the U.S. presence remained strong.

As debate over U.S. policy heightened in 1983, Reagan named Henry Kissinger to head a bipartisan commission to study Central America. The Committee's report, although providing considerable evidence that the basic problems on the isthmus were socio-economic, concluded with an endorsement of the military policies of the Reagan government. It also called, however, for a massive economic and social aid program, which the Reagan government also began to implement. While U.S. officials continued to insist that U.S. combat troops would not be employed in Central America, it increasingly appeared that U.S. objectives would not likely be achieved without U.S. forces, and the 1983 U.S. Marine invasion of Grenada suggested Reagan's willingness to consider that alternative.

These hard line policies failed either to arrest the growing guerrilla power in El Salvador or to topple the Sandinista government, but they further polarized Central American politics and increased the violence which has claimed more than 100,000 lives during the past five years. It also undermined the efforts in 1983-84 of the Contadora Group to find a pacific solution to the conflicts.

Optimism regarding peace and rekindling of the spirit of unity and cooperation toward economic and social progress was a scarce commodity by 1985. The gap between Central American expectations and achievements was wider than ever, and the affluence of the few stood in sharp contrast to the rapid population growth that has expanded the depressing poverty of the majority to alarming proportions. Despite much modernization, the people of these states still carry a heavy colonial burden, both materially and psychologically. The creole mentality of small elites who remain dominant and willingly collaborate with foreign interests is disappearing only slowly. Widespread corruption, the heritage of an underpaid and poorly trained bureaucracy, resistance to structural change, and protection of position and wealth characterize the elites everywhere.

Independence brought the creole elites to power. The Liberal revolutions challenged their absolute hold and enlarged the middle sectors, so that late in the twentieth century the small elites no longer control everything. Middle- and working-class interests are now challenging the oligarchies created by the Liberal revolutions and demanding a more equitable distribution of wealth and power. The social revolutions which have characterized the past half-century of Central American history are not nearly completed.

The myriad parties, factions, fronts, and organizations that characterize the political spectrum of each Central American state sometimes obscure the four broad concentrations of ideological, social, and economic interests that vie for control on the isthmus today: 1) The traditional Right, defending the Liberal-Positivist development models of the last century in an effort to save the privileged position of the old order. While it is often badly divided, with planter, merchant, and military factions, it remains united in its fear of "communism" and any serious restructuring of the society. 2) Moderate reformist parties, best represented by the Christian Democrats in El Salvador and Guatemala, but also by the Conservative Party of Nicaragua, who reject the Liberal-Positivist tradition, but who seek progress by moderate, gradual reforms that can accommodate the old elites as well as the masses. 3) Social Democrats who want thorough-going restructuring, with a much greater public sector role, although retaining private investment and development. Although often Marxist in ideology, these groups tend to be intensely anti-communist and look toward western Europe for models of socialist-capitalist synthesis. And 4) Marxist-Leninists who seek by revolution to establish socialist regimes along Cuban or eastern European lines.

While much of the media attention focuses on the first and fourth of these groups, those of the center are in fact quite strong and if peace can be restored there is room for optimism that those elements can begin to solve Central America's formidable problems. While chances of reunion now seem more unlikely than at any time since 1839, the logic of union remains irresistible. If peace returns and more popular governments gain power, then the hopes of Francisco Morazán and Salvador Mendieta for a single Central American republic may yet come to fruition. But for the immediate future, while cooperation at many levels will probably resume, it is just as likely that Central America will remain divided into five sovereign states with strong nationalistic elements that emphasize their unique differences rather than their common problems.

Political Chronology

1501	Rodrigo de Bastidas, first European to set foot on Central America, discovers Isthmus of Darién.
1502	Christopher Columbus sails along coast from Bay Islands to Panama, giving many place names.
1504	Bastidas returns to Daríen, captures 600 Indian slaves.
1506-08	Juan Díaz de Solís and Vicente Yáñez discover Amatique Bay and sail along Central American coast, searching for westward passage.
1509	First Spanish settlements on mainland of America established under leadership of Alonso de Ojeda and Diego de Nicuesa.
1510	Ojeda founds settlement on Gulf of Urabá (Darién), but returns to Santo Domingo when he is wounded. Vasco Núñez de Balboa emerges as leader of Darién.
	Requerimiento provides for "legal" war against Indians by Spaniards.
1512	War breaks out between Cakchiquel, in alliance with Aztec, and Quiché in Guatemalan highlands.
1513	Laws of Burgos. Balboa discovers Pacific Ocean (South Sea). Pedro Arias de Avila (Pedrarias Dávila) named Governor of Castilla del Oro.
1514	Iximché (Cakchiquel capital) nearly destroyed entirely by fire. Pedrarias takes command at Darién.
1517	Balboa executed at Darién. Francisco Fernández de Córdoba

284

killed in expedition against Maya in Yucatán. Carlos I (Holy
Roman Emperor Charles V) becomes King of Spain. Spanish
Crown authorizes African slavery as substitute for Indian labor
in America.

1518   Juan de Grijalva leads expedition from Cuba to coast of Yucatán, but fails to establish a settlement.

1519   Expedition of Fernando Cortés to Mexico, news of which brings
suspension of war between Cakchiquel and Quiché. Pedrarias
founds Panama City. Hernán Ponce de León and Juan de Castañeda explore Pacific coast of Costa Rica.

1521   Quiché resume war against Cakchiquel.

1522   Gil González launches exploration of Pacific coast of Central
America and moves into Costa Rica and Nicaragua. Andrés
Niño discovers Gulf of Fonseca.

1523   Carlos I orders Cortés to search both coasts for route through
the hemisphere. Luis Marín, one of Cortés' officers, establishes
Espíritu Santo, first European settlement in Chiapas. Gil González returns to Panamá, claiming to have baptized 32,000 Indians in Nicaragua.

1524   Pedro de Alvarado conquers Guatemala, defeating Tecúm Umán
at Xelajú, then is defeated by the Pipiles at Cuscatlán in El Salvador. Alvarado establishes Santiago de Guatemala at Iximché.
Pedrarias sends Francisco Hernández de Córdoba and Hernando
de Soto into Nicaragua to challenge claim of Gil González. Hernández de Córdoba establishes León and Granada. Gil González
sails to Honduras, bringing first European woman and first African to Central America; he marches to Nicaragua, but is forced
to return out of fear of Hernández de Córdoba's larger force.
Cristóbal de Olid sails to Honduras from Mexico and establishes
Triunfo de la Cruz. Cortés sends Francisco de las Casas to Honduras to discipline Olid, but Olid captures him; later, Las Casas
and González overpower and murder Olid. Francisco Pizarro
sails from Panamá for Peru.

1524-30   Cakchiquel revolt against Spaniards.

1525   Cortés marches across Petén to Honduras, successfully securing
Honduras against Hernández de Córdoba. Juan López de Aguirre
establishes Trujillo, Honduras, on orders from Francisco de las
Casas. Alvarado conquers Pipil and establishes San Salvador at
Cuscatlán. Carlos I grants Honduras to Diego López de Salcedo,
who takes command in Trujillo on October 27, 1526; Cortés'
governor, Alvaro de Saavedra Cerón, does not contest.

1526   Pedrarias executes Hernández de Córdoba in Nicaragua and extends his control into Honduras. Pedro de los Ríos replaces Pedrarias as governor of Castilla del Oro. Pedro Portocarrero continues pacification of Guatemala as Alvarado returns to Spain.

1527   Captaincies General established in Guatemala and Nicaragua under respective commands of Alvarado and Pedrarias. Jorge de Alvarado lays out new site for Santiago de Guatemala (Ciudad Vieja).

1528   Pedrarias proposes interoceanic route across Nicaragua as rival to Panamanian route. Martín Estete and Gabriel de Rojas explore Pacific coast to El Salvador, claiming it for Pedrarias. Jorge de Alvarado marches to region and reasserts Guatemalan authority. San Salvador reestablished in Valley of la Bermuda. Toribio de Motolinía establishes Concepción Convent in Granada.

1530   Pedro de Alvarado begins shipbuilding on Pacific coast. Luis de Moscoso establishes San Miguel, El Salvador.

1531   Diocese of Nicaragua established. Pedrarias dies in Léon. Poor government and disorder characterize successive Nicaraguan governments. Mob under leadership of Diego Méndez assassinates Lt. Governor of Trujillo, Vasco de Herrera; misrule and anarchy characterize subsequent years.

1534   Diocese of Guatemala established. Alvarado establishes Realejo, Nicaragua, and sails for Peru, returning the following year. Pedro de Andagoya reports that construction of a waterway through Panama is not feasible.

ca. 1535   Bartolomé de las Casas arrives in Nicaragua and establishes Dominican Convent.

1535   Audiencia established at Panama. Cristóbal de la Cueva opens communications between Guatemala and Honduran Caribbean coast. Deteriorating conditions in Honduras lead to Alvarado taking over jurisdiction there.

1536   Chiapas transferred from Diocese of Tlaxcala to Guatemala. Bartolomé de las Casas precipitates major Church-State conflict in Nicaragua over Indian treatment; he finally leaves, taking Dominican friars to Guatemala.

1536-39   Alvarado reaches agreement in 1536 with Francisco de Montejo: Alvarado to have jurisdiction in Honduras, Montejo in Yucatán. Alvarado establishes Puerto de Caballos in Honduras, but in 1537 Montejo receives royal appointment as Governor of Honduras; a subsequent agreement (1539) endorsed by the Crown restores Honduras to Alvarado.

1537-38   French corsairs begin to attack Central American settlements on Caribbean.

1538   Diocese of Chiapas authorized, but not effected until 1545.

1538-43   Panama is seat of authority for Spanish territory from Nicaragua southward throughout Spanish South America.

1539   Diocese of Honduras established at Trujillo. Bishop of Panama, Tomás de Berlarga, fails in attempt to colonize Costa Rica. Alonson Calero sails along coast from Nombre de Dios to Honduras.

1540   Alonso de Cáceres establishes Comayagua, Honduras. Diego Gutiérrez expedition to Costa Rica ends in failure. Alvarado leaves Guatemala for northern Mexico, taking troublesome Indian chiefs into exile with him.

1541   Cabildo of Santiago de Guatemala, upon learning of Alvarado's death (June 29, 1541), gives authority to his widow, Beatriz de la Cueva, on September 9; two days later she is killed and the city destroyed by earthquake and flood; survivors name her brother, Francisco de la Cueva, as Governor.

1542   Santiago de Guatemala (Antigua) reestablished in Panchoy Valley. Francisco Marroquín, first Bishop of Guatemala, plays major role in early development of Santiago (1535-63).

1543   New Laws resisted in Central America, but gradually enforced, causing modification of labor system. Audiencia de los Confines ordered established, with jurisdiction over region from Tabasco, Yucatán, and Chiapas southward through Panama; it is installed in 1544 with administrative seat at Gracias, Honduras.

1543-47   Baltolomé de las Casas attempts pacific conquest of the Verapaz.

1545   San Salvador moved to its present site in the Valley of las Hamacas.

1549   Audiencia de los Confines moved from Gracias to Santiago de Guatemala.

1550   Panama separated from jurisdiction of Audiencia de los Confines. Contreras brothers in Nicaragua and Panama revolt in an effort to regain the control their father had held in Nicaragua; Pedro de la Gasca comes from Peru to suppress the revolt, but family feuds and disorders continue to make Nicaraguan development violent in the sixteenth century.

1556   Carlos I abdicates, leaving Spanish crown to his son, Felipe II.

1557   Descendants of Columbus surrender all claims to rights on Central American territory in return for title and pension.

1558   Accession of Elizabeth I of England begins period of active English privateering against Spanish shipping in the Caribbean.

1560   Tabasco and Yucatán removed from jurisdiction of Audiencia de los Confines.

1561   Juan de Cavallón leads first successful colonizers into Costa Rica.

1562-65 Juan Vázquez de Coronado continues conquest of Costa Rica and establishes Cartago.

1563   Audiencia de los Confines ordered moved to Panamá; Central American territory divided between Panama and New Spain, with a Captain General to remain in Guatemala.

1567   Audiencia of Guatemala ordered reestablished; it is installed in 1570, with jurisdiction over territory from Chiapas through Costa Rica.

1578   Silver discoveries result in growth of Tegucigalpa and its separation from Comayagua's administrative authority until 1788.

1582   Jesuits arrive in Kingdom of Guatemala.

1587   England's Elizabeth I challenges Spain's claim to unconquered lands of the Western Hemisphere.

1588   Defeat of the Spanish Armada begins decline of Spanish naval strength and increase of foreign maritime activity in the Caribbean.

1598   Felipe III becomes King of Spain.

1601   Road opened between Cartago and Chiriquí stimulates mule raising.

1605   Puerto Santo Tomás de Castilla established on north coast of Guatemala after freebooter attack on Puerto de Caballos; Guatemalan Caribbean port relocated at several sites on Amatique Bay and Golfo Dulce during colonial period.

1610   Léon, Nicaragua, moves to new site to escape further earthquake and volcanic damage.

1621   Felipe IV becomes King of Spain.

1622   Costa Rican request for union with Panama denied.

1630   English Puritans establish colony on Providence Island: English logcutters begin to operate on eastern coast of Central America soon thereafter.

1635   San Vicente, El Salvador, established as center for indigo trade.

1638   British logcutters and buccaneers operating in Belize from about this date. Settlement develops gradually.

1642   British take Roatán Island.

1643   Dutch sack Trujillo and Spanish abandon that port until 1789.

1655   British take Jamaica, providing a base for contraband trade with isthmus.

1660   José de Pineda Ibarra establishes first printing press in Central America. Freebooters burn Puerto Caballos, then march inland and take San Pedro Sula.

1662   Dutch settlement is developing at Bluefields, Nicaragua.

1665   English buccaneers burn Granada; Realejo also sacked. Buccaneers under Morgan and Mansfield march inland in Costa Rica, but fail to reach highlands. Carlos II becomes King of Spain.

1651-67 Exemplary work of Friar Pedro de San José de Betancur in Guatemala results in establishment of Bethlehemite Order.

1670-90 Buccaneers make many forays into interior of Nicaragua and Costa Rica. British recognize Spanish sovereignty in Belize, but English logcutters and buccaneers continue to develop settlement.

1671   Panama City moved to new site after destruction by Henry Morgan.

1676   University authorized in Guatemala, but not officially opened as the University of San Carlos until 1681.

1697   Popular uprising in Guatemala put down with force; results in organization of new urban guard. Tayasal, last Maya stronghold, captured by Spanish force from Yucatán under command of Martín de Ursúa y Arizmendi.

1698-99 William Paterson sets up unsuccessful Scottish colony at Darién.

1699   Joint Guatemalan-Yucatecan expedition against Lacandones fails.

1700   Accession to the Spanish throne of the Bourbon Felipe V, setting off War of the Spanish Succession (1701-14).

1705   Ministerial system inaugurated in Spanish government.

1706-16 Toribio de Cosío y Campa is progressive Captain General of Guatemala.

1712-13 Tzendale Indian rebellion in Chiapas suppressed.

1714   Honduras Company founded, but fails to profit.

1729-31 *Gazeta de Goathemala,* first Central American newspaper, published.

1731   Royal mint authorized for Kingdom of Guatemala; first coins minted in 1733.

1733	British driven from Belize by Governor of Yucatán, Antonio de Figueroa y Silva, but they soon return.
1736	San José de Costa Rica established.
1739	War of Jenkins' Ear brings new attacks to Central American coasts; Captain Edward Vernon seizes and destroys Portobelo.
1745	By decree of 1742 Archdiocese of Guatemala established, with jurisdiction over entire Kingdom, making ecclesiastical jurisdiction conform to political boundaries.
1746	Fernando VI becomes King of Spain.
1747	Mosquito Indians, operating under orders of Governor of Jamaica, drive Spanish from Matina Valley, Costa Rica.
1748	Guatemala Company formed, but fails to profit.
1751	Temple dedicated to the "Black Christ" built at Esquipulas, Guatemala. Audiencia of Panamá terminated.
1752	Liquor monopoly established in Kingdom of Guatemala.
1754	Large Spanish expedition from the Petén fails to capture Belize.
1755	British build fort at Belize.
1756	Riot in Santiago de Guatemala against prohibition of certain liquors. Mosquito Indians, supported by British, kill Costa Rican Governor in Matina Valley fighting.
1759	Carlos III becomes King of Spain, inaugurates most important of Bourbon Reforms.
1763	Treaty of Paris. British agree to demolish their fortifications around the Bay of Honduras, but are allowed to continue cutting wood there. Soon after, Sir William Burnaby writes a Code of Laws; it provides a framework of government and justice for the Belize settlers for many years.
1766	British Free Trade Act facilitates illicit Central American trade with British West Indies. Uprising in Guatemala against establishment of the tobacco monopoly and rising taxation stemming from Spanish expenditures in Seven Years' War (1756-63).
1767	Jesuits expelled.
1774	Intercolonial trade between Guatemala, Peru, New Spain, and New Granada is permitted.
1776	As a result of earthquakes of 1773, Santiago de Guatemala moved to its present site in Valley de la Hermita.
1778	Spanish Free Trade Act opens Kingdom of Guatemala to wider commerce.
1779-83	Spain declares war on England in 1779. Spanish drive the British from Belize. British capture Omoa, and British-supported

Mosquito Indians retake Matina, where they exact tribute from residents there until 1841, but British invasion of Nicaragua fails. Captain General Matías de Gálvez retakes Omoa and develops expanded defense, production, commerce, and public works in the Kingdom.

1780   Serious smallpox epidemic in Guatemala City. Vaccination employed for first time in Central America; it succeeds in stemming epidemic.

1783   Peace of Paris ends American Revolution. British agree to evacuate Mosquito Coast and recognize Spanish sovereignty all along Central American coast, but Spanish recognize right of British subjects to cut wood at Belize; a new treaty in 1786 confirms this agreement.

1786   Intendants appointed for Nicaragua, Honduras, El Salvador, and Chiapas.

1788   Comayagua and Tegucigalpa consolidated into single administrative unit under intendancy system until 1812. Carlos IV becomes King of Spain.

1789   French Revolution begins; Spanish involvement in wars that result leads to expanded foreign trade for Kingdom of Guatemala.

1793   Spain allies with Britain against French Republic. Central America permitted to receive Philippine goods directly through Realejo and Acajutla. New *Gazeta de Guatemala* begins publication.

1796   Spain joins in alliance with France, resulting in renewed British attacks on Central America. British reoccupy Bay Islands, bring in "Black Caribs" from St. Vincent Island. Spanish establish San Juan del Norte.

1797   Neutrals permitted to trade with Central America; United States trade is especially favored, but British ships sometimes pose as North American. Permission revoked in 1799, but traders continue to come.

1800   Royal Order of 1799 suppresses Guatemalan *Sociedad Económica*; it is restored in 1811.

1801-11 Captain General Antonio González Mollinedo y Saravia faces severe economic crises in Central America; major increases made in royal requests for funds to pay for war. Inflation, crop failures, and interdiction of trade place great economic stress on colony.

1803   Carlos IV orders that San Andrés Island and Mosquito Coast as far north as Cape Gracias a Dios belong to Viceroyalty of New Granada.

1804   War resumes between Spain and England. Mosquito Indians get military aid from British. Privateering increases along Caribbean coast.

1808   Carlos IV abdicates; Joseph Bonaparte placed on Spanish throne. Guatemalan government declares its allegiance to Fernando VII, rejecting Napoleonic rule. Simón Bergaño y Villegas, editor of the *Gazeta de Guatemala* (1802-7), deported at behest of Archbishop.

1809   Ayuntamiento of Guatemala expresses grievances to the Spanish Supreme Central Junta.

1811   News of Hidalgo revolt in Mexico alarms authorities in Guatemala. José M. Delgado leads independence uprising in San Salvador; José de Aycinena, appointed as Intendant, restores peace. Abortive independence attempt in Nicaragua is also crushed by a royalist force from Guatemala.

1811-18   Captain General José de Bustamante y Guerra imposes strong rule.

1812   Cortes of Cádiz establishes Constitutional Monarchy and inaugurates liberal regime. Central American signers of the 1812 Constitution include Manuel de Llano (Chiapas), Antonio Larrazábal (Guatemala), José Avila (El Salvador), José F. Monejón (Honduras), José A. López de la Plata (Nicaragua), and Florencio Castillo (Costa Rica); Cortes appoints José de Aycinena to a Council of State. University at León established; revolt against Spanish rule fails in Tegucigalpa, but Tegucigalpa wins administrative separation from Comayagua. Election of ayuntamientos in Central America results in emergence of political factions.

1813   *Diputaciones provinciales* decreed for Guatemala and Léon; later, one is also established at Ciudad Real. Belén conspiracy in Guatemala exposed.

1814   Fernando VII restored to Spanish throne; he annuls Constitution of 1812 and all acts of juntas in Spain and America; old ayuntamientos restored. Revolt in El Salvador led by Manuel José de Arce fails.

1815   Indians in San Juan Ostuncalco rebel against Alcalde, who attempted to stop pagan religious practices.

1816   Mosquito King, George Fredrick II, crowned at Belize, reestablishing British protectorate over Mosquito Coast.

1817   Inquisition reestablished in Guatemala.

1818-21   Carlos Urrutia y Montoya is last Spanish Captain General of
          Central America.

1819   Gregor MacGregor temporarily takes and holds Portobelo.

1820   Riego revolt in Spain restores Constitution of 1812. Pedro Mo-
          lina begins publication of *El Editor Constitucional;* José Cecilio
          del Valle responds with *El Amigo de la Patria.*

1821   Sub-Inspector Gabino Gáinza assumes power from ailing Urru-
          tia. Guatemala and provincial governments declare independ-
          ence from Spain, but differ on subsequent course of action.
          Independent states begin to gain in authority at expense of Gua-
          temala, as federalism becomes major political issue. Panama de-
          clares independence from Spain, becomes part of Gran Colombia.

1822   Central America annexes itself to Mexican Empire. Vicente
          Filísola is new Captain General, as Agustín Iturbide becomes
          Emperor. Kingdom of Guatemala divided into three comandan-
          cias, with capitals at Ciudad Real, Guatemala, and León. San
          Salvador opposes annexation to Mexico.

1823   Filísola conquers El Salvador and incorporates it into Mexican
          Empire; fighting breaks out in Nicaragua and Costa Rica over
          annexation issue. Iturbide overthrown in Mexico. Central Amer-
          ica declares absolute independence (July 1) and forms the
          United Provinces of Central America. A provisional junta, com-
          posed of Pedro Molina, Antonio Rivera Cabeza and Juan Vi-
          cente Villacorta, organizes new government and inaugurates
          republican reforms. Chiapas remains with Mexico. Military
          uprising in Guatemala, led by Captain Rafael Ariza y Torres,
          suppressed (September 13-14); pro-Spanish revolt led by José
          María Martínez Wallop crushed a week later.

1824   Republican constitution ratified by all five states.

1824-33   Juan Mora Fernández's administration in Costa Rica gives that
          state a stability not enjoyed by others in early independent
          period.

1825   J. M. Delgado inaugurated as Bishop of El Salvador in opposi-
          tion to Archbishop of Guatemala. Manuel J. Arce elected Presi-
          dent of Central America by federal congress. Costa Rican diocese
          separate from Nicaragua's established. Treaty of Friendship and
          Commerce signed between United States and Central America;
          ratified 1826.

1826	Britain acquires Mexican claim to Belize. Congress of Panamá.
1826-29	Arce deposes Liberal state government of Guatemala and joins with Conservatives in reorganizing federal government, touching off bloody three-year civil war between Liberals and Conservatives. Mob in Quezaltenango assassinates Liberal Lt. Governor of Guatemala; Mariano de Aycinena becomes new Guatemalan Governor (1827-29). Francisco Morazán leads Liberals to victory by 1829.
1829-38	Liberals in control, vindictive toward Conservatives, embark upon radical anticlerical and liberal economic and political program; serious conflicts between state and federal authority throughout region. Costa Rica secedes (August 1829 to May 1830).
1830	Dionisio Herrera becomes Chief of State of Nicaragua and succeeds in bringing about some order after a decade of strife.
1829-30	Growing Spanish threat; in 1832 pro-Spanish insurgents take and hold Omoa until dislodged by Central American troops.
1830-31	Panama is twice briefly independent from Gran Colombia.
1831-38	Mariano Gálvez, Chief of State of Guatemala, launches boldest Liberal and anticlerical policies until overthrown by Rafael Carrera.
1832	University of San Carlos suppressed in favor of lyceums and academies.
1833	*Noticioso Universal*, Costa Rica's first newspaper, begins publication at Alajuela.
1834	Federal capital moved from Guatemala to San Salvador, which becomes a Federal District in 1835. José Cecilio del Valle elected President of Central America, but dies before votes are counted; Morazán then reelected.
1835	Braulio Carrillo establishes Conservative dictatorship in Costa Rica and makes San José as capital; rules 1835-37 and 1838-42.
1837-40	Cholera epidemic strikes Central America. Peasant revolts, beginning at San Juan Ostuncalco, spread throughout Guatemala, leading to general uprising. War of the *Montaña* brings Rafael Carrera to power in Guatemala as Gálvez government collapses when Liberals quarrel among themselves. Federal Vice President José G. Salazar killed by Carrera's troops. Los Altos departments secede from Guatemala and establish a new state under the leadership of Marcelo Molina, in alliance with Morazán. Central American Congress allows states to go their separate ways; Nicaragua, Honduras, and Costa Rica secede in 1838.

1839-42   Liberal program dismantled in Guatemala; Hispanic institutions restored.

1839-43   British seize Bay Islands and San Juan del Norte.

1839-47   Carrera's Conservative ally, Francisco Ferrera, dominates Honduras.

1839-65   Carrera dominates Guatemala and much of the rest of Central America. Conservative caudillos and a strong clergy characterize the period.

1840   Carrera defeats Morazán, forcing him to go into exile in David, Panama; Carrera restores Guatemalan rule in Los Altos. Honduran Liberals defeated at El Potrero, near Tegucigalpa. Mexican troops occupy Soconusco.

1840-46   Carrera establishes Conservative Francisco Malespín in El Salvador; Malespín rules until assassinated (1846).

1840-41   Panama secedes from New Granada under rights granted in 1831 Constitution, remains independent for nearly two years.

1841   Braulio Carrillo establishes himself as lifetime dictator of Costa Rica.

1842   Morazán ousts Carrillo in San José and tries to reestablish Central American union, but is soon overturned; Morazán executed (September 15). Honduras, El Salvador, and Nicaragua agree to union at Chinandega, but fail to establish it successfully. Anti-Liberal alliance of Central American states is signed in Guatemala. British blockade coast.

1840-45   Religious orders reestablished in Central America.

1843   British government formally accepts Mosquito Coast protectorate. Guatemala contests Mexican occupation of Soconusco.

1845-51   Conservative Trinidad Muñoz maintains shaky control of Nicaragua.

1846   Bidlack-Mallarino Treaty between United States and New Granada guarantees U.S. rights over Panama transit route; Ratified 1848.

1847   Guatemala declares itself a "Republic," it is first in Central America to change name from "State." Other four states eventually take similar action. Hise-Selva Treaty signed between United States and Nicaragua provides for U.S. rights in Nicaragua. (Although never ratified, it reflected growing North American interest and involvement on the isthmus and resulted from Nicaraguan attempts to solicit U.S. aid against Britain; it was significant in bringing about Clayton-Bulwer Treaty of 1850.)

1847-52   Juan N. Lindo Zelaya's Conservative administration in Honduras provides order and, uniquely, allows a Liberal to take office peacefully in 1852.

1847-53   Caste War in Yucatán.

1848   Carrera resigns in face of poular uprising and secession of Los Altos.

1848-50   British occupy San Juan del Norte, renaming it Greytown.

1849   Carrera returns to power in Guatemala as armed forces chief, but Mariano Paredes remains as President until 1851. Nicaragua makes concessions to Cornelius Vanderbilt and associates for isthmian route; Vanderbilt develops profitable route by 1854. British seize Tigre Island in Gulf of Fonseca; Nicaragua and Honduras cede their claims on island to United States in effort to check British. Guatemala and Costa Rica sign Treaties of Friendship and Commerce with Great Britain.

1849-59   After seven years of disorder, Juan Rafael Mora Porras brings orderly, Conservative government to Costa Rica.

1850   Clayton-Bulwer Treaty between the United States and Great Britain signed.

1851   Carrera defeats Liberal unionists at San José la Arada, ending serious Liberal threat to Guatemala for nearly two decades.

1850-55   Panama Railway constructed, resulting in sharp transfer of Central American commerce from Caribbean to Pacific ports.

1852   Compromise begins between León and Granada, eventually leading to Managua becoming Nicaraguan capital.

1854   Carrera is made Perpetual President of Guatemala, and holds office until death (1865). U.S. Navy bombards Greytown, Nicaragua (San Juan del Norte).

1855   Río San Juan changes course and destroys Greytown; William Walker and associates arrive in Nicaragua to assist Liberals; Walker gains control of the army, becoming President in 1856.

1855-56   Carrera restores Conservative rule in Honduras, replacing Trinidad Cabañas with Santos Guardiola, who dominated Honduras until his assassination (1862).

1856-57   Mora leads Central American resistance (National War) against Walker. Walker surrenders on May 1, 1857; Walker's attempt to launch second invasion of Nicaragua thwarted by U.S. officials. Subsequent attempts in 1858 and 1859 also foiled by U.S. agents.

1857-93   Conservatives dominate Nicaragua.

1858   Nicaragua grants canal concession to Felix Belly and Paris associates.

1859   Guatemala agrees to recognize British sovereignty in Belize in return for construction of a road from Guatemala City to the Caribbean coast; British agree to turn over Bay Islands to Honduras. Gerardo Barrios, first of the "New Liberal" rulers of Central America, becomes President of El Salvador.

1859-68   Montealegre family dominates Costa Rica.

1860   Walker captured and executed near Trujillo; Mosquito Indian reservation (7000 sq. miles) designated by treaty with Nicaraguan government. By Treaty of Managua, Britain relinquishes all claims to Nicaraguan east coast.

1862   Belize Settlement becomes Colony of British Honduras.

1863   Carrera invades El Salvador and replaces Gerardo Barrios with Conservative Francisco Dueñas. United States claims Swan Islands.

1865   Carrera dies; his designee, General Vicente Cerna, continues Conservative rule in Guatemala to 1871.

1867   General Serapio Cruz declares against Cerna, beginning Liberal Revolution. It succeeds in 1871.

1870   British Honduran legislature abolishes itself.

1870-82   Tomás Guardia, New Liberal dictator of Costa Rica, breaks power of old, landholding, Conservative families.

1870-   Strong Positivist influence evident in Central American govern-
1900   ments and constitutions; most governments are dedicated to material progress: they encourage railroad construction, foreign investment, and port development, and they are anticlerical.

1871   Liberal Revolution in El Salvador replaces Dueñas with Santiago González; Miguel García Granados and Justo Rufino Barrios lead revolt in Guatemala, breaking Conservative dictatorship.

1873   J. R. Barrios becomes dictator of Guatemala, aids Liberals in Honduras. British bombard Omoa to protect British commercial interests.

1876   Barrios intervenes in Honduras and places Marco Aurelio Soto in power.

1878   French company acquires rights to dig canal through Panama.

1880   Tegucigalpa established as Honduran capital.

1883	Differences with Barrios lead to resignation of Soto in Honduras; another Barrios protégé, Luis Bográn Baraona, continues the Liberal domination to 1891.
1885	Barrios killed at Chalchuapa, El Salvador, ending his ambitions of reestablishing the Central American union by military power.
1885-90	Bernardo Soto continues Liberal trends in Costa Rica.
1889	Conservative José Joaquín Rodríguez (Constitutional Democrat) defeats Ascensión Esquivel (Progressive Liberal), and Liberals allow him to take office. Since election of 1889 Costa Rica has generally had free popular political participation. Maritime Canal Company incorporated in U.S. to build Nicaragua Canal; extensive surveys follow. French Panama Canal Company goes bankrupt.
1890- 1902	Conservatives (José Joaquín Rodríguez and Rafael Iglesias) dominate Costa Rica. Iglesias intrigues against Nicaraguan government of José Santos Zelaya.
1893- 1909	Zelaya is Liberal dictator in Nicaragua.
1894	Last British intervention on Mosquito Coast; Mosquito Coast fully incorporated into Nicaragua.
1895	British blockade Corinto; U.S. mediation brings settlement.
1895-99	Major steps taken toward formation of Republic of Central America behind leadership of Salvador Mendieta, but projects fail in 1899; Mendieta organizes Central American Unionist Party.
1898	President José M. Reyna Barrios assassinated in Guatemala.
1898- 1920	Manuel Estrada Cabrera's iron-fisted dictatorship in Guatemala is longest uninterrupted one-man rule in Central American history.
1899	United Fruit Company formed.
1899- 1903	"Thousand Days War" in Colombia brings violence to Panama.
1901	Walker Commission recommends building canal in Nicaragua; second Hay-Pauncefote Treaty abrogates Clayton-Bulwer Treaty, leaving U.S. free to develop canal route unilaterally.
1903	Panama declares independence from Colombia; U.S. quickly recognizes Panama and negotiates favorable canal treaty.
1906	Nicaragua, Costa Rica, El Salvador, and Honduras sign Corinto Convention, agreeing to submit disputes to a Central American arbitration tribunal. U.S. and Mexico mediate war between Gua-

temala and El Salvador, leading to Marblehead Pact, San José Conference, and Central American cooperative peace-keeping machinery. Britain finally relinquishes all claims or interest in Mosquito Coast.

1907   Zelaya attempts to impose union on Central America by interfering in political affairs of Honduras and El Salvador; this leads to new U.S. and Mexican peace initiative. Washington Conference results in establishment of Central American Court of Justice.

1907-31 Meléndez family dominates El Salvador.

1909   Overthrow of Zelaya is followed by instability in Nicaragua, which prompts U.S. financial and military intervention (1912-33).

1914   Panama Canal opened.

1916   Bryan-Chamorro Treaty between U.S. and Nicaragua leads to collapse of Central American Court of Justice.

1917   Federico Tinoco Granados seizes power in Costa Rica by a coup, but cannot get recognition of United States or other nations; he resigns in 1919. Attempted Central American union of all five states, on Honduran initiative, fails when Nicaragua refuses to cooperate.

1921   Overthrow by military of Guatemalan "Unionist" government ends tripartite republic initiative of Guatemala, El Salvador, and Honduras; Socialist Labor Unification (Guatemala) affiliates with Communist Party of Mexico.

1923   Washington Conference results in new Central American treaties, but fails to promote union. Violence breaks out in Honduras when Tiburcio Carías Andino wins plurality in presidential election but Congress denies him office; U.S. mediation results in new election without Carías as a candidate, but his National Party's candidate, Miguel Paz Baraona, wins.

1924-36 Costa Rica dominated by Conservatives Ricardo Jiménez Oreamuno and Cleto González Víquez.

1925   Regional Workers Federation (FRO) meets violent repression in El Salvador.

1927   Tipitapa Agreements provide basis for U.S. occupation of Nicaragua and subsequent election.

1928-34 Augusto César Sandino leads Nicaraguan guerrillas against U.S. occupation.

1931-44 Jorge Ubico and Maximiliano Hernández Martínez establish

	strong dictatorships in Guatemala and El Salvador, respectively.
1932	Peasant uprising in El Salvador suppressed with great bloodshed.
1932-48	Tiburcio Carías Andino is dictator of Honduras.
1933	Guatemalan-Honduran border dispute in Río Motagua Valley settled, largely in Guatemala's favor, by special arbitration tribunal.
1934	Sandino murdered in Managua by members of Nicaraguan National Guard; Guard chief Anastasio Somoza dominates country until 1956.
1936	Reformist National Republican Party (PRN) wins in Costa Rica with León Cortés Castro as President. U.S.-Panama Canal treaty renegotiated. U.S. gives up protectorate powers over Panama and agrees to nonintervention.
1940	Rafael Angel Calderón Guardia (PRN) wins in Costa Rican election; more radical group dominates Costa Rica to 1948; León Cortés Castro leaves PRN to form more conservative Democratic Party.
1944	Hernández Martínez and Ubico resign in face of increased violence and protests.
1945	New Constitution embodies principles of Guatemalan Revolution.
1945-50	Juan José Arévalo heads reformist administration in Guatemala.
1948	Otilio Ulate wins Costa Rican presidential election, but Calderón Guardia and PRN attempt to retain power. José Figueres leads Army of National Liberation successfully against government, beginning period of dominance for Figueres in Costa Rican politics.
1949	Francisco J. Arana assassinated in Guatemala, and revolt of Guardia de Honor follows. It is the most serious of twenty-two military coups attempted against Arévalo.
1950	Costa Rica abolishes army.
1950-54	Jacobo Arbenz elected President of Guatemala; during his administration revolutionary reforms are intensified and there is increased Communist infiltration of the government.
1950-60	Revolutionary Party of Democratic Union (PRUD) dominates El Salvador under leadership of Major Oscar Osorio.
1951	Meeting of foreign ministers lays groundwork for formation of the Organization of Central American States (ODECA).
1952	Guatemalan Labor Party (PGT) organized from dissolved Communist Party (PCG) and Revolutionary Workers' Party (PROG). Guatemalan agrarian reform law goes into effect.
1953-58	Figueres administration in Costa Rica brings modest social and

economic reform, but fails to improve Costa Rican standard of living significantly.

1954 Organization of American States "Declaration of Solidarity" against intervention of International Communism is directed against Arbenz government; after east European arms arrive in Guatemala, Carlos Castillo Armas overthrows Arbenz with aid of Honduras, Nicaragua, and U.S. Castillo Armas becomes chief of state and restores Conservative rule. George Price's leftist Peoples United Party (PUP) wins election in Belize and provides more progressive leadership and movement toward independence. Ramón Villeda Morales wins substantial plurality, but is denied presidency of Honduras as Julio Lozano Díaz seizes power.

1956 Anastasio Somoza assassinated in León. His sons, Luis and Anastasio, continue family domination of Nicaragua to the present.

1957 Castillo Armas assassinated; period of instability and violence begins in Guatemala.

1957-63 After overthrow of a military regime which had relieved the ailing Lozano in 1956, Villeda Morales wins a free election and provides more progressive government in Honduras.

1958 Common market plan developed and treaty signed.

1958-63 Following period of instability, Conservative Miguel Ydígoras Fuentes elected President of Guatemala.

1959-60 Border skirmishes between Costa Rica and Nicaragua.

1960 José María Lemus and PRUD overthrown in El Salvador by civilian-military group with slightly leftist tendencies under junta headed by Colonel César Yanes Urías. Leftist revolt suppressed in Guatemala, but survivors form MR-13 guerrilla movement under leadership of Lt. Marco Aurelio Yon Sosa and Luis A. Turcios Lima; guerrilla fighting continues throughout the decade. After three years of skirmishing, Nicaragua-Honduras border is settled by International Court of Justice.

1961 Guatemalan and Nicaraguan governments support launching of Bay of Pig invasion against Cuba. Hurricane "Hattie" wrecks Belize City, leading to decision to build Belmopan, fifty miles inland.

1961-67 Rightist military coup in El Salvador ousts Yanes Urías. Lt. Col. Julio A. Rivera, head of Party of National Conciliation (PCN), dominates state through 1967.

1963 Military, led by Minister of Defense Enrique Peralta Azurdia, ousts Ydígoras and pursues hard line against leftists. Ubico's remains returned from Louisiana to Guatemala for state funeral and internment. Guatemala breaks diplomatic relations with Great Britain over question of sovereignty in Belize. Central American Defense Council (CONDECA) established by Guatemala, El Salvador, Nicaragua, and Honduras with strong U.S. support.

1963-71   Military removes Villeda Morales and returns Conservatives to control in Honduras. Col. Osvaldo López Arellano establishes mild military dictatorship (1965-71).

1964   British Honduras gains limited self-rule, with steps toward absolute independence. Panamanian riots against U.S. sovereignty bring new negotiations on canal question.

1966   Hernández Martínez murdered on his Honduras estate in labor dispute.

1967   Heart attack kills Luis Somoza, leaving Anastasio ("Tachito") Somoza in control of Nicaragua.

1967-72   PCN continues military rule in El Salvador under Col. Fidel Sánchez Hernández.

1969   Brief war between Honduras and El Salvador stems from demographic problems and border dispute; common marked damaged.

1970   José Figueres returns to presidency of Costa Rica.

1971   Pressing economic problems aggravated by war with El Salvador result in a national unity coalition of Conservative and Liberal parties in Honduras; Dr. Ramón Ernesto Cruz elected president.

1972   PCN maintains power in El Salvador against strong challenge of Christian Democrat José Napoleon Duarte. Earthquake devastates Managua, leading to tightening of Somoza dictatorship in Nicaragua. López Arellano takes over as president of Honduras again (December).

1973   British Honduras' name formally changed to Belize.

1974   Daniel Oduber wins Costa Rican presidency, continuing Figueres's PLN in power. General Kjell Langerud García wins Guatemalan presidency. Tachito Somoza wins another term as Nicaraguan president. Hurricane "Fifi" wreaks havoc on Honduran north coast.

1975   Col. Juan Alberto Melgar Castro leads coup in April which overthrows López Arellano in Honduras. Peasant uprisings suppressed in July. Guerrilla Army of the Poor (EGP) launches guerrilla activity in northern Quiché Department, Guatemala.

1976   Earthquake causes massive damage to central Guatemala and western Honduras; less serious damage in El Salvador. PCN sweeps Salvadoran congressional and municipal elections, as most of opposition refuses to participate; leftist guerrilla activity grows in El Salvador, led by People's Revolutionary Army (ERP). New disclosures of bribes offered by United Brands to Honduran officials in addition to 1974 U.S. $1.25 million payment. FSLN founder, Carlos Fonseca Amador, killed in clashes with Nicaraguan Guardia Nacional. Panamanian strong-man Omar Torrijos visits Cuba for talks with Fidel Castro, putting pressure on U.S. regarding Panama Canal.

1977   Guatemala rejects U.S. military aid when Jimmy Carter links it to greater human rights observance. U.N. General Assembly adopts resolution favoring independence for Belize by vote of 126-4, with 13 abstentions. Nicaraguan church hierarchy criticizes government for abuses of human rights, charging the Guardia Nacional with a "reign of terror"; Sandinistas step up attacks. General Carlos Humberto Romero wins Salvadoran presidential election, denounced as fraudulent by opposition; Archbishop Oscar Romero boycotts President Romero's inauguration. U.S. and Panama sign Panama Canal treaties, ratified by Panamanian plebiscite on October 23.

1978   Assassination on January 10 of Pedro Joaquín Chamorro, editor of La Prensa, sparks general uprising against Somoza dynasty; FSLN forms mass organizations to mobilize population against Somoza; Edén Pastora (Comandante Zero) captures the National Palace on August 22; Costa Rica breaks relations with Somoza government; guerrillas launch coordinated offensive in September, combined with general strike; General Fernando Romeo Lucas García becomes President of Guatemala in controlled election, pursues repressive, anti-communist policies; civilians dominate Lucas's cabinet (9 civilians, 3 military); rejuvenated Rebel Armed Forces (FAR) renew guerrilla activities. Bloodless coup in Honduras replaces President Melgar with junta headed by Gen. Policarpo Paz García. PCN wins legislative assembly and municipal elections in El Salvador with negligible opposition; PDC refused to name candidates in opposition because they believed elections would not be fairly conducted. U.S. ratifies Panama Canal treaties and Panama accepts modifications made by U.S. Senate; Minister of Education Aristedes Royo succeeds Omar Torrijos as President of Panama, but Torrijos remains head of National Guard. Rodrigo Carazo Odio of Unity Coalition wins Costa Rican presidency; case of

Robert Vesco continues to smoulder in Costa Rica, as Vesco is denied Costa Rican citizenship and forbidden to return to Costa Rica.

1979   Full-scale Sandinista offensive begins on May 29 with invasion from Costa Rica; U.S. newsman Bill Stewart (ABC-TV) killed by National Guard forces on camera, causing increased hostility toward Somoza government in U.S.; general strike begins in June, closing 80 percent of Nicaraguan businesses; Somoza resigns on July 17 and flees to Paraguay, where Argentine radicals assassinate him on Sept. 17, 1980. Somoza's successsor, Francisco Urcuyo Malianos, flees to Guatemala on July 18; Sandinistas seize government on July 19, with Sandinista-controlled junta installed the next day (Daniel Ortega Saavedra, Alfonso Robelo Callejas, Sergio Ramírez, Violeta Barrios de Chamorro, and Moisés Hassan Morales). Reformist officers headed by Colonels Adolfo Majano and Jaime Abdul Gutiérrez overthrow Romero government in El Salvador (October 15). Unrest in Honduras causes cancellation of elections scheduled for April 1980; labor strife especially noticeable, sometimes violent, both urban and agricultural. Transfer of Panama Canal Zone from U.S. to Panama (October 1).

1980   Civilian progressives, Guillermo Ungo and Román Mayorga, resign from Salvadoran junta in January; Archbishop Romero, after writing an open letter to Jimmy Carter asking the U.S. not to send arms to the Salvadoran government, is assassinated on March 24; Democratic Revolutionary Front (FDR) formed by the three principal leftist political organizations and their military wings; J. N. Duarte is named to the junta in March and replaces Colonel Majano as its president on December 22, but without command of the army; Duarte launches agrarian reform; El Salvador and Honduras agree to a peace treaty formally ending the 1969 "soccer war," although details regarding the border remain in dispute. Sandinistas move Nicaragua toward the left with government institutions subservient to FSLN Directorate; U.S. indicates for first time in late 1980 that it believes Sandinistas are assisting Salvadoran guerrillas. Liberals win 52 percent of votes in election for Honduran Assembly, but fail to gain majority of seats; illegal leftist parties fail in bid to encourage large-scale absenteeism. Rapid inflation and economic problems in Costa Rica lead to labor unrest. Continued political polarization in Guatemala with widespread violence, as

Vice-President Francisco Villagrán Kramer resigns in opposition
to right-wing violation of human rights.

1981   U.S. resumes military sales to Guatemala, sends 55 military advisers to El Salvador, suspends economic assistance programs to
Nicaragua, and begins CIA support of counterrevolutionaries
(FDN); Secretary of State Alexander Haig attacks "large-scale
shipments of Soviet military supplies" and cites rapid growth of
Nicaragua armed forces, charging that Nicaragua and Cuba are
supplying arms to the Salvadoran guerrillas. Sandinistas consolidate position in Nicaragua, as junta is reduced to three
members. Belize gains independence (September 21) within
British Commonwealth; British security force stays on to protect
it from Guatemala. Liberals win Honduran elections, Dr. Roberto Suazo Córdova receiving about 54 percent of votes and an
absolute majority in the Assembly. General Torrijos dies in
small plane crash, which is followed by political turmoil; Torrijos's security chief, Manuel Antonio Noriega, eventually
emerges as Commander of the Defense Force (formerly National Guard) and Panama's new strong man.

1982   Costa Ricans elect Luis Alberto Monge as President in a clear
victory for PLN; U.S. aid helps Costa Rica meet foreign debt
problems. Guatemalan military coup ousts General Lucas on
March 23 and installs a junta headed by Gen. Efraín Ríos
Montt, who assumed the presidency on June 9; Ríos continues
hard line policy against guerrillas after a brief, unsuccessful
amnesty; Guatemalan National Revolutionary Unity (URNG)
formed as umbrella group for rebel groups. Rightest coalition
headed by Major Roberto D'Aubisson defeats Duarte's PDC in
legislative elections in El Salvador. Duarte resigns presidency,
replaced by Alvaro Magaña Borjo, while D'Aubisson becomes
president of the Assembly. Hostility escalates between U.S. and
Nicaragua, as in March the U.S. makes public reconnaissance
photos demonstrating sizable Nicaraguan military buildup. Ar-
gentine-trained Honduran Defense Minister, Gustavo Alvarez
Martínez, expands Honduran army to 20,000 under Suazo government, in close cooperation with U.S.

1983   Pope John Paul II visits Central America, highlighted by an ugly
confrontation with Sandinistas; Pope confirms Arturo Rivera y
Damas as Archbishop of El Salvador, a blow to Salvadoran
rightists who had hoped for a more conservative appointment;
visit to Guatemala strained by Ríos Montt's refusal to grant

clemency to six guerrillas, executed on eve of the Pope's arrival.
Salvadoran military intrigues and shakeups impede action
against the FMLN guerrillas. Ríos Montt ends stage of siege
in Guatemala in March, allowing amnesty for those exiled and
permitting political parties to function once more; Guatemalan
economy continues to falter; military coup in August ousts Ríos
Montt and installs Defense Minister Oscar Humberto Mejías
Victores; in October the Interamerican Human Rights Commission scores Guatemalan violations and cites the army for the
"very gravest violations of human rights including the destruction, burning, and pillaging of entire villages"; a U.N. subcom-
mittee declares Guatemala to be in a state of war and recom-
mends the recognition of belligerency status to the URNG.
Leader of Honduran Communist Party assassinated on Jan. 29
in San Pedro Sula. Nicaragua expels three U.S. diplomats accused of trying to assassinate Sandinista leaders for the CIA;
when U.S. responds by closing Nicaraguan consulates in the
U.S., Nicaragua removes visa requirements for U.S. citizens;
Edén Pastora's Revolutionary Democratic Alliance (ARDE)
aircraft begin bombing military installations in Managua, apparently aided by the CIA. Ronald Reagan announces his
Caribbean Basin Initiative in speech to OAS; U.S. policy continues to insist that Nicaragua is threat to peace in Central
America; Central American Defense Council (CONDECA)
resurrected; President Monge declares Costa Rica "perpetually
and actively neutral" in any armed conflict around the world.
Diplomats of México, Venezuela, Panama, and Colombia meet
on Contadora Island, Panama, to seek solution to violence and
crisis in Central America. Panama complains that U.S. is violating spirit of Canal treaties in its new wage scale that pays
lower wages for workers hired after 1978.

1983-84   Major expansion of U.S. military presence in Honduras, with
as many as 300 U.S. military advisers and up to 7000 U.S.
troops participating in maneuvers near the Salvadoran and
Nicaraguan borders; border skirmishes and sea-air attacks common along Nicaragua-Honduras border, some involving U.S.
forces. Mosquito Indians migrating into Honduras (at least
20,000 since 1979).

1984   U.S. fleets operating off both coasts of Nicaragua; Kissinger
Report defends arms aid to El Salvador and calls for military
and economic aid to friendly Central American nations, while

recognizing serious social and economic inequities. Nicaragua announces elections for Nov. 4, 1984, but opposition boycotts and Daniel Ortega wins easily; as church-state relations worsen, Pope John Paul II admonishes Sandinistas for expelling ten foreign Roman Catholic priests; split furthered when Archbishop Miguel Obando y Bravo declares his support for the opposition. Duarte defeats D'Aubisson in Salvadoran presidential election and takes office; U.S. Congress passes Salvadoran military aid bill within a few days after the election; growing Costa Rican concern over use of Costa Rican territory by ARDE; Pastora wounded when a bomb explodes in his headquarters. Major shakeup in Honduran military, as younger officers oust Alvarez and his cronies after growing anti-US demonstrations in Honduras. International outcry against mining of Nicaraguan harbors. Nicaragua takes case to World Court (The Hague); U.S. rejects Court's jurisdiction, but stops mining. In first Panamanian presidential election since 1968, 82-year-old Arnulfo Arias Madrid (running on opposition coalition including his own Authentic Panamanian Party and the Christian Democratic Party) claimed victory over government (Revolutionary Democratic Party) candidate Nicolás Ardito-Barletta, but Election Tribunal declares Ardito the winner; when Panama Canal Commission (5 U.S. and 4 Panamanian members) extends special privileges to U.S. employees and operators of the Canal, Panama accuses U.S. of violating 1978 treaty by discriminating against local workers.

A Selective Guide to the
Literature on Central America

The number of publications dealing with Central America is very great, despite the fact that there are still gaps on many aspects of its history and development. There has been an enormous surge of historical publication during the past decade, especially of materials relating to recent history. The following bibliographical essay cites much of this literature for both the general reader and the specialist. It concentrates for the most part on books, however; periodical literature and unpublished (or obscurely published) theses and dissertations constitute important sources of additional information and interpretation on the region which the serious student should also consult. Many items listed in the first edition (1976) of this work have been deleted here in favor of newer publications.

The first section surveys a selection of materials in the English language for the general reader. The second is devoted to a selection of travelers' accounts. The third and most extensive section deals with the history of the isthmus. Subsequent sections treat the economy, inter-state relations, the society, culture, and the arts. The final section discusses bibliographies and current periodicals of the region. To save space, the following abbreviations have been used for places of publication: Buenos Aires, B.A.; Boston, Bos.; Guatemala, Gua.; London, Ln.; Los Angeles, L.A.; Managua, Man.; New Orleans, N.O.; New York, N.Y.; San José, S.J.; San Salvador, S.S.; Tegucigalpa, Teg.; and Washington, Wash.

I. SELECTED WORKS IN ENGLISH

Still very useful for the details of Central America from the sixteenth through the nineteenth century is H. H. Bancroft, *History of Central America* (3 vols., San Francisco, 1886-87). More recent general histories of value include F. D. Parker, *The Central American Republics* (Ln., 1964), which contains much data on the social, cultural, and economic growth of the isthmus, and Mario Rodríguez, *Central America* (Englewood Cliffs, N.J., 1965), a brief but succinct interpretation of modern Central America. Although uneven in quality, the U.S. Army *Area Handbooks/Country Studies* series (Wash., 1970-85), for all the Central American states provide a variety of statistical and factual data, particularly for recent years. The series of *Historical Dictionaries* of the Latin American countries published by the Scarecrow Press are also of uneven quality, but are nevertheless useful for reference, as is Glen Taplin, *Middle American Governors* (Metuchen, N.J., 1972), in the same series. For the geography of the region, see Robert West and John Augelli, *Middle America: Its Lands and Peoples* (2d ed., Englewood Cliffs, N.J., 1976). Jacques May and Donna McLellan, *The Ecology of Malnutrition in Mexico and Central America* (N.Y., 1972), offers a wealth of detail and statistical data on the medical geography of the region. An excellent introduction to the people and customs of the area is R. N. Adams, *Cultural Surveys of Panama–Nicaragua–Guatemala–El Salvador–Honduras* (Wash., 1957). Useful for their description of the evolution of the culture and society of Central America are Eric Wolf, *Sons of the Shaking Earth* (Chicago, 1959); William Sanders and Barbara Price, *Mesoamerica, the Evolution of a Civilization* (N.Y., 1968); Mary Helms, *Middle America, A Culture History of Heartlands and Frontiers* (Englewood Cliffs, N.J., 1975); and Nathan Whetten, *Guatemala: The Land and the People* (N.Y., 1961). Doris Stone, *Pre-Columbian Man Finds Central America* (Cambridge, Mass., 1972), is an excellent introduction to the archaeology of Central America. Problems of life and development in the tropics are outlined in Marston Bates, *Where Winter Never Comes. A Study of Man and Nature in the Tropics* (N.Y., 1953). A wide assortment of current statistical data may be found in the *Statistical Abstract of Latin America* (L.A., 1958-, annual). The *South American Handbook* (Ln. & Bath, 1924-, annual) provides a handy guide to basic current information on each Central American state.

Several monographic studies offer more detail on historical topics or periods. Murdo MacLeod, *Spanish America: A Socioeconomic History, 1520-1720* (Berkeley, 1973), is a masterful description and analysis of the sixteenth and seventeenth centuries. W. L. Sherman, *Forced Native Labor in Sixteenth Century Central America* (Lincoln, 1979) is both informative and insightful regarding Spanish enslavement of the Indian population in the early colonial period. M. L. Wortman, *Government and Society in Central America, 1680-1840* (N.Y., 1982), provides an overview of the Bourbon century and federation period, which if less impressive than MacLeod's treatment is nonetheless convenient. Troy Floyd, *The Anglo-Spanish Struggle for Mosquitia* (Albuquerque, 1967), details the colonial rivalry for the eastern coast of Central America. J. T. Lanning's two works, *The University in the Kingdom of Guatemala* (Ithaca, 1955), and *The Eighteenth Century Enlightenment in the University of San Carlos de Guatemala* (Ithaca, 1956), are major contributions to the understanding of colonial academic life and its role in the society.

Mario Rodríguez, *The Cádiz Experiment in Central America, 1808-*

1826 (Berkeley, 1978), brilliantly describes the origin of Central American liberalism and its roots in the Spanish constitutional experiment of 1812, while Louis Bumgartner, *José del Valle of Central America* (Durham, 1963), illuminates the life and career of one of Central America's most important leaders during the time political independence was achieved. T. L. Karnes, *Failure of Union: Central America, 1824-1975* (Tempe, Az., 1975), surveys the repeated failures at federation. Mary Holleran, *Church and State in Guatemala* (N.Y., 1949), is a reliable study of the church-state conflict in nineteenth-century Central America and provides valuable insight into the broader political issues of the period. R. L. Woodward, Jr., *Class Privilege and Economic Development: The Consulado de Comercio of Guatemala, 1793-1871* (Chapel Hill, 1966), describes a major institution in the economic development and political structure of Guatemala, while W. J. Griffith, *Empires in the Wilderness: Foreign Colonization and Development in Guatemala, 1834-1844* (Chapel Hill, 1965), explores in depth efforts to establish foreign colonies on Central American shores. Rodríguez, Woodward, Miriam Williford, and Griffith, in *Applied Enlightenment: 19th-Century Liberalism* (N.O., 1972), explore further the political conflicts of the nineteenth century. Rodríguez, *A Palmerstonian Diplomat in Central America* (Tucson, 1964), traces the influential career of Frederick Chatfield. M. W. Williams, *Anglo-American Isthmian Diplomacy, 1815-1915* (Wash. & Ln., 1916), is still a useful introduction to that subject, but has been greatly supplemented by a number of monographs treated later in this essay along with many works on the William Walker episode. The Liberal modernization efforts in the late nineteenth century is carefully described in D. J. McCreery, *Development and the State in Reforma Guatemala* (Athens, Ohio, 1983).

The twentieth century has received more attention, but much of it has been of rather transitory quality. A few works have lasting value, however. Neill Macaulay, *The Sandino Affair* (Chicago, 1967); William Kamman, *A Search for Stability, 1925-1933* (Notre Dame, Ind., 1968); Richard Millett, *Guardians of the Dynasty* (Maryknoll, N.Y., 1977); and John Booth, *The End and the Beginning* (Boulder, 1982) all reveal especially well important aspects of Nicaraguan history, and the collection of essays edited by T. W. Walker, *Nicaragua in Revolution* (N.Y., 1982), offers perceptive views of the Sandinista Revolution. Walker has also written a recent overview of Nicaraguan political history, "Nicaragua: From Dynastic Dictatorship to Social Revolution," for the forthcoming second edition of H. J. Wiarda and H. F. Kline, *Latin American Politics and Development*. Peter Rosset and John Vandermeer (eds.), *The Nicaragua Reader* (N.Y., 1983), provide a useful collection of materials on the Sandinista Revolution.

David Browning's *El Salvador, Landscape and Society* (Oxford, 1971), is the most important work ever written on Salvadoran history. T. F. Anderson has shed light on two important periods with his *Matanza* (Lincoln, 1971), on the 1932 revolution, and *The War of the Dispossessed* (Lincoln, 1981), on the 1969 "soccer war." See also his *Politics in Central America* (N.Y., 1982) for an overview of the recent politics of Guatemala, El Salvador, Honduras, and Nicaragua. The most perceptive work coming out of the "soccer war" is William Durham, *Scarcity and Survival in Central America: Ecological Origins of the Soccer War* (Stanford, 1979). On more recent events in El Salvador, see S. A. Webre, *José Napoleón Duarte and the Christian Democratic Party in Salvadoran Politics, 1960-1972* (Baton Rouge, 1979); Enrique Baloyra, *El Salvador in Transition* (Chapel Hill, 1982); Tommie Sue Montgomery, *Revolution in El Salvador* (Boulder, 1982); J. A. Dunkerley, *The Long War: Dictatorship and Revolution in El Salvador* (Ln., 1982); and a useful anthology by M. E. Gettleman *et al.* (eds.), *El Salvador: Central America in the New Cold War* (N.Y., 1981).

On Honduras see J. A. Morris, *Honduras: Caudillo Politics and Military Rulers* (Boulder, 1984).

K. J. Grieb has given us a detailed study on a *Guatemalan Caudillo, the Regime of Jorge Ubico, 1931-1944* (Athens, Ohio, 1979). Earlier works on the Guatemalan Revolution and its overthrow by K. H. Silvert, *A Study in Government: Guatemala* (N.O., 1954), and R. M. Schneider, *Communism in Guatemala, 1944-54* (N.Y., 1958), have been recently supplemented by José Aybar, *Dependency and Intervention: The Case of Guatemala in 1954* (Boulder, 1979), R. H. Immerman, *The CIA in Guatemala* (Austin, 1982), and S. C. Schlesinger and S. Kinzer, *Bitter Fruit* (N.Y., 1982). R. N. Adams, *Crucifixion by Power* (Austin, 1970) offers perceptive analyses and insights into the structure of society in Guatemala, while Thomas and Marjorie Melville, *Guatemala, the Politics of Land Ownership* (N.Y., 1971), help to understand the problems of that country since 1954. A useful collection of readings on contemporary Guatemala is J. L. Fried *et al.* (eds.), *Guatemala in Rebellion: Unfinished History* (N.Y., 1983).

In addition to his excellent study of Central American political leaders found in *The Democratic Left in Exile* (Miami, 1974), Charles Ameringer has contributed to our understanding of recent Costa Rican history with his biography of José Figueres, *Don Pepe* (Albuquerque, 1978), and a survey of the country's politics since about 1930 in *Democracy in Costa Rica* (N.Y., 1982). J. P. Bell, *Crisis in Costa Rica* (Austin, 1971) remains the best account in English of the 1948 revolution.

On Belize there are now several useful histories, including Narda Dob-

son's general *History of Belize* (Ln., 1973), O. N. Bolland, *The Formation of a Colonial Society* (Baltimore, 1977), Wayne Clegern, *British
Honduras, Colonial Dead End, 1859-1900* (Baton Rouge, 1967), and
C. H. Grant, *The Making of Modern Belize* (Cambridge, 1976). In the
first of a projected three or four volumes, Father John Maher has reprinted
a selection of articles on Belizean history from *Belizean Studies* in his
Readings in Belizean History (Belize, 1978).

A perceptive collection of essays on contemporary Central America as a
whole is S. C. Ropp and J. A. Morris (eds.), *Central America, Crisis and
Adaptation* (Albuquerque, 1984). Another is R. S. Leiken (ed.), *Central
America, Anatomy of Conflict* (N.Y., 1984). On U.S. policy in the region
see Walter LaFeber, *Inevitable Revolutions, The United States in Central
America* (N.Y. & Ln., 1983). For reviewing recent events, Jack Hopkins
(ed.), *Latin America and Caribbean Record* (N.Y., 1948-   , annual), is
an excellent annual reference work written by leading specialists on the
region.

II.   TRAVEL ACCOUNTS

The observations of travelers and foreign residents often provide an enormous source of information. Central America has a particular wealth of
such literature, especially for the nineteenth and twentieth centuries. Such
accounts must be used with care because of the peculiar biases and interests of their authors and their individual shortcomings in observation.
Their value varies depending on the topic of interest, and thus the following list is only a representative selection.

Few foreign travelers came to Central America during the colonial period and fewer still wrote accounts. There are some notable exceptions,
however. For the sixteenth century there is the *Relación breve y verdadera
de algunas cosas de las muchas que sucedieron al padre Fray Alonso Ponce
en las Provincias de la Nueva España . . . escrita por dos religiosos, sus
compañeros* (2 vols., Madrid, 1873). The work has been indexed by Grace
Metcalf in *Boletín Bibliográfico de Antropología Americana* 7 (1943-44),
pp. 56-84. Also very informative and entertaining, but subject to distor-
tions stemming from the author's fierce anti-Spanish bias at the time he
wrote the account, is Thomas Gage, *New Survey of the West-Indies*, origi-

nally published in London in 1648, with several subsequent editions under a variety of titles. Lionel Wafer, a physician who accompanied a buccaneering expedition, described the isthmus in *A New Voyage and Description of the Isthmus of America* (Ln., 1699). Later, another Englishman, John Cockburn, described his adventures in *A Journey over Land from the Gulf of Honduras to the Great South Sea* (Ln., 1735). An early view of the British settlements on the eastern coast is provided by Captain George Henderson, *An Account of the British Settlement of Honduras* (Ln., 1809).

Independence brought more visitors to the isthmus. F. D. Parker, *Travels in Central America, 1821-1840* (Gainesville, Fla., 1970), examines and analyzes the most important of these early accounts, while Ricardo Fernández Guardia assembled and translated a selection of the nineteenth-century travel accounts in his *Costa Rica en el siglo XIX* (S.J., 1929). One of the first of the British accounts to appear during the first decade of independence was Orlando Roberts, *Narrative of Voyages and Excursions on the East Coast and in the Interior of Central America* (Edinburgh, 1827), in which he pointed to the advantages of direct commerce with the natives of the Nicaraguan coast. Life in Guatemala was depicted in *A Brief Memoir of the Life of James Wilson* (Ln., 1829), and in Henry Dunn, *Guatimala, or, the Republic of Central America, in 1827-8* (Ln., 1829). Also useful are the observations of the British diplomat, George A. Thompson, *Narrative of an Official Visit to Guatemala from Mexico* (Ln., 1829). Dutch accounts are J. Haefkens, *Reize naar Guatemala* (2 vols., Hague, 1827-28), and, by the same author, *Central Amerika, vit een geschiedkundig, aardrijskundig en statistiek oogpunt beschouwd* (Dordrecht, 1832). Extremely useful for explaining economic conditions in the early republic is L. H. C. Obert, *Mémoire contenant un aperçu statistique de l'état de Guatemala* (Bruxelles, 1840). The first major North American account was George Washington Montgomery, *Narrative of a Journey to Guatemala in Central America, in 1838* (N.Y., 1839). It was soon followed by one of the most perceptive and informative accounts ever to be written about Central America, that of U.S. envoy John Lloyd Stephens, *Incidents of Travel in Central America, Chiapas, and Yucatan* (2 vols., N.Y., 1841). About the same time Thomas Young published a revealing description of the Honduran north coast and Bay Islands, *Narrative of a Residence on the Mosquito Shore* (Ln., 1842). Useful accounts and descriptions of the decade of the 1840's include Philippe la Renaudière, *Mexique et Guatemala* (Paris, 1843); the pro-Liberal autobiographical account of Joseph Sue, *Henri le Chancelier: Souvenirs d'un voyage dans* l'*Amérique Centrale* (Paris, 1857); Robert Dunlop, *Travels in Central America* (Ln., 1847); Frederick Crowe, *The Gospel in Central America* (Ln., 1850); and John Baily, *Central America* (Ln., 1850).

The latter half of the nineteenth century experienced the peak of travel literature popularity, and a number of notable accounts described Central America. By far the most informative were the works of E. G. Squier, the U.S. envoy to Central America, written in the 1850's and dealing principally with Honduras and Nicaragua, but providing much data on the other states as well. C. F. Reichardt, *Centro-Amerika* (Braunschweig, 1851), has an excellent map and notes on the principal towns. There were several important French accounts at mid century: the French *chargé d'affaires*, Victor Herrán, *Notice sur les cinq états du Centre-Amérique* (Bordeaux, 1853); André Cornette, *Relation d'un voyage de Mexico á Guatémala dans la cours de l'année 1855* (Paris, 1858); Charles E. Brasseur de Bourbourg, *Aperçus d'un voyage dans les états de San-Salvador et de Guatémala* (Paris, 1857); and Arthur Morelet, *Voyage dans l'Amérique Centrale, l'ile de Cuba, et le Yucatan* (2 vols., Paris, 1857). An English edition of Morelet, *Travels in Central America*, appeared in London in 1871. Another useful European impression is Karl Ritter von Scherzer, *Travels in the Free States of Central America* (Ln., 1857). The astute observations of the Chilean *chargé d'affaires*, Francisco Solano Astaburuaga, made principally from Costa Rica, are found in his *Repúblicas de Centro América* (Santiago de Chile, 1857). An important U.S. account was William V. Wells, *Explorations and Adventures in Honduras, comprising sketches of travel in the gold regions of Olancho, and a review of the history and general resources of Central America* (N.Y., 1857). Sympathetic descriptions of William Walker's foray into Central America are Walker's own *The War in Nicaragua* (Mobile, Ala., 1860); and Lawrence Oliphant, *Patriots and Filibusterers* (Ln., 1860). Detailed descriptions of the isthmus in the following decade are Wilhelm Marr, *Reise nach Central-Amerika* (2 vols., Hamburg, 1863); Felix Belly, *À travers l'Amérique Centrale* (2 vols., Paris, 1868); and Frederick Boyle, *A Ride across a Continent: A Personal Narrative of Wanderings through Nicaragua and Costa Rica* (Ln., 1868). The wife of a British diplomat, Mrs. H. G. Foote published her perceptive observations of Central America in the 1860's in her *Recollections of Central America and the West Coast of Africa* (Ln., 1869). J. W. Boddam-Wetham, *Across Central America* (Ln., 1877), describes Guatemala, including the Verapaz, Los Altos, and the Petén, in the early years of the Barrios regime, with detailed information on economic and social conditions. The perceptive French vice-consul in El Salvador, Joseph Laferrière, recorded his impressions in *De Paris à Guatémala;*

notes de voyages au Centre-Amérique, 1866-1875 (Paris, 1877). Other
valuable French accounts of the period are Louis Verbugghe, *À travers
l'Isthme de Panama* (Paris, 1879); and Alexandre Lambert de Sainte-
Croix, *Onze mois au Mexique et au Centre-Amérique* (Paris, 1897). Otto
Stoll published a descriptive account, *Guatemala: Reisen und Schilderun-
gen aus den Jahren 1878-1883* (Leipzig, 1886), as well as a pioneering
ethnographical work on the Guatemalan Maya, *Zur Ethnographie der
Republik Guatemala* (Zürich, 1884). British accounts by Mary Lester
(Maria Soltera, pseud.), *A Lady's Ride across Spanish Honduras* (Edinburgh & Ln., 1884), and Anne and Alfred Maudslay, *A Glimpse of
Guatemala and some Notes on the Ancient Monuments of Central America* (Ln., 1899), are both entertaining and informative. Social and political data is blended exotically with zoological and botanical information in
Thomas Belt, *The Naturalist in Nicaragua* (Ln., 1874). The best of
many North American accounts written during the late nineteenth century is Helen Sanborn (the Chase & Sanborn coffee heiress), *A Winter in
Central America and Mexico* (Bos., 1866). Others are E. A. Lever, *Central America* (N.O., 1885); Frank Vincent, *In and Out of Central America* (N.Y., 1890); Cecil Charles, *Honduras: The Land of Great Depths*
(Chicago, 1890); Hezekiah Butterworth, *Lost in Nicaragua* (Bos. & Chicago, 1898); R. H. Davis, *Three Gringos in Venezuela and Central America* (N.Y., 1896); and Albert Morlan, *A Hoosier in Honduras* (Indianapo-
lis, 1897). Henry Blaney, *The Golden Caribbean* (Bos., 1900), is valuable
for its descriptions of the Central American banana lands and its lovely
water colors of Central American ports and cities at the turn of the century. J. W. G. Walker, who headed the canal commission, wrote a valuable account based on his activities in Nicaragua, *Ocean to Ocean: An
Account, Personal and Historical, of Nicaragua and its People* (Chicago,
1902).

The early twentieth century saw a continuation of the popularity of
travel accounts, but their quality seems to have suffered, for many are little
more than rehashes of earlier accounts and reinforcements of older prejudices. The classic among such trash is G. L. Morrill, *Rotten Republics*
(Chicago, 1916). More objective is Nevin Winters, *Guatemala and her
People of Today* (Bos., 1909). More detailed description is provided in
C. W. Domville-Fife, *Guatemala and the States of Central America*
(N.Y., 1913). Other descriptive accounts are Frederick Palmer, *Central
America and its Problems; an Account of a Journey from the Rio Grande
to Panama* (N.Y., 1910); G. P. Putnam, *The Southland of North Amer-
ica* (N.Y. & Ln., 1913); and W. H. Koebel, *Central America* (Ln.,
[1917]). Perceptive accounts by Spaniards are José Segarra and Joaquín

Julía, *Escursión por América: Costa Rica* (S.J., 1907); and Jacinto Ca-
pella, *La ciudad tranquilla (Guatèmala)* (Madrid, 1916). The experiences
of the first U.S. Ph.D. candidate doing dissertation research on the isthmus
are recalled in a fascinating account by Dana Munro, *A Student in Central America, 1914-1916* (N.O., 1983).

Several travel accounts illuminate the years between the World Wars,
beginning with R. W. Babson, *A Central American Journey* (Yonkers,
N.Y., 1920). Eugene Cunningham describes in lively style his overland
journey through the isthmus in *Gypsying through Central America* (N.Y.,
1922). Similar is Morley Roberts, *On the Earthquake Line: Minor Adventures in Central America* (Ln., 1924), which pays greater attention to
social conditions and customs. L. E. Elliott, *Central America, New Paths
in Ancient Lands* (Ln., 1924), provides greater detail, with some historical
material. Wallace Thompson, *Rainbow Countries of Central America*
(N.Y., 1926), is descriptive and informative. Arthur Ruhl, *The Central
Americans* (N.Y. & Ln., 1928), offers impressions of these countries on
the eve of the Great Depression.

Aldous Huxley, *Beyond the Mexique Bay* (N.Y. & Ln., 1934), is de-
lightful as well as informative. His fascination with Guatemala is shared
by several others who wrote travel accounts in the 1930's, notably J. H.
Jackson, *Notes on a Drum* (N.Y., 1937); Addison Burbank, *Guatemala
Profile* (N.Y., 1939); Vera Kelsey and Lilly de Jongh Osborne, *Four
Keys to Guatemala* (N.Y., 1939); and Erna Fergusson, *Guatemala* (N.Y.
& Ln., 1938). Frances Emery-Waterhouse, the wife of a United Fruit
Company engineer, provides a revealing account of life in the banana
country of Guatemala in the late 1930's and early 1940's in *Banana Para-
dise* (N.Y., 1947). William Krehm, *Democracies and Tyrannies of the
Caribbean* (Westport, Ct., 1984), is a vivid day-by-day account of events
as seen by a *Time* Magazine reporter in the 1940's.

Since the war there has been a flurry of travel accounts, many of which
do no more than gloss over the region's picturesque scenery and people.
Some, however, provide insightful comment on the politics and social and
economic conditions. Ralph Hancock, *The Rainbow Republics* (N.Y.,
1947), provides a guide for travelers which reflects conditions and ap-
pearances in the mid 1940's. Jean Hersey, *Halfway to Heaven, A Guatemala Holiday* (N.Y., 1947), offers more sentimental insight into Guatemalan life. Hakon Morne, *Caribbean Symphony* (N.Y., 1955), describes
the adventures of a Finnish couple in Panama, Costa Rica, and Nicaragua.
Maria Schwauss, a German woman, describes her experiences in Guatemala in *Tropenspiegel: Tagebuch einer deutschen Frau in Guatemala*
(Halle, 1949). David Dodge, *How Lost Was my Weekend* (N.Y., 1948),

is an amusing and irreverent description of the problems of a foreign writer attempting to establish residence there. Maud Oakes, *Beyond the Windy Place, Life in the Guatemalan Highlands* (N.Y., [1951]), recounts her experiences in Todos Santos and Huehuetenango. Tord Wallstrom, *Wayfarer in Central America* (N.Y., 1955), is a Swedish journalist's perceptive observation. Lilly de Jongh Osborne, *Four Keys to El Salvador* (N.Y., 1956), is a useful introduction, and Donald E. Lundberg, *Adventure in Costa Rica* (Tallahassee, Fla., 1960, 2nd ed., S.J., 1968), provides a great deal of specific information on that country. Nicholas Wollaston, *Red Rumba: A Journey through the Caribbean and Central America* (Ln., 1962), includes a number of interesting interviews with ordinary citizens. Hans Helfritz, *Zentralamerika; die Länderbrücke im Karibishen Raum* (Berlin, 1963), contains detailed descriptions of the region. Selden Rodman, *Road to Panama* (N.Y., 1966), is a travel guide with chapters on each country from Mexico to Panama. Albert Lisi, *Round Trip from Poptún, A Journey in Search of the Maya* (N.Y., 1968), describes adventures in highland Guatemala and the Petén. Very useful is the impressionistic travel guide, containing some current political, social and economic description, prepared by Hilda Cole Espy and Lex Creamer, Jr., *Another World: Central America* (N.Y., 1970). Paul Kennedy, an American journalist, has provided a useful survey of the current scene in his *Middle Beat: A Correspondent's View of Mexico, Guatemala, and El Salvador* (N.Y., 1971). The articles describing the travels in Central America of Luis Marañón Richi, the Secretary to the Spanish Minister of Commerce, *Centroamérica paso a paso* (Madrid, 1968), are descriptive and perceptive. Doug Richmond, *Central America: How to Get There and Back in One Piece with a Minimum of Hassle* (Tucson, 1974), reflects the situation in the 1970's. Among current travel guides, see the latest edition of *The South American Handbook* (a misnomer) (Ln. and Bath, 1924- , annual), or *Fodor's Central America* (N.Y., 1980-).

III. HISTORY

A. *General Histories and Reference Works*

Few comprehensive histories of the isthmus exist in any language. Most Central American histories have traditionally been preoccupied with the Hispanic period. The major work is Ernesto Chinchilla Aguilar, *Historia de Centroamérica* (3 vols., Gua., 1974-77), which is very useful, but is heavily weighted toward the pre-Columbian and Hispanic periods, with less than half of the final volume devoted to independent Central America. Parker and Karnes, already mentioned, survey significant aspects, but neither is truly comprehensive. Bancroft was published a century ago. Dana Munro, *The Five Republics of Central America* (N.Y., 1918), surveys the nineteenth century, but is most useful for detail and analysis of the early part of the twentieth century. C. F. S. Cardoso and Héctor Pérez Brignoli, *Centroamérica y la economía occidental* (1520-1930) (S.J., 1977), outline the economic history of the region, while insight into the political structure and history of Central America can be gained from Fernando Guier, *La función presidencial en Centroamérica* (S.J., 1973). A broader work is Antonio Batres Jáuregui, *La América Central ante la historia* (3 vols., Gua., 1916-49), but it contains nothing after 1921. Of more antiquarian than historical value is Federico Hernández de León, *El libro de las efemérides* (6 vols., Gua., 1925-63), which contains a chapter of historical data for each day of the year. Miguel A. Gallardo (comp.), *Cuatro constituciones federales de Centro América y las constituciones políticas de El Salvador* (S.S., 1945), provides a useful compilation of the federal constitutions from 1824 to 1921.

The military history of Central America through about 1920 is surveyed in some detail in J. N. Rodríguez, *Estudios de historia militar de Centroamérica* (Gua., 1930); and Pedro Zamora Castellanos, *Vida militar de Centro América* (Gua., 1934). The latter deals with the national period.

More numerous are works dealing with individual countries. Chester Lloyd Jones, *Guatemala, Past and Present* (Minneapolis, 1940), and William Brigham, *Guatemala, the Land of the Quetzal* (N.Y., 1887), both still have value, but are out of date both in content and methodology. Mario Rosenthal, *Guatemala, the Story of an Emerging Latin American Democracy* (N.Y., 1962) provides additional data on the mid-twentieth century despite its overly optimistic title, as does the brief but useful work of Selden Rodman, *The Guatemala Traveler: A Concise History and Guide* (N.Y., 1971). Works on recent Guatemalan history are dealt with elsewhere in this essay. Clemente Marroquín Rojas, *Historia de Guatemala* (Gua., 1971), is injudicious in its use of the facts, but offers interesting hypotheses in its nationalistic interpretations. A thoughtful Marxist treatment of Guatemalan history is Carlos Guzmán-Böckler y Jean-Loup Herbert, *Guatemala: una interpretación histórico social* (México, 1970). Pedro Zamora Castellanos details the military history, principally since independence, in *Nuestros cuarteles* (Gua., 1932). Gilberto Valenzuela Reyna, *Guatemala y sus gobernantes* (1821-1958) (Gua., 1959), briefly sketches Guatemala's chiefs of state. Luis Mariñas Otero, *Las constituciones de Guatemala* (Madrid, 1958), is valuable both for its documents and its commentary. Although disappointing in some of its entries, R. E. Moore, *Historical Dictionary of Guatemala* (Metuchen, N.J., 1967), is a handy reference. J. L. Arriola, *El libro de las geonimías de Guatemala; diccionario entimológico* (Gua., 1973), describes thousands of Guatemalan place names. The most detailed economic geography is Alfredo Guerra Borges, *Geografía económica de Guatemala* (2 vols., Gua., 1969-73).

For Honduras, Luis Mariñas Otero, *Honduras* (Madrid, 1963), is easily the most complete history, but see also Morris, *Honduras* (Boulder, 1984). Mariñas also compiled *Las constituciones de Honduras* (Madrid, 1962). Mario Argueta and Egardo Quiñónez, *Historia de Honduras* (2d ed., Teg., 1979), is a useful traditional history. W. S. Stokes, *Honduras, an Area Study in Government* (Madison, Wis., 1950), is an introduction to the country, with emphasis on the mid-twentieth century. Rómulo Durón y Gamero, *Bosquejo histórico de Honduras, 1502 a 1921* (San Pedro Sula, 1927), is a brief political survey. An excellent anthology of readings and documents on Honduras within the context of New World history is Héctor Pérez Brignoli, *et al.* (eds.), *De la sociedad colonial a la crisis de los años 30* (Teg., 1972). Honduran labor history is treated by Victor Meza, *Historia del movimiento obrero hondureño* (Teg., 1980); and Mario Posas, *Luchas del movimiento obrero hondureño* (S.J., 1981). Marcelino Bonilla, *Diccionario histórico-geográfico de las poblaciones de Honduras* (2d ed., Teg., 1952), has a little reference value, and Carlos A. Aguilar B., *Texto de enseñanza de la geografía de Honduras* (2 vols., Teg., 1969-70), is a complete school geography.

In addition to Browning's brilliant study of land use in El Salvador, Alastair White, *El Salvador* (N.Y., 1973), offers a brief historical overview, but its principal value is for the 1960's. Philip Russell, *El Salvador in Crisis* (Austin, 1984), also traces Salvadoran development since the Spanish conquest but concentrates on the recent history. Rodolfo Barón Castro has made a monumental study of the development of the Salvadoran population from pre-Columbian times through 1942, *La población de El Salvador* (Madrid, 1942). Several Salvadoran historians provide a review of the basic political developments, but they offer little along socio-economic lines; however, a brief survey is provided by Roque Dalton, *El Salvador* (Havana, 1963). Manuel Vidal, *Nociones de historia de Centro América* (*especial para El Salvador*) (5th ed., S.S., 1957), is useful for placing El Salvador in the context of Central America, but thin on the twentieth century. Similarly, José Figeac, *Recordatorio histórico de la república de El Salvador* (S.S., 1938), offers much detail on the nineteenth century, rather cursory coverage of the colonial period, and nothing on the twentieth century. Francisco Gavidia, *Historia moderna de El Salvador* (S.S.,

1917-18; 2d ed., 1958), extends only to 1814. Jorge Lardé y Larín, *El Salvador: Historia de sus pueblos, villas y ciudades* (S.S., 1957), details local history, while a large number of biographical sketches and a brief account of the founding of San Salvador is provided in the Academia Salvadoreña de la Historia, *San Salvador y sus hombres* (S.S., 1938). María and Freddy Leistenschneider, *Gobernantes de El Salvador* (S.S., 1980), provides a handy reference for biographical data on El Salvador's chiefs of state, and they also have begun to publish a series of volumes on individual Salvadoran chief executives. J. N. Rodríguez Ruíz, *Historia de las instituciones jurídicas salvadoreñas* (S.S., 1951), is a competent history of Salvadoran judicial development to the mid-twentieth century. Philip Flemion, *Historical Dictionary of El Salvador* (Metuchen, N.J., 1972), is among the best in that series. The multi-volume *Diccionario histórico-enciclopédico de la República de El Salvador,* published since 1927 in a variety of formats, is a sometimes inconsistent and confusing series of historical materials, but it contains much of value. The *Diccionario geográfico de la República de El Salvador,* published irregularly by the Dirección General de Estadística y Censos in San Salvador since 1940, provides a handy guide to place names. For Salvadoran constitutions, see Ricardo Gallardo, *Las constituciones de El Salvador* (2 vols., Madrid, 1961).

Nicaraguan historians, who have been severely handicapped by the destruction of the national archives in the earthquake of 1931, have yet to produce a satisfactory general history of their country, although the Sandinista Revolution has prompted much hasty publication. Claribel Alegría and D. J. Flakoll, *Nicaragua, la revolución sandinista: una crónica política* (México, 1982), concentrates principally on recent history. The broad lines of Nicaraguan history have been well laid out by David Radell in his Ph.D. dissertation, *An Historical Geography of Western Nicaragua: The Spheres of Influence of León, Granada and Managua, 1519-1965* (Berkeley, 1969). Notable in his effort to combine Nicaraguan nationalism with Marxist ideology is Jaime Wheelock Román, *Native Roots of the Nicaraguan Anticolonial Struggle* (N.Y., 1979 [original Spanish edition, México, 1974]). H. K. Meyer, *Historical Dictionary of Nicaragua* (Metuchen, N.J., 1972), is a handy, although occasionally inaccurate, reference. Traditionally, many Nicaraguan historians have concentrated on local history of antiquarian nature or on retelling the story of the William Walker episode or the U.S. intervention of 1912-33. Sara Barquero, *Gobernantes de Nicaragua, 1825-1947* (2d ed., Man., 1945), provides very brief sketches of the chiefs of state. Andrés Vega Bolaños, *Gobernantes de Nicaragua* (Man., 1944), provides greater detail and principal documents from their administrations, but only for the period 1821-58. The best early histories are those of Tomás Ayón, *Historia de Nicaragua desde los tiempos más remotos hasta 1852* (3 vols., Man., 1882-89; 3d ed., 1977), which despite its title extends only to 1821; and J. D. Gámez, *Historia de Nicaragua desde los tiempos pre-históricos hasta 1860 en sus relaciones con España, México y Centroamérica* (3d ed., Man., 1975), especially useful for diplomatic history. Gámez also wrote an informative history of the Mosquito coast, *Historia de la costa de Mosquitos, hasta 1894,* a useful sequel to Floyd's *Anglo-Spanish struggle for Mosquitia,* which extends only to 1790. A brief survey may be found in T. W. Walker, *Nicaragua, Land of Sandino* (Boulder, 1981). Traditional political histories of some utility include Alberto Medina, *Efemérides nicaragüenses, 1502-1941* (Man., 1945); Alejandro Cole Chamorro, *145 años de historia política en Nicaragua* (Man., 1967); and Manuel Castrillo Gámez, *Proceres nicaragüenses y artículos históricos* (Man., 1961). A. S. Aguilar, *Reseña histórica de la diócesis de Nicaragua* (Madrid, 1958), contains both documents and detailed commentary on the ecclesiastical history. For the many Nicaraguan constitutions, see Emilio Alvarez Lejarza, *Las constituciones de Nicaragua* (Madrid, 1958).

The development of a strong school of history at the University of Costa Rica has resulted in the growth of considerable monographic production of high quality in recent years, and has begun to produce some more general works, notably Carlos Meléndez Ch., *Historia de Costa Rica* (S.J., 1979); J. L. Vega Carballo, *Historia social y económica de Costa Rica: fuentes y bibliografía* (S.J., 1977), *Hacia una interpretación del desarrollo costarricense* (4th ed., S.J., 1973), and *La formación del estado nacional en Costa Rica* (S.J., 1981); and J. A. Cordero, *El ser de la nacionalidad costarricense* (2d ed., S.J., 1980). Samuel Stone, *Dinastía de los conquistadores* (S.J., 1976), studies in great depth the political and genealogical ties among Costa Ricans from the Conquest to the present in a model of scholarship and ingenuity. The vivid portrayal of *Costa Rican Life* (S.J., 1944), by John and Mavis Biensanz has been admirably rewritten and updated as *Los costarricenses* (S.J., 1979) and *The Costa Ricans* (Englewood Cliffs, N.J., 1983) by Richard, Karen and Mavis Biesanz. Several older histories still have some utility, including C. L. Jones, *Costa Rica and Civilization in the Caribbean* (Madison, 1935); Carlos Monge A., *Historia de Costa Rica* (S.J., 1947); Ricardo Fernández Guardia, *Cartilla histórica de Costa Rica* (S.J., 1909, with many subsequent editions); and León Fernández Guardia, *Historia de Costa Rica*. A major nineteenth-century history is Francisco Montero Barrantes, *Elementos de historia de Costa Rica* (2 vols., S.J., 1892-94). Montero also wrote a descriptive *Geografía de Costa Rica* (Barcelona, 1892). Hernán Peralta compiled the

Constituciones de Costa Rica (Madrid, 1962). Vladimir de la Cruz, *Las luchas sociales en Costa Rica, 1870-1930* (S.J., 1980), provides a history of the emergence of the labor movement in Costa Rica, but see also Edwin Chacón León, *El sindicalismo en Costa Rica* (S.J., 1980).

Narda Dobson's *History of Belize* (Ln., 1973) is the most comprehensive general history of Belize, although she ignores major Spanish sources. A Mexican approach, with greater emphasis on the modern period is M. E. Paz Salinas, *Belize, el despertar de una nación* (México, 1979). Other useful surveys include D. A. G. Waddell, *British Honduras: A Historical and Contemporary Survey* (Ln., 1961); W. D. Setzekorn, *Formerly British Honduras* (2d ed., Athens, Ohio, 1981); John Burdon, *Brief Sketch of British Honduras, Past, Present and Future* (Ln., 1927); William Donohoe, *A History of British Honduras* (Montreal, 1946); and Archibald Gibbs, *British Honduras: An Historical and Descriptive Account of the Colony from Its Settlement, 1670* (Ln., 1883). The early history of settlement is treated by O. N. Bolland, *The Formation of Colonial Society: Belize from Conquest to Crown Colony* (Baltimore, 1977). See also Bolland and Assad Shoman, *Land in Belize, 1765-1871* (Mona, Jamaica, 1977). The diplomatic history of the settlement to the twentieth century is R. A. Humphreys, *The Diplomatic History of British Honduras, 1638-1901* (Ln., 1961).

Greater attention has been given to the Panama transit route than to the history of the country generally, but there are several useful surveys: Ernesto Castillero R., *Historia de Panamá* (7th ed., Panamá, 1962); David Howarth, *Panama, Four Hundred Years of Dreams and Cruelty* (N.Y., 1966); Guy Vattier, *Les Grandes Heures de l'histoire de Panama* (Paris, 1965); and John and Mavis Biesanz, *The People of Panama* (N.Y., 1955). John Niemier, *The Panama Story* (Portland, Ore., 1968), tells Panama's history since 1850 as reflected in the Panama *Star & Herald.* Manuel Alba C., *Cronología de los gobernantes de Panamá, 1510-1967* (Panamá, 1967), provides biographical sketches of its chiefs of state. A useful reference work is Basil and A. K. Hedrick, *Historical Dictionary of Panama* (Metuchen, N.J., 1970). Andrés Achong, *Orígenes del movimiento obrero panameño* (Panamá, 1980), and M. A. Gandásegui, hijo, *et al., Las luchas obreras en Panamá, 1850-1978* (Panamá, 1980), are serious studies of the history of Panamanian labor. See also the section on twentieth-century Panama in III-F, below.

B. Pre-Columbian Central America

The literature on the Indian ancestors of Central America, particularly on the Maya, is vast, and the works mentioned here are intended only as an introduction to the study of pre-Columbian life. Susan F. Magee (comp.), *Mesoamerican Archaeology, A Guide to the Literature and Other Information Sources* (Austin, 1981), suggests sources for the study of Central American Indians, but the most valuable tool is Robert Wauchope *et al.* (eds.), *Handbook of Middle American Indians* (Austin, 1964-76, with later supplements) which contains articles by the leading scholars on various aspects of Indian studies. A basic reference work, with a review of the literature, is R. E. Taylor and C. W. Meighan (eds.), *Chronologies in New World Archaeology* (N.Y., 1978).

An excellent introduction to the Indian civilizations of all of Central America is Doris Stone, *Pre-Columbian Man Finds Central America* (Cambridge, Mass., 1972), which treats more fully than do most general works the non-Mayan parts of the isthmus. The best general history of the Maya is S. G. Morley, G. W. Brainerd, and R. J. Sharer, *The Ancient Maya* (4th ed., Stanford, 1983). Other useful surveys include Norman Hammond, *Ancient Maya Civilization* (New Brunswick, N.J., 1982); J. S. Henderson, *The World of the Ancient Maya* (Ithaca, N.Y., 1981); and J. Eric Thompson, *The Rise and Fall of Maya Civilization* (2d ed., Norman, Okla., 1966). Thompson's *Maya History and Religion* (Norman, Okla., 1970), contains a series of thoughtful essays on Mayan history which provide fresh insight and updating. See also R. E. W. Adams (ed.), *The Origins of Maya Civilization* (Albuquerque, 1977). Thirteen scholars discuss the causes of the collapse of the lowland Maya civilization in Patrick Culbert (ed.), *The Classic Maya Collapse* (Albuquerque, 1973). A useful study of early Maya scholars is R. L. Brunhouse, *In Search of the Maya, The First Archaeologists* (Albuquerque, 1973). See also Robert Wauchope, *They Found the Buried Cities* (Chicago, 1965).

English translations of Adrián Recinos's Spanish versions of the highland Maya epics have been published by the University of Oklahoma Press at Norman: *Popol Vuh* (1950) and *Annals of the Cakchiguels* (1953). The latter also includes a translation of the *Title of the Lords of Totonicapán*. A more careful recent translation of the Popol Vuh, directly from the Quiché and using all available sources, is Munro Edmonson, *The Book of Counsel, The Popol Vuh of the Quiché Maya of Guatemala* (N.O., 1971). Robert Carmack has provided a detailed study of written sources for Quichean history in his *Quichean Civilization: The Ethnohistorical, Ethnographic, and Archaeological Sources* (Berkeley, 1973); and *The*

Quiché Mayas of Utatlán, The Evolution of a Highland Guatemalan Kingdom (Norman, 1981). See also Carmack and D. T. Wallace (eds.), *Archaeology and Ethnology of the Central Quiché* (Albany, [1976]); Murdo MacLeod and Robert Wasserstrom (eds.), *Spaniards and Indians in Southeastern Mesoamerica: Essays on the History of Ethnic Relations* (Lincoln, 1983); and J. W. Fox, *Quiché Conquest: Centralism and Regionalism in Highland Guatemalan State Development* (Albuquerque, 1978).

A guide to the archaeology of Central America, with many pictures, is Claude Baudez, *Central America* (Ln., 1970). See also Joyce Kelly, *The Complete Visitor's Guide to Mesoamerican Ruins* (Norman, Okla., 1982). There is much excellent scholarship on Maya ruins and relics. Tatiana Proscouriakoff, *A Study of Classic Maya Sculpture* (Wash., 1950), is among the most useful of volumes. Two especially noteworthy photographic renderings of Maya ruins and relics are Merle Greene's rubbings, *Maya Sculpture* (Berkeley, 1972); and Francis Robicsek, *Copán, Home of the Mayan Gods* (N.Y., 1972). The best and most up-to-date book on the archaeology of lower Central America is Frederick Lange and Doris Stone (eds.), *The Archaeology of Lower Central America* (Albuquerque, 1984). On Honduras the best general work is Roberto R. Reyes Mazzoni, *Introducción a la arqueología de Honduras*, 2 vols. (Teg., 1976). P. F. Healy, *Archaeology of the Rivas Region, Nicaragua* (Waterloo, Ont., 1980), is a detailed description of a section of the Pacific coastal plain of Nicaragua. On Costa Rica see Doris Stone, *Pre-Columbian Man in Costa Rica* (Cambridge, Mass., 1977); and Luis Ferrero Acosta, *Costa Rica precolombina* (2d ed., San José, 1977).

A useful map of Mesoamerica, extending from Mexico through Honduras and El Salvador, is the National Geographic Society, *Archaeological Map of Middle America* (Wash., n.d.). The scale is 1:2,250,000.

C. *The Hispanic Period* (1502-1821)

Murdo MacLeod, *Spanish Central America* (Berkeley, 1973), and Miles Wortman, *Government and Society in Central America* (N.Y., 1982), provide a survey of colonial Central American history. Both have ample bibliographies which go well beyond the following review. Note also that several of the works mentioned in Section III-A are principally histories of the Spanish period.

There are several major chronicles and contemporary accounts of the colonial period. Gonzalo Fernández de Oviedo y Valdés, *Historia general y natural de las Indias* (5 vols., Madrid, 1959), originally published in the mid-sixteenth century, is a passionate account of the conquest of the isthmus by an arch foe of Pedrarias. Bartolomé de las Casas tells his story in the polemical *Breve relación de la destrucción de las Indias Occidentales* (México, 1957) and in the more historical *Historia de las Indias* (3 vols., México, 1965). The *Colección Somoza* (17 vols., Madrid, 1955-57), edited by Andrés Vega Bolaños, provides documents on Nicaragua during the first half of the sixteenth century. The first major history of Central America was that of Antonio de Remesal, *Historia general de las Indias Occidentales, y particular de la Gobernación de Chiapa y Guatemala* (2 vols., Madrid, 1964-66), first published in 1619. Toribio de Motolinía, *Memorias e historia de los indios de la Nueva España* (Madrid, 1970), also includes some description of Central America. A fuller description is found in the fifth book of Antonio Vásquez de Espinosa, *Compendium and Description of the West Indies* (Madrid, 1969). An important description of the Vera Paz and Lacandón region of Guatemala is the 1635 account by Martín Alfonso Tovilla, *Relaciones histórico-descriptivas de la Verapaz, el Manché y Lacandón, en Guatemala* (Gua., 1960). The late-seventeenth-century work of Francisco Antonio de Fuentes y Guzmán, *Recordación florida* (2 vols., Gua., 1933), offers great detail on the social and economic life of the kingdom. Long delayed in publication, the chronicle of a Dominican friar, Francisco Ximénez, *Historia de la provincia de San Vicente de Chiapa y Guatemala* (3 vols., Gua., 1967), was written about 1700. Francisco Vásquez, *Crónica de la Provincia del Santísimo Nombre de Jesús de Guatemala* (4 vols., Gua., 1937-44), treats the history of the Franciscan order in Guatemala through the seventeenth century. A valuable description written in the eighteenth century is Pedro Cortés y Larraz, *Descripción geográfico-moral de la Diócesis de Goathemala, 1768-1770* (2 vols., Gua., 1958). Antonio Gutiérrez y Ulloa describes the province of El Salvador as it was in 1807 in *Estado general de la provincia de San Salvador* (S.S., 1962). Near the close of the colonial era Domingo Juarros wrote his informative *Compendio de la historia de la ciudad de Guatemala* (2 vols., Gua., 1936), which is considerably more than just a history of the capital city. Soon thereafter, a translation by John Baily provided an abridged English edition, *A Statistical and Commercial History of the Kingdom of Guatemala* (Ln., 1823).

Of the traditional histories of Central America the most well known is José Milla and Augustín Gómez Carillo, *Historia de la América Central desde 1502 hasta 1821* (5 vols., Madrid, 1892-1905). The first two volumes, written by Milla, cover the period through 1686. Another very useful work, written shortly after the close of the period, is that of Archbishop Francisco de Paula García Peláez, *Memorias para la historia del antiguo*

Reyno de Guatemala (3 vols., Gua., 1851-52). The burst of historical writing around the close of the nineteenth century produced several colonial surveys in addition to the Bancroft volumes. Some, such as M. M. de Peralta, *Costa Rica, Nicaragua y Panamá en el siglo XVI, su historia y sus limites* (S.J., 1883), were stimulated by the boundary disputes among the states. Among those on Costa Rica is León Fernández, *Historia de Costa Rica durante la dominación española* (Madrid, 1889). A Honduran point of view came from Eduardo Martínez López, *Historia de Centro América* (Teg., 1907); and a Salvadoran one from Santiago Barberena, *Historia de El Salvador* (2 vols., S.S., 1914-17). Ayón's *Historia de Nicaragua*, mentioned earlier, is still the standard for colonial Nicaragua. Later, Nicaraguan Sofonías Salvatierra, *Contribución a la historia de Centroamérica* (2 vols., Man., 1939), offered some new materials and viewpoints, particularly on economic history, based on his research in Spain. J. Antonio Villacorta Calderón, *Historia de la Capitanía General de Guatemala* (Gua., 1942), became the standard colonial history at mid-century. More recent works, notably André Saint-Lu, *Condition colonial et conscience créole au Guatemala (1524-1821)* (Paris, 1970), Severo Martínez Peláez, *La patria del criollo: ensayo de interpretación de la realidad colonial guatemalteca* (Gua., 1970), Germán Romero-Vargas, *Les structures sociales du Nicaragua au XVIIIe siècle* (Lille, 1977), and Lowell Gudmundson, *Estratificación socio-racial y económica de Costa Rica: 1700-1850* (S.J., 1978), have emphasized the social history to a greater degree than older works and have explored the development of the creole mentality. A careful and useful study of colonial scribes is Jorge Luján Muñoz, *Los escribanos en las Indias Occidentales y en particular en el Reino de Guatemala* (Gua., 1977).

There are several accounts of the discovery and conquest of Central America. See J. H. Parry and R. J. Keith (eds.), *New Iberian World, A Documentary History of the Discovery and Settlement of Latin America to the Early 17th Century,* 5 vols. (N.Y., 1984), especially Vol. III, *Central America and Mexico,* for commentary and a large collection of contemporary documents translated to English. C. L. G. Anderson, *Old Panama and Castilla de Oro* (Wash., 1911) surveys the exciting early days in Panama, supplemented by his *Life and Letters of Vasco Núñez de Balboa* (Westport, Ct., 1941); Kathleen Romoli, *Balboa of Darien* (Garden City, N.Y., 1953); and Octavio Méndez Perreira, *Núñez de Balboa, el tesoro del Dabaibe* (2d ed., B.A., 1943). Mary Helms, *Ancient Panama, Chiefs in Search of Power* (Austin, 1979), relates the history of Panamanian Indian elites during the Spanish conquest. Pablo Alvarez Rubiano has written a documentary history on *Pedrarias Dávila* (Madrid, 1944).

S. J. Mackie edited Pedro de Alvarado's *Account of the Conquest of Guatemala in 1524* (N.Y., 1924), and J. E. Kelly wrote a popular biography, *Pedro de Alvarado: Conquistador* (Port Washington, N.Y., 1932). More thorough is Adrián Recinos, *Pedro de Alvarado, Conquistador de México y Guatemala* (México, 1952). Among the most valuable of studies of the conquest and early colonization period are Sherman's, *Forced Native Labor in Sixteenth Century Central America* (Lincoln, 1979) and Peter Gerhard, *The Southeast Frontier of New Spain* (Princeton, 1979). Also useful are Salvador Rodríguez Becerra, *Encomienda y conquista: Los inicios de la colonización en Guatemala* (Sevilla, 1977); Robert Chamberlain, *Conquest and Colonization of Yucatán, 1517-1550* (Wash., 1948), and *Conquest and Colonization of Honduras, 1502-1550* (Wash., 1953). See also Frans Blom, *The Conquest of Yucatán* (Bos., 1936); R. H. Valle, *Cristóbal de Olid, conquistador de México y Honduras* (México, 1950); and Ricardo Fernández Guardia, *History of the Discovery and Conquest of Costa Rica* (N.Y., 1913; original Spanish ed., S.J., 1905). Carlos Meléndez, *Juan Vásquez de Coronado, conquistador y fundador de Costa Rica* (S.J., 1966); and Victoria Urbano, *Juan Vásquez de Coronado y su ética en la conquista de Costa Rica* (Madrid, 1968), are both excellent biographies of the conqueror of Costa Rica. Other useful works on the period include Juan Contreras y López de Ayala, *Vida del segoviano Rodrigo de Contreras, gobernador de Nicaragua (1534-1544)* (Toledo, 1920), with its large documentary appendix; Rodolfo Barón Castro, *Reseña histórica de la villa de San Salvador* (Madrid, 1950), thoroughly documented but covering only the period 1525-46; Carlos Molina Argüello, *El gobernador de Nicaragua en el siglo XVI* (Sevilla, 1949); Ernesto Alvarado García, *Los forjadores de la Honduras colonial* (Teg., 1928) and *El significado histórico de la ciudad de Gracias* (Teg., 1936).

International rivalry has been the subject of extensive historical writing, although considerably more attention has been paid to the Caribbean island areas than to the mainland. Of particular utility for students of Central America are R. A. Humphreys, *Diplomatic History of British Honduras, 1638-1901* (Ln., 1961); J. A. Calderón Quijano, *Belice, 1663(?)-1821* (Sevilla, 1944); and Troy Floyd, *The Anglo-Spanish Struggle for Mosquitia* (Albuquerque, 1967). John Prebble, *The Darien Disaster* (N.Y., 1968), is the most complete of a stream of works on William Paterson's ill-fated isthmian colony. Pedro Pérez Valenzuela has made notable contributions with *Historia de piratas: los aventoras del mar en la América Central* (Gua., 1936), and *Santo Tomás de Castilla: apuntes para la historia de las colonizaciones en la costa atlántica* (Gua., 1955).

Several studies of colonial institutions have offered glimpses into life and society in the kingdom. Silvio Zavala, *Contribución a la historia de las instituciones coloniales en Guatemala* (4th ed., Gua., 1967), deals with labor institutions in the colonial period and compares them with those of México. L. B. Simpson, *The Repartimiento System of Native Labor in New Spain and Guatemala* (Berkeley, 1938), is a brief but classic description of the system in Guatemala. S. A. Webre, "El cabildo de Santiago de Guatemala en el siglo XVII: una oligarquía criolla cerrada y hereditaria?" *Mesoamérica* 2 (1981), 1-19, is a valuable study of the seventeenth-century society of the capital of the kingdom. Manuel Rubio Sánchez, *Alcaldes mayores* (2 vols., S.S., 1979), is a thorough study of El Salvador's colonial *alcaldes mayores, justicias mayores,* governors, intendents, *corregidores,* and *jefes políiticos.* Carlos Meléndez Ch., *Conquistadores y pobladores: orígenes histórico-sociales de los costarricenses* (S.J., 1982), brings together a variety of the author's studies on colonial land and colonization. The late H. H. Samayoa Guevara made significant contributions to colonial historiography with his *Implantación del regimen de intendencias en el Reino de Guatemala* (Gua., 1960) and *Los gremios de artesanos en la ciudad de Guatemala, 1524-1821* (Gua., 1962). J. C. Pinto Soria has written a number of interesting studies on Guatemala's colonial development, which are synthesized in his *Raices históricas del estado en Centroamérica* (2d ed., Gua., 1983). See also Pinto and Edelberto Torres, *Problemas en la formación del estado nacional en Centroamérica* (S.J., 1983). M. A. Burkholder and D. S. Chandler, *From Impotence to Authority: The Spanish Crown and the American Audiencias, 1687-1808* (Columbia, Mo., 1977), describe the eighteenth-century trend toward greater peninsular authority in the Guatemalan and other audiencias. R. J. Shafer, *Economic Societies in the Spanish World, 1763-1821* (Syracuse, N.Y., 1958), has an excellent chapter on the Guatemalan Economic Society, but more detail is provided in J. L. Reyes M., *Apuntes para una monografía de la Sociedad Económica de Amigos del País* (Gua., 1964), and Elisa Luque Alcaide, *La sociedad económica de amigos del país de Guatemala* (Sevilla, 1962). R. L. Woodward, Jr., details the role of the merchant guild in *Privilegio de clase y desarrollo económico, Guatemala 1793-1871* (S.J., 1981), with documentary appendices not included in the earlier English edition. Marco Antonio Falla, *La factoria de tabacos de Costa Rica* (S.J., 1972), and V. H. Acuña Ortega, *Historia económica del tabaco: época colonial* (S.J., 1974), are both useful studies of the tobacco industry in Costa Rica. A useful work on colonial land and settlement in Costa Rica is Carlos Meléndez, *Costa Rica, tierra y poblamiento en la colonia* (S.J., 1977). Manuel Rubio Sánchez has made major contributions to the economic history of the isthmus with his studies, based on thorough archival research, on *Comercio terrestre de y entre las provincias de Centroamérica* (Gua., 1973), *Historia del añil or xiquilite en Centro América* (2 vols., S.S., 1976), *Historia del puerto de la Santísima Trinidad de Sonsonate o Acajutla* (S.S., 1977), *Historia del puerto de Trujillo* (3 vols., Teg., 1975), and *Historia de El Realejo* (Man., 1975). In addition to several detailed articles on the eighteenth-century economy, Francisco de Solano has written an informative work, *Los Maya del siglo XVIII* (Madrid, 1976). A major reference work on colonial Guatemala (except for El Petén), to be published by CIRMA in Antigua Guatemala, is Lovell, Lutz, and Swezey's forthcoming work on the colonial demography of southern Guatemala.

C. H. Lutz, *Historia sociodemográfica de Santiago de Guatemala, 1541-1773* (Antigua, Gua., and South Woodstock, Vt., 1982), is a brilliant and painstaking study of Antigua Guatemala. J. J. Pardo, *Efemérides de la Antigua Guatemala, 1541-1779* (3d ed., Gua., 1984) is a very extensive chronology of events relating to the city's history. The standard work on the architecture of that city is Sidney Markman, *Colonial Architecture of Antigua Guatemala* (Philadelphia, 1966), but V. L. Annis, *The Architecture of Antigua Guatemala, 1543-1773* (Gua., 1968), is also a beautifully illustrated guide. Other important contributions to colonial urban history include D. T. Kinkead (ed.), *Urbanization in Colonial Central America* (Sevilla, 1985), Ernesto Chinchilla Aguilar, *El ayuntamiento colonial de la ciudad de Guatemala* (Gua., 1961), and Pedro Pérez Valenzuela, *La nueva Guatemala de Asunción* (2d ed., 2 vols., Gua., 1964), which details the 1773 destruction of the Guatemalan capital and its move to, and early years in, its present location. Inge Langenberg, *Urbanisation und Bevölkerungsstruktur der Stadt Guatemala in der ausgehenden Kolonialzeit* (Cologne, 1981), has written a more thorough socio-demographic study of the early history of Nueva Guatemala. José Reina Valenzuela, *Comayagua antañona, 1537-1821* (Teg., 1968), and Carlos Meléndez Ch., *La ciudad de Lodo: Cartago* (S.J., 1964), are among the few descriptions of colonial cities in the rest of Central America.

The Church has received some attention from historians, although they have been hindered by the inaccessibility of ecclesiastical archives in Central America. A major reference work by the director of the Guatemalan ecclesiastical archive is Agustín Estrada Monroy (comp.), *Datos para la historia de la Iglesia en Guatemala* (Gua., 1973). Lewis Hanke, *The Spanish Struggle for Justice in the Conquest of America* (Philadelphia, 1949), is the best introduction to the voluminous work on Bartolomé de las Casas, but see also H. R. Wagner and H. R. Parish, *The Life and Writings of Bartolomé de las Casas* (Albuquerque, 1967). On Guatemala's

Bethlehemite order, see José García de la Concepción, *Historia betlemítica* (Sevilla, 1723; 2d ed., Gua., 1956), and David Vela, *El Hermano Pedro en la vida y en las letras* (Gua., 1935). Among other studies on the Church see Ernesto Chinchilla Aguilar, *La inquisición en Guatemala* (Gua., 1953); and Andrés Saint Lu, *La Vera Paz, esprit évangelique et colonisation* (Paris, 1968).

The intellectual history of colonial Central America is best treated in Constantino Láscaris Comneno, *Historia de las ideas en Centroamérica* (S.J., 1970). Carlos Meléndez provides a brief survey of the eighteenth century in *La ilustración en el antiguo reino de Guatemala* (S.J., 1970). See also T. B. Irving, "On the Enlightenment in Central America," in A. O. Owen (ed.), *The Ibero-American Enlightenment* (Urbana, Ill., 1971).

D. Independence (1800-23)

The best introduction to the period of independence is Mario Rodríguez, *The Cádiz Experiment* (Berkeley, 1978), which goes considerably beyond J. M. García Laguardia's perceptive *Origenes de la democracia constitucional en Centroamérica* (S.J., 1971) and his documentary collection, *La genesis del constitucionalismo guatemalteco* (Gua., 1971). A detailed and scholarly treatment of the period is also provided by Oscar Benítez Porta, *Secessión pacífica de Guatemala de España* (Gua., 1973). In contrast to Benítez, Arturo Valdés Oliva, *Centro América alcanzó la libertad al precio de su sangre* (Gua., 1965), emphasizes the violence of the period. Still useful, also, is Ramón Salazar's narrative *Historia de veintiún años* (Gua., 1928) and his collection of biographical sketches, *Los hombres de la independencia* (Gua., 1899), several of which have been more recently reprinted. H. H. Samayoa Guevara, *Ensayos sobre la independencia de Centroamérica* (Gua., 1972), deals with several themes in the period leading to independence, including studies of Alejandro Ramírez and Fray Matías de Córdova. See also Francisco Peccorini Letona, *La voluntad del pueblo en la emancipación de El Salvador* (S.S., 1972); Chester Zelaya, *Nicaragua en la independencia* (S.J., 1971); Ricardo Fernández Guardia, *La independencia: historia de Costa Rica* (3d ed., S.J., 1971); Rafael Obregón, *Costa Rica en la independencia y en la federación* (S.J., 1977); and Guillermo Mayes, *Honduras en la independencia de Centro América y anexión a México* (Teg., 1931). More detailed on Honduras is Antonio Vallejo, *Compendio de la historia social y política de Honduras* (2d ed., Teg., 1926), which treats only the period 1811-29. See also Pedro Zamora

Castellanos, *El grito de la independencia* (Gua., 1935); and Virgilio Rodríguez Beteta, *Ideología de la independencia* (Paris, 1926).

Documents relative to annexation to Mexico were compiled by R. H. Valle, *La anexión de Centro América a México* (6 vols., México, 1924-49). For a careful study of that question see Gordon Kenyon, "Mexican Influence in Central America, 1821-1823," *Hispanic American Historical Review* 41 (1961), 175-205. H. G. Peralta, *Agustín Iturbide y Costa Rica* (2d ed., S.J., 1968), focuses on the period with particular reference to Costa Rica. Francisco Barnoya Gálvez, *Fray Ignacio Barnoya, prócer ignorado* (Gua., 1967), details the efforts of a Catalonian friar who played an active, if unsuccessful, role in preventing the separation of Chiapas from Guatemala. César Brañas, *Antonio Larrazábal, un guatemalteco en la historia* (2 vols., Gua., 1969), provides a detailed but undocumented account of a key figure of the Cádiz period. Other useful biographical works covering the period include Carlos Meléndez's anthology, *Próceres de la independencia centroamericana* (S.J., 1971); and Arturo Aguilar, *Hombres de la independencia de Nicaragua y Costa Rica* (León, 1939). Enrique del Cid Fernández, *Don Gabino de Gaínza y otros estudios* (Gua., 1959), treats Spain's last ruler in Guatemala. Rubén Leyton Rodríguez traces the careers of José Cecilio del Valle and Pedro Molina in *Valle, padre del panamericanismo* (Gua., 1955), and *Doctor Pedro Molina, o Centro América y su prócer* (Gua., 1958). The most enlightening book on del Valle's role is Bumgartner, *José del Valle* (Durham, N.C., 1963), but Ramón Rosa's late-nineteenth-century *Biografía de José Cecilio del Valle* (Teg., 1971) still has utility, as do the newer Central American interpretations of Pedro Tobar Cruz, *Valle, el hombre—el político—el sabio* (Gua., 1961), and Ramón López Jiménez, *José Cecilio del Valle, Fouché de Centro América* (Gua., 1968). Rosa's study was originally published as an introduction to the collection he edited with Rómulo E. Durón, *Obras de D. José Cecilio del Valle* (Teg., 1906 [1914]). Molina's and Valle's important periodicals, *Editor constitucional* and *El Amigo de la Patria*, were reprinted in Guatemala in 1969.

Considerable work has been done, especially by Salvadorans, on José Matías Delgado. Notable among these works are M. A. Durán, *Ausencia y presencia de José Matías Delgado en el proceso emancipador* (S.S., 1961); Rodolfo Barón Castro, *José Matías Delgado y el movimiento insurgente de 1811* (S.S., 1962); Ramón López Jiménez, *José Matías Delgado y de León; su personalidad, su obra y su destino* (S.S., 1962); Carlos Meléndez, *El presbítero y doctor don José Matías Delgado en la forja de la nacionalidad centroamericana* (S.S., 1962); and J. S. Guandique, *Presbítero y doctor José Matías Delgado* (S.S., 1962).

Carlos Meléndez and José Villalobos have shed considerable light on Costa Rican events during the period in the brief but valuable biography of the neglected Costa Rican military and naval leader, *Gregorio José Ramírez* (S.J., 1973).

E.   The Nineteenth Century (1823-1900)

The best-known history of nineteenth-century Central America is by the Guatemalan Lorenzo Montúfar, *Reseña histórica de Centro América* (7 vols., Gua., 1878-87). Although Montúfar vehemently proclaimed his objectivity, his Liberal leanings are obvious throughout the book, which extends only to 1860. Subsequent histories, including Bancroft, have relied heavily on his work, and the influence of his interpretations has thus been very great. Somewhat more balanced, but also devoted almost exclusively to political history is J. A. Villacorta Calderón, *Historia de la República de Guatemala* (Gua., 1960). More recent interpretation of the Liberal impact on Guatemala are found in Rodríguez *et al.*, *Applied Enlightenment* (N.O., 1972). For an overview of the Liberal-Conservative struggle and impact on modern Central America, see R. L. Woodward, Jr., "The Rise and Decline of Liberalism in Central America: Historical Perspectives on the Contemporary Crises," *Journal of Inter-American Studies and World Affairs* 26 (Aug. 1984), 291-312. Useful accounts of individual states in the nineteenth century are headed by J. L. Vega Carballo, *La formación del estado nacional en Costa Rica* (S.J., 1981); and Catarino Castro S., *Honduras en la primera centuria, 1821-1921* (Teg., 1921).

Studies of Francisco Morazán and the Central American federation dominate much of the historiography of the early years of independence. Andrés Townsend Ezcurra, *Las Provincias Unidas de Centroamérica: Fundación de la República* (2d ed., S.J., 1973), details the events surrounding the declaration of independence and establishment of the republic. After Karnes, *Failure of Union* (Tempe, Az., 1975), the most useful work on the attempted union is Alberto Herrarte, *La unión de Centroamérica* (2d ed., Gua., 1964). Also useful is Herrarte's brief but instructive summary, *El federalismo en Centroamérica* (S.J., 1972); P. J. Chamorro y Zelaya, *Historia de la federación de la América Central, 1823-1840* (Madrid, 1951); Rodrigo Facio, *Trayectoria y crisis de la federación centroamericana* (S.J., 1949) and *La federación de Centroamérica: sus antecedents, su vida y su disolución* (S.J., 1960); J. T. Calderón, *El ejército federal de la República de Centroamérica* (S.S., 1922); and Enrique Ortiz Colindres, *La República Federal de Centroamérica a la luz del derecho internacional* (S.S., 1963).

Nineteenth-century biographies of Morazán, notably Ramón Rosa, *Historia de Francisco Morazán* (Teg., 1971); Lorenzo Montúfar, *Morazán* (S.J., 1970); José Beteta, *Morazán y la federación* (Gua., 1888); and Eduardo Martínez López, *Biografía del General Francisco Morazán* (Teg., 1931), firmly established the Liberal mythology around Morazán, a mythology which has been broken only slowly. A large number of twentieth-century biographies have added relatively little to what those studies tell us. Two notable exceptions are J. A. Zúñiga Huete, *Morazán, un representativo de la democracia americana* (México, 1947); and Ricardo Dueñas, *Biografía del General Francisco Morazán* (S.S., 1962). The standard work in English is the brief but carefully researched work of R. S. Chamberlain, *Francisco Morazán, Champion of Central American Federation* (Miami, 1950). Two interesting comparative studies, both, unfortunately of low scholarly standards, are Carlos Ferro, *San Martín y Morazán* (Teg., 1971), favorable toward the Central American; and Clemente Marroquín Rojas, *Francisco Morazán y Rafael Carrera* (Gua., 1965), bitterly attacking the Morazán myth. See also W. J. Griffith (ed.), "The Personal Archive of Francisco Morazán," *Philological and Documentary Studies*, Vol. 2, No. 6 (N.O. [M.A.R.I. Publication No. 12], 1977), 197-286.

Other biographical studies have offered greater enlightenment on the federation period. Treatment of Arce by Rolando Velásquez, *Carácter, fisionomía y acciones de don Manuel José Arce* (S.S., 1949), provides basic data, but Philip Flemion, "States Rights and Partisan Politics: Manuel José Arce and the Struggle for Central American Union," *Hispanic American Historical Review* 53 (1973), 600-618, is more objective and offers a guide to additional sources. Adam Szaszdi provides excellent insights into the period in his account of a foreign military adventurer, *Nicolás Raoul y la República Federal de Centro-América* (Madrid, 1958). Antonio Batres Jáuregui presents a brief but balanced view of *El Dr. Mariano Gálvez y su época* (2d ed., Gua., 1957), but J. L. Arriola offers greater depth in his *Gálvez en la encrucijada* (México, 1961). Too numerous to mention here are a large number of monographic studies and articles on other figures of the federation period.

In addition to Arce's *Memoria* (4th ed., S.S., 1959), there are several useful memoirs of the period, notably the Liberal *Memorias del Benemérito General Francisco Morazán* (Paris, 1870); *Memorias del General Miguel García Granados* (2 vols., Gua., 1893); and the Conservative Manuel Montúfar y Coronado, *Memorias para la revolución de Centro América* (Jalapa, México, 1832). The most useful contemporary accounts, however, are those of the historian, Alejandro Marure, *Bosquejo histórico de las revoluciones de Centro América desde 1811 hasta 1834* (unfinished, Gua., 1837), and his sketchy chronology, *Efemérides de los hechos notables acaecidos en la república de Centro-América desde 1821 hasta 1842* (Gua., 1844). Carlos Meléndez Ch. has compiled the *Mensajes presidenciales, 1824-1906* (3 vols., S.J., 1981) for Costa Rica. Other helpful accounts of the early years of independence are J. A. Cevallos, *Recuerdos salvadoreños* (2d ed., S.S., 1964); Francisco Ortega, *Nicaragua en los primeros años de su emancipación política* (Paris, 1894); Rómulo Durón y Gamero, *Historia de Honduras* (Teg., 1956), which covers only the 1820's, and Rodolfo Cerdas, *Formación del estado en Costa Rica* (2d ed., S.J., 1978).

The Conservative years were largely neglected by Liberal historians, but there has recently been renewed interest in the period, although much of the work is confined to periodical articles and unpublished theses. Several Guatemalans have concentrated on Rafael Carrera's rise to power, notably Pedro Tobar Cruz, *Los montañeses* (2 vols., Gua., 1959-71). Manuel Cobos Batres, *Carrera* is an unscholarly, but interesting defense of Carrera. Much more valuable to an understanding of the period are Luis Beltranena Sinibaldi, *Fundación de la República de Guatemala* (Gua., 1971); Enrique del Cid Fernández, *Origen, trama y desarrollo del movimiento que proclamó vitalicia la presidencia del General Rafael Carrera* (Gua., 1966); and Ramón Salazar, *Tiempo viejo, recuerdos de mi juventud* (2d ed., Gua., 1957). A key figure in the Carrera administration, is described by Antonio Batres Jáuregui, *José Batres Montúfar; su tiempo y sus obras* (Gua., 1910); and by José Arzú, *Pepe Batres íntimo; su familia, su correspondencia, sus papeles* (Gua., 1940).

Useful works dealing with other caudillos of the period include a little collection of contemporary views of *Braulio Carillo* (2d ed., S.J., 1972), edited in 1900 by Francisco Yglesias, and the sympathetic treatment of Emmanuel Thompson, *Defensa de Carrillo: un dictador al servicio de América* (S.J., 1945). Unscholarly and of limited value, but nevertheless suggestive, is Medardo Mejía, *Trinidad Cabañas, soldado de la república federal* (Teg., 1971). An important aspect of the later Nicaraguan Conservative rule is dealt with in great detail by Franco Cerutti, *Los Jesuitas en Nicaragua en el siglo XIX* (S.J., 1984).

Historians, especially Nicaraguans, Costa Ricans, and North Americans, have paid an inordinate amount of attention to the William Walker and other filibustering episodes. The most useful volume is still the old standard, W. O. Scroggs, *Filibusters and Financiers* (N.Y., 1916). Among the enormous volume of other works, the following are the most reliable: Jerónimo Pérez, *Memorias para la historia de la revolución de Nicaragua y de la guerra nacional contra los filibusteros* (2 vols., Man., 1865-73); Lorenzo Montúfar, *Walker en Centro América* (2 vols., Gua., 1887); Ildefonso Palma Martínez, *La guerra nacional, sus antecedentes y subsecuentes tentativas de invasión* (Man., 1956); Rafael Obregón, *La campaña de tránsito, 1856-1857* (S.J., 1956); Julio Raudales Soto, *Cinco ejércitos y un objeto común* (Teg., 1976); Virgilio Rodríguez Beteta, *Transcendencia nacional e internacional de la guerra de Centro América contra Walker y sus filibusteros* (Gua., 1960); J. R. Dueñas Van Severen, *La invasión filibustera de Nicaragua y la guerra nacional* (S.S., 1962); Albert Carr, *The World and William Walker* (N.Y., 1963); Alejandro Hurtado Chamorro, *William Walker: ideales y propósitos* (Granada, 1965); Enrique Guier, *William Walker* (S.J., 1971); Frederick Rosengarten, *Freebooters Must Die!* (Wayne, Pa., 1976); R. E. May, *The Southern Dream of a Caribbean Empire, 1854-1861* (Baton Rouge, 1973); and C. H. Brown, *Agents of Manifest Destiny, the Life and Times of the Filibusters* (Chapel Hill, 1980). Among contemporary accounts, in addition to Walker's own *War in Nicaragua* (Mobile & N.Y., 1860), the most revealing are W. V. Wells, *Walker's Expedition to Nicaragua* (N.Y., 1856); Peter Stout, *Nicaragua, Past, Present and Future* (Philadelphia, 1859); and Charles Doubleday, *Reminiscences of the Filibuster War in Nicaragua* (N.Y., 1886). The extensive chapters 5-14 of J. J. Roche, *The Story of Filibusters* (N.Y. & Ln., 1891), were translated to Spanish, *Historia de los Filibusteros* (S.J., 1908 and 1980). Alejandro Bolaños, *El filibustero Clinton Rollins* (Man., 1976), exposes Rollins as a purely fictional creation of journalist H. C. Parkhurst.

Works treating other aspects of foreign penetration form an important body of the literature on nineteenth-century Central America. L. D. Langley, *Struggle for the American Mediterranean: United States-European Rivalry in the Gulf-Caribbean, 1776-1904* (Athens, Ga., 1976), is an excellent overview. In addition to Griffith, *Empires in the Wilderness* (Chapel Hill, 1965); Rodríguez, *A Palmerstonian Diplomat* (Tucson, 1964); and Williams, *Anglo-American Isthmian Diplomacy* (Wash. & Ln., 1916), see R. A. Naylor, "The British Role in Central America prior to the Clayton-Bulwer Treaty of 1850," *Hispanic American Historical Review* 40 (1960), 361-82, and his forthcoming *Penny Ante Imperialism: The Mosquito Shore and the Bay of Honduras, A Case Study in British Informal Empire*. Watt Stewart, *Keith and Costa Rica* (Albuquerque, 1964), tells the story of the founder of the banana trade and beginnings of the United Fruit Company. See also Anita Gregorio Marchie, *Imported Spices: Anglo American Settlers in Costa Rica in the Nineteenth Century* (S.J., 1981). Cyril Allen, *France in Central America* (N.Y., 1966), details the interesting career of French canal agent Felix Belly. Virgilio Rodríguez Beteta surveys the British role unsympathetically in *La política inglesa en Centro América durante el siglo XIX* (Gua., 1963). Pablo Levy, *Notas geográficas y económicas sobre la república de Nicaragua* (2d ed., Man., 1976), in a marvelous description of that country around 1870, reflects the substantial foreign interest there. Andrés Vega Bolaños focuses on the British threats from Belize from 1840 to 1842 in *Los atentados del superintendente de Belice* (Man., 1971). Joseph Fabri, *Les Belges au Guatemala, 1840-1845* (Bruxelles, 1955), tells the little-known story of Belgian activities. Wayne Clegern, *British Honduras, Colonial Dead End, 1859-1900* (Baton Rouge, 1967), focuses on the decline of Belize and the transfer of economic interests there from British to United States hegemony. Clegern also edited the enlightening 1887 memorandum of Alfred Maudslay to Lord Salisbury, *Maudslay's Central America: A Strategic View in 1887* (N.O., 1962).

Interest in an interoceanic route was, of course, closely related to much of the foreign activity, especially in Nicaragua and Panama. Thomas Schoonover, "Imperialism in Middle America: United States, Britain, Germany, and France Compete for Transit Rights and Trade, 1820s-1920s," in *Eagle Against Empire* (Aix-en-Provence, 1983), 41-57, is an excellent overview. David Folkman, *The Nicaragua Route* (Salt Lake City, 1972), and J. H. Kemble, *The Panama Route, 1848-1869* (Berkeley, 1943), are two excellent surveys of the efforts during the mid-nineteenth century in these areas. Special aspects of the story are dealt with ably in Ricardo Jinesta, *El Canal de Nicaragua y los intereses de Costa Rica en la magna obra* (S.J., 1964), and J. L. Schott, *Rails across Panama: The Story of the Building of the Panama Railroad, 1849-1855* (N.Y., 1967). The nineteenth-century history of Panama is surveyed by Catalina Arrocha Graell, *Historia de la independencia de Panamá: sus antecedentes y sus causas, 1821-1903* (Panamá, 1953). Easily the best work on the building of the canal is David McCullough, *Path Between the Seas* (N.Y., 1977). Gerstle Mack, *The Land Divided* (N.Y., 1944), remains one of the more thorough works covering isthmian canal projects, while M. P. Duval, *Cadiz to Cathay* (Stanford, 1940), and *And the Mountains Will Move* (Stanford, 1947), are still useful.

A number of historians have occupied themselves with the Liberal Revolution. Among studies of Gerardo Barrios especially notable is Italo López Vallecillos, *Gerardo Barrios y su tiempo* (2 vols., S.S., 1965). Other useful works on Barrios include José Gámez, *Gerardo Barrios ante la posteridad* (Man., 1901), principally a collection of documents; and Emiliano Cortés, *Biografía del Capitán General Gerardo Barrios* (S.S., 1965). Rodolfo Cardenal, *El poder eclesiástico en El Salvador, 1871-1931* (S.S., 1980), discusses Liberal policy toward the Church in El Salvador, while Rafael Guidos Véjar, documents *El ascenso del militarismo en El Salvador* (S.S., 1980) from 1871 to 1935. The standard history of the Guatemalan Liberal Revolution is Mariano Zeceña, *La revolución de 1871 y sus caudillos* (Gua., 1898), but more recently J. M. García Laguardia, *La reforma liberal* (Gua., 1972), has provided an excellent description and analysis of the Guatemalan political experience. See also his *El pensamiento liberal de Guatemala: antología* (S.J., 1977). D. J. McCreery, *Development and the State in Reforma Guatemala* (Athens, Ohio, 1983), superbly describes the economic development philosophy and process under Barrios, while H. J. Miller, *La iglesia y el estado en Guatemala en el tiempo de Justo Rufino Barrios* (Guatemala, 1976), details Barrios's anticlerical policy. There are several biographies of Barrios which offer additional data on the period, notably Paul Burgess, *Justo Rufino Barrios* (N.Y., 1926); V. M. Díaz, *Barrios ante la posteridad* (Gua., 1935); and C. D. Rubio, *Biografía del General Justo Rufino Barrios* (Gua., 1935). Enrique Guzmán Selva, *Diario íntimo* (Man., 1912), is a valuable eyewitness record of personalities in Guatemala in the last year of Barrios's regime (1884-85). A catalogue of the economic legislation during the Barrios regime has recently been compiled by Roberto Díaz Castillo, *Legislación económica de Guatemala durante la reforma liberal* (Gua., 1973). José Reina Valenzuela and Mario Argueta, *Marco Aurelio Soto, Reforma liberal de 1876* (Teg., 1978), relates the biography of Honduras's major Liberal caudillo. Ramón Rosa's principal writings were gathered together by R. H. Valle and Juan Valladares R., *Oro de Honduras* (2 vols., Teg., 1948-54). Aro Sanso, *Policarpo Bonilla* (México, 1936), contains a biography and documents, as well as useful shorter studies by R. H. Valle and Ricardo Alduvin, all relating to Bonilla's administration. Insight into Liberal economic policy in Honduras is provided by Kenneth Finney, "Rosario and the Election of 1887: The political economy of mining in Honduras," *Hispanic American Historical Review* 59 (1979), 81-107. See also Mario Posas and Rafael del Cid, *La construcción del sector público y del estado nacional en Honduras, 1876-1979* (S.J., 1981). On the delayed Nicaraguan Liberal Revolution, see Charles Stansifer, "José Santos Zelaya: A New Look at Nicaragua's Liberal Dictatorship," *Revista Interamericana* 7 (Fall 1977), 468-85; and, for a Conservative criticism, J. J. Morales, *De la historia de Nicaragua de 1889-1913* (Granada, 1963), of which only Part I, covering 1889-1909, was published. Manuel Castrillo Gámez, *Reseña histórica de Nicaragua . . . desde el año 1887 hasta fines de 1895* (Man., 1963), provides much data on his arrival to power. Carlos

Meléndez, *Dr. José María Montealegre* (S.J., 1968), treats the career of
an important nineteenth-century Costa Rican. Jacqueline West de Cochez
has edited the writings of a noted Panamanian Liberal, Pablo Arosemena,
Estudios (Panamá, 1982).

F.   *The Twentieth Century*

The Liberal ascendancy over most of Central America continued in the
early twentieth century, with the dictatorship of Estrada Cabrera and
Zelaya being especially noticeable. Neither has received adequate historical
treatment to date. Among the few useful works on the Estrada period in
Guatemala are the firsthand accounts of Adrián Vidaurre, *Los últimos
treinta años de la vida política de Guatemala* (Habana, 1921); Carlos
Wyld Ospina, *El autócrata; ensayo político-social* (Gua., 1929); and Rafael Arévalo Martínez, *¡Ecce Pericles!* (Gua., 1945). J. R. Gramajo, *Las
revoluciones exteriores contra el expresidente Estrada Cabrera* (2 vols.,
Mazatenango, 1937-43), also contains documents and commentary on the
period. Carlos Cuadra Pasos, *Historia de medio siglo* (2d ed., Man., 1964),
surveys Nicaragua in the first third of the twentieth century. P. F. Martin,
Salvador in the Twentieth Century (Ln., 1911), offers a comprehensive
view of El Salvador in the early years of the century. N. E. Alvarado, *La
revolución de 19* (Teg., 1967), provides detail on Honduran politics of
1919 and after. Eugenio Rodríguez Vega, *Los días de don Ricardo* (S.J.,
1971), provides insight into Costa Rican development during the first
half of the century in his review of the life and work of Ricardo Jiménez,
while Hugo Murillo Jiménez, *Tinoco y los Estados Unidos* (S.J., 1981),
details the events surrounding the regime of Federico Tinoco, 1917-19.
Jeffrey Casey has documented the rise of the Costa Rican banana port,
Limón, 1880-1940 (S.J., 1979). Marina Volio, *Jorge Volio y el Partido
Reformista* (S.J., 1974), studies one of Costa Rica's most important political reformers. There is a considerable volume of polemical unionist
literature in the early twentieth century, the most valuable of which are
Salvador Mendieta, *La enfermedad de Centro-América* (3 vols., Barcelona, 1910-34) and *Alrededor del problema unionista de Centro América*
(2 vols., Barcelona, 1934). These five volumes offer copious description
and analysis of Central America's early-twentieth-century problems. For
a study of Mendieta's career see W. H. Mory, *Salvador Mendieta: Escritor
y apostol de la unión centroamericana* (Birmingham, Alabama, 1971).

The heavy-handed role of the United States early in this century has
occupied the attention of several historians. Among the more general
works, Dana Munro, *Intervention and Dollar Diplomacy, 1900-1921*

(Princeton, 1964) and *The United States and the Caribbean Republics,*
1921-33 (Princeton, 1974), provides excellent coverage of Central America, as does Lester Langley, *The United States and the Caribbean in the*
Twentieth Century (Athens, Ga., 1980), and more specifically, his *Banana*
Wars, An Inner History of American Empire (Lexington, Ky., 1983).
Still useful are W. H. Callcott, *The Caribbean Policy of the United States,*
1890-1920 (Baltimore, 1942); and H. C. Hill, *Roosevelt and the Carib-*
bean (N.Y., 1927). H. B. Deutsch, *The Incredible Yanqui* (Ln., 1931),
describes the career of soldier of fortune Lee Christmas. Vicente Saenz,
Rompiendo cadenas (3d ed., B. A., 1961), first published in 1931, represents the anti-U.S. sentiment which interventionism engendered. More
recent U.S. economic influence is attacked by Susan Bodenheimer *et al.,*
La inversión extranjera en Centroamérica (2d ed., S.J., 1975).

The United States presence was most obvious in Panama and Nicaragua. Among the extensive literature on the Panama Canal episode the
following are most useful: Walter LaFeber, *The Panama Canal* (N.Y.,
1978), covering subsequent U.S.-Panamanian relations as well; James
Bryce, *South America: Observations and Impressions* (N.Y., 1912), containing extensive description; Philippe Bunau-Varilla, *Panama, The Crea-*
tion, Destruction and Reconstruction (Ln., 1913), revealing his role in
the affair. D. A. Arosemena (comp.), *Documentary Diplomatic History*
of the Panama Canal (Panamá, 1961), provides a collection of the principal documents for the period 1826-1955. See also D. C. Miner, *The*
Fight for the Panama Route (N.Y., 1940); and Oscar Terán, *Del tratado*
Hay-Herán al tratado Hay-Bunau-Varilla (2 vols., Bogotá, 1936). The
best overview of Panamanian politics in the twentieth century is S. C.
Ropp, *Panamanian Politics: From Guarded Nation to National Guard*
(N.Y., 1982). Other studies focusing on the canal and its politics, includ-
ing more recent relations with the U.S., are Ernesto Castillero Pimentel,
Panamá y los Estados Unidos (Panamá, 1952); Lawrence Ealy, *Yanqui*
Politics and the Isthmian Canal (Pennsylvania State University, 1971);
Ernesto Castillero Reyes, *Historia de la comunicación interoceánica y de*
su influencia en la formación y en el desarollo de la entidad nacional
panameña (Panamá, 1941); R. J. Alfaro, *Medio siglo de relaciones entre*
Panamá y los Estados Unidos (Panamá, 1953); Jules Dubois, *Danger over*
Panama (N.Y., 1964); Larry Pippin, *The Remón Era: An Analysis of a*
Decade of Events in Panamá, 1947-1957 (Stanford, 1964); and a handy
biographical reference, J. A. Ortega C., *Gobernantes de la República de*
Panamá, 1903-1968 (Panamá, 1965).

The period of U.S. intervention in Nicaragua has been the subject of
a variety of studies of uneven quality. Nicaraguan accounts have been

either passionately against or apologetic for the U.S. role, but seldom objective. Among the general works on the period, Isaac Cox, *Nicaragua and the United States, 1909-1927* (Bos., 1927); and H. L. Stimson, *American Policy in Nicaragua* (N.Y., 1927), are carefully written defenses of U.S. policy. A less objective, but still informative pro-U.S. account is H. H. Denny, *Dollars for Bullets: The Story of American Rule in Nicaragua* (N.Y., 1929). Highly critical is J. A. H. Hopkins and Melinda Alexander, *Machine-Gun Diplomacy* (N.Y., 1928). More scholarly is William Kamman, *A Search for Stability 1925-1933* (Notre Dame, Ind., 1968). Zelaya's own account of his overthrow, *La revolución de Nicaragua y los Estados Unidos* (Madrid, 1910), is interesting if not thoroughly illuminating. Roscoe Hill, *Fiscal Intervention in Nicaragua* (N.Y., 1933), details the financial questions from the bankers' point of view. Marvin Goldwert, *The Constabulary in the Dominican Republic and Nicaragua: Progeny and Legacy of United States Intervention* (Gainesville, 1962), traces the longer term effects of the intervention. In addition to Macaulay's sympathetic work, other useful accounts on Sandino include Lejeune Cummins, *Quijote on a Burro: Sandino and the Marines* (México, 1958); Gregorio Selser, *Sandino, General de hombres libres* (2d ed., S.J., 1974); and Rodolfo Cerdas, *Sandino, el APRA y la Internacional Comunista* (S.J., 1979).

A number of recent studies have improved our understanding of the dictatorships growing out of the Great Depression. Kenneth Grieb, *Guatemalan Caudillo* (Athens, Ohio, 1979), dispassionately describes the Ubico regime. Among a number of scathing attacks on Ubico, Efraín de los Ríos, *Ombres contra hombres* (3d ed., 2 vols., Gua., 1969), is the most useful to the historian. Col. F. E. Ardón F., *El Señor General Ubico* (Gua., 1968), offers a defense of the regime, while Carlos Samayoa Chinchilla, *El dictador y yo* (Gua., 1950), is a more critical view.

David Luna dealt with the regime of Hernández Martínez in his *Análisis de una dictadura fascista latinoamericana* (S.S., n.d.). On the bloody suppression of the communist revolt of 1932 see, in addition to Anderson, *Matanza* (Lincoln, Neb., 1971), Roque Dalton, *Miguel Marmol* (S.J., 1972); Jorge Arías Gómez, *Farabundo Martí* (S.J., 1972); and Rodolfo Cerdas, *Farabundo Martí, la Internacional Comunista y la insurrección salvadoreña de 1932* (S.J., 1982). Francisco Morán, *Las jornadas cívicas de abril y mayo de 1944* (S.S., 1979) details the overthrow of Hernández Martínez.

There is a need for more serious study of Honduras, but J. A. Morris, *Honduras: Caudillo Politics and Military Rulers* (Boulder, 1984), provides a fine overview. Gilberto González y Contreras, *El último caudillo* (México, 1946), is a measured defense of Tiburcio Carías. Roberto Bardini, *Conexión en Tegucigalpa: El somocismo en Honduras* (México, 1982), is critical of Honduran support of the *contras* against Nicaragua.

The literature on the Somozas is more extensive, led by Richard Millett, *Guardians of the Dynasty* (Maryknoll, N.Y., 1977), which carefully documents the role of the *Guardia Nacional*. P. J. Chamorro Cardenal, *Estirpe sangriente: los Somoza* (B.A., 1959), and L. G. Cardenal, *Mi rebelión* (México, 1961), are especially vocal in their denunciations of the Somozas. Bernard Diederich, *Somoza and the Legacy of U.S. Involvement in Central America* (N.Y., 1981) provides a more objective account, while Anastasio Somoza Debayle, as told to Jack Cox, gives his own account in *Nicaragua Betrayed* (Bos. & L.A., 1980). See also S. P. Huntington, *Political Order in Changing Societies* (New Haven, 1965). Another biographical account of the Somoza years is Eduardo Crawley, *Dictators Never Die: A Portrait of Nicaragua and the Somoza Dynasty* (N.Y., 1979). T. W. Walker, *The Christian Democratic Movement in Nicaragua* (Tucson, 1970), analyzes the development of a new opposition party in Somoza's dictatorship, while Jaime Wheelock Román, *Imperialismo y dictadura* (5th ed., México, 1975), is a biting condemnation in a Marxist framework by one of the Sandinista comandantes.

Costa Rica's twentieth-century history has focused on the Revolution of 1948, and J. P. Bell, *Crisis in Costa Rica* (Austin, 1971), leads the field on that event, while Charles Ameringer has produced a useful overview of recent Costa Rican history in his *Democracy in Costa Rica* (N.Y., 1982). Excellent analyses of Costa Rican political development in this century include Carlos Araya Pochet, *Historia de los partidos políticos: Liberación Nacional* (S.J., 1968), and J. L. Vega Carballo, *La crisis de la democracia liberal en Costa Rica* (S.J., 1972) and *Poder político y democracia en Costa Rica* (S.J., 1982). Among other important works on the 1948 revolution and its aftermath are Oscar Aguilar Bulgarelli, *Costa Rica y sus hechos políticos de 1948* (S.J., 1969); Harry Kantor, *The Costa Rican Election of 1953* (Gainesville, 1958); B. H. English, *Liberación Nacional in Costa Rica* (Gainesville, 1971); Charles Denton, *Patterns of Costa Rican Politics* (Bos., 1971); J. L. Busey, *Notes on Costa Rican Democracy* (Boulder, 1967); Hugo Navarro Bolandi, *La generación de 48* (México, 1957); J. E. Romero P., *La social democracia en Costa Rica* (S.J., 1977) and *Partidos políticos, poder y derecho* (S.J., 1979); J. M. Salazar Mora, *Calderón Guardia* (S.J., 1980) and *Política y reforma en Costa Rica* (S.J., 1981); and biographies of José Figueres by Charles Ameringer, *Don Pepe* (Albuquerque, 1978), and Alberto Baeza Flores, *La lucha sin fin* (México, 1969).

The literature on the Guatemalan Revolution is extensive. The definitive work remains to be written, although Mario Monteforte Toledo, *La revolución de Guatemala, 1944-1954* (Gua., 1975), is a useful attempt. Marxist overviews by Jaime Díaz Rozzotto, *El carácter de la revolución guatemalteca* (México, 1958) and *La Révolution au Guatemala* (Paris, 1971), are helpful although they overlook many of the sources, but so also do the anti-Arbenz accounts such as Daniel James, *Red Design for the Americas: Guatemalan Prelude* (N.Y., 1954). Several excellent studies have treated specific aspects of the Revolution, notably R. N. Adams, *Crucifixion by Power* (Austin, 1970); K. H. Silvert, *A Study in Government: Guatemala* (N.O., 1954); Leo Suslow, *Aspects of Social Reform in Guatemala* (Hamilton, N.Y., 1949); A. C. Bush, *Organized Labor in Guatemala, 1944-49* (Hamilton, N.Y., 1950); and R. M. Schneider, *Communism in Guatemala* (N.Y., 1958). See also M. López Larrave, *Breve historia del movimiento sindical guatemalteco* (Gua., 1979). Studies of Arévalo include Pedro Alvarez Elzondo, *El Presidente Arévalo y el retorno a Bolívar* (México, 1947); and M. B. Dion, *Las ideas sociales y políticas de Arévalo* (México, 1958). Arévalo has written a series of autobiographical accounts of his early life, *La inquietud normalista, estampas de adolescencia y juventud, 1921-1927* (S.S., 1970), *La Argentina que yo viví, 1927-1944* (México, 1974), and a memoir of the crucial period between the fall of Ubico and his inauguration as President in 1944-45, *El candidato blanco y el hurracán* (Gua., 1984). Among his other voluminous works, the most well known are *Istmania, tierras del istmo* (Gua., 1945); *The Shark and the Sardines* (N.Y., 1961), a bitter condemnation of U.S. imperialism in Latin America; and *Anti-Kommunism in Latin America* (N.Y., 1963). Among many personal accounts of the Revolution, several are notable. Manuel Galich describes the Ubico regime and its overthrow in *Del pánico al ataque* (Gua., 1949), and continues in exile with a defense of the Revolution in *¿Por qué lucha Guatemala? Arévalo y Arbenz: dos hombres contra un imperio* (B.A., 1956). José García Bauer, *Nuestra revolución legislativa* (Gua., 1948), outlines the program of the Revolution. Arcadio Ruiz Franco, *Fermentos de lucha: hambre y miseria* (Gua., 1950), is the account of a worker and student in the printing industry. Guillermo Toriello, Arbenz's foreign minister, defends his regime in *La batalla de Guatemala* (México & Santiago de Chile, 1955); as does literary figure Luis Cardoza y Aragón in *Guatemala, las líneas de su mano* (México, 1955) and *La revolución guatemalteca* (México, 1955). Carlos Samayoa Chinchilla, *El quetzal no es rojo* (Gua., 1956), defends Arbenz, while attacking both American imperialism and international communism. Mario Efraín Nájera Farfán, *Los estafadores de la* *democracia, hombres y hechos en Guatemala* (B.A., 1956), is critical of Arbenz. One of the important labor leaders of the Revolution, Carlos Pellecer, in *Renuncia al comunismo* (México, 1963), later renounced the communist role in which he had cooperated. Gregorio Selzer, *El guatemalazo: la primera guerra sucia* (B.A., 1954), attacks the U.S. role in Arbenz's overthrow. More recently, that role has been thoroughly exposed by José Aybar, *Dependency and Intervention* (Boulder, 1979); R. H. Immerman, *The C.I.A. in Guatemala* (Austin, 1982); and Schlesinger and Kinzer, *Bitter Fruit* (Garden City, N.Y., 1982).

A valuable account of U.S. perceptions of Central America in the immediate post-war era is Thomas Leonard, *The United States and Central America, 1944-1949* (Alabama, 1984).

Guatemala since the Revolution has been treated by R. N. Adams, *Crucifixion by Power* (Austin, 1970), Mario Rodríguez, *Central America* (Englewood Cliffs, N.J., 1965), G. E. Aguilar Peralta, *La violencia en Guatemala como fenómeno político* (Cuernavaca, 1971), and Thomas and Marjorie Melville, *Guatemala, the Politics of Land Ownership* (N.Y., 1971). Miguel Ydígoras Fuentes, *My War with Communism* (Englewood Cliffs, N.J., 1963), defends his regime of the early 1960's. Eduardo Galeano, *Guatemala, Occupied Country* (N.Y., 1969), provides insight into the violence and guerrilla warfare that has plagued Guatemala since 1954, as does Ricardo Falla, *Quiché rebelde* (Gua., 1978). A fairly comprehensive, radical analysis of the period by the North American Congress on Latin America is Jonas and Tobis, *Guatemala* (N.Y., 1974), with several updates in *NACLA Report on the Americas* (1975-present). An anthology on recent Guatemalan history is J. L. Fried *et al.* (eds.), *Guatemala in Rebellion: Unfinished History* (N.Y., 1983).

The 1969 war between Honduras and El Salvador elicited a flurry of polemical defenses from both countries, but the best study on the conflict is Durham's *Scarcity and Survival* (Stanford, 1979). Also useful are Anderson, *War of the Dispossessed* (Lincoln, Neb., 1981), M. J. R. Martz, *Central American Soccer War: Historical Patterns and Internal Dynamics of OAS Settlement Procedures* (Athens, Ohio, 1978); James Rowles, *El conflicto Honduras-El Salvador y el orden jurídico internacional* (1969) (S.J., 1980); and M. V. Carías and Daniel Slutsky, *La guerra inutil* (S.J., 1971).

On the recent crises on the isthmus, R. S. Leiken (ed.), *Central America, Anatomy of Conflict* (N.Y., 1984), is an excellent collection of essays, and S. C. Ropp and J. Morris (eds.), *Central America, Crisis and Adaptation* (Albuquerque, 1984), provide a superb analysis of the recent history of each country. See also Anderson, *Politics in Central America* (N.Y.,

1982). The Centro de Estudios Internacionales of the Colegio de México has published an exceptionally perceptive collection of essays on *Centroamérica en crisis* (México, 1980), which is especially useful for understanding Latin American points of view. Some provocative essays are also found in Richard Millett and Marvin Will (eds.), *The Restless Caribbean* (N.Y., 1979), and Richard Feinberg (ed.), *Central America: International Dimensions of the Crisis* (N.Y., 1982). Mark Falcoff and Robert Royal (eds.), *Crisis and Opportunity in Central America and the Caribbean* (Wash., 1984), bring together key spokesman for the U.S., Cuba, Nicaragua, and the Salvadoran guerrillas in a stimulating anthology. Another collection of readings and documents was prepared by the Stanford Central American Action Network, *Revolution in Central America* (Boulder, 1983). Marlene Dixon and Susanne Jonas (eds.), *Revolution and Intervention in Central America* (San Francisco, 1984), features documents from El Salvador, Guatemala, and Nicaragua in its defense of the left. Philip Berryman, *Religious Roots of Rebellion* (Maryknoll, N.Y., 1984), describes how the Church has influenced social change in each country in Central America and complements Penny Lernoux's *Cry of the People* (N.Y., 1980), a moving description of the growth of liberation theology and the "people's church." Earlier views of the Church in Central America are Isidoro Alonso, *La iglesia en América Central y el Caribe* (Madrid, 1962); Rodolfo Cardenal, *Acontecimientos sobresalientes de la Iglesia en Honduras, 1900-1962* (Teg., 1979); and B. J. Calder, *Crecimiento y cambio de la iglesia católica guatemalteca* (Gua. & Austin, 1970).

U.S. policy in response to these crises is dealt with especially well by Cole Blasier, *The Hovering Giant* (Pittsburgh, 1976); and Walter LaFeber, *Inevitable Revolutions, the United States in Central America* (N.Y., 1983). See also Richard Allen White, *The Morass. United States Intervention in Central America* (N.Y., 1984); and Wolf Grabendorff and Heinrich Krumweide (eds.), *Policy Change in Central America: Internal and External Dimensions* (Boulder, 1984). An articulate criticism of Reagan's Central American policy is Piero Gleijeses, *Tilting at Windmills: Reagan in Central America* (Wash., 1982). An important document of U.S. policy toward Central America in the 1980's is the Kissinger Commission's, *Report of the National Bipartisan Commission on Central America* (Wash., 1984), with its voluminous annex. Views from the left are found in Roger Burbach and Patricia Flynn (eds.), *The Politics of Intervention: The United States in Central America* (N.Y., 1983). B. B. Levine (ed.), *The New Cuban Presence in the Caribbean* (Boulder,

1983), deals with the Cuban involvement in Central America, while Cole Blasier, *The Giant's Rival: The USSR and Latin America* (Pittsburgh, 1983) looks at the Soviet role.

The Salvadoran crisis is dealt with ably by Enrique Baloyra, *El Salvador in Transition* (Chapel Hill, 1982); Tommie Sue Montgomery, *Revolution in El Salvador* (Boulder, 1982); and J. A. Dunkerley, *The Long War: Dictatorship and Revolution in El Salvador* (Ln., 1982). S. A. Webre, *José Napoleón Duarte and the Christian Democratic Party of El Salvador, 1960-1972* (Baton Rouge, 1979), is a splendid study of the rise of the Salvadoran Christian Democratic Party and its leader. J. R. Brockman tells the story of the martyred Archbishop of El Salvador in *The World Remains: A Life of Oscar Romero* (Maryknoll, N.Y., 1982). See also Liisa North, *Bitter Grounds: Roots of Revolt in El Salvador* (Toronto, 1982); Robert Armstrong and Janet Shenk, *El Salvador: The Face of Revolution* (Boston, 1982); and S. W. Schmidt, *El Salvador, América's Next Vietnam?* (Salisbury, N.C., 1983). Cynthia Arson, *El Salvador: A Revolution Confronts the United States* (Wash., 1982), relates the struggle well to U.S. policy. Norma de Herrera, *La mujer en la revolución salvadoreña* (México, 1983), describes women in the Salvadoran revolution. Gettleman *et al.* (eds.), *El Salvador: Central America in the New Cold War*, brings together a useful collection of readings on the conflict there.

On the Sandinista Revolution, the best overall treatments are found in J. A. Booth, *The End and the Beginning* (Boulder, 1982); and David Nolan, *FSLN, The Ideology of the Sandinistas and the Nicaraguan Revolution* (Miami, 1984), but there are many other works dealing with it. T. W. Walker has edited an excellent collection of essays, *Nicaragua in Revolution* (N.Y., 1982), and plans a second volume soon. Belden Bell (ed.), *Nicaragua, An Ally under Siege* (Wash., 1978), defends the Somoza dynasty, while George Black, *Triumph of the People, the Sandinista Revolution in Nicaragua* (Ln., 1981), and Henri Weber, *Nicaragua, the Sandinista Revolution* (Ln., 1981), offer sympathetic views of the Sandinistas. A critical account of the Sandinista treatment of the Church is Humberto Belli, *Nicaragua: Christians Under Fire* (S.J., [1983]). Rosset and Vandermeer (eds.), *The Nicaragua Reader, Documents of a Revolution under Fire* (N.Y., 1983), provide a variety of documents and commentary on the revolution.

The most useful work on modern Belize is C. H. Grant, *The Making of Modern Belize: Politics, Society and British Colonialism in Central America* (Cambridge, 1976).

IV. THE ECONOMY

C. F. S. Cardoso and Héctor Pérez Brignoli, *Centro América y la economía occidental* (S.J., 1977), have provided an outline of Central American economic history to 1930, which is partially extended by Pérez and Yolanda Baires Martínez, "Growth and Crisis in the Central American Economies, 1950-1980," *Journal of Latin American Studies* 15 (1983), 365-98, and, in the same issue, V. Bulmer-Thomas, "Economic Development Over the Long Run—Central America Since 1920," pp. 269-94. Another useful Central American approach, within the dependency school, is Mario Monteforte Toledo, *Central America, subdesarrollo y dependencia* (2 vols., México, 1972). Tom Barry et al., *Dollars and Dictators, a Guide to Central America* (Albuquerque, 1982), is a revealing study of the influence of foreign investment in Central America along with sketches of each country. Joseph Grunwald (ed.), *Latin America and World Economy* (Beverly Hills, 1978), also includes well-informed commentary on Central America. Gary Wynia, *Politics and Planners: Economic Development in Central America* (Madison, 1972), still has value for understanding the process of economic planning and development on the isthmus. The *Statistical Abstract of Latin America* (L.A., 1955-present) provides useful statistical data on each country. Inforpress Centroamericana prepares an annual *Análisis económicos y políticos sobre la región* (Gua., 1982-), providing a great deal of objective, current information on the region as a whole and on each state. For more detail consult the statistical annuals published by the governments of each country. Up-to-date demographic tables may be obtained from the International Data Base of the U.S. Bureau of the Census.

With the exception of studies on economic integration, treated later, most of the work on Central America has been at the state level. Valentín Solórzano Fernández, *Historia de la evolución económica de Guatemala* (2d ed., Gua., 1978), is the nearest thing to a comprehensive economic history of Guatemala. More limited, but containing much information, is the International Bank for Reconstruction and Development, *The Economic Development of Guatemala* (Wash., 1951). A revealing study of economic development under Arévalo and Arbenz is J. H. Adler, E. H. Schlesinger, and E. C. Olsen, *Public Finance and Economic Development in Guatemala* (Palo Alto, 1952). Several important articles on Guatemalan economic development were reprinted in the Seminario de Integración Social Guatemalteco, *Economía de Guatemala* (Gua., 1958). David Luna, *Manual de historia económica de El Salvador* (S.S., 1971), is a brief survey, particularly for the post-independence period. El Salvador's development after World War II is discussed in a series of contemporary publications: H. C. Wallich *et al.*, *Public Finance in a Developing Country: El Salvador—A Case Study* (Cambridge, Mass., 1951); B. F. Hoselitz, *Industrial Development of El Salvador* (N.Y., 1954), a United Nations study; G. P. Turner, *An Analysis of the Economy of El Salvador* (L.A., 1961); and M. S. Conyer, *El Salvador: Its Agriculture and Trade* (Wash., 1963). Each makes a rather narrow contribution to understanding the threshold period of quickening economic development, while D. R. Reynolds, *Rapid Development in Small Economies: The Example of El Salvador* (N.Y., 1967), provides an overview of the postwar period and comparison with other small nations. There is little economic data on Honduras, but Vincent Checchi *et al.*, *Honduras, a Problem in Economic Development* (N.Y., 1959), provides data on the 1950's. Nicaragua also suffered from lack of scientific study before the Sandinista Revolution. The IBRD study, *Economic Development of Nicaragua* (Baltimore, 1953), while useful, does not come up to the standards set in the volume covering Guatemala. More recently, a series of publications by the Banco Central de Nicaragua helped to fill the void, and the Centro de Investigaciones y Estudios para la Reforma Agraria has carried on important regional studies, as notably, for example, Jaime Wheelock Román (ed.), *La Mosquitia en la revolución* (Man., 1981). Costa Rican development has been more carefully researched. Stacy May *et al.*, *Costa Rica: A Study in Economic Development* (N.Y., 1952), provides basic coverage, but the most useful economic history is Tomás Soley Güell, *Historia económica y hacendaria de Costa Rica* (2 vols., S.J., 1947-49). Mitchell Seligson, *Peasants of Costa Rica and the Development of Agrarian Capitalism* (Madison, 1980), is very informative. For the more recent period see Carlos Araya Pochet, *Historia económica de Costa Rica, 1950-1970* (S.J., 1975). Lowell Gudmundson, *Hacendados, políticos y precaristas: la ganaderia y el latifundismo guanacasteco, 1800-1950* (S.J., 1983 [1984]), provides a detailed examination of an important agricultural region of Costa Rica. For contemporary Costa Rica see V. H. Céspedes *et al.* (Academia de Centroamérica), *Costa Rica: una economía en crisis* (S.J., 1983) and *Problemas económicas en la década de los 80* (S.J., 1983). Norman Ashcraft applies dependency theory to Belize in his *Colonialism and Underdevelopment: Processes of Political Economic Change in British Honduras* (N.Y., 1973). See also N. S. Carey Jones, *Patterns of a Dependent Economy: The National Income of British Honduras* (Cambridge, Eng., 1953).

Important studies dealing with aspects of agricultural development throughout Central America are Craig Dozier, *Indigenous Tropical Agriculture in Central America: Land Use, Systems and Problems* (Wash.,

1958); and George Ordish, *Man, Crops and Pests in Central America* (Ln., 1964). The agricultural history of Costa Rica has been dealt with in a massive, informative chronology, Alberto Saenz Maroto, *Historia agrícola de Costa Rica* (Universidad de Costa Rica, 1970). Agricultural studies on Guatemala which are especially informative include Julio Castellanos Cambranes, *Introducción a la historia agrícola de Guatemala* (Gua., 1978); L. B. Fletcher *et al.*, *Guatemala's Economic Development; The Role of Agriculture* (Ames, Iowa, 1971); and A. C. Martínez-Holgado, *Le secteur agricole du Guatemala* (Austin, 1969). There is a wealth of information in Escuela Facultativa de Ciencias Económicas de Occidente y Comité Interamericano de Desarrollo Agrícola, *Tenencia de la tierra y desarrollo socio-económico del sector agrícola en Guatemala* (2d ed., Gua., 1971). Dealing with Honduras in great detail is the OAS publication, *Informe oficial de la misión 105 de asistencia técnica directa á Honduras sobre reforma agraria y desarrollo* (2 vols., Wash., [c. 1963]).

Coffee and bananas have, understandably, received considerable attention. A. Alvarado, *Tratado de cafecultura práctica* (2 vols., Gua., 1935-36), details the growth of coffee culture in Guatemala, but also see Manuel Rubio Sánchez, "Historia del comercio del café en Guatemala, siglos XVIII y XIX," *Anales de la Sociedad de Geografía e Historia de Guatemala* 50 (1977), 167-93; D. J. McCreery, "Coffee and Class: The Structure of Development in Liberal Guatemala," *Hispanic American Historical Review* 56 (1976), 438-60; and C. F. S. Cardoso, "Historia económica del café en Centroamérica, siglo XIX," *Estudios Sociales Centroamericanos* 4(No. 10) (1975), 9-55. For Costa Rica see Jaime Daremblum, *El auge del café y la apertura de la economía costarricense* (S.J., 1979); and Carolyn Hall, *El café y el desarrollo histórico-geográfico de Costa Rica* (S.J., 1976) and *Formación de una hacienda cafetelera, 1889-1911* (S.J., 1978). H. B. Arthur and G. L. Beckford, *Tropical Agribusiness Structures and Adjustments—Bananas* (Bos., 1968), explains modern methods of production and marketing bananas. Studies on the United Fruit Company are numerous. C. M. Wilson, the principal apologist for the company, traces its history in *Empires in Green and Gold* (N.Y., 1947). Its early development in Central America is also glorified in F. U. Adams, *Conquest of the Tropics* (N.Y., 1914), while Stacy May and Galo Plaza, *The United Fruit Company in Latin America* (Wash., 1958), defended it more recently. Charles Kepner, *Social Aspects of the Banana Industry* (N.Y., 1936); Kepner and Jay Soothill, *The Banana Empire* (N.Y., 1931; reprinted, N.Y., 1967); Carleton Beals, *Banana Gold* (Philadelphia, 1932); Richard LaBarge, *Impact of the United Fruit Company on the Economic Development of Guatemala, 1946-1954* (N.O.,

1960); Alfonso Bauer Paíz, *Cómo opera el capital yanqui en Centro-américa: el caso de Guatemala* (México, 1956); and Julio Castelló, *Así cayó la democracia en la guerra de la United Fruit* (Havana, 1961), all treat United Fruit more critically. Virgilio Rodríguez Beteta, *No es guerra de hermanos sino de bananos* (2d ed., Gua., 1969), concentrates on the fruit company's role in the boundary dispute between Honduras and Guatemala in the early twentieth century. The decline of the company is documented in a fascinating work by T. P. McCann, *An American Company: The Tragedy of United Fruit* (New York, 1976). McCann, a former public relations officer for the company, is sympathetic in his treatment of Samuel Zemurray and highly critical of Eli Black. T. L. Karnes details the story of another major banana company in *Tropical Enterprise: The Standard Fruit and Steamship Company in Latin America* (Baton Rouge, 1978).

Manuel Rubio Sánchez has dealt with the histories of a number of other important Central American export commodities. In addition to his work on indigo mentioned earlier, he has dealt with "El Cacao," *Anales de la Sociedad de Geografía e Historia de Guatemala* 31 (1958), 81-129; and "La grana o cochinilla," *Antropología e Historia de Guatemala* 13 (1961), 15-46. See also C. A. Rosas Alvarado, *El cacao en la economía colonial de Costa Rica, siglos XVII y XVIII* (S.J., 1975).

Fiscal and monetary policies have not attracted much historical study in Central America, but there are a few notable exceptions. The standard older work is J. P. Young, *Central American Currency and Finance* (Princeton, 1925), but Dana Munro, *The Five Republics of Central America* (N.Y., 1918), is also useful. On coinage, H. F. Burzio, *Diccionario de la moneda hispanoamericana* (3 vols., Santiago de Chile, 1956-58), is an indispensable reference for the colonial period, as is the profusely illustrated work of Kurt Prober, *Historia numismática de Guatemala* (2d ed., Gua., 1973). Arturo Castillo Flores, *Historia de la moneda de Honduras* (Teg., 1974), concentrates on the period since independence. See also C. F. Hidalgo, *De estructura económica y banca central: la experiencia de Honduras* (Madrid, 1963). For Nicaragua, see Luis Cuadra Cea, *Aspectos históricos de la moneda de Nicaragua* (Man., 1963). For nineteenth-century Costa Rica, see Cleto González Víquez, *Historia financiera de Costa Rica* (2d ed., S.J., 1977). Tomás Soley Güell, *Historia monetaria de Costa Rica* (S.J., 1926); and Rodrigo Facio, *La moneda y la banca central en Costa Rica* (2d ed., México, 1973), are other early accounts, but a more complete history is Rufino Gil Pacheco, *Ciento cinco años de vida bancaria en Costa Rica* (3d ed., S.J., 1975). More recently, under the encouragement of government and international agen-

cies, more attention has been given to this area. The national banks and
statistical departments of all the Central American states regularly publish
statistical reports on all aspects of their economies, as has the Secretariat
of the Central American Integration Movement (SIECA) in Guatemala.

Transportation and communications developments have been touched
upon by many writers, but few have focused their studies on this important
area. W. R. Long, *Railways of Central America and the West Indies*
(Wash., 1925), is an early survey, and there are a few descriptions of
railways in individual countries, but no comprehensive analysis exists.
The Banco Central de Integración Económica, *Regional Program of Central
American Highways* (Teg., 1963), developed in the 1960's. P. F.
Barreda, *Geografía e historia de correos y telecomunicaciones de Guatemala*
(Gua., 1960), offers a rudimentary history of the postal service in
Guatemala. Cristina Chamorro B., *Las primeras bases de infraestructura
en Nicaragua, 1875-1936* (Man., 1976), offers a survey of the foundations of infrastructure in Nicaragua.

The Central American Common Market has attracted considerably more
attention, although much of it is very narrow in scope and significance
and interest has waned since the decline of the CACM. W. R. Cline and
Enrique Delgado (eds.), *Economic Integration in Central America*
(Wash., 1978); R. Q. Shaw, *Central America: Regional Integration and
National Political Development* (Boulder, 1978); V. Bulmer-Thomas,
"The Central American Common Market," in A. El-Agraa (ed.), *International
Economic Integration* (Ln., 1982); and Gabriel Siri, *El Salvador
and Economic Integration, An Econometric Study* (Lexington, Mass.,
1984), have largely superseded earlier works, a bibliography of which
James Cochrane has provided in "Movement toward Economic Integration
in Latin America," *Southeastern Latin Americanist* 18 (June 1974), 4-7.
Related to the common market development is the high degree of aid
programs and international agency involvement in Central America since
World War II, a topic explored in detail by J. F. McCamant, *Development
Assistance in Central America* (N.Y., 1968).

V. INTER-STATE RELATIONS

Gordon Ireland, *Boundaries, Possessions and Conflicts in Central and
North America and the Caribbean* (Cambridge, Mass., 1941), is the
standard work for the many boundary disputes in Central American history.
Laudelino Moreno, *Historia de las relaciones interstatuales de Centro
América* (Madrid, 1928), is more detailed. Among other treatises, the

following will provide a beginning for such study: Antonio Vallejo, *Historia documentada de los limites entre la República de Honduras y las de Nicaragua, El Salvador y Guatemala* (*desde 1524 hasta 1890*) (Teg., 1938); Felipe Rodríguez S., *El Golfo de Fonseca en el derecho pública centroamericano: La doctrina Meléndez* (S.S., 1917); L. M. Bloomfield, *The British Honduras-Guatemala Dispute* (Toronto, 1953); W. J. Bianchi, *Belize: The Controversy between Guatemala and Great Britain over the Territory of British Honduras in Central America* (N.Y., 1959); and David Vela, *Nuestro Belice* (Gua., 1939).

Manuel Castro Ramírez reviewed the work of the Central American Court of Justice in *Cinco años de la Corte de Justicia* (S.J., 1918), while Ernesto Martín edited the Court's principal records in *Anales de la Corte de Justicia* (7 vols., S.J., 1911-18).

The history of the Organization of Central American States (ODECA) is explored in Marco Tulio Zeldón, *La ODECA: sus antecedentes históricos y su aporte al derecho internacional americano* (S.J., 1966). A guide to United Nations activity in Central America is J. V. Moreno, *Las Naciones Unidas en el ámbito centroamericano* (S.S., 1970). Works on the 1969 "Soccer War" have been dealt with in Section III-F, but mention should be made here of Martz, *Central American Soccer War:* (Athens, Ohio, 1978), and Rowles, *El conflicto Honduras-El Salvador* (S.J., 1980).

VI. THE SOCIETY

There is a vast literature on the society of Central America, particularly for Guatemala and Costa Rica. While most of it is the work of sociologists or anthropologists, there are few attempts at synthesis of the entire area. R. N. Adams, *Cultural Surveys* (Wash., 1957), is an excellent introductory survey, and his *Crucifixion by Power* (Austin, 1970) provides perceptive analyses of national institutions in Guatemala. See also Adams *et al., Community Culture and National Change* (N.O., 1972). Edelberto Torres Rivas describes Central American society in the framework of its historical development in economic dependency in his *Interpretación del desarrollo social centroamericano* (2d ed., S.J., 1971). Also very suggestive in explaining the class structure of much of rural Central America is Rodolfo Stavenhagen, *Clases, colonialismo y aculturación* (Gua., 1968). Carlos Araya Pochet, *Origen y desarrollo de la burguesía agroexportadora en Centroamérica: los casos de Costa Rica y Guatemala* (*1840-1900*) (S.J., 1977), compares Guatemala and Costa Rica in the nineteenth century. J. L. Vega Carballo takes an historical approach in his brilliant *Hacía una interpretación de desarrollo costarricense* (4th ed., S.J., 1983). Santiago Montes Mozo, *Etnohistoria de El Salvador: El Guachival Centroamericano* (2 vols., S.S., 1977), is a fine contribution to Salvadoran ethnohistory. On Honduras, see Antonio Murga Frassinetti, *Enclave y sociedad en Honduras* (Teg., 1978). Luis Barahona J., *El gran incognita* (S.J., 1953), offers a sociological description of the Costa Rican peasant. For Guatemala, the series of sociological, anthropological, and economic studies published by the Seminario de Integración Social Guatemalteca have greatly increased the literature on that state. There have been far more important village case studies in Central America than can possibly be mentioned here, again with a preponderance in Guatemala. Among the most useful of these are the pioneering work of Webster McBryde, *Sololá* (N.O., 1933); Charles Wagley, *Santiago Chimaltenango* (2d ed., Gua., 1957); John Gillin, *The Culture of Security in San Carlos* (N.O., 1951); Ruth Bunzel, *Chichicastenango* (N.Y., 1952); Melvin Tumin, *Caste in a Peasant Society* (Princeton, 1952); Sol Tax, *Penny Capitalism: A Guatemalan Indian Economy* (Wash., 1953); and R. E. Hinshaw, *Panajachel: A Guatemalan Town in Thirty-Year Perspective* (Pittsburgh, 1975). Also notable are Sakari Sariola, *Social Class and Social Mobility in a Costa Rican Town* (Turrialba, 1954); Manning Nash, *Machine Age Maya* (Glencoe, Ill., 1958), which describes the impact of a textile factory on a Guatemalan Indian village; Rubén Reina's exhaustive description of Chinautla, *Law of the Saints* (N.Y., 1966); and Pedro Carrasco, *Sobre los indios de Guatemala* (Gua., 1982), containing articles and documents on the Indians of the Guatemalan highlands. A thorough study of the Verapaz region of Guatemala is Arden King, *Cobán and the Verapaz, History and Cultural Process in Northern Guatemala* (N.O., 1974); and Robert Carmack has made major contributions with his *Quichean Civilization* (Berkeley, 1973); *Historia social de los Quichés* (Gua., 1979); and, with John Early and Christopher Lutz (eds.), *Historical Demography of Highland Guatemala* (Albany, 1982). R. A. Naylor, "Guatemalan Indian Attitudes toward Land Tenure," *Journal of Inter-American Studies* 9 (1967), 619-39, is a provocative essay. See also Donald Thompson, *Maya Paganism and Christianity: A History of the Fusion of Two Religions* (N.O., 1954). The *Handbook of Middle American Indians* provides extensive coverage of the Indians and their bibliography.

Relatively little work has been done on the African in Central America, but Carlos Meléndez and Quince Duncan offer an uneven but informative group of studies in *El negro en Costa Rica* (S.J., 1972). See also M. D. Olien, *The Negro in Costa Rica: The Role of an Ethnic Minority in a Developing Society* (Winston-Salem, 1970). For a review of literature on the colonial period, see Thomas Fiehrer, "Slaves and Freedmen in Colonial Central America," *Journal of Negro History* 64 (1979), 39-57.

Manuel Rubio Sánchez, *Status de la mujer en Centroamérica* (Gua., 1976), has made an introductory study of the status of women in Central American history, while Margaret Randall has described women in the Sandinista Revolution in *Sandino's Daughters* (Vancouver, B.C., 1981).

Regarding population movement and urbanization, Jorge Arias de Blois, *La población de Centroamérica y sus perspectivas* (Gua., 1966), is a helpful addition to William Vogt's pioneering neo-Malthusian study, *The Population of El Salvador and Its Natural Resources* (Wash., 1946). Bryan Roberts, *Organizing Strangers* (Austin, 1973), points to specific problems of urbanization in Guatemala City. Bruce Herrick and Barclay Hudson describe Costa Rican problems in *Urban Poverty and Economic Development: A Case Study of Costa Rica* (N.Y., 1981). Jacobo Schifter, Lowell Gudmundson, and Mario Solera, *El Judío en Costa Rica* (S.J., 1984), describe the Jewish community in Costa Rica, highlighting the Polish immigration of the 1930's, the migrant experience, and the establishment of community institutional life since then. Daniel Goldrich, *Sons of the Establishment* (Chicago, 1966), is an interesting comparative study of elite youth in Panama and Costa Rica. Oscar Arias Sánchez, *Grupos de presión en Costa Rica* (S.J., 1971), offers a brief but perceptive study of the political role of Costa Rican pressure groups. Other excellent Costa Rican studies are Daniel Camacho Monge, *Organización económica y social de Costa Rica* (S.J., 1967), and J. A. Booth, *Características sociográficas de las regiones periféricas de Costa Rica* (S.J., 1974).

VII. CULTURE AND THE ARTS

There are no satisfactory comprehensive guides to cultural development of Central America, or even to individual states, although Charles Stansifer, *Cultural Policy in the Old and the New Nicaragua* (Hanover, N.H., 1981), has written an interesting essay comparing cultural policies under the Somozas and the Sandinistas. Ramón Salazar, *Historia del desenvolvimiento intelectual de Guatemala* (Gua., 1897), offers a good introduction through the nineteenth century for Guatemala, and R. H. Valle, *Historia de las ideas contemporáneas en Centro-América* (México, 1960), is a useful catalogue of the leading thinkers of the isthmus. Specific areas of intellectual development have been treated with varying degrees of scholarly care. Constantino Lascaris has followed up his extensive *Desa-*

rrollo de las ideas en Costa Rica (2d ed., S.J., 1975) with an *Historia de las ideas en Centroamérica* (S.J., 1970). One of the most thorough works on philosophical development in Central America is Jesús Amurrio G., *El positivismo en Guatemala* (Gua., 1966).

The history of Central American literature has not been adequately recorded, but L. A. Díaz Vasconcelos, *Apuntes para la historia de literatura guatemalteca* (2d ed., Gua., 1950), is a standard reference for the colonial period. Joquim de Montezuma de Carvalho (ed.), *Panorama das literaturas das Américas de 1900 a actualidad* (4 vols., Nova Lisboa, Angola, 1958-63), despite its unlikely place of publication provides a handy reference to literary developments in each of the Central American states during the first half of the twentieth century. Another useful reference work is the Pan American Union, Division of Philosophy and Letters, *Diccionario de la literatura latinoamericana: América Central* (2 vols., Wash., 1963). Useful works dealing with individual states include David Vela, *Literatura guatemalteca* (2 vols., Gua., 1943); Seymour Menton, *Historia crítica de la novela guatemalteca* (Gua., 1960); Otto Olivera, *La literatura en publicaciones periódicas de Guatemala, siglo XIX* (N.O., 1974); Néstor Bermúdez, *Escritores de Honduras (perfiles fugaces)* (2 vols., Habana, 1939-41); Jorge Eduardo Arellano, *Panorama de la literatura nicaragüense* (Man., 1977); S. F. White (ed.), *Poets of Nicaragua: A Bilingual Anthology, 1918-1979;* J. F. Toruño, *Desarrollo literario de El Salvador* (S.S., 1958); María B. de Membreño, *Literatura de El Salvador* (S.S., 1959); Abelardo Bonilla, *Historia de la literatura costarricense* (2 vols., S.J., 1957-61); and Anita Herzfeld and Teresa Cajiao Salas, *El teatro de hoy en Costa Rica* (S.J., 1973). It is impossible here to list the anthologies or works of even the major Central American literary figures, but some mention may be made of biographical studies of a few. Antonio Batres Jáuregui compared two important earlier Guatemalan literary giants in his *Landívar e Irisarri* (Gua., 1896), while Richard Callan has written *Miguel Angel Asturias* (N.Y., 1970), but see also Callan, Gerard Flynn, and Kenneth Grieb, *Essays on Miguel Angel Asturias* (Milwaukee, 1973). Walter Payne relates the life and work of a noted Guatemalan historian and literary light in *A Central American Historian, José Milla (1822-1882)* (Gainesville, 1957). The life and work of a more modern Central American historian has been sympathetically treated by Oscar Acosta, *Rafael Heliodoro Valle, vida y obra* (Teg., 1964). Among the many studies on Rubén Darío, Edelberto Torres, *La dramática vida de Rubén Darío* (4th ed., Barcelona, 1966), is the most complete and popular, but C. D. Watland, *Poet-errant: A Biography of Rubén Darío* (N.Y., 1965), will provide English readers with some insight into the life and work of the Nicaraguan poet. Other Nicaraguan literary lights are featured in J. E. Arellano, *Diccionario de las letras nicaragüenses* (Man., 1982); Xavier Zavala Cuadra (ed.), *Homenaje a Pablo Antonio Cuadra*, a special issue of the *Revista del Pensamiento Centroamericano* 37(no. 172) (1982); and J. L. Smith (ed.), *An Annotated Bibliography of and about Ernesto Cardenal* (Tempe, Az., 1979).

J. F. Figeac, *La libertad de imprenta en El Salvador* (S.S., 1947); Antonio Zelaya C., *Cien años de libertad de prensa en Costa Rica, 1843-1943* (S.J., 1943); and J. H. Montalván, *Breves apuntes para la historia del periodismo nicargüense* (León, 1958), have little analytical or critical content as histories of journalism, but they offer a chronology of events in the publishing history of those states. Italo López Vallecillos, *El periodismo en El Salvador* (S.S., 1964), is a more substantial work.

The standard survey on Central American education is George and Barbara Waggoner, *Education in Central America* (Lawrence, Ks., 1971), but it is supplemented by a number of works on individual countries. Carlos González Orellana, *Historia de la educación en Guatemala* (2d ed., Gua., 1970), is informative and thorough. L. F. González Flores, *Historia del desarrollo de la instrucción pública en Costa Rica* (2 vols., S.J., 1945-61), is informative but extends only to 1884. More substantial is his detailed *Historia de la influencia extranjera en el desenvolvimiento educacional y científica de Costa Rica* (2a ed., S.J., 1976). Miguel de Castillo Urbina, *Educación para la modernización en Nicaragua* (B.A., 1972), and *La educación primaria nicaragüense* (Man., 1968), provide considerable detail on the system under the Somozas. Carlos Tunnermann Bernheim, *Hacía una nueva educación en Nicaragua* (Man., 1980), describes the Sandinista effort to develop education. A more detailed description is J. B. Arrién, *Nicaragua: revolución y proyecto educativo* (Man., 1980). Charles Stansifer, *The Nicaraguan National Literary Crusade* (Hanover, N.H., 1981), describes the Sandinista literacy campaign, as do Sheryl Hirshon and Judy Butler, *And also Teach Them to Read* (Westport, Ct., 1983). Several careful studies have been done on the teaching of history in Central America. Martín Alvarado R., *La enseñanza de la historia en Honduras* (México, 1951), is rather limited in scope and utility, but Carlos Molina Argüello, *La enseñanza de la historia en Nicaragua* (México, 1953), Pedro Tobar Cruz, *La enseñanza de la historia en los tres movimientos educacionales de Guatemala en el siglo xix: Gálvez, Pavón, Barrios* (Gua., 1953), and Héctor Samayoa G., *La enseñanza de la historia en Guatemala* (*desde 1832 hasta 1852*) (Gua., 1959), are all major works. Several works treat various aspects of university history; they are led by Lanning's two classic volumes on colonial Guatemala, *The*

University in the Kingdom of Guatemala (Ithaca, N.Y., 1955), and *The Eighteenth Century Enlightenment in the University of San Carlos de Guatemala* (Ithaca, N.Y., 1956). Esteban Gardiola Cubas, *Historia de la Universidad de Honduras en la primera centuria de su fundación* (Teg., 1952), traces the institution's history to 1930, and M. A. Durán does the same for El Salvador in *Historia de la Universidad de El Salvador* (S.S., 1941). Rafael Obregón L. has focused on nineteenth-century university administration in *Los rectores de la Universidad de Santo Tomás de Costa Rica* (S.J., 1955). Jorge Eduardo Arellano, *Historia de la Universidad de León* (2 vols., León, 1973-74), is a careful and detailed history of Nicaragua's first university. A broader look at Central American universities, reflecting their strengths and weaknesses, is found in a collection of essays by Carlos Tunnermann, *Pensamiento universitario centroamericano* (S.J., 1980). Carlos Martínez Durán, *Las ciencias médicas en Guatemala* (3d ed., Gua., 1964), is a major contribution to the history of medicine in Guatemala. Rafael Alvarado Sarria, *Breve historia hospitalaria de Nicaragua* (León, 1969), provides only a sketchy synopsis for Nicaragua.

Indigenous culture is for the most part dealt with elsewhere, but mention here may be made of Lila O'Neale, *Textiles of Highland Guatemala* (Wash., 1945); Carmen L. Petterson, *Maya of Guatemala, Life and Dress* (Gua., 1976); Marilyn Anderson, *Guatemalan Textiles Today* (N.Y., 1978); Anne Pollard Rowe, *A Century of Change in Guatemalan Textiles* (N.Y., 1981); Lilly de Jongh Osborne, *Indian Crafts of Guatemala and El Salvador* (Rev. ed., Norman, 1975); and Ann Parker and Avon Neal, *Molas: Folk Art of the Cuna Indians* (N.Y., 1977). There is substantial periodical literature on the folklore of Guatemala. Marcial Amas Lara, *El Folklore guatemalteco en la tradición y leyenda a través de los siglos* (Gua., 1970), is not scholarly, but it will provide a convenient introduction. For the other states the following will provide a general survey: Enrique Peña Hernández, *Folklore de Nicaragua* (Masaya, 1968); Francisco Pérez Estrada, *Ensayos nicaragüenses* (Man., 1976); Evangelina Quesada de Núñez, *Costa Rica y su folklore* (S.J., 1957); Gonzalo Chacón, *Tradiciones costarricenses* (3d ed., S.J., 1964); and Ministerio de Cultura de El Salvador, *Recopilación de materiales folklóricos salvadoreñas* (S.S., 1944). Most interest in the fine arts has been focused on the pre-Columbian period and on colonial architecture. Exceptions worth noting are V. M. Díaz, *Las bellas artes en Guatemala* (Gua., 1934); and Ernesto Chinchilla Aguilar, *Historia del arte en Guatemala, 1524-1962* (Gua., 1963). Marcial Armas Lara, *Origen de la marrimba, su desenvolvimiento y otros instrumentos músicos* (Gua., 1970), presents not altogether convincing evidence that the marimba originated among the Maya, but in the process he contributes to the available literature on indigenous musical instruments. See also José Saenz Poggio, *Historia de la música guatemalteca desde la monarquía española hasta fines del año 1877* (Gua., 1878), and Rafael Vásquez, *Historia de la música en Guatemala* (Gua., 1950), especially useful for showing nineteenth-century musical activity.

VIII.   BIBLIOGRAPHIES AND CURRENT PERIODICALS

General bibliographies of Latin America seldom give Central America adequate coverage, but are nevertheless good starting places. C. C. Griffin (ed.), *Latin America: A Guide to the Historical Literature* (Austin, 1971), and the *Handbook of Latin American Studies* (Cambridge, Mass., 1936-51, & Gainesville, 1951-   ), along with the *Bibliographic Index* (N.Y., 1973-   ); ABC-Clio, *Latin American Politics, A Historical Bibliography* (Santa Barbara, 1984); R. L. Delorme (comp.), *Latin America, 1979-1983, A Social Science Bibliography* (Santa Barbara, 1984), which updates an earlier 1967-79 edition (Santa Barbara, 1980); A. E. Gropp (comp.), *A Bibliography of Latin American Bibliographies* (Metuchen, N.J., 1968, with 1971 supplement); S. A. Bayitch (comp.), *Latin America and the Caribbean, a Bibliographical Guide to Works in English* (Coral Gables, 1967); J. R. Wish, *Economic Development in Latin America: An Annotated Bibliography* (N.Y., 1966); M. H. Sable (ed.), *A Guide to Latin American Studies* (L.A., 1967); and S. D. Brunn (comp.), *Urbanization in Developing Countries: An International Bibliography* (East Lansing, 1971). For relations with the U.S. see D. F. Trask, Michael Meyer, and R. R. Trask, *A Bibliography of United States–Latin American Relations since 1810* (Lincoln, Neb., 1968, with an extensive supplement in 1979); and Dean Burns (ed.), *Guide to American Foreign Relations since 1770* (Santa Barbara, 1982). An analysis of national bibliographies for Central America is found in Irene Zimmerman, *Current National Bibliographies of Latin America: A State of the Art Study* (Gainesville, 1971). The Pan American Union's *Index to Latin American Periodical Literature* (8 vols., Bos., 1961), with *Supplement* (2 vols., Bos., 1965), and *Index to Latin American Periodicals* (10 vols., Metuchen, N.J., 1961-71), have been succeeded by the *Hispanic American Periodicals Index* (L.A., 1975-   , annual) for lists of periodical articles. *Historical Abstracts* (Santa Barbara, 1955-   ) provides brief abstracts for most articles dealing with the post-1775 period in journals throughout the world.

A major tool for the student of Central American history is K. J. Greib (ed.), *Research Guide to Central America and the Caribbean* (Madison, 1985), which contains both historiographical articles and guides to the principal archives and libraries containing Central American materials. Computer searches of major bibliographical databases, such as the Library of Congress and other major research libraries are also now available and can be of great assistance in the formation of bibliographies on specific subjects. Many serials, including *Historical Abstracts* and *Dissertations Abstracts International,* may also be searched quickly by computer. These computer services have reduced the need for printed bibliographies, but specific topical or area bibliographies are useful where computer services are unavailable or impractical.

The standard bibliography of works published in the Kingdom of Guatemala is José Toribio Medina, *La imprenta en Guatemala* (1660-1821) (Santiago de Chile, 1910). Medina failed to discover all the colonial imprints, however, so there have been a number of supplementary works, most notably that of Gilberto Valenzuela, *La imprenta en Guatemala, algunas adiciones . . .* (Gua., 1933). Most useful for the colonial period is Sidney Markman, *Colonial Central America* (Tempe, Az., 1977). See also Eleanor Adams, *A Bio-bibliography of Franciscan Authors in Colonial Central America* (Wash., 1953); J. E. O'Ryan, *Bibliografía guatemalteca de los siglos XVII y XVIII* (2d ed., Gua., 1960); and Murdo MacLeod, "Modern Research on the Demography of Colonial Central America: A Bibliographical Essay," *Latin American Population History Newsletter* 3(Nos.3/4) (1983), 23-39.

Bibliographies for the separate states cover the period since independence (and sometimes the colonial period as well), but an excellent overview of the literature through the mid-twentieth century is provided by W. J. Griffith, "The Historiography of Central America since 1830," *Hispanic American Historical Review* 45 (1965). Clio Press's World Bibliographical Series, with its goal of producing a selective, annotated bibliography of all fields, emphasizing works in English, for every country in the world, has begun to have an impact on Central American bibliographies. Franklin Woodman (comp.), *Guatemala* (Oxford, 1981) is less comprehensive than other Central American volumes to date, but it is nonetheless a good introduction to Guatemalan bibliography. The most detailed bibliography on Guatemala since independence, although now much out of date, is found in vols. 3-10 of Gilberto Valenzuela Reyna (ed.), *Bibliografía guatemalteca* (Gua., 1961-64), although its chronological organization limits its usefulness. J. L. Reyes M., *Bibliografía de la imprenta en Guatemala (adiciones 1769-1900)* (Gua., 1969), adds items that Medina and Valenzuela overlooked.

R. L. Woodward, Jr. (comp.), *Belize* (Oxford, 1980), in the World Bibliographical Series, is the most comprehensive annotated bibliography yet produced for that country. An extensive but unannotated list of works on Belize is, Clarence Minkel and Ralph Alderman (eds.), *A Bibliography of British Honduras, 1900-1970* (East Lansing, 1970).

Woodward has also compiled the World Bibliographical Series volume for *Nicaragua* (Oxford, 1983), which is supplemented by an excellent series of topical bibliographies published by the Biblioteca of the Banco Central de Nicaragua under the supervision of René Rodríguez Masís and several bibliographical publications of the Instituto de Estudio del Sandinismo edited by Jorge Eduardo Arellano, as well as Arellano's *Cuadernos de Bibliografía Nicaragüense* (Man., 1981-   ). A basic guide to older Nicaraguan historiography in Spanish is Carlos Molina Argüello, "Bibliografía historiográfica de Nicaragua," *Inter-American Review of Bibliography* 4 (1954), 9-22. Arellano and George Elmendorf are presently undertaking to publish a union list of all Nicaraguan publications in their "Proyecto de Bibliografía Nicaragüense."

For Honduras the most comprehensive bibliography is M. A. García, *Bibliografía hondureña, 1620-1960* (2 vols., Teg., 1971-72).

El Salvador is in need of a modern bibliography, although extensive lists are appended to many of the works published on El Salvador listed elsewhere in this essay. A World Bibliographical Series volume on El Salvador is currently in preparation by R. L. Woodward, Jr., and Michael Fry.

For Costa Rica, the standard older work is Luis Dobles Segreda, *Indice bibliográfico de Costa Rica,* 9 vols., S.J., 1927-36). The *Anuario bibliográfico costarricense* (S.J., 1959-71, annual), lists current publications through 1969. J. A. Lines, *Libros y folletos publicados en Costa Rica durante los años 1830-1849* (S.J., 1944), is a bibliography on the early years of independence.

Eleanor DeSelms Langstaff (comp.), *Panama* (Oxford, 1982), another World Bibliographical Series volume, is the best contemporary guide to Panamanian bibliography. Manuel Lucena Salmoral, *Historiografía de Panamá* (Panamá, 1967), is a basic bibliography of Panamanian history.

Specific topical bibliographies are too numerous to list here except for a few of the most important. The Tropical Science Center in San José has published a series of anthropological bibliographies on aboriginal Central America. Aubyn Kendall, *The Art and Archaeology of pre-Columbian Middle America* (Bos., 1977), is an annotated bibliography of works in

English. Sara de Mundo Lo, *Index to Spanish American Collective Biography: Volume 3—The Central American and Caribbean Countries* (Bos., 1984), presents approximately 1000 annotated listings, mostly on Central America, for biographies containing information on three or more individuals. K. S. Kapp presents an annotated list of 277 *Central America Early Maps up to 1860* (North Bend, Ohio, 1974). Joyce Waddell Bailey (ed.), *Handbook of Latin American Art* (3 vols., Santa Barbara, 1984-85), is a bibliographic compilation by more than seventy scholars of both published and unpublished items from the late nineteenth century through 1983 relating to Latin American art from pre-Columbian times to the present.

Most of the North American and European journals dedicated to Latin American studies until the current crises published articles dealing with Central America only occasionally. Among those which do so most often are the *Hispanic American Historical Review* (Baltimore, 1918-22, Durham, N.C., 1926- , quarterly); *Journal of Inter-American Studies and World Affairs* (Gainesville, Fla., 1959-64, Coral Gables, Fla., 1965- , quarterly); *Latin American Perspectives* (Riverside, Ca., 1974- , tri-annual); *Caribbean Studies* (Río Piedras, P.R., 1961- , quarterly); *The Americas* (Wash., 1947- , quarterly); *Inter-American Economic Affairs* (Wash., 1947- , quarterly). The *Latin American Research Review* (Austin, 1965- , tri-annual) publishes frequent bibliographical and methodological essays. The *Inter-American Review of Bibliography* (Wash., 1951- , quarterly) publishes bibliographical articles, book reviews, and a guide to current publications. Excellent coverage of current economic developments can be found in the *Quarterly Economic Review* (Ln., 1956- , quarterly). For business trends see *Business Latin America* (N.Y., 1966- , weekly). See also the *Economic Bulletin for Latin America* (United Nations, 1956- , semi-annual). Current events are covered in *Latin America Weekly Report* (Ln., 1979- , weekly); *Latin American Regional Reports: Mexico & Central America* (Ln., 1979- , monthly); *Latin America Press* (Lima, 1969- , weekly); and *Latin American Index* (Wash., 1973- , monthly). See also the radical *NACLA Report on the Americas* (N.Y., 1967- , monthly). Some which deal more specifically with Central America are *Inforpress Centroamericana* (Gua., 1972- , weekly); and its subsidiary publications, *Central America Report* (Gua., 1974- , weekly), a weekly review of business and politics; and *La Gaceta* (Gua., 1972- , weekly), which contains government decrees and other official documents; *Mesoamerica* (S.J., 1982- , monthly); *Central America Bulletin* (formerly *El Salvador Bulletin*) (Berkeley, 1981- , monthly); *¡Guatemala!* (Oakland, Calif., 1978- , irregular).

The number of scholarly journals in Central America has increased slightly over the past decade. Notable are the *Estudios Sociales Centroamericanos* (S.J., 1972-   , tri-annual); and *Anuario de Estudios Centroamericanos* (S.J., 1972-   , annual). The *Revista del Pensamiento Centroamericano* (Man., 1960-72, monthly; 1975-   , quarterly) has a broader scope of interests but continues to be the leading Nicaraguan independent journal. The Nicaraguan Ministry of Culture has published a number of journals, of which the most important, featuring principally literary articles which emphasize the Revolution, is *Nicarauac* (Man., 1980-   , bimonthly). Pablo Antonio Cuadra continues to publish the independent *El Pez y la Serpiente* (Man., 1960-   , semi-annual) dedicated to the arts and poetry. An important new journal which has gained stature is *Mesoamérica* (Antigua Guatemala, 1980-   , annual), published by the Centro de Investigaciones Regionales de Mesoamérica. *ECA, Estudios Centroamericanos* (S.S., 1945-   , monthly), continues to be one of the best social science reviews in Central America, and is especially useful for its documentation of the civil war and political crises in El Salvador. Other important Central American journals include the *Anales de la Academia de Geografía e Historia de Guatemala* (Gua., 1924-   , irregular); *Revista de Geografía e Historia de Honduras* (Teg., 1904-   , irregular); *Revista de Historia* (Heredia, C.R., 1975-   , irregular); *Antropología e Historia de Guatemala* (Gua., 1949-   , semiannual); *Revista de la Universidad de Costa Rica* (S.J., 1945-   , irregular); *Universidad de San Carlos* (Gua., 1945-   , annual); *Guatemala Indígena* (Gua., 1961-62, 1968-   , quarterly); *Repertorio Centro Americano* (Heredia, 1964-   , irregular); *Tiempo Actual* (S.J., 1976-   , monthly); *Revista de Filosofía* (S.J., 1957-   , irregular); *Economía: Revista del Instituto de Investigaciones Económicas y Sociales* (Gua., 1962-   , quarterly, although recently much in arrears); *Economía Política* (Teg., 1962-   , irregular); and two journals published since 1973 by the Belize Institute of Social Research and Action at St. John's College in Belize City, *Belizean Studies* (formerly *National Studies*) and the *Journal of Belizean Affairs*.

Central America has many newspapers, although television has begun to make inroads on their circulation. The leading daily papers in each state are: *El Imparcial, El Gráfico, Prensa Libre,* and *La Palabra* in Guatemala; *Diario de Hoy, La Prensa Gráfica,* and *El Mundo* in San Salvador; *El Tiempo, La Prensa,* and *La Tribuna* in Tegucigalpa (*El Tiempo* and *La Prensa* also publish a San Pedro Sula edition); *La Prensa, Barricada,* and *Nueva Diario* in Managua; *La Nación, La República,* and *La Prensa Libre* in San José; *The Belize Times* in Belize; and *La Estrella, El Matutino, La Prensa,* and *La Crítica* in Panama.

Tables

TABLE I. ESTIMATES OF CENTRAL AMERICAN POPULATION (1500-2025)

Year	Population	Year	Population
1500	7,000,000	1945	8,141,493
1778	805,339	1955	9,155,000
1810	1,000,000	1965	12,515,000
1824	1,287,491	1975	17,670,000
1855	2,000,000	1985	24,218,000
1915	4,915,133	2000	37,178,000
1930	6,018,880	2025	65,113,000

NOTE: Panama not included in these estimates.

TABLE 2. POPULATION, AREA, AND DENSITY

Country	Est. 1985 Population (thousands)	Area (000 sq. miles)	Density (per sq. mile)	Population Growth (1970-81)
Belize	165	10.1	16.3	2.1
Costa Rica	2,504	19.6	127.8	2.8
El Salvador	5,677	8.1	700.9	3.0
Guatemala	8,442	42.0	201.0	2.9
Honduras	4,400	43.3	101.6	3.2
Nicaragua	3,020	57.1	52.8	2.4
Panama	2,137	28.8	74.2	2.4
Total	26,345	209.0	126.1	2.7

SOURCES: Based on Organization of American States, *Statistical Bulletin of the OAS*, Vol. 4 (3/4) (Washington, 1982); *The 1984 South American Handbook* (Bath, Eng., 1984); Inforpress Centroamericano, *Centroamérica 1982, análisis económicos y políticos sobre la región* (Guatemala, 1982); Inter-American Development Bank, *Economic and Social Progress in Latin America 1982* (Washington, 1982).

TABLE 3. MAJOR CITIES

City	Elevation (ft.)	Population (1985 est.)
Belize City	3	56,362
Guatemala City	4,927	1,500,000
Managua, Nicaragua	180	791,800
Panama City	10	492,850
San José, Costa Rica	3,845	660,000
San Pedro Sula, Hond.	200	254,000
San Salvador, El Sal.	2,230	1,117,850
Santa Ana, El Sal.	2,850	445,700
Tegucigalpa, Honduras	3,303	890,420

SOURCES: Estimates based on *Demographic Yearbook 1981* (N.Y., 1983); *The 1984 South American Handbook* (Bath, England, 1983); *Statistical Abstract of Latin America*, Vol. 22 (L. A., 1983); G. T. Kurian, *Encyclopedia of the Third World* (N.Y., 1982); and Economic Commission for Latin America, *1981 Statistical Yearbook for Latin America* (Santiago de Chile, 1983).

TABLE 4. GROSS DOMESTIC PRODUCT, WHOLESALE PRICE INDEX,
CONSUMER PRICE INDEX, AND URBAN POPULATION (1965-84)

Country & Year	GDP (millions of 1980 US$)	GDP (per capita 1980 US$)	Wholesale Price Index 1980 = 100	Consumer Price Index 1980 = 100	Urban Population (% of total)
Belize					
1980		1,038.0			
Costa Rica					
1965	1,380.8	926.7	21.4	31.5	
1970	1,970.1	1,138.8	24.9	35.7	43.0
1975	2,641.4	1,347.7	54.3	67.8	43.9
1980	3,410.3	1,515.7	100.0	100.0	47.0
1981	3,254.8	1,433.8	158.7	137.1	
1982	3,053.0	1,316.0	344.3	260.6	
1983			434.2	346.8	
1984 (Jan.-Mar.)				378.2	
El Salvador					
1965	1,962.6	669.8	32.1	34.0	
1970	2,439.7	709.2	34.9	35.8	
1975	3,183.0	793.8	54.1	54.2	39.7
1980	3,342.1	703.6	100.0	100.0	42.8
1981	3,024.5	612.2	105.8	114.8	
1982	3,662.0	732.0	122.0	128.2	
1983			134.0	145.0	
1984 (Jan.-Mar.)				157.2	
Guatemala					
1965	3,687.9	836.3	34.0	37.3	33.6
1970	4,878.5	925.7	37.8	40.2	
1975	6,402.4	1,026.0	60.4	60.3	35.6
1980	8,454.6	1,164.5	100.0	100.0	36.5
1981	8,529.7	1,140.3	111.8	111.4	
1982	7,930.0	1,030.0	105.1	111.8	37.0
1983			105.0	119.6	
1984 (Jan.-Apr.)				128.3	
Honduras					
1965	1,216.7	558.1		42.0	
1970	1,518.8	575.3		46.9	23.2
1975	1,703.8	551.4		63.7	32.2
1980	2,420.4	655.9		100.0	37.7
1981	2,445.0	640.1		110.0	36.8
1982	2,801.0	707.3		121.5	

TABLE 4. (*Continued*)

Country & Year	GDP (millions of 1980 US$)	GDP (per capita 1980 US$)	Wholesale Price Index 1980 = 100	Consumer Price Index 1980 = 100	Urban Population (% of total)
1983	2,945.0	718.0		131.9	
1984 (Jan.-Apr.)				136.0	
Nicaragua					
1965	1,688.7	1,042.4			
1970	2,036.3	1,112.7			47.6
1975	2,609.1	1,207.9		41.6	49.8
1980	2,219.4	813.0		100.0	55.0
1981	2,412.5	855.5		116.7	59.2
1982	2,394.0	942.0		154.8	
1983				202.8	
1984					
Panama					
1965	1,616.0	1,308.5	30.9	47.0	
1970	2,341.7	1,635.3	33.2	50.8	47.6
1975	2,977.1	1,774.2	62.4	71.9	49.8
1980	3,711.1	1,953.2	100.0	100.0	56.0
1981	3,846.5	1,982.7	110.0	107.3	54.7
1982	3,494.0	1,755.0	119.9	111.8	
1983			122.0	114.0	

SOURCES: *América en Cifras* (Washington, 1974); *World Military Expenditures and Arms Trade 1963-1973* (Washington, 1975); *El Salvador en Gráficas* (San Salvador, 1973); *Anuario Estadístico 1972* (Managua, 1974); Organization of American States, *Statistical Bulletin of the OAS* 4 (3/4) (1982); SIECA, *Estadísticas macroeconómicas de Centroamérica 1979-1983* (Guatemala, 1984). G. T. Kurian, *Encyclopedia of the Third World* (N.Y., 1982); *Quarterly Economic Review of Nicaragua, Costa Rica, Panama* (London, 1984); *Quarterly Economic Review of Guatemala, El Salvador, Honduras* (London, 1984); *Statistical Abstract of Latin America*, Vol. 22 (L.A., 1983); Economic Commission for Latin America, *1981 Statistical Yearbook* (Santiago de Chile, 1983); and Inter-American Development Bank, *Economic and Social Progress in Latin America 1982* (Washington, 1982).

TABLE 5. CENTRAL AMERICAN REAL GDP GROWTH RATES, 1960-82

Country	1960-70	1970-80	1980	1981	1982
Costa Rica	5.9	5.6	.8	−4.6	−5.9
El Salvador	5.6	3.2	−9.0	−9.5	−4.9
Guatemala	5.5	5.6	3.7	.9	−3.5
Honduras	5.0	4.8	2.8	1.0	−2.0
Nicaragua	6.9	.9	10.0	8.7	−1.0
Panama	8.0	4.7	4.9	3.6	1.0
Latin American Region	5.7	6.1	5.5	1.5	−.5

SOURCE: Organization of American States, *Statistical Bulletin of the OAS*, Vol. 4 (3/4) (Washington, 1982).

TABLE 6. CENTRAL AMERICAN EXPORT COMMODITIES (1980)
(Millions of US$)

Commodity	Costa Rica	Salvador	Guatemala	Honduras	Nicaragua	Panama
Bananas	201.2	–	82.7	228.0	–	61.6
Coffee	246.5	624.2	465.0	204.1	165.7	–
Cotton	–	87.2	166.1	–	30.3	–
Meat	70.7	–	29.1	60.7	58.6	–
Sugar	40.6	–	69.3	–	–	0.1
Total Exports	1,017.8	1,073.6	1,557.1	829.4	450.4	360.3

SOURCE: Organization of American States, *Statistical Bulletin of the OAS*, Vol. 4 (3/4) (Washington, 1982).

TABLE 7. CENTRAL AMERICAN COFFEE EXPORTS, 1983-84
(In thousands of 60 kilo bags)

Country	Exports	% of Latin American Coffee Exports
Costa Rica	1700	4.04
El Salvador	2600	6.18
Guatemala	2101	5.00
Honduras	1100	2.62
Nicaragua	860	2.05
Panama	75	.18
TOTAL C. A.	8436	20.07

SOURCE: U.S. Department of Agriculture.

TABLE 8. CENTRAL AMERICAN MILITARY EXPENDITURES (1965-82)

Country Date	Armed Forces (thousands)	Armed Forces p/1000 pop.	Military Expenditures as % of GNP	Military Expenditures per capita (1981 US$)
Costa Rica				
1965	2	1.3	n/a	n/a
1970	2	1.2	n/a	n/a
1975	2	1.0	.6	6
1980	3	1.3	.7	7
1981	3	1.2	.6	5
1982	4	1.5	n/a	n/a
El Salvador				
1965	4	1.4	1.2	9
1970	4	1.1	1.0	8
1975	8	2.0	1.2	10
1980	12	2.5	2.4	18
1981	13	2.8	3.3	25
1982	25	5.4	4.1	29
Guatemala				
1965	10	2.2	1.1	8
1970	13	2.5	1.6	14
1975	13	2.1	1.2	12
1980	15	2.1	1.3	15
1981	16	2.2	1.3	15
1982	17	2.3	1.7	18
Honduras				
1965	5	1.9	1.4	8
1970	6	2.2	1.0	7
1975	12	3.8	2.0	11
1980	7	1.2	1.7	4
1981	8	1.5	1.9	5
1982	8	1.4	1.6	4
Nicaragua				
1965	5	3.2	1.5	11
1970	6	3.1	1.5	14
1975	5	2.3	1.8	22
1980	15	6.0	5.7	52
1981	40	15.4	6.9	65
1982	75	27.8	n/a	n/a
Panama				
1965	4	3.3	.1	6
1970	5	3.5	.2	9
1975	8	4.7	2.5	13
1980	8	4.2	.7	13
1981	9	4.5	.7	13
1982	10	5.0	.8	14

SOURCES: *World Military Expenditures and Arms Trade 1963-1973* (Washington, 1975); *World Military Expenditures and Arms Transfers 1972-1982* (Washington, 1984).

TABLE 9. CENTRAL AMERICAN EXTERNAL DEBT SERVICE, 1972-82

9-A. AS A PERCENTAGE OF GROSS NATIONAL PRODUCT

Country	1972	1974	1976	1977	1978	1979	1980	1981	1982
Costa Rica	2.8	3.2	3.6	4.7	8.9	5.3	4.7	3.7	16.0
El Salvador	.9	1.5	1.6	2.4	1.0	1.0	1.2	1.3	2.3
Guatemala	2.0	.9	.3	.3	.5	.6	.8	.6	1.0
Honduras	1.0	1.2	2.3	6.1	6.8	8.9	7.1	7.5	6.8
Nicaragua	3.8	3.5	4.3	5.0	5.2	3.8	3.7	7.2	10.1
Panama	4.1	7.6	5.2	7.6	23.5	14.0	14.3	13.4	9.9
Average for Lat. America	1.6	2.4	3.0	3.8	4.6	5.2	4.5	6.7	7.1

9-B. TOTAL PER CAPITA EXTERNAL DEBT (US$)

Country	1972	1974	1976	1977	1978	1979	1980	1981	1982
Costa Rica	112.6	158.0	266.6	355.3	448.0	594.6	729.0	816.0	1115.9
El Salvador	29.7	45.2	63.7	62.4	76.7	91.1	107.2	134.4	234.8
Guatemala	18.8	18.9	32.7	41.5	54.4	68.4	77.2	91.5	174.8
Honduras	42.5	57.3	143.2	180.2	220.8	257.8	317.6	365.2	417.7
Nicaragua	120.7	221.8	293.6	373.5	402.8	421.6	620.8	700.2	816.3
Panama	227.2	348.6	635.5	750.7	1033.8	1115.1	1183.3	1220.4	1750.0
Average for Lat. America	96.5	160.5	254.5	304.4	379.3	441.5	493.3	573.0	779.1

SOURCE: Organization of American States, *Statistical Bulletin of the OAS*, Vol. 4 (3/4) (Washington, 1982).

TABLE 10. PUBLIC FINANCE: TAXATION & EXPENDITURES, 1980

Country	Tax Revenues as % of Total Current Revenues	Tax Revenues as % of GDP	Income & Property Taxes as % of Tax Revenues	Total Cur. Rev. as % of GDP	Total Expenditures as % of GDP
Costa Rica	92.68	11.92	25.46	12.86	20.71
El Salvador	95.14	11.36	31.54	11.94	18.60
Guatemala	90.83	8.63	14.80	9.51	14.21
Honduras	91.31	13.73	33.87	15.03	22.85
Nicaragua	89.16	17.68	16.82	19.83	28.30
Panama	74.51	16.52	44.54	22.17	27.21

SOURCE: Organization of American States, *Statistical Bulletin of the OAS*, Vol. 4 (3/4) (Washington, 1982).

TABLE 11. PHYSICAL QUALITY OF LIFE INDEX
(On an ascending scale with 100 as the maximum)

Country	1976	1980
Costa Rica	87	86
El Salvador	67	66
Guatemala	53	59
Honduras	50	57
Nicaragua	53	54
Panama	81	81
Mexico	75	76
United States	95	95

SOURCE: George Thomas Kurian, *Encyclopedia of the Third World* (N.Y., 1982).

Index

Chiapas, remains with Mexico, 91; migration to, 244
Chichén Itzá, Yuc., 14
Chicle, 159
Childs, O. W., 137
Chinandega, Nic., 140
Chiquimula, Gua., 101
Cholera, 8, 99, 104-5, 141, 294
Christian Base Communities, 252
Christian Democratic parties, 225, 282
  El Salvador, 251-53, 282, 302-7
  Guatemala, 245, 247, 282
  Panama, 307
Church, Roman Catholic
  activities, 34-41, 56, 107, 109, 113-14, 117-18, 169, 212-13, 241, 252, 261, 279, 303
  anticlericalism, 63-64, 93, 101-2, 153, 169, 220, 241, 258
  conversion of the Indians, 21-22, 29, 34-35
  economic activity of, 40-41, 56, 60, 63, 241
  liberation theology, 246, 252, 258, 261
  social mobility in, 78
  William Walker and, 140
CIA. See Central Intelligence Agency
Cigar and cigarette smoking, 206
Ciudad Real, Chis. (San Cristóbal de las Casas), 9, 35, 82, 292, 293
Ciudad Vieja, Gua., 9, 31, 32
Cleveland, Grover, 187
Climate, 8
Cobán, Gua., 40, 44, 150
Cochineal, 19, 70, 90, 97, 99, 114, 128, 130, 131, 150
Cockfighting, 206
Coffee, 96, 128, 130-31, 147-60 passim, 176, 178, 181, 213-14, 218, 219, 229, 244, 260, 366
Cofradías, 212
Cojutepeque, E. S., 5, 152, 153
Cole, Byron, 139-40
Colombia, 135, 137, 189-91, 266
Columbia, Christopher, 25-26, 29, 284
Comandante Zero, 303

Comayagua, Hon., 9, 35, 36, 166, 219, 287, 288, 291
Communications, 48-49, 130, 163, 179, 206
Communist Party of Guatemala (PCG), 233, 235-36, 240, 300
Communists, 209, 216, 219, 224-40 passim, 253, 255-56, 261, 282, 299, 306-7
Composición, 56
Comte, Auguste, 156
Condillac, Étienne B. de, 62
Conferation of Latin American Workers (CTAL), 233
Congress of Panama, 294
Conquest, Spanish, 15-16, 25-35 passim
Conservative Party
  Costa Rica, 215, 225
  Honduras, 257
  Nicaragua, 219-23, 260-62, 282
  post-1840, 111-55 passim
  United Provinces, 92-111 passim
Constitutions
  1812 (Spain), 82-88 passim
  1824 (United Provinces), 93, 94, 112, 293
  1945 (Guatemala), 233-34, 300
  1949 (C.R.), 226-27
  1950 (E.S.), 250
  1956 (Guatemala), 241
Consulado de Comercio, 49-50, 68-70, 73, 83, 87, 90, 113
Construction industry, 206
Contadora Plan, 266-67, 281, 306-7
Contraband trade, 51-54, 64-65, 81, 86-87
Contras, 258-59, 263, 265-67, 280
Contreras brothers, 287
Copán, Hon., 12, 13, 14
Córdoba, Alejandro, 231
Corinto, Nic., 128, 138, 147, 162, 187, 191, 298
Corn. See Maize
Corn Islands, Nic., 197
Coronado, Juan Vásquez de, 33, 288
Corporatism, 269
Corruption and graft
  colonial period, 51, 60, 88
  Costa Rica, 226, 227